D1357688

Monte Cassino

A German View

Rudolf Böhmler
Translated by R.H. Stevens

Foreword by Peter Caddick-Adams

Pen & Sword
MILITARY

First published in German in 1956 by Maximilian Verlag GmbH & Co
English translation first published in 1964
This edition published in Great Britain in 2015 by
Pen & Sword Military
an imprint of
Pen & Sword Books Ltd
47 Church Street
Barnsley
South Yorkshire
S70 2AS

Copyright © Maximilian Verlag GmbH & Co.
KG/E.S. Mittler & Sohn, 1956
Copyright foreword © Peter Caddick-Adams

ISBN 978 1 47382 846 9

Typeset in Ehrhardt by
Mac Style Ltd, Bridlington, East Yorkshire
Printed and bound in the UK by CPI Group (UK) Ltd,
Croydon, CR0 4YY

Pen & Sword Books Ltd incorporates the imprints of Pen & Sword
Archaeology, Atlas, Aviation, Battleground, Discovery, Family
History, History, Maritime, Military, Naval, Politics, Railways, Select,
Transport, True Crime, and Fiction, Frontline Books, Leo Cooper,
Praetorian Press, Seaforth Publishing and Wharncliffe.

For a complete list of Pen & Sword titles please contact
PEN & SWORD BOOKS LIMITED
47 Church Street, Barnsley, South Yorkshire, S70 2AS, England
E-mail: enquiries@pen-and-sword.co.uk
Website: www.pen-and-sword.co.uk

Contents

Maps

Foreword

As the sun glints down at me, reflected from the snow still clinging to the peaks around Monte Cassino, I am very happy to introduce this new edition of Rudolf Böhmler's account of the fighting here in 1944. Although published in German in 1956, it first appeared in English only in 1964 and immediately caused a stir as one of the most vivid accounts of the Second World War written from a German standpoint. There are relatively few German soldiers' voices of the fighting in Italy, and almost none translated into English. Accordingly, my well-thumbed, 50-year-old copy of Böhmler is fast disintegrating and a replacement edition has been long overdue. This volume is something of a rarity and its reappearance is an important reminder of the effectiveness of German fighting methods, excellent low-level leadership, to which Böhmler adds a useful analysis of Allied military strategy in that campaign. It is a reliable, objective account penned by a battalion commander, who had a somewhat wider perspective of the battles in which he fought than those who served under him. Although his book is actually a wider history of the Italian campaign, Böhmler really comes into his own when describing the battles at Cassino, where he led his battalion, and for which he was awarded the Knight's Cross on 26 March 1944.

Rudolf Böhmler was born in Weilimdorf, a suburb of Stuttgart, on 12 June 1914 – just days the fatal shots which ushered Europe into the First World War. Aged 20, he joined the army in 1933 and served as a *leutnant* in Infantry Regiment 55. He was one of the very first *Fallschirmjäger* volunteers, transferring to the Luftwaffe in 1939. Even before the massive deployment of paratroops to Crete in May 1941, Bohmler had served in Poland and Holland, winning both classes of Iron Cross. For his leadership on the Russian Front in 1942, he was awarded the German Cross in Gold on 3 April and was promoted to Major in 1943; by this time he had already been wounded twice.

Böhmler's unit was the I Battalion of the 3rd *Fallschirmjäger* (Parachute) Regiment, commanded by *Oberst* Ludwig Heilmann. Both men knew each other well, having served together as *Fallschirmjäger* commanders since jumping into Crete (May 1941), then serving on the Eastern Front until redeployed to counter the Allied invasion of Sicily (Operation Husky, July–August 1943). That December, they fought a very effective delaying action against Canadian troops in the region of Ortona, on the Italian Adriatic coast, before arriving at Cassino. The *Fallschirmjäger* were thus already veterans of several campaigns and regarded as an elite 'fire brigade', to be rushed to areas where the fighting was most dangerous and enemy break-ins anticipated. Armed with a high proportion of automatic weapons and grenades, but weak in artillery and transport (which couldn't be dropped into battle), German parachute forces were trained to anticipate chaos, be prepared to find themselves behind enemy lines, and always to understand their mission, and take offensive action in support of it – without orders, if need be. This gave them the edge over other Wehrmacht units, and a reputation for getting things done quickly, though with an excessively high casualty rate.

Heilmann's regiment was one of three regiments in *Generalleutnant* Richard Heidrich's First *Fallschirmjäger* Division, which took over the Cassino sector in late February 1944. Böhmler gives us a handy Order of Battle of the division as at 26 February. With other divisions – whose activities Böhmler also recounts – they formed part of XIV Panzer Corps, led by General der Panzertruppen Fridolin von Senger und Etterlin. The latter general wrote his own memoirs, including an account of the Cassino fighting, published in German as *Krieg in Europa* in 1960 and in English as *Neither Fear Nor Hope* in 1963. Read together, Senger and Böhmler remind the student of World War Two that it was still the bitter fighting of 1914–18 that haunted the collective memory of Europe's warriors. Senger had served in that earlier war, which claimed the life of his brother; whilst at the beginning of his chapter on 'The Defenders of Town and Abbey', Böhmler reminds his readers 'As their fathers had stood up to the fury of Verdun and the battles of the Somme a quarter of a century before, their sons now stood fast in the face of the terrifying material onslaught with which the enemy was destined to destroy them'.

Böhmler's opponent, the New Zealander Corps commander General Sir Bernard Freyberg, was also a prisoner of his Great War experiences – where he won three DSOs and a Victoria Cross but lost two of his brothers – and haunted by the utter devastation of Passchendaele. Once Freyberg discovered the *Fallschirmjäger* were in possession of Cassino – the very same troops who had trounced him out of Crete in 1941 – the adoptive New Zealander (he was a Briton by birth) seems to have surrendered to a sense of retribution, which resulted in exactly the same kind of destruction that he and Senger had witnessed in the First World War. Instead of the awesome quantities of artillery used in 1916 at Verdun and the Somme, to which Böhmler was referring, Freyberg requested its 1944 equivalent – the application of airpower on a massive scale which reduced town and abbey to rubble and dust.

Under the ruins lay Böhmler and the remnants of his battalion. 'It was a picture as gruesome as any that the fields of Flanders had had to offer in the First World War', he wrote. His chapter on the Second Battle of Cassino describes the bombing of the town on 15 March, as seen through his own eyes and those of his men: 'Tensely we waited in our holes for the bombs to drop. Then they came. The whining scream of their approach, the roar of their explosions, and the noise of the aircraft themselves mingled with echoes flung back from the hills to produce and indescribable and infernal bedlam of noise. The whole earth quaked and shuddered under the impact. Then – a sudden silence'.

Here a technical note will be in order. The Allies identify four battles of Cassino. The first – overseen by the American Mark Clark – began on 17 January 1944 and saw several sequential actions, made all along the 25-mile length of the Rapido-Gari-Garigliano rivers, from Cassino to Minturno, where it enters the Tyrrhenian Sea. These attacks, made in conjunction with an amphibious assault at Anzio (22 January) represented an attempt to *bypass* the natural fortress of Cassino, whilst also drawing German reserves to the area, away from Anzio. It was the terrain and weather which defeated the Allies as much as the Germans, which saw all Clark's various divisions exhausted and spent by 11 February. With the second and third battles, attempts to outflank Cassino were abandoned in favour of attritional head-on assaults, commanded by Freyberg. The Allies generally reckon the second battle to have begun with the bombing of the abbey on 15 February, and the third with the bombing of the town on 15 March. A pause then ensued whilst the Allies returned to the formula of assaults all along the river line, beginning on 11 May, but massively reinforced and in good weather. These eventually resulted in the penetration of the German defences around Cassino, whilst Polish troops secured the Allied right flank, capturing the elusive abbey, and French troops swarmed through the Aurunci mountains on the left.

Though Allied narratives speak of four battles, Böhmler discusses only three. This is because he fuses the first and second battles into one, referring to the initial assault 'which started on 17 January and ended on 18 February' as the first. Thus his second battle, the destruction of the town, is understood in most English language accounts to represent the third struggle for this corner of the Gustav Line, where the terrain formed what another historian of the campaign,

John Ellis, called 'a vile tactical puzzle'. But who are we to complain? Böhmler had arrived with the rest of the 3rd *Fallschirmjäger* Regiment on 20 February, in the aftermath of the destruction of the abbey on the fifteenth, and his account up till then is largely narrative and analytical. Thereafter he lets his eyes do the talking and it is his impressions of the fight for Cassino town and abbey that leave their mark on the reader.

At the time of publication, there was great controversy over the destruction of this world famous landmark, founded by St Benedict in 529 AD, with the German armed forces generally cast as villains occupying the undamaged religious buildings for their tactical utility. Böhmler went to great lengths to research the validity of these claims, and was able to interview many of the Germans, Italian civilians and monks who had witnessed the dramas of only ten years earlier, before their memories had dimmed. Other authors have trodden the same path, including my own *Ten Armies In Hell* (2012) and the general conclusion – certainly reinforced by the fact that the devout Catholic aristocrat General von Senger was a lay member of the Order of St Benedict – is that the Germans seem to have respected the status of the monastery, to the extent that they evacuated the art treasures in it to the Vatican. Only once the buildings had been reduced to rubble by Allied bombers on 15 February did the Germans occupy the excellent defensive positions in the ruins so helpfully created by the Allied pilots – as the conventions of war allowed them to do.

Böhmler was researching and writing in 1954-55, when the nature of the Cold War had shifted radically in Europe. In the face of an ever-stronger Soviet threat, on 9 May 1955 West Germany had joined NATO, followed by the establishment of the Bundeswehr on 12 November. Böhmler's account was therefore, also to re-establish the credibility of the new German armed forces. The Russian front and Normandy were both too brutal and riddled with war crimes to provide much pride in German military activity, but with the Italian theatre in 1944 (although war crimes were perpetrated later on, particularly against partisans), many Germans felt they had achieved respect and integrity as opponents. On the slopes of Cassino, truces were arranged, stretchers borrowed and punctiliously returned. Bohmler observed that 'The Gurkhas gave their opponents – and not only the wounded – cigarettes, chocolates, offered them a swig from their water bottles and in many other small ways demonstrated the esteem in which they had held a worthy foeman'. All Allied accounts of Cassino support these anecdotes of decency by all sides.

Occasionally, Böhmler is carried away, or magnifies the achievements of the *Fallschirmjäger*. On 19 March 1944 the Allies used armour to break into the monastery area – much to the Germans' surprise, for it was thought that tanks could not get onto the high ground. Böhmler's account of his parachutists leaping from tank to tank, hurling mines about, destroying every armoured vehicle, does not accord with Allied After Action Reports of the engagement, where few relatively few armoured crewmen were lost and most damaged or bogged tanks recovered. But this should not detract from the authenticity of this work – the men were from another battalion, and events not personally witnessed by the author.

After Cassino, Rudolf Böhmler was promoted to *Oberstleutnant* (Lieutenant-Colonel) and command of the 4th *Fallschirmjäger* Regiment on 20 August 1944. The end of the war saw him as *Oberst* (Colonel) commanding the *Fallschirmjäger* Officer School at Bosco Chiese, north of Verona. By the time of his death in November 1968, he had become the major authority on German parachute actions, just when the Bundeswehr was forming a new *Fallschirmjäger* unit. Leutnant Joseph 'Jupp' Klein, a veteran of nearly 200 parachute jumps, who commanded a company of *Fallschirmjäger* engineers at Monte Cassino, recalled to me that Böhmler was 'a natural leader, who maintained a spirit of optimism when all around seemed dark'. A fellow company commander, Leutnant Hermann Volk, who after the war became a priest, recollected to me in 2007, 'Yes, Böhmler – now there was a man we would follow anywhere.'

Peter Caddick-Adams
Monte Cassino and Oxford, April 2015

Chapter 1

The Downfall of Mussolini

The grim fate which was to bring Mussolini to his ignominious end was hastened from two directions—by the army and by the Fascist Party itself. Behind the army stood the King, behind the party only those who still waxed fat on its bounty and were determined to preserve their privileges—even over the dead body of the Duce. In actual fact, Mussolini dragged both of them, King and Party, down to destruction with him.

In the preparations for the *coup d'état* a particularly active part was played by the Crown Princess, Maria José, an energetic and ambitious woman, who had never been friendlily disposed towards the Dictator. In her eyes he was an upstart, who should never have been allowed to attain the high position that he had. When the tide turned decisively in North Africa in the second half of 1942 and Italy was on the road to defeat, Maria José felt that her hour had come. She sought and succeeded in making contact with senior military officers, whom she hoped to persuade to intervene. One was the aged Marshal Caviglia, another was Marshal Pietro Badoglio. For Badoglio, too, was no friend of Mussolini. The aversion which in his heart of hearts he had always felt for him turned into implacable hatred when Mussolini, attributing to him the blame for the failure of the offensive in Albania, removed him from his post as Chief of Staff, Armed Forces, on 6 December 1940. This was a slight which Badoglio had never forgotten.

In the Italian Army Badoglio was held in high esteem. In the First War he had served in the field and as a staff officer with a distinction that was rewarded by the conferring on him of the title of Marchese di Sabotino. After the war he was for some years Italian Ambassador in Brazil. In 1926 he was promoted to Marshal of Italy and appointed Governor of Libya. In 1933 the King appointed him Chief of Staff, Armed Forces. When Marshal de Bono was seen to be making no progress in the Abyssinian war, he was replaced by Badoglio, who within six months brought the campaign to a successful conclusion. Honoured with the title of Duke of Addis Ababa, he returned to his post of Chief of the General Staff, where he remained until Mussolini sent him into the wilderness.

In his heart, he had never sided with his German ally. His sympathies, as was generally and well known, had always been with the West. When the scales of war moved steadily in favour of the Allies at the beginning of 1943, his friends urged him to approach the King and beg him to dismiss Mussolini. At first Badoglio was averse to the idea, though this did not prevent him from putting out feelers. The year before he had had a long and detailed discussion with the Crown Princess in the vicinity of Cogno, and this had been followed by numerous further conferences between these two important figures. Maria José impetuously insisted that the time had now come to get rid of Mussolini and his Fascist spectre. But the only channel through which this could be accomplished was the Villa Savoia and the King himself. The monarch, however, did not consider that the time for action had yet come; nor did he change his mind when he heard Badoglio's appreciation of the situation and his proposals for dealing with it. For by this time Badoglio was determined to set the wheels in motion. He very quickly persuaded the Minister of the Royal Household, Prince Acquarone, who had once served as his aide-de-camp, to support his conspiracy; and from him Badoglio learnt that the King, too, was now in favour of swift action. The time had now come to win over the waverers and the faint-hearted.

As in Germany in 1944, so now in Italy, only the army was in a position to do this. It alone possessed both the requisite organization and adequate material power; and Badoglio knew how to deal with the army. His task was made much easier by the fact that the new Chief of Staff, Colonel-General Ambrosio, entirely agreed with his views. With Prince Acquarone and Ambrosio he quickly decided to arrest Mussolini and a number of the more senior party officials. Of primary importance was the neutralizing of the Fascist Militia and its Black Shirt battalions, and, above all, of the 'M' Armoured Division, stationed near Rome. Ambrosio thought he could achieve this within three weeks. He and Acquarone now set about creating the secure and reliable system of communication which they would require to direct the activities of those officers and officials of Police Headquarters and the Ministry of the Interior who supported their cause. In good time a detachment of Carabinieri was stationed in the vicinity of the Villa Savoia.

At the end of June Badoglio held a series of discussions with Bonomi and other politicians on the subject of his intention to form a Cabinet composed of all the political parties which had been driven underground by the Fascists. About this there seemed to be no difficulty; but what really was difficult was how first to unseat Mussolini and then to seize power. In addition, 'there remained one insuperable obstacle—the breaking away from the Germans and the declaration of an armistice. Through the medium of confidential agents I had been able to establish contact with prominent British officials in Switzerland. These latter, however, could give no assurances whatever, and the sole result was that the British Government was informed that I was seeking every possible means of reaching an understanding with them.'* Badoglio, of course, had no illusions regarding how Hitler would react to the defection of Italy. Only the help of the Allies could save him from the rubbish heap. But if he wished to come to an agreement with the Western powers, he would first have to rid himself of the Germans; and that, in all conscience, was a tough problem.

While Badoglio was thus spreading his net, a second group of conspirators were also spinning their web—Mussolini's own immediate entourage. They saw disaster coming and were anxious to leave the heaving deck and get safely ashore before the leaking ship of state plunged with them to the bottom of the sea. The King heard all about these machinations but remained a passive spectator. It would be better, he thought, to leave it to the Fascist pack to bring the quarry to bay and then to step in and personally deliver the *coup de grâce*. But once that was done, the pack would, of course, have to be put under lock and key forthwith.

The leading spirits in the Party Leaders' Group were Count Dino Grandi and Count Galeazzo Ciano. Grandi had for many years been Ambassador to the Court of St James's. He was regarded as an Anglophile and an opponent of the Duce's foreign policy. The 8 February 1943, the day on which he had been compelled to give up his post as Minister of Justice, had left Grandi at a dead end; the same applied to Count Ciano whom, in the government reshuffle, his father-in-law had tucked out of harm's way as Ambassador to the Vatican. Both these ambitious politicians had thus been shorn of power. The Party Big Men, who set about forcing the downfall of Mussolini immediately after the beginning of the invasion of Sicily, were unanimous in their determination to see that control of the country did not fall into the hands of any other group. The Fascist Party, they were

* Badoglio, *Italy in the Second World War.*

resolved, must maintain its predominant position in the State. There was general agreement, too, regarding Mussolini's successor. The Duce was to be replaced by a triumvirate consisting of Grandi, Ciano and Federzoni. There was no agreement, however, regarding the fate of Mussolini after he had been deposed; some wished to see him completely and irrevocably removed from public life, while others were in favour of retaining him as a puppet, without power or credit. His military successor was to be the King himself.

Mussolini's bad state of health at the time was very convenient for the conspirators. The Duce was suffering from a recurrence of an old malady, an inflammation of the duodenum, presumed to be of syphilitic origin. And now the word was being passed round Rome and the other cities that the Duce was very ill and was seriously considering retiring. The party plotters zealously added fuel to this fire, in order to conjure up the impression that Mussolini was a spent force and that the appointment of a successor was both inevitable and urgent.

Thanks to the invasion of Sicily, the ball was slowly set in motion. On 12 July the Party Secretary, Scorza, issued an appeal to the party leaders to go out into the countryside and urge the population to remain steadfast in their resolve. But before doing so, these leaders wanted to hear from Mussolini himself the truth about the state of affairs. Accordingly, they were received by the Duce at the Palazzo Venezia on 16 July. In the course of a lively debate, Farinacci urged Mussolini to convene a meeting of the Fascist Grand Council as quickly as possible and place the facts before it. Pressed by the majority to do so, Mussolini much against his will at last gave way and fixed 24 July for the convening of the Council.

Now, with the assistance of Ciano, Grandi set about sharpening the point of his deadly spear. He drafted an 'Order of the Day', a resolution demanding the termination of Mussolini's dictatorship and the assumption of power by the King. This order of the day met with the approval—before ever a vote was taken on it in Council—of most of the members of the Grand Council. Mussolini's days were numbered.

It was during this period that the meeting between Hitler and Mussolini took place at Feltre on 19 July. The Germans taking part were Keitel and Warlimont from Supreme Headquarters, von Mackensen (the Ambassador to Rome), and General von Rintelen. The Italian delegation consisted of Colonel General Ambrosio, Bastiani the Under Secretary of State for Foreign Affairs, and Alfieri, the Ambassador to Berlin. Mussolini was plainly in a very depressed frame of mind. After the receipt of the negative German reply to the demand for weapons made on 21 June, the Italian Chief of Staff had reproached him heavily and had painted the blackest possible picture of Italy's desperate military plight. In Ambrosio's view

Italy was quite incapable of continuing to wage war. He had therefore insisted that the Duce should tell Hitler, tersely and quite bluntly, that the country was tottering on the verge of collapse.

At Feltre Hitler opened the proceedings with a two-hour monologue on the conduct of total war, in the course of which he aimed an oblique but emphatic smack at the Italians by saying that he could continue to wage total war for as long as the auxiliary resources of the European countries, and of the Balkans in particular, remained at his disposal. Hitler's speech was not translated, so his Italian audience were able only to follow the broad gist of it. Mussolini listened in silence, and when Hitler ended, he made no reply.

In the middle of the conference came the shattering news that Rome had been bombed. Mussolini was horrified. So the Allies were not even going to spare the Eternal City! Two hundred and seventy Flying Fortresses and Liberators had wrought havoc in the marshalling yards at Littorio and Termini, and the adjacent residential areas of San Lorenzo had been lain waste. At the same time 320 medium bombers had attacked the Roman airfields. This was a terrible blow to the Italians. But even this nightmare news failed to goad Mussolini to speak plainly to Hitler and clear the air.

When the conference ended, Ambrosio, Alfieri and Bastiani reproached the Duce for not having then and there made Italy's desperate plight clear to Hitler and told him the blunt truth. Driven into a corner, Mussolini promised to do so during the drive to the Treviso airfield. But even then he could not bring himself to confess that he was at the end of his tether. All he did was to ask for further German reinforcements.

Keitel and Ambrosio also had an opportunity for a brief talk during the drive. Keitel demanded that the Italian High Command should take measures to guarantee the security of the lines of communication across the Messina Straits and should send further troops to reinforce the defences of Calabria. The whole of southern Italy, he said, should at once be declared to be a theatre of war; on the German side he was ready to transfer forthwith two infantry divisions to south Italy, provided the Italians did likewise. Finally the German Field-Marshal asked that a German liaison staff should be allowed to join the headquarters of the Italian Seventh Army in southern Italy. Ambrosio received these demands with reservation. In the end he replied that he hoped to be able to obtain a reply from the Duce very soon. The next day Mussolini's reply, agreeing to the German demands almost in their entirety, reached German Supreme Headquarters.

When Mussolini flew back to Rome on the morning of 20 July, dense clouds of smoke formed an admirable landmark for the pilot of his aircraft.

The Roman railway stations were still burning. The population was in a state of hysterical despair. Badoglio, who had visited the stricken districts, was greeted with angry shouts and demands that this futile war be stopped at once.

In the afternoon Mussolini was received in audience by the King, who met him with furrowed brow and an anxious expression on his face. Victor Emmanuel, too, emphasized that Italy could not hold out much longer. Sicily, he said, was practically lost, the morale of the troops was bad, and Italy had been deceived by Germany. Mussolini ended his reply by saying that he hoped to put an end to the Italo-German alliance by 15 September. All this shows only too clearly how far removed Mussolini's ideas were from the stern reality of the situation. That evening he sent for Ambrosio and told him that he had now decided to write a letter to Hitler, telling him that Italy was no longer able to continue the fight. Greatly agitated, the Chief of Staff retorted that there had been ample opportunity to do so at the Feltre conference; the letter Mussolini now proposed sending, he said, would simply be pitched into the waste-paper basket in Berlin. The Duce, he continued, had ignored all his previous warnings, and he there-fore did not feel able any longer to share the responsibility with him and requested to be relieved of his post. This, however, was not permitted. The King and Badoglio had need of the Chief of Staff, devoted to their cause, to help them overthrow Mussolini and the Fascists. But the proposed letter to Hitler was never written.

A few days later the Fascist Grand Council belaboured the man to whom all its members owed their high position. It was 24 July. In the morning the Duce had received first Grandi and then the Commander-in-Chief, South. When Field-Marshal Kesselring entered Mussolini's office, the Duce greeted him with the words: 'You know Grandi? He has just been here, and we had a long discussion. We are in complete agreement, and Grandi remains faithful to me.'

On the same day the German Ambassador, von Mackensen, reported to Kesselring that Mussolini was in no danger and was complete master of the situation! In the afternoon the storm burst about Mussolini's head. At five o'clock the Grand Council met in the Palazzo Venezia. A heavy, tense atmosphere prevailed, which boded no good. The meeting opened with the reading out of Grandi's *Ordine del Giorno*. He started off with admirably turned and pompous phrases. The thoughts of the Fascist Grand Council, meeting at this grave hour of dire peril, he declaimed, turn first and foremost to those heroic warriors of all arms, who, side by side with the proud inhabitants of Sicily, those most shining examples of the unshakeable faith of the Italian people, are so worthily upholding the traditions of gallantry and selfless devotion to duty of our armed forces.

And he ended rather tamely with a request that the King should now please reassume active command of the armed forces.*

Grandi was followed by Mussolini, who defended his policy. At great length he described the assistance that Italy had received from Germany, enumerating in detail 220,000 tons of aviation petrol, 421,000 tons of crude oil, 2,500,000 tons of steel and 40,000,000 tons of coal. Turning to Grandi's resolution, he asserted that this was tantamount to presenting the King with a blank cheque; it meant that the latter and not the Grand Council would have the power to make decisions and that Fascism itself would thereby be exposed to mortal danger.

When Mussolini ended, Grandi opened the discussion. He attacked the Duce with unwonted acerbity, and was followed by Ciano who confined himself to hurling abuse at the Germans. Nearly all the members of the Grand Council had their say. Towards midnight Scorza proposed that the meeting be adjourned and continued the next day. This was sharply opposed by Grandi who insisted that their business must be completed without delay. He was, of course, already aware that the King had completed all the arrangements for Mussolini's arrest on 25 July. At last, at about three o'clock in the morning, the Council cast its votes. Grandi's resolution was carried by nineteen votes to seven, with one abstention. In addition to Grandi and Ciano, Alfieri and the aged Marshal de Bono, who had taken part in the march on Rome, had also turned their backs on the Duce.

Mussolini's fate was thus sealed. He made no attempt to oppose it with any show of force. The die had been cast against him, and he no longer had the inner strength of will to resist. Without further ado, he submitted. After the voting, when he asked who should convey the Council's decision to the King, Grandi sprang to his feet and cried: 'You yourself!' Mussolini then declared the meeting closed with the words: 'It is you who have provoked this crisis in the régime.' In reality, sentence of death had already been passed on Fascism.

The news of the Council's decision spread through Rome with the speed of the wind. Excitement was intense. There were open demonstrations against Fascism, some of which ended in blows.

Mussolini, who in contrast to most of his opponents in the Grand Council had spent the rest of the night in his own residence, set off as usual at nine o'clock the next morning for his office, as though nothing had happened. During the morning he telephoned to the Villa Savoia to ask that the King should grant him an audience. After that he received the Japanese Ambassador and a number of other prominent people. About

* At the beginning of the war Mussolini had assumed the post of Supreme Commander, Armed Forces.

noon, accompanied by General Galbiati, the Chief of the Militia, he visited the areas of the city which had been badly damaged in the air raid. When he returned to the Villa Torlona, the King's reply awaited him. The Duce was requested to be at the Villa Savoia at 4 p.m. Devoid of any misgivings and dressed, as he always was for an audience with the King, in civilian clothes, Mussolini arrived at the King's residence at the hour appointed. The monarch, of course, had been fully informed of the events of the previous night; all he now had to do was to close the trap. The ensuing conversation was of brief duration. Mussolini was reluctant to admit that the resolution of the Grand Council affected him personally in any way. But the King pointed out that the Grand Council was a constitutional organ of the State and as such derived its authority from the constitution. Its decrees, therefore, were equally binding on both the monarch and the head of the government. In that case, Mussolini retorted, if that were the King's view, he had no option but to tender his resignation. 'And I accept it forthwith,' replied the King. Taken utterly aback, Mussolini reeled as though hit by an unexpected blow. At that moment he may well have recalled the words he used to von Rintelen in 1939, when he said that any government which led its people into disaster as the Polish Government had done, had no option but to resign.

The King accompanied Mussolini to the door and shook him by the hand as he took his leave. But as the Duce strode towards his car, a captain of Carabinieri to his surprise came over to him and stated that the King had entrusted him with the protection of the Duce's person. At the same time he pointed to an ambulance standing nearby and invited Mussolini to get in. Without protest the Duce clambered into his prison on wheels, which took him to the Carabinieri barracks that for the time being were to be his place of confinement.

During the night he received a letter from Badoglio, in which the latter assured him that he would come to no harm and that he had been placed in custody solely for his own protection. Would he please say, Badoglio concluded, where he would prefer to take up his ultimate abode? Mussolini replied that he would like to go to his summer residence in northern Italy, Rocca delle Cominate. The Prefect of the provincial administration in question, however, demurred, and his protestation that he would be quite unable to guarantee Mussolini's safety caused Badoglio to move his prisoner to Gaeta on the night of 27/28 July and from there to ship him across to the island of Ponza.

While Mussolini's fate was thus being settled in the Villa Savoia, Badoglio, surrounded by a group of trusted friends, had remained at home, ready to pounce. The tension eased when, at about five o'clock in the afternoon, Prince Acquarone arrived with the eagerly awaited news of the events of the previous hour. At the same time he brought an order for Badoglio to report forthwith to the King. The latter, said the Prince, had now made up his mind to entrust the forming of a government to the Marshal. The game was won! Not Grandi but Badoglio was to be the next Prime Minister.

At the Villa Savoia Badoglio submitted his proposed list of Ministers to the King, and on it were names such as Bonomi, Casati, Einaudi—representatives, that is, of all the major political parties. The King, however, had already drafted a list of his own, all experts in their own particular sphere. The dismissal of the Duce had caused great indignation among the Germans, and the King, obviously, did not wish further to exacerbate them by forming a government composed entirely of Mussolini's non-Fascist political opponents.

The measures taken by the new government were dictated to a large extent by the anticipated reactions of the Germans. It was impossible for Badoglio to announce, as the Italian people were hoping, Italy's immediate withdrawal from the war. Such an announcement would have forced Hitler's hand and compelled him to intervene. The danger of any such intervention could be obviated, the Government hoped, by the issue of two proclamations, which were already complete in draft form when the King received his new Prime Minister. Both were broadcast, one by Badoglio and the other by the King himself, in the late evening. In both the King and Badoglio called upon the Italian people to redouble their war efforts and declared that Italy would unflinchingly fight on at the side of her German ally 'until final victory had been won'.

During the night of 25/26 July Rome—and all Italy—was cleansed of Fascism. In the capital the news of Mussolini's dismissal had led to scenes of wild and frantic enthusiasm; and all through the night a vast mass of humanity, intoxicated with joy, roamed through the streets of the Eternal City. Enemies of the former régime started a witch hunt against Fascists, and Badoglio set his henchmen on the tracks of the senior party officials. Many, however, succeeded in fleeing in good time to safety. Grandi was on his way to Portugal, Ciano *en route* for Germany and Farinacci had sought refuge in the German Embassy. Among those caught was Count Cavallero, a former Chief of the General Staff.

Fascism disappeared overnight like a ghost whom the earth had swallowed. By 26 July there was hardly a single Fascist emblem to be seen in the whole of Rome. With pickaxes and hammers the people had set about demolishing these insignia of a régime which had perished miserably thanks to its feet of clay and the corruption with which it had been permeated.

As always happens when a dictator is toppled from his throne, people shot up like mushrooms, who had 'always been anti-Fascist'—without, admittedly, having previously themselves realized it. Opportunists made a rush for the flesh-pots, doing their utmost to brush aside the men who for years on end had had the courage to oppose Fascism. 'Many acted in perfectly good faith, inspired solely by the desire to see freedom and order re-established in the land. Many, too, were moved by hatred, born of the injustices they had suffered. But there were also those—and truth, bitter though it may be, compels me to say that there were not a few of them— who were actuated solely by avarice and the hope of getting a good job. And it was these latter, of course, who were the most clamorous.'*

Contrary to expectation, the assumption of power by the new Government took place without any opposition. Only General Galbiati, the Chief of Staff of the Fascist Militia, seems to have contemplated opposing the new régime with his Black Shirt battalions, but Badoglio's intervention persuaded him to vacate the field in favour of General Armellini, an old and trusted friend of the Prime Minister. The 'M' Armoured Division, too, remained passive. Command of it was taken over by Count Calvi di Bergolo, the King's son-in-law, and it was then renamed the Centauro Division.

The Germans in Rome were completely flabbergasted when they heard the news of the *coup d'état*. Even as late as the evening of 25 July Field-Marshal Kesselring had urgently requested audience of the King. This the King had refused to grant, for there was always the fear that the Germans might intervene before the new Government was firmly in the saddle. But he promised to receive the Field-Marshal the next day. Before the audience, Kesselring went to see Badoglio, who reiterated the sentiments he had expressed in his broadcast and begged Kesselring not to make things difficult for him. To the Field-Marshal's question regarding the whereabouts of Mussolini he replied: "That is known to the King alone.'

Victor Emmanuel received the Commander-in-Chief, South, with a great show of friendship. He, too, repeated that Italy would remain true to the alliance, that she would, indeed, redouble her war effort. When Kesselring tried again to find out where Mussolini was, the King answered: 'That is known to Badoglio alone.' Although the attitude adopted by the King and his government was both dishonest and evasive, the Field-Marshal accepted the King's word and the official assurances of the head of the Government.

Führer Headquarters was not in the least surprised to hear of the Italian *coup d'état*. Ever since May, since the defeat in Tunisia, Hitler had been expecting a political upheaval in Italy and the defection of his Italian ally. His whole attitude towards the Italians was based on this suspicion and a

* Badoglio, *Italy in the Second World War.*

deep sense of mistrust. This it was that had caused him to concentrate large armies in Austria and southern France, so that he would have strong forces ready to hand in the event of Italian defection. When the news of Mussolini's fall reached Führer Headquarters, it did so in the middle of a conference concerning the strengthening of the armies in question. Hitler foamed with rage. Once again he had 'been proved right'. In the initial paroxysm of his fury his first inclination was 'to drive without any ado into Rome and arrest the Government, the King—the whole bag of them—especially the Crown Prince and Badoglio'.* His rancour was also directed against the German representatives in Rome, who, he considered, had allowed themselves to be well and truly duped. Kesselring's days seemed to be numbered, while von Mackensen (the Ambassador), and General von Rintelen were recalled and were given no further employment. Field-Marshal von Richthoven and the German Air Attaché, General Ritter von Pohl, also came under suspicion, but were nevertheless allowed to remain at their posts. Nor did Mackensen's successor, Dr Rahn, bask in the sunshine of Hitler's approbation.

To the Western powers Mussolini's fall came as a surprise. Militarily they were not in the least prepared for it. Churchill, of course, had consistently urged his allies to carry the war to the Italian mainland and destroy Fascism. But the Americans put on the brake and held back. On 17 July Allied aircraft had dropped leaflets on Rome, calling upon the Italian people in the name of Roosevelt and Churchill to overthrow Mussolini and surrender. No military preparations had, however, been made to exploit the Duce's downfall by a swift *coup de main*. Eisenhower's hands were tied by the campaign in Sicily; and reserves and the transport and landing craft necessary to create a strong force and launch it at once against the peninsula were not available. For the Western powers had other objectives in view, in addition to Italy, for the second half of 1943; and in this way they allowed Hitler the requisite time to appreciate the potential consequences of Mussolini's downfall and to consolidate his own position in Italy.

* Chester Wilmot, *The Struggle for Europe*.

Chapter 2

Italy Capitulates

Mussolini's downfall, occurring as it did during a period of unbroken military failures, inevitably shook the Berlin-Rome Axis to its very foundations. The effect was all the more shattering because, with the Duce, Fascism, too, vanished like a ghost.

Hitler, as a friend of Mussolini, not only felt that the Duce's fall was a personal affront to himself, but was also equally shocked by the realization that a handful of men had sufficed to topple the mighty dictator from his throne. Then again, the swift sweeping away of the inherently corrupt Fascist system must, he felt, have given the German people food for thought, and it was quite possible that this, too, might have repercussions in Germany.

Above all, however, the downfall of his friend was regarded by Hitler as the first step towards capitulation by Italy, the probability of which had now to be taken seriously into consideration. The—to his mind—shameful and degrading way in which Mussolini had been removed from the stage of world affairs did nothing to mitigate his furious anger. Whereas hitherto his mistrust had been confined to the Royal House and its entourage, he now had grave misgivings about the Italian Government and the leaders of the armed forces as well. The lack of any success by his allies in the Mediterranean theatre and the failure of the Italian divisions on the eastern front now seemed to him to be links in one and the same chain of treachery. In his deep resentment he gave no thought to the fact that in 1940, too, against a France on the brink of collapse and a weak but gallant Greece, Italian arms had achieved no success worth mentioning.

His reaction, then, to the events of 25 July was violent in the extreme. He had no doubt whatever that the new Government was determined to break off the alliance, to betray its German brothers-in-arms and to make common cause with the Western powers; and memories of Italy's attitude in 1914–15 may well have strengthened his conviction.

In the first flush of his anger he decided to seize Rome by a *coup de main* and without further ado to arrest the Royal Family and all the political and military chiefs. With this object in view—and without informing even the Commander-in-Chief, South, to say nothing of the Italian Supreme Command—he transferred the 2 Parachute Division (General Ramcke) by air from southern France to Pratica di Mare, just south of Rome, and ordered the 3 Panzer Grenadier Division, which was a little to the north of the capital, to stand by to move to its support at the appropriate moment. Since these moves could not take place without Kesselring's co-operation, however, he was forced at the last moment to take the Field-Marshal into his confidence. Kesselring, not unnaturally, opposed the whole idea. Thus brutally to put an end to a brotherhood-in-arms of long standing by a *coup de main* which, without positive proof of Italy's shady intentions, would be contrary to every code of military ethics, was, to Kesselring's mind, out of the question. On the other hand, Hitler's second precautionary measure—the immediate transfer of German divisions to northern Italy—was readily acceptable to him.

From 26 July German forces from southern France, the Tyrol and Styria poured over the Alpine passes and on into Tuscany. They dismantled, probably with some glee, the mountain fortifications constructed by the Italians against Germany, occupied the main lines of communication, defiles and bridges and announced for all to hear that they had come to put Mussolini back on his throne.

The eight divisions in question, to which later a mountain brigade was added, were not, as one would have supposed, placed under the command of the Commander-in-Chief, South, but were organized as Army Group B, under Field-Marshal Rommel, who with his staff remained for the time being in Munich.

In Rome, too, there was feverish activity. After the new Cabinet had taken the oath, Badoglio informed Hitler officially by telegram of the constitution of the new Government and suggested a meeting in northern Italy, to be attended also by the King. He did this, presumably, with a view to doing what Mussolini had not had the courage to do at Feltre, namely, to tell Hitler bluntly that Italy was at the end of her resources and could no longer continue the war.

Hitler himself did not reply. But through the normal channels he informed the Italian Foreign Minister that he had discussed the situation in detail with the former head of the government at Feltre on 19 July and therefore saw no reason for a further conference at the highest level. Instead, he suggested that the Foreign Ministers and the military chiefs should meet at Tarvisio on 6 August. It is possible that fear may have caused him to refuse the Italian invitation. He may well have felt that, on Italian soil, Badoglio might ambush him as he had done Mussolini. Badoglio, on the other hand had suggested a meeting in Italy 'because I was quite sure that if I had gone to Germany I should never have returned'.*

The problem now facing the Italian Premier was whether or not it would be advisable to accept the German suggestion. He decided to accept, for had he rejected it he would only have heightened German suspicion, whereas by accepting he would at least not increase it. At the worst, his acceptance might perhaps give the Allies the impression that Italy intended to remain loyal to the Axis and would honour the assurances given by the King and himself and fight on. He was determined, however, to do his best to counteract any such impression. 'I had become convinced of the vital necessity of marking time with the Germans for as long as possible and of doing my utmost in the meanwhile to get in touch with the Anglo-Americans.'†

His immediate task, then, was somehow or other to mollify his future allies before sitting down at the conference table with his current brothers-in-arms at Tarvisio. This he succeeded in doing.

Some of the measures taken by the Germans were certainly not of a kind that might have persuaded the Italians not to break off the alliance after all. But it is a gross exaggeration to assert, as is sometimes done today, that these measures simply drove the Italians into the arms of the Allies. Badoglio's vanity had been hurt by the very lively concern shown by Hitler and other leading Germans regarding Mussolini's fate, while he himself was ignored and had not even been vouchsafed the courtesy of a direct reply by Hitler to his invitation.

He was annoyed, too, when Hitler on 29 July sent his friend Mussolini a birthday present of the works of Nietzsche, bound in blue leather, with the inscription in the first volume: 'Adolf Hitler to his friend, Benito Mussolini.' He was equally furious over the birthday telegram sent to Mussolini by Göring. He was also full of complaints regarding Farinacci's flight to the German Embassy. The German Ambassador was fully entitled,

* Badoglio, *Italy in the Second World War.* † Ibid.

he conceded, to afford asylum to a political fugitive, but this flight, aided and abetted by the Germans, of one of the leading Fascists was, in his opinion, a gross violation of Italian sovereignty. All these, however, were mere pin-pricks in comparison with the march of Rommel's Army Group into upper Italy and the surprise appearance of the 2 Parachute Division at the gates of the Italian capital.

Hitler's decision to occupy upper Italy without even consulting the Italian Supreme Command was undoubtedly based on the assumption that, in the event of Italy's capitulation, the Italians intended to block the Alpine passes and seal off the other main routes of communication in northern Italy. For Germany, the results of such measures would have been incalculable. For one thing it would have meant that the German divisions in central and southern Italy would have been starved out, and it might well have constituted an open invitation to the Allies to carry out a major landing in these areas. Kesselring condemned this as a devilish plan, 'for,' he said, 'as a reward for all the comradeship and help we had so unstintingly given and all the sacrifices we had made, it could not be adequately described by any other words.'

The dispositions of their major formations seems rather to support the assumption that the Italian High Command was, indeed, contemplating some such sinister action. For whereas in southern Italy, where the danger of invasion was greatest, there were only three Italian divisions, in the relatively secure north there were no less than seven, which, together with seven further divisions that the Italians demanded should be withdrawn from southern France and the Balkans, would have constituted a most formidable threat to their former allies.

Equal suspicion was aroused in German minds by the Italian High Command's efforts to ensure that as strong German forces as possible should be concentrated in the south. 'There could be only one possible motive behind the suggested moves, namely, to ensure that as strong German forces as possible should be removed as far as possible from their native land and lines of supply and communication and thus be presented to the Allies as a dowry.'* The correctness of the assumption is further confirmed by Badoglio's repeated insistence, during his armistice negotiations with the Allies, that strong Allied forces should be landed north of Rome. Had this occurred, the fate of the German divisions in southern Italy would have been sealed.

The measures taken by German Supreme Headquarters naturally provoked a response from the Italians. It consisted firstly of verbal and written protests by both government and the Italian Supreme Command, who regarded Hitler's chess moves as a gross violation of Italian

* Kesselring, *Soldat bis zum letzten Tag.*

sovereignty, and secondly of the concentration of strong Italian forces in the vicinity of the capital and the naval port of La Spezia. In the Rome area alone a battle group of more than five divisions was in the process of rapid formation.

This Army Corps was under the command of General Carboni, a trusted friend of the new Prime Minister and a man well known for his anti-German sympathies. That alone gave ample food for thought. The sudden appearance of Italian armoured formations, among them the Centauro Armoured Division, in this battle group was also regarded as significant. Hitherto, the Comando Supremo had fearfully—or, perhaps, with more sinister motives—kept its armour far away from the fronts. Now, all of a sudden, here they were! This, too, gave food for thought.

Initially Carboni's divisions took up positions in light fieldworks, behind swiftly operable road blocks and more or less 'at ease'. But there was little doubt that, when the time came, they would turn their weapons on their former allies. Two further divisions were grouped round La Spezia, with the obvious object of protecting the fleet from being seized by the Germans.

These precautions, most unusual between allies and taken by both sides alike, threatened to transform the already existent feeling of mutual distrust into an open and irreparable breach. To avert this danger, the 'General attached to the headquarters of the Italian Armed Forces', General von Rintelen, flew to Führer Headquarters on 2 August. What he was there told was very much the reverse of flattering to the Italian ally. His efforts to ease the intolerable tension met with but little success; all he managed to achieve was to cause the temporary postponement of the arrest, planned for the next day, of the King and the Government until after the Tarvisio conference. Hitler remained adamant in his conviction that nothing could turn Badoglio from his intention of joining the Allied camp.

In contrast to the angry suspicion which overshadowed the relations between the two Governments and their respective High Commands, the mutual confidence between the fighting troops remained for the most part unaffected. For this, the bonds forged during the North African campaign may well have been responsible, even though the attitude of the Italian soldiers regarding the imminent invasion of Sicily had left the Germans with little confidence in their determination to put up a fight. For any illusions of that kind Sicily was still too fresh in their minds. Relations between the German commanders and their opposite numbers remained equally good, even after the fall of Mussolini. More than anyone else, it was Field-Marshal Kesselring who was most anxious to maintain a cordial understanding. Most sincerely he strove to preserve that feeling of mutual trust between Germans and Italians, the corner-stone of which, in his eyes, was the assurance given by the King and repeated officially by Badoglio.

The faith he displayed in the integrity of his allies, his—in Hitler's opinion—too great a readiness to see the Italian point of view and to concede it was all in keeping with the man's character. General Westphal, who worked in close collaboration with Kesselring long enough to be able to form an authoritative opinion, has the following to say: 'Trust in his fellow men and a frank and generous nature were the salient features of his character. These qualities manifested themselves in many ways—in his giving the whole of his income and fortune to bring joy or help to some of his subordinates or their dependents and to needy Italian friends; and again, in the constancy of his affection for the Italian people, not always understood by others, during 1943 and 1944.'* At Führer Headquarters the Field-Marshal was regarded—not without justification—as an Italo- phile. Hitler therefore decided that he should retain his command only for as long as it remained necessary to deal with the Italians on a more or less friendly basis. Behind him, in northern Italy, stood Rommel, specially selected for the task of opening, at the appropriate moment, a new chapter in Italo-German relations. This moment, however, never materialized. Italophile though he undoubtedly was, Kesselring emerged in brilliant fashion from the whole wretched business of the Italian capitulation.

He had himself repeatedly tried to mitigate Hitler's deep-rooted mistrust of the King and the new Government, but without success. Eventually, on 22 August, he found himself compelled to revise his ideas, when Hitler told him on that date that he had irrefutable proof of Badoglio's treachery. This information placed obligations on him which he could not ignore. But it also put him in a most anomalous position. He, an officer of absolute integrity and a man who conducted all his affairs with frank honesty, was now called upon to act with the same 'flexibility' with which the Italians had been acting for weeks, perhaps months, in their dealings with him. Now, for him, too, his right hand was not to be allowed to know what his left hand was doing.

To deal with the contingency of a sudden defection by Italy the O.K.W. issued directives to ensure the safety of the German divisions in that country and the neutralization of the Italian Armed Forces. The code word 'Axis' was to be the signal for immediate and drastic action—the Italian Army was to be disarmed, the Italian soldiers were to be transferred as 'military internees' to Germany, all aircraft and anti-aircraft artillery was to be seized, the Italian fleet was to be prevented from putting to sea, with the object of incorporating it later in the German Navy, and all supply dumps and focal points on the lines of communication were to be taken

* Westphal, *Heer in Fesseln.*

over. In addition, the Field-Marshal gave orders for the evacuation of Calabria, Sardinia and Corsica. All these orders in connexion with 'Axis' were, on principle, passed on verbally by the Field-Marshal to be acted upon as soon as an armistice was announced.

It is worth noting that Kesselring was opposed to the wholesale arrest of the Italian troops. He thought that this would not only be very difficult to carry out, but that it could also prove to be a dangerous move. Subsequent events fully justified his view.

The great question-mark, however, remained Rome itself. If Carboni's Army Corps showed even a modicum of fighting spirit and if somehow or other it were reinforced by a drop of Allied paratroops, the Germans would find themselves in dire peril. O.K.W. itself feared the worst. 'Hitler greatly feared that the Italians were planning a St Bartholomew's eve for the Germans, while the latter were making all preparations for a counter-attack against them.'* This applied not only to Rome, but to the whole of Italy. But the capital was the nerve-centre; whoever controlled Rome would be the master of southern Italy.

The new Foreign Minister, Guariglia, who up till now had been the Ambassador in Ankara, arrived in Rome on 29 July. Before he left Turkey, he gave the Turkish Foreign Minister to understand that he regarded a radical change in Italian foreign policy as inevitable. Mussolini's downfall, he said, should be regarded as the first step and as the beginning of the disintegration of the Berlin-Rome Axis. He had also asked the Minister to pass on this information to the Allied representatives accredited to the Turkish Government. Having assumed office, Guariglia immediately made contact with the British and American *chargés d'affaires* at the Holy See. His query whether these two diplomats were in a position to set up a channel of communication between their own and the Italian Foreign Ministries was answered in the negative 'on account of a lack of technical equipment'.

In both Badoglio's and Guariglia's view, the imminence of the Tarvisio conference made it imperative that they should act swiftly.

In an atmosphere reminiscent of the days of the Borgias, the opening of the capitulation negotiations was entrusted to the Marquis d'Ayeta. As Ciano's *chef de Cabinet* and a man with family connexions in the United States, he seemed to be the right person to take the first steps.

On 2 August he left Rome for Lisbon. On the day following his arrival he asked for an interview with the British Ambassador, Campbell, letting it be known that he had an important communication from the Italian Government to pass on. Campbell was quite prepared to receive the Italian negotiator and gave him the opportunity of fulfilling his mission

* Westphal, *Heer in Fesseln.*

on 4 August. The latter started off by describing the hopelessness of Italy's situation, coupling his remarks with an assurance that Badoglio was most anxious to surrender, but that his liberty of action was being seriously restricted by the Germans. Hitler, he said, was already suspicious, and the Italians were therefore compelled to attend the Tarvisio conference—not, of course, to reaffirm the Axis alliance, but simply to lull German suspicions.

This first feeler by the Badoglio Government came as no surprise to the Western powers. As early as the end of July the British Foreign Office and the General Staff had set about the task of drafting terms of capitulation for Italy, and by the first week in August had completed the draft. Churchill, the old fox, knew what was coming! D'Ayeta's arguments were convincing, and on 5 August Churchill telegraphed his views on the situation to the President of the United States, saying that the King and Badoglio had no option but to pretend to wish to fight on, and that this they would continue to assure the Germans at Tarvisio. 'But,' he said, 'this will be only pretence. The whole country is only longing for peace. . .'*

The next day Guariglia and Ribbentrop met at Tarvisio. The two Supreme Headquarters were represented by Ambrosio and Keitel. The Italian Foreign Minister succeeded without much difficulty in convincing his German colleague of Italy's 'loyalty'. But 'a shot in the arm' delivered by Hitler on the telephone stiffened the attitude of the German negotiators.

The ensuing conference between Keitel and Ambrosio led to no positive result. The Italian Chief of Staff complained about the German move into upper Italy and demanded that Rommel's Army Corps should be placed under the command of the Comando Supremo and transferred to the front in south Italy! The Italian portion of the Brenner railway line he proposed to 'secure', he said, with two Alpini divisions. In addition, the Comando Supremo proposed to withdraw the Italian Fourth Army from southern France and three divisions from the Balkans and concentrate them in the threatened motherland.

Keitel justified the measures taken by Germany in upper Italy by pointing out that it was essential to safeguard the German lines of communication and by drawing attention to the possibility of an Allied air landing in that area. He made the investment of further German divisions in south Italy dependent upon the transfer to the threatened south of the Italian divisions at present being retained in the north.

Neither side wanted to take the first step. The Italians felt that their shabby intentions had been unmasked, the Germans were playing for safety and had no intention of voluntarily putting their heads into the noose.

* Churchill, *The Second World War*, Vol. V.

While tempers in Tarvisio were getting more and more heated, a certain Signor Berio presented himself at the British Embassy in Tangiers. As an emissary of the Italian Foreign Minister, he repeated the latter's plea that the Allies should have patience with the Italians and give them time to free themselves from their German toils. He let it be understood that the Italian Government was most sincere in its desire to negotiate and that he himself had been granted plenipotentiary powers to do so. A week later Berio returned to Rome with a demand for 'unconditional surrender' as the sole reward of all his efforts.

Next, on 12 August, a military mission under General Castellano and camouflaged as a delegation from one of the civilian Ministries, travelled by diplomatic train to Lisbon. Castellano took advantage of the fact that he was passing through the Spanish capital to make contact with Sir Samuel Hoare, the British Ambassador to Madrid. He informed the latter that he had been authorized by the King and Badoglio to state that the Italian Government was firmly determined to break off the alliance with Germany at the first possible moment. That, however, was not the whole story! His country, Castellano continued, was prepared to transfer all its available forces to the Allied camp and to take up the fight against the Reich side by side with the Western allies. It would, of course, be appreciated, he said, that his government would not be in a position to implement this volte-face until after the Allied armies had set foot on the Italian mainland. But the most succulent bait, at which it was felt the Allies would certainly snap with great eagerness, came at the end. 'If the Allied powers are prepared to accept the proposals of my government,' said Castellano, 'I am in a position to hand over to their representatives all the files and maps of the Italian General Staff in so far as they refer to the German forces in Italy. You will receive precise details regarding the dispositions, movements, strengths and armament of the German forces.'

This was Italy's thanks to an ally who had shed so much blood on her behalf! Now their German brothers-in-arms were to be ruthlessly sacrificed by the Italians in a frantic effort to save their own skins at the last moment. This offer to betray military secrets (which was implemented a few days later) overstepped by far the lengths to which it was permissible to go in an endeavour to negotiate an armistice that was recognized by all to be unavoidable. History will condemn this act as an indelible blemish on the names of Italy's rulers at the time.

Hoare immediately informed Eden, who in turn passed on the information to Churchill, then at sea in the *Queen Mary* on his way to the Quebec conference. The latter instructed his Foreign Secretary to enter into negotiations with the Italian Government, but only in so far as was consistent with military requirements. 'These instructions,' writes

Jacques Mordal, 'were quite superfluous, since Castellano was ready to sign anything which would make it possible for him to join forces with the Allies against Germany.'*

On 15 August, the same day that Castellano was with Sir Samuel Hoare, representatives of the German and Italian Supreme Commands, led respectively by Jodl and Roatta, met in Bologna. Rommel was also present. From the outset the atmosphere was extremely tense, and the tension found concrete expression in the security measures ordered personally by Hitler and put into practice by the '*Leibstandarte*'. General von Rintelen's remark that he considered these measures wholly superfluous and would himself vouch for the safety of the German paratroops drew from Jodl the retort: 'Don't you know the history of the Italian Renaissance?'

The negotiations followed very much the same lines as those at Tarvisio. Jodl again demanded that the German and Italian divisions in northern Italy should be placed under the command of Field-Marshal Rommel, who would be responsible directly to German Supreme Headquarters, and suggested that the Commander-in-Chief, South, should come under the direct orders of the King. The first of these demands was bluntly rejected by Roatta. As regards Field-Marshal Kesselring, he said he would prefer to see him placed under the command of Italian Supreme Headquarters—in other words, under Ambrosio, one of the chief architects of the treachery in process of preparation. Only on the question of the withdrawal of the Italian Fourth Army from southern France was agreement reached, though even here Jodl could not refrain from remarking that it would interest him to know whether this army would be used in southern Italy against the British or in the north against the Germans. This provoked Roatta to the furious reply: 'How dare you! We are no traitors to go over to the enemy in the middle of a battle!'

For all these fine words, the Italians were already in close touch with the other side. Castellano's interview with Sir Samuel Hoare had been the signal for the start in earnest of negotiations. On instructions from Roosevelt and Churchill, Eisenhower had sent his Chief of Staff, Walter Bedell Smith and his intelligence officer (Ic), the British General Kenneth Strong, to Lisbon as negotiators. On 19 August at 10.30 p.m. they met Castellano at the residence of the British Ambassador.

Bedell Smith opened the proceedings with the words: 'General Eisenhower is prepared to accept the unconditional surrender of the Italian Government', and thrust into the hands of the bewildered Italians a sheet of paper, containing the Allies' armistice conditions. Castellano recovered swiftly from the shock and put forward the views of his own Government,

* Jacques Mordal, *Cassino.*

ending with the words: 'The King and Badoglio are burning to join hands with their Western friends and with their help to drive the Germans out of our country.'

There then followed a recommendation from Badoglio that Eisenhower should land with at least fifteen divisions in the vicinity of Leghorn and Ancona and thus pinch off the leg of the boot well to the north and save Rome from the Germans. In that case, of course, Kesselring's eight divisions and most of 2 Air Fleet would be caught in the trap. Here, indeed, was the proof of Badoglio's cunning intention of presenting the German troops in south Italy to the Allies 'as a dowry'.

Apart from the fact that the Western powers were not, in any case, in a position, in view of the relatively small numbers of landing craft at their disposal, to throw any such major forces ashore (even in Normandy they landed only five divisions in the first wave), the landing areas suggested by the Italians were far beyond the range of their land-based fighter aircraft. Had the original plan of the U.S. Chiefs of Staff—to follow up the Sicilian campaign with invasions of Corsica and Sardinia—been put into operation, then, admittedly, the Spitfires and Lightnings could have reached Leghorn; and in that case the Allies would have been spared the battles in south Italy which, according to Churchill, were among the most bitter of the whole war. The battles of Cassino, with their immense expenditure of war material, would not have been fought and the peace of the monastery of St Benedict would have remained undisturbed. Be that as it may, Bedell Smith, following the instructions of his lord and master, was not prepared even to discuss the Italian proposals. Churchill and Roosevelt had decreed that the King and Badoglio must first place their necks in the Caudian yoke, before they could be permitted to hoist their flag beside those of the Allies. Once Italy and the Italian fleet were firmly in their hands, then the Allies might consider allowing the Italians to take an active part in the struggle against Germany.

The armistice negotiations continued throughout the night. When Castellano could see no other way out, he unrolled before the eyes of the Allied representatives a map of Italy, upon which everything that could possibly be of interest to them was neatly entered: the dispositions and assembly areas of the German forces, their order of battle and defensive localities in the threatened coastal areas, the whereabouts of staff headquarters and supply dumps—in short, everything that the Italian General Staff knew about their allies. This act of treachery was responsible for the death not only of a very great number of German soldiers, but also of thousands of Italian civilians.

For reasons of security, Badoglio had refrained from creating any channel of communication with Castellano. When, after ten days, the latter had still not returned, Badoglio lost patience and sent General Zanussi as an additional negotiator to Lisbon. With him went the British General Carton de Wiart, V.C., a prisoner of war in Italian hands.

The reasons for bringing this much-decorated British officer out of his P.O.W. camp were obvious, but even his appearance in Lisbon did nothing to improve the climate of the negotiations. Zanussi himself had been directed to go on from the Portuguese capital to London, to plead at the highest level for an Allied landing north of Rome. Instead, however, he was sent to Eisenhower's headquarters in Algiers, where he acted as a sort of liaison officer and, with the aid of a wireless set given to him by the Allies in Lisbon, kept the Commander-in-Chief informed of the defensive measures being taken by the Germans.

In return for the handing over to him of the German dispositions, Eisenhower promised to curtail his air offensive against Italy 'as far as he was able'. Future air raids were, in theory, to be directed solely against the Germans. In practice, however, things worked out very differently. It is true that the attacks were concentrated on the German lines of communication, but the carpet of bombs which came hurtling down on the focal points thereof also wrought havoc in the Italian cities and caused grave shortages of food supplies for the civilian population. All this, of course, was grist to the mill of the Communists, who were once again creating a great uproar in northern Italy and Apulia and had to be suppressed by force of arms. Nothing, however, could silence the calls for peace, especially in Rome, which had been hit by a second heavy air raid on 13 August.

On 28 August Castellano at last returned to Rome. His journey home had been delayed by the late arrival of the Italian Ambassador to Chile, who had been recalled and in whose train he was to travel from Lisbon.

The surrender terms came as a bitter disappointment to Rome. Badoglio's hopes that he would be welcomed with open arms by the Allies had not been realized and his wishes and recommendations had been completely ignored. The Allies had formulated their hard conditions with an eye solely to their own interests—free access to the whole of Italy for the further prosecution of the war against Germany, evacuation of the territories occupied by the Italians, surrender of the fleet and the air arm; in short—complete and utter subjection. And these were only the purely military terms imposed; the political, economic and financial conditions were not to be made known until a future date. It was further laid down that Eisenhower would announce the conclusion of the armistice over the Algiers radio six hours before the invading Allied army landed, and that Badoglio should immediately issue a similar proclamation over the Italian radio network. The Italian Government was given until 30 August to reply.

On 31 August Castellano again met Bedell Smith, this time at Cassibile, near Syracuse. He was empowered to say that the Italian Government would accept the armistice terms, provided that strong Allied forces were landed on the Tuscan coast. Once again he mentioned fifteen divisions, the force which Badoglio considered necessary to ensure the success of the enterprise. He again enumerated the difficulties with which Badoglio was faced and added that the situation had deteriorated in the meanwhile, since the Germans were hastily transferring more troops to Italy.

Castellano also persisted obstinately in his efforts to find out the time, place and strength of the invasion, in order, he said, to enable the Italians to support the landing. This, indeed, was a praiseworthy gesture on his part, but Bedell Smith nevertheless took good care to give him no inkling of Allied intentions. He had no means of knowing for certain that the Italians were not playing an extremely subtle game and that anything he told them might not be passed on to the Germans the next day!

Jacques Mordal, a Frenchman and a good European, sums up the situation accurately: 'It must certainly be very difficult for people who mutually distrust each other to reach an agreement; for it must be remembered that the Italians were about to betray their former allies—an act reminiscent of similar action on their part in the past. The stab in the back of 10 June 1940 was not a thing to be readily forgotten.' And, after quoting Field-Marshal Alexander, he continues: 'What caused the Italian Government to capitulate was not so much a recognition of the justice of the Allied cause and of democracy, but rather the fact that the Italian statesmen had decided —as they had done on a previous occasion—that the time had now come to rush to the assistance of the victors.'*

In short, Bedell Smith remained icily unresponsive. He did not feel, he said, that he was in a position to negotiate on the basis of the Italian Government's demands. The only choice he could offer the latter was between 'yes' and 'no'. If the answer was 'no', however, then the Italian Government would have to face the certainty of further air attacks on Rome and a ruthless stepping-up of the war in the air.

This rejection of all their proposals, passed on by Castellano the same day, drove the King and his Government into a corner from which there was no escape. Sink or swim, they now saw themselves at the mercy of Germans and Allies alike, and they had no option but to dare a leap into the unknown.

Accordingly, on 1 September, Badoglio, Ambrosio and Guariglia decided to accept the conditions imposed upon them, and, after the King's consent had been obtained, Castellano flew back once more to Sicily. There, at 5.30 p.m. on 3 September, the armistice was signed in an

* Jacques Mordal, *Cassino*.

olive grove near Cassibile. The instrument of unconditional surrender bore the signatures of Bedell Smith and Castellano.

Once again, with the over-ebullient temperament of his race (he was a Sicilian), Castellano pressed Bedell Smith now at long last to tell him of the Allied invasion plans. This time the latter was a little more forthcoming and dropped a hint that the Italians might expect a landing some time between 10 and 15 September and probably on the 12th. The British Eighth Army, he said, had landed that morning at the southernmost point of Calabria, with the object of pinning down strong German forces in the south. The main landing, however, would be aimed, on the day appointed, at the Germans further north. In addition he could divulge, he said, the gratifying news that Eisenhower had decided to drop the U.S. 82 Airborne Division in the vicinity of the capital, in order, with it and with Carboni's help, to hold Rome against the Germans.

Eisenhower's distrust of Badoglio, which was largely responsible for the attitude he had adopted, was the reason for his once again withdrawing Ridgway's 82 Division from General Clark's Salerno Army. The latter did not accept Eisenhower's decision without protest, for in his plan he had counted on the 82 Airborne to seal off the Volturno crossings. Who, he asked, were now to bar the way to the advance of the German reserves, coming, it was anticipated, primarily from the north?

Initially, however, the need to give Badoglio swift military support and keep him firm to his purpose seemed to the Allied Commander-in-Chief to be the more important; for in the Italian General's palpable terror at the thought of the expected German reaction there lurked the danger of yet another volte-face on the part of the Italian Government. And that was a thing that had to be forestalled.

As may well be imagined, Castellano's report evoked a sigh of relief in Rome. Now they were free of at least one horrible anxiety. If the date of the main invasion remained fixed for 12 September, they would have a good week in which to prepare for the landing of Ridgway's Division, in accordance with the instructions which Bedell Smith had given them. According to these latter, if the Germans had occupied the airfields in Rome, the Italians were to construct a number of landing strips south of the capital for the transport planes and were to have ready to hand motor transport and ample fuel supplies for the swift transportation of the American paratroops to Rome. Bedell Smith had further stated that in good time before the landing of the 82 Division was due to take place a senior American officer would be sent to Rome to co-ordinate plans with the Italian General Staff. As there seemed to be no particular hurry, Ambrosio went off to northern Italy on family business, and Carboni showed no great eagerness to prepare his divisions for the coming events. Then, on

8 September, Brigadier Maxwell-Taylor, Ridgway's deputy, exploded his bombshell.

On the night of 7/8 September, this doughty officer, accompanied by Colonel Gardiner of Air Transport Command, arrived in Rome. The two Americans had boarded an Italian corvette at the island of Ustica, north of Palermo, and had been put ashore at Gaeta. From there they had been driven to Rome in a closed car. Maxwell-Taylor wished to see the Chief of the General Staff. But as Ambrosio was on leave, Carboni suggested that he should see Badoglio. At about 2 p.m. he arrived at the Prime Minister's house, accompanied by the two Americans. The Italians were thunderstruck when Maxwell-Taylor told them of Eisenhower's intention to announce the armistice that very night. Badoglio was the first to recover his wits and protested that all preparations were being made on the assumption that the landing would take place on 12 September and that they could not possibly be completed immediately. Furthermore, he added, the four airfields in Rome were firmly in German hands and this again meant that further measures would have to be taken. In short, he finished, the 82 Airborne's landing could not yet take place. When Carboni added his quota, asserting that his Corps still required a few days to obtain its full stock of fuel and ammunition, Maxwell-Taylor began to fear that the operation of his Division would end in disaster. He wirelessed his unfavourable impressions to Eisenhower, who without hesitation cancelled the whole enterprise.

This, of course, meant the giving up of any idea of seizing the Italian capital by a sudden assault; in this way the Allies abandoned an operation which would have ensured a victorious conclusion of the campaign before ever the first shot had been fired. It is true, certainly, that the Italians had failed to make the requisite preparations for Ridgway's landing. But was that entirely their fault? Hardly—the Allies should have fixed 8 September as the latest date for the completion of Italian arrangements. Instead, they had led the Italians erroneously to believe that they had until 12 September. That was the first mistake. The second was the sending of Maxwell-Taylor to Rome too late. A successful co-ordination of plans with Carboni's Corps in so short a time—Ridgway's landing was planned for the night of 8/9 September—was impossible, since there remained a large number of measures which the Italian units had to complete by the evening of 8 September at the latest, but for which the orders had not yet been issued.

Would the 82 Airborne, in any case, have been strong enough to force a decision? It may well be that it would have become entangled with its 'opposite number' under Ramcke and be tied down before reaching Rome. Even that, however, would not have caused irreparable damage. Behind Ridgway's Division stationed in Sicily was the admirable British 1 Airborne

Division in Tunisia, which could very swiftly have been dropped on Rome.

One further important fact must be borne in mind. An Allied air landing in the vicinity of Rome would not only have put some 'stiffening' into Carboni's Corps, but also, and more important, would have restrained the King, the Government and the General Staff from fleeing incontinently from the capital and leaving the army and the people in the lurch. The machinery of State and the operational command of the armed forces would have continued to function, and the task of disarming the Italian forces would have confronted the Germans with a problem difficult to solve.

Finally, Churchill's pipe-dream that the German divisions would be forced to retire to northern Italy would have been swiftly realized.

The drama was approaching its climax. After his interview with Maxwell-Taylor, Badoglio sent a wireless signal to Eisenhower in Algiers, in which he most urgently, and with some justification, beseeched him to postpone the proclamation of the armistice at least until 12 September. On the afternoon of 8 September Maxwell-Taylor and Gardiner flew back to Eisenhower's advanced headquarters in Tunis. With them went General Rossi, the Italian Deputy Chief of Staff, who had been entrusted with the mission of reiterating the request for the postponement of the armistice proclamation and of explaining the vital importance of the landing north of Rome which the Italians had requested. His mission, however, was overtaken by the flurry of events.

In Algiers Badoglio's wireless signal came as a bombshell. Eisenhower's staff completely lost their nerve and repeated Badoglio's signal to the Combined Chiefs of Staff in Washington, with a request for further instructions. At the same time they sent the text of the signal to Eisenhower himself in Tunis. The latter, imbued with a deep mistrust of Badoglio, decided to act at once, fearing that the Italian Government might after all change its mind at the last moment. . . . 'I replied in a peremptory telegram that regardless of his action I was going to announce the surrender at six-thirty o'clock as previously agreed upon and that if I did so without simultaneous action on his part Italy would have no friend left in the war.'*

This reply reached Rome at 5.30 p.m. Its effect was shattering. Badoglio, on the verge of a nervous collapse, decided to call a meeting of the Italian Privy Council for 6.15 p.m. in the Quirinal. But now blow followed blow. At 5.45 p.m. Reuter announced the Italian surrender over the British radio. This caused Galli, the Propaganda Minister, who had not been let into the secret of the negotiations, to issue an immediate *démenti*. The Privy Council met in an atmosphere of tense anxiety and desperation. In addition to the King, Badoglio and the Minister of the Royal Household, the

* Eisenhower, *Crusade in Europe.*

meeting was attended by Ambrosio, who had meanwhile returned from northern Italy, the Ministers of the three Services, the Foreign Minister, an officer representing Roatta, who at that moment was conferring with Westphal, Carboni and a Major Marchesi, an officer on Castellano's staff.

The meeting had scarcely started when the news came that at 6.30 p.m. Eisenhower had announced Italy's surrender over the Algiers radio. The moment for swift action had arrived. Some of those present, however, were now learning for the first time that the government had been negotiating with the Allies for weeks and that the armistice had, in fact, been signed as long ago as 3 September. This merely added to the confusion. The Italians found it very difficult to decide what they should do. Some of the generals, Carboni among them, accused the Allies of having broken their word and were in favour of repudiating the armistice—influenced, no doubt, to a considerable extent by their fears regarding German reactions. Badoglio himself was unable to make up his mind and suggested that the King should disassociate himself from his Prime Minister on the grounds that the latter had acted without his knowledge. In the end, the youngest member present, Major Marchesi, stood up and argued passionately in favour of acceptance of the armistice terms, basing his arguments on the obviously disastrous consequences of a repudiation.

With this view the King agreed, and Marchesi's motion was carried. At 7.45 p.m. Badoglio announced the Privy Council's decision. After fighting for three and a half years at the side of her German ally, Italy had capitulated unconditionally.

After Montgomery's leap across the Straits of Messina, the main invasion was obviously close at hand and was the subject of a conference on 7 September between Field-Marshal Kesselring and the new Italian Minister of the Marine, de Courten. Co-operation between the two had so far always run smoothly and, as far as the Field-Marshal was concerned, without any hint of mistrust. 'Admiral de Courten,' says Kesselring in his memoirs, 'was always very friendly and generally did his utmost to meet my wishes.'* At this moment, therefore, on the threshold of the decisive battle, he felt that he could confidently rely on the vigorous support of the Italian fleet.

De Courten declared that now that the enemy was about to strike directly at the Italian mainland, the fleet would certainly not be content to remain at anchor in its ports. It would put to sea at once from La Spezia and set course for the sea area to the west of Sicily in an effort to engage the Mediterranean fleet and destroy the invading forces before they reached the Italian coast. They would conquer, he asserted, or go down with flags

* Kesselring, *Soldat bis zum letzten Tag.*

flying. There would be no 'Scapa Flow' as far as the Italian Navy was concerned! To Kesselring's question as to when he would like the German Air Liaison Commando to embark, de Courten replied: 'Not until the ships are about to put to sea, if you don't mind. For you know, of course, that the enemy intelligence is keeping a particularly sharp eye on the fleet.'

The Italian played his part in masterly fashion. He had spoken with deep and passionate emotion, and there were tears in his eyes when he referred to the German blood, from his mother's side, that flowed in his veins. The effect was all that he could have desired. 'Neither to Kesselring nor myself did the thought occur that this was most probably all a ruse to lull German suspicions of the impending cruise of the Italian fleet to internment in Malta.'*

The next day both the Italians and the Allies put their cards down on the table. The prelude consisted of a heavy, two-hour attack by Flying Fortresses on Kesselring's and von Richthoven's headquarters in Frascati. Casualties were heavy. The two German staffs lost about a hundred men, while of the Italian civilian population more than a thousand men, women and children were killed.

Two interesting facts emerged from this attack. Firstly, in one of the bombers that was shot down was found a map, upon which the location of the headquarters of the two Field-Marshals was precisely pin-pointed. This, of course, was the handiwork of Ambrosio and Castellano. Secondly, within a few minutes of the start of the attack, fire engines and rescue squads from Rome were on the outskirts of Frascati, in spite of the fact that the headquarters were a good twelve miles from the metropolis. A truly remarkable feat! But not one that was in the least appreciated by those who knew for certain that the attack had been delivered with the pre-knowledge of the Italian Government!

For the moment there occurred no change in the relations between the German and Italian military authorities. Immediately after this attack, which took place around noon, Westphal went to Army Headquarters to see Roatta. The penny did not drop until the late afternoon, when Jodl and Ribbentrop asked the Commander-in-Chief and the German Embassy respectively whether the announcement by the British radio that Italy had capitulated was true. Both Kesselring and Rahn (who had succeeded von Mackensen on 31 August) were taken completely by surprise and were quite unable to confirm the ominous news. The Field-Marshal's inquiries in Rome met with the reply that the report was a swindle, perpetrated by the enemy propaganda. Rahn, after making a few abortive telephone calls, went personally to the Foreign Ministry, where Guariglia, who had just

* Westphal, *The German Army in the West.*

returned from the Privy Council meeting, greeted him with the words: 'I have the honour to inform you that Italy has just capitulated.'

As the news spread, the Italian people burst into one great paean of jubilation. Happy, excited men and women roamed the streets, soldiers and civilians embraced one another, bonfires were lighted on the surrounding hills and the clergy called the people to thanksgiving services. All Italy was caught up in a turmoil, as though she were celebrating the greatest victory in her history.

Sobriety followed quickly on the heels of this intoxication, when the German Army went swiftly into action. 2 Parachute Division received the order to move. It surged forward towards Rome, overrunning portions of Carboni's Corps, and the next morning was engaged in heavy street fighting on the outskirts of the capital itself. From Frascati the code signal 'Axis' went forth, and all over Italy German troops, including the divisions of Rommel's Army Group, were at once on the move.

In the midst of the reports pouring in from Rome came the news of the Allied landing at Salerno. To headquarters in Frascati this came rather as a relief. They now knew where the enemy was and what he was up to, and they could act accordingly. The first essential remained, however, the clearing-up of the situation in Rome itself. This task was entrusted to the Air Force General Student, whose XI Air (Parachute) Corps had been transferred from southern France to the area south of Rome at the end of July. Ramcke's Division and the 3 Panzer Grenadier Division, holding Latium to the north, were also placed under Student's command.

Student's first move was to launch the attack of 2 Parachute Division against the capital; his second was directed against Italian Army Head-quarters in Monterotondo, to which it had been transferred after the second air raid on the Eternal City and the Italian Government, to obviate further attacks, had declared Rome an 'open city'.

For the neutralization of this very considerable military headquarters, a parachute assault battalion in Foggia under the command of Major Gericke had been briefed weeks before. Gericke was an old hand and a thruster, who had been with paratroops ever since their formation. In a Storch helicopter he had already made a personal reconnaissance and had selected dropping areas and objectives; after that he had bluffed his way by car into the place itself and inspected the area of his future operations on the spot. What he had seen there had not been exactly encouraging. The whole of Monterotondo was one large fortress, with concrete emplacements, road blocks and strong anti-aircraft defences, consisting mostly of German 8·8cm. guns. This, he realized, could well prove to be a tough nut to crack.

In spite of acts of sabotage by the Italians on the telephone lines, Gericke received orders to move in such good time that he was able to take off at 6.30 a.m. on 9 September in 52-Ju troop-carrying aircraft. His force suffered its first casualties from anti-aircraft fire on the fly-in and during the drop. After some hard fighting, the battalion thrust its way into Monterotondo itself, and by the afternoon it had surrounded the fortress-like castle in which, it was presumed, the senior officers were housed. Eventually this stubbornly defended bulwark was taken by storm, and fifteen officers and 200 men surrendered. Roatta, however, was not among them. The bird had long since flown and was now in Pescara, waiting for an aircraft to take him south.

In the late afternoon even the stout-hearted Gericke began to feel a little anxious, when his depleted forces were attacked by an armoured division advancing from Rome. His efforts, in view of the overwhelmingly superior forces against him, to come to some reasonable understanding at first met with no response at all from the Italians. Eventually, however, armistice negotiations initiated by the Commander-in-Chief, South, put an end to the fighting and led to an agreement. Gericke, who was allowed to march out under arms, handed over the bitterly contested town to the Italians on 11 September and on the same day made contact with the German forces on the outskirts of Rome.

And what of the Eternal City itself? First and foremost, when the news of the Italian surrender was received, O.K.W. had straightway written off Rome and the forces of the Commander-in-Chief, South! Field-Marshal Kesselring received no further orders from Führer Headquarters and from that quarter no more help, obviously, was to be expected. Hitler had from the outset reconciled himself to the loss of eight *élite* divisions. It is difficult to understand how he could bring himself thus lightly to accept so grievous a loss after the previous catastrophes of Stalingrad and 'Tunisgrad', as the people now referred to the recent tragedy in Tunisia. Could he not see that the 'boot' of Italy formed a perfect counterpart to the British Isles as a base for the strategic air offensive against the Reich? Why, then, did he leave Rommel's Army Group far away from the decisive area and doing nothing, while round Rome and in southern Italy German troops were fighting for their lives and at Salerno the fate of the Allied invasion hung by a thread? The answer is to be found in Hitler's conviction (shared incidentally by Rommel) that, because of her long coastline, Italy could not be successfully defended south of the Etruscan Apennines, far away to the north. Any attempt to defend south Italy would, in his view, have led to disaster, if the Allies made full use of the sea flanks, the whole long stretches of which could not possibly be protected; and that the Allies would do so he was quite convinced.

Field-Marshal Kesselring did all he could to prevent the developments envisaged by Führer Headquarters. The first step in this direction was to clear up the situation in Rome.

When the landing confidently expected north of Rome failed to materialize, the 3 Panzer Grenadier Division was brought up to the capital and its advent very considerably strengthened the German position. It was still doubtful, however, whether the forces under Student would be able to contain Carboni's Corps for any length of time. But above all it was the possibility of an air drop in the vicinity of Rome that was causing the greatest anxiety at Frascati, particularly since no more than two battalions could be spared for the defence of the Roman airfields. Westphal's comments reflect the anxiety felt by all in the face of this deadly danger: 'On 9 September and the days following, therefore, all eyes and binoculars turned skywards whenever the rumble of engines was heard. . . . We only breathed freely after the evening dusk had descended, for large-scale landings at night were improbable.'*

In this connexion it is perhaps of interest to note in parentheses that the Allies always preferred to arrange their parachute drops during the hours of darkness. Had this fact been realized at Frascati, the staff would doubtless have had many sleepless nights to add to their other worries.

When no landing from the air had occurred by the evening of 9 September and Carboni's Corps, with the exception of the units at Monterotondo, had remained passive, Westphal suggested that the Italians should be invited to surrender. There was just a chance that they might agree.

And, indeed, the invitation was accepted instantly, and the aged Marshal Caviglia, the victor of Vittorio Veneto, readily offered to conduct the negotiations. Carboni's men laid down their arms and were allowed to depart with all honour to their homes. Kesselring promised to recognize Rome as an open city and to station only two companies of military police in the capital.

This success did not, however, prevent Führer Headquarters from expressing keen displeasure at the free discharge of the Italian troops. Those above failed entirely to realize that it was only the promise of freedom that had persuaded the Italian divisions to surrender. It really seemed as though they attached more importance to filling up the P.O.W. camps than to preserving the German divisions in Italy from destruction!

With the surrender and disbanding of Carboni's Corps a great deal had been gained. By and large we had parted company amicably with our former allies—thanks also, in no small measure, to the state of complete bewilderment in which the Italians found themselves. But now the way to the German Tenth Army, which was engaged in heavy fighting at Salerno, was opened; through the canals which Carboni had temporarily

* Westphal, *The German Army in the West.*

blocked, the stream of supplies, fuel, munitions and food started once more to flow freely southwards. Of no less importance was the taking-over of the network of long-distance communication, without which the Commander-in-Chief, South, would have found it impossible to exercise effective command.

For this much at least the Germans had reason to be thankful. There still remained the question whether the Italians in other localities had taken up arms against their erstwhile allies; but this danger, too was averted. Contrary to expectation, the disarming of the Italian forces was completed swiftly and almost without incident. Only in a very few places had there been any shooting or serious conflict between Germans and Italians. In some quarters this unfortunately led to the belief that a Prussian corporal and a dozen men were sufficient to disarm a whole Italian division. Of course the Italian soldiers, like the rest of the Italian people, were war weary and longing to get home to their beloved spaghetti. But had they received orders from Rome to cross swords with the Germans and defend themselves in earnest, the game would probably not have ended with this checkmate of the Italians.

It must not be forgotten that the Italian soldier, too, had fought and bled for his country; and while, perhaps, he could not compare in steadiness under pressure and dogged determination with his German brother-in-arms, when on the offensive he nevertheless displayed noteworthy *élan* and very frequently quite outstanding gallantry. To quote but a few examples, the Italians had no reason to be ashamed of their submariners. Of the 122 submarines in the Italian Navy, eighty-five had perished fighting; or of the 'Decima M.A.S.', Prince Borghese's 10th E-boat Flotilla, whose daring and successful operations against British ports and men-of-war had won for them the esteem and respect of their opponents. Worthy of a place beside these are also the paratroops of the Folgore Division, which, trained by General Ramcke, had brought great honour to their instructor in North Africa. Nor must the courage with which the Italian soldiers faced the grim winter of 1940/41 in Albania be forgotten. Thousands of them were stricken by frostbite and lost both feet—because they had been sent into a winter campaign without canvas-protected boots. The crucial factor had been the utterly inadequate equipment and the antiquated weapons, which had proved quite incapable of meeting the demands of modern war. This was the real fly in the ointment, and for this the Italian soldier was in no way to blame. The responsibility rested squarely on the shoulders of the political and military leaders who, with wholly inadequate resources and devoid of any conception of strategy, declared war on a world power.

No less irresponsible was the action of the new leaders who in the early dawn of 9 September ignominiously took to their heels and fled, leaving their unfortunate people and the army to whatever fate awaited them. This abject failure, which sheds so glaring a light on the character of the weaklings concerned, evoked indignation throughout Italy and nowhere more vehemently than in the armed forces; for it was the latter more than anyone else who found themselves in a most awkward predicament and with no one to whom to turn for guidance. To this day many Italians are severely critical of Badoglio, whom they regard as the man responsible and whose halo as 'the saviour of his country' very quickly faded away.

What, then, lay behind this headlong flight of the Royal Family, the Government and the General Staff? On the eve of 8 September, after the acceptance of the armistice terms, the Italian Privy Council agreed that the Royal Family, the Head of the Government and the Chief of the General Staff should proceed at once to the War Ministry, the sole place which seemed to offer some measure of security, and spend the night there.

After the armistice had been proclaimed, Badoglio himself went to the War Minister's office, where he went early to bed. Whether he was by this time past caring or was simply physically exhausted, the fact remains that during the hours in which the fate of Italy was being settled, the Head of her Government was sleeping peacefully in his bed. At four o'clock in the morning he was rudely awakened by Roatta with the shattering news of the successful German parachute drop on the capital. Fighting was already in progress at the Porta San Paolo, Roatta said, and it would only be a question of time before the Germans reached the centre of the city. The danger that the King and the Government would be taken prisoner was acute in the extreme, Roatta continued, and it was essential that they should get away at once by the only way still open to them, the Via Tibertina. He had already given orders to Carboni, he said, to retire to Tivoli and there take up a defensive position. (This move, incidentally, was never executed.)

In spite of the numerically overwhelming superiority of the Italian forces, Badoglio confirmed Roatta's irresponsible orders and agreed that they must leave at once. To the King, to whom he immediately went, he painted the situation in the gloomiest possible colours and he did not have much difficulty in persuading the monarch that the time to flee had come. Nevertheless, Victor Emmanuel himself seems to have had some misgivings, for Badoglio says: 'I insisted, however, that the responsibility for a departure in the direction of Pescara was mine and mine alone.'*

On the evening of 8 September the La Spezia Squadron raised steam and as darkness fell stole quietly out of port. Its nucleus, consisting of the modern battleships *Roma, Italia* and *Vittorio Veneto*, was protected by five

* Badoglio, *Italy in the Second World War.*

cruisers, twelve destroyers and two torpedo boats. At the same time the light forces in Genoa weighed anchor and joined the main fleet during the night. Under the command of Admiral Bergamini the whole force then set course for the sea area to the west of Sardinia. Below deck the rumour went round that the fleet was making for the Balearic Islands, where it would be interned. When the fleet changed course and turned southwards, the crews thought: 'Well—we're going to have a go at the enemy after all.' It was only after the German air attack that they learnt that Malta and internment there was the purpose of their voyage.

In accordance with the Allies' instructions, the fleet maintained course along the western coast of Sardinia, where, at 9 a.m. on 9 September it made contact with British patrols. But the Germans, too, had begun to smell a rat, and about 3 p.m. a strong formation of *Luftwaffe* bombers appeared on the scene. The fleet turned away eastwards in the vain hope of reaching the Gulf of Asinara in northern Sardinia. At 3.30 p.m. the first bombs hurtled down on the *Italia*, scoring a hit near the bridge, but without causing much damage. *Roma* was less lucky. At 3.41 she was hit by a bomb immediately in rear of one of her turrets. The ship at once lost way and listed sharply to starboard. Ten minutes later a direct hit on the port side sealed her fate. A great tongue of flame shot more than 300 feet into the air, and Bergamini's flagship began to sink. At 4.18 the waves closed over the proud ship and she sank, taking the Admiral and most of the crew to the bottom with her. Admiral Oliva, who now assumed command, detached a cruiser and a destroyer to pick up survivors and then follow the main body to Malta.

From Malta 'H' Squadron, with the battleships *Warspite* and *Valiant*, was sailing westwards to meet the Italian fleet. Britannia, ruler of the seas, was about to gather her most glittering prize, and from her seamen a great cheer broke out when at 6 a.m. on 10 September the Italian fleet hove in sight. All eyes were riveted on the *Savoia* as a British prize crew went aboard the Italian flagship. It was, indeed, a memorable moment in the proud history of the Royal Navy, when 'H' Squadron took station ahead of the enemy battle fleet.

On this 10 September Eisenhower and Cunningham enjoyed the greatest triumph they had hitherto known in their Service careers. To the north of Cape Bon, on board the destroyer *Hambledon*, they watched the defeated enemy plough his way through the waters of the 'Mare Nostro' in the wake of a British squadron. For Cunningham, who had been chasing the Italian Navy for more than three years, it was a particularly unforgettable moment. 'To me it was a most moving and thrilling sight. To see my wildest hopes of years brought to fruition and my former flagship the *Warspite*, which had struck the first blow against the Italians three years before, leading her erstwhile opponents into captivity, filled me with the deepest emotion and lives with me today.'*

On the afternoon of this noteworthy day the Tarento Squadron dropped anchor in the Grand Harbour in Malta. It consisted of the fairly old battleships *Duilio* and *Doria*, three cruisers, two destroyers and four torpedo boats under command of Admiral Da Zara. On 9 September, while *en route* from Tarento to Malta, Da Zara had passed a British squadron, consisting of two battleships, five cruisers and a number of destroyers, carrying the 1 Airborne Division to Tarento. 'As the two fleets passed each other, there was a moment of tension. There was no guarantee that the Italian fleet would observe the terms of surrender and would not, at long last, show fight.'† The Allies did not trust the Italians, even after they had hauled down their flag.

On the morning of 11 September the La Spezia Squadron steamed into the St Paul's Harbour in Malta. On the same day, Cunningham made a signal to the Admiralty: 'Be pleased to inform their Lordships that the Italian Battle Fleet now lies at anchor under the guns of the fortress Malta.'‡

Still more Italian ships arrived, among them the battleship *Giulio Cesare* and the aircraft-carrier *Miraglia*. But Malta was too small to accommodate this great armada for any length of time. On 14 September, therefore, the battleships *Italia* and *Vittorio Veneto* (which, incidentally, with their thirty knots were faster than their British escorts), and a number of cruisers and destroyers were ordered to proceed to Alexandria.

The 'former naval person' had every excuse for treating himself to an extra Havana. The surrender of the Italian Fleet was something well worth celebrating! The capital ships were stripped of their armament, but the cruisers and destroyers rendered invaluable service on convoy escort duties. In one way, of course, de Courten had been right. There had, indeed, been no 'Scapa Flow', in that the Italians had not scuttled their fleet. But equally they had no one of the calibre of Admiral von Reuter.

The tragic chapter of the Italian capitulation ended with the liberation of Mussolini. His stay on the island of Ponza had been of short duration. After 'a little bird' had told everyone in Rome where he was, Badoglio had him transferred to the sea fortress of Maddalena, between Corsica and Sardinia. Even this place, however, did not strike him as being altogether safe from a possible German surprise attack. He therefore moved the Duce once more, under conditions of the most rigorous secrecy, to the 10,000-foot plateau of Gran' Sasso d'Italia, where he was hermetically sealed off from the outer world in the winter sports hotel, Campo d'Imperatore.

---

* A. B. Cunningham, *A Sailor's Odyssey.*   † Eisenhower, *Crusade in Europe.*
‡ A. B. Cunningham, *A Sailor's Odyssey.*

As everyone knows, Hitler was from the outset determined by some means or other to secure the liberation of his friend. He entrusted the preparations for, and the execution of, the rescue to General Student, whose Army Corps at that time was still in the Nîmes area. At the end of July Hitler summoned him to Führer Headquarters in Rastenberg to discuss the practical possibilities with him in person. After this conference Student, with Skorzeny aboard his He-111, flew direct to Rome. The first essential was to find out where Mussolini was. This task was given to Skorzeny, to whom some thirty men of the security branch were attached. The actual rescue, the purely military execution of the plan, was entrusted to the Lehr Parachute Battalion under the command of Major Mors.

After weeks of searching, Skorzeny thought he had located the Duce in the Campo d'Imperatore Hotel. Although he was by no means certain that he was right, the enterprise was fixed for Sunday 12 September— not, as has often been stated, by Skorzeny, but by Student, who was responsible for the whole enterprise. At about 2 p.m. a company of paratroops under the command of Lieutenant Freiherr von Berlepesch, packed into transport gliders, landed on an undulating hillock in the immediate vicinity of the hotel. Skorzeny was with them. At his urgent request, Student had given him permission to accompany the party. Another guest was the Carabinieri General Soliti, who had been given the task of persuading Mussolini's warders to hand him over. Contrary to expectation everything went well. The Italians, who at first had mistaken the German paratroops for Americans, offered no resistance and were only too pleased to come out of the whole business unscathed. At the funicular station in the valley below, everything also went according to plan. The station was occupied without resistance by Major Mors and his battalion, which had marched there on foot. A few moments later, Captain Gerlach, who was to take Mussolini off in his helicopter, also landed. Again Skorzeny begged 'almost on his knees' to be allowed to accompany Gerlach and the latter acceded to his urgent pleas. After a hair-raising take-off, in which the overladen Storch narrowly escaped plunging into the yawning abyss below, Gerlach flew to Rome, where a waiting He-111 took over Mussolini and Skorzeny and flew them to Hitler.

Himmler lost no time in telling the whole world that Skorzeny was the hero who had rescued the Duce; and to this day Skorzeny is known all the world over as 'the man who liberated Mussolini'. Captain Gerlach, however, as the man in charge, puts things in their proper perspective: 'When I look back after ten years on the events of the late summer of 1943, I am more than ever convinced that it is idle to quarrel over who deserves the credit for having rescued Mussolini. It was a team effort, in which everyone did his best and in which the co-operation of all concerned was the key to our success. There is only one man who can with justice claim to be Mussolini's rescuer, and that is General Student, who planned and directed the whole operation and bore the sole responsibility for it.'*

Almost as soon as it had been accomplished, the liberation of Mussolini gave rise to the comment that the Duce had merely exchanged one warder for another and at the best had been transferred from the hands of Badoglio into those of Hitler. This, people said, explained why the Saló Republic pursued its course as a shameful satellite, at the head of which stood a dictator, enchained by the Germans and devoid of all lustre and repute. It is true, of course, that after the débâcle of 25 July Hitler no longer placed any great trust in his friend and for that reason had cut down the sovereignty of the Social Republic (the official designation of the Fascist rump in Italy) to nothing more than a façade. But one fact must not be forgotten. Mussolini's willingness to place himself at the head of the 'Republic' saved central and upper Italy from being treated by Hitler as enemy territory. The German troops there moved about as they would have done in the country of any ally, though Mussolini kept a sharp eye on all their comings and goings. It was not long before the following wisecrack was being bandied round among the Germans: 'Hitler decorated the people who brought Mussolini here from the Gran' Sasso with the Knight's Cross; but anyone who would take him back there would deserve the Oak Leaves as well!'

Those in 'the other Italy' who believed that the Allies would now accept Badoglio as a partner on equal terms were destined to be bitterly disillusioned. In fact, he fared no better than his Fascist opponents. Whereas at Lake Garda there was only the German Ambassador to keep an eye on things, in Brindisi the Allies established a complete military government in the ante-room of the monarchical Cabinet. Badoglio had no option but to reconcile himself as best he could to the presence of foreign troops, and violations of the sovereignty of his government by the Western powers were inevitable. Nor could they in any way be mitigated by the soft words which the Allies, statesmen and soldiers alike, poured in such abundant measure into his ears. On 11 September, for example, Roosevelt and Churchill sent him a telegram from Quebec: 'The German terror in Italy will not last much longer. The Germans will be exterminated in their own country.'

To sum up, Badoglio's patience was being put to a severe test, and co-operation with the Allies was most certainly not being made easy for him. Before they were willing to grant monarchist Italy the status of a 'co-belligerent power', they demanded the written acceptance of the political and economic clauses of the armistice. Only when this had been

* Gerlach, in *Der deutsche Fallschirmjaeger*.

done would they regard the wholesale capitulation of Italy as complete in all aspects. Many authoritative critics, however, consider that it was just this insistence on 'unconditional surrender' that was responsible for the subsequent disappointing course of the Italian campaign. Fuller says: 'As we shall soon see, this foolishness, conceived by President Roosevelt and Mr Churchill at Casablanca, trapped the British and the Americans into tactically the most absurd and strategically the most senseless campaign of the whole war. "Unconditional surrender" transformed the "soft under-belly" into a crocodile's back; prolonged the war; wrecked Italy; and wasted thousands of American and British lives.'*

To put a final stop to this 'foolishness' Badoglio sailed in a cruiser to Malta on 28 September. There he was received aboard H.M.S. *Nelson* with full military honours, a nice gesture, but not one likely to make it in any way easier for him to sign the instrument of unconditional surrender. This he nevertheless did, after a vain attempt to secure some mitigation of the harsh terms imposed, on 29 September in the presence of Eisenhower, the three Commanders-in-Chief, Alexander, Cunningham and Tedder, and the Governor of Malta, Lord Gort. The ceremony was followed by a discussion with Eisenhower, who raised the question of an Italian declaration of war on Germany, a thought that had been at the back of Badoglio's mind for some time. Therein, in his eyes, lay the only prospect not only of avoiding utter ruin and desolation, but also of ensuring for himself a seat at the victor's table—a hope, incidentally, which was realized only to an extremely modest degree.

On 13 October the Italian Ambassador in Madrid handed to his German colleague the Badoglio Government's declaration of war. Six weeks later the first of Badoglio's troops were in the forefront at Cassino, and there then began that tragic period of fratricidal war, in which Italy was torn into two. In all conscience, a sorry heritage of unconditional surrender!

* Fuller, *The Second World War.*

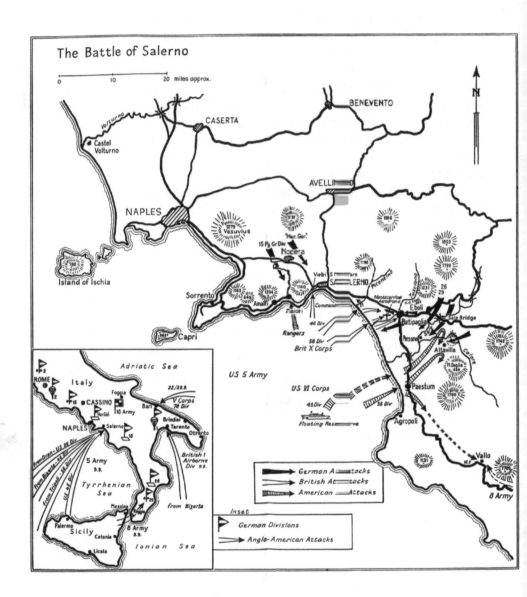

The Battle of Salerno

0   10   20 miles approx.

Chapter 3

The Landing in Italy

It was not until six weeks after Mussolini's fall that the Allies set foot on the Italian mainland. A great opportunity had gone begging. The Western powers had failed to gather the crop which had sprung up thanks to Badoglio's *coup d'état* and the Italian surrender. Victory over Italy had been thrust so swiftly upon them that it caught them unprepared and unable to exploit it. For, during the summer of 1943, their attention had not been focused on Italy, but rather on south-east Asia, on the Pacific and on north-west Europe. At first sight this may seem to have been a departure from the overall Western strategy as decided at the Washington conference of December 1941 by Churchill, Roosevelt and the Combined Chiefs of Staff Committee. Then it had been agreed to concentrate the whole of the war effort of the United States and Great Britain in the first instance on the defeat of Germany and her European allies. Only after Germany had been defeated would the offensive against Japan begin.

This had been a bold decision and one which reflects credit on Roosevelt's courage, for it was entirely contrary to the wishes of his countrymen. The American people were filled with a bitter hatred of the Japanese, who had descended like a thunderbolt from the skies at Pearl Harbor, and they were imbued with a burning desire for bloody revenge. What did the Americans care about Europe, when the torch of war had been brandished in the Pacific—their very own parish! Yet, in spite of this the President decided—Germany first. This decision was undoubtedly the result of his realization that emotion can play no part in the framing of strategy, which must be based solely on political and military reality and objectives.

These latter were clear for all to see. The Russian colossus had only just begun to recover from the heavy blows it had received and was now in process of halting the German onslaught at the gates of Moscow. Even so, whether in the long run Stalin would gain the upper hand was a very open question. On the other hand, if once Hitler overthrew Russia he might be able to build up so formidable a military force that the Western powers' chances of ultimate victory would be slender in the extreme.

Like that of Russia, the fate of Great Britain was indissolubly linked to the European theatre of war; and Britain's position, too, was critical. The high shipping losses she had suffered at the hands of the German U-boats and the uncertainty of the outcome in Libya gave rise to grave anxiety and a feeling that there might well be worse to come. Neither Britain nor Russia could release any appreciable forces for use against Japan. On the other hand, if the Americans launched a single-handed offensive against the Japanese, there was a real danger that, having achieved victory in the Pacific, they would be compelled to attack Fortress Europe side by side with a Britain and a Russia, exhausted, bled white and battle-weary, if, indeed, capable of waging further war at all. There remained, then, no alternative. It had to be: first victory in Europe and then all together against Japan.

But—how was victory in Europe to be achieved? To discuss this question with the British, Roosevelt sent his Chief of Staff, General Marshall, and his personal representative, Harry Hopkins, to London in April 1942. In principle, the British accepted Marshall's thesis that the decisive blow against Germany would have to be delivered across the Channel and through the west European countries; but they were mildly shocked when he came out with the suggestion that a landing should be made on the Cotentin peninsula in 1942, with the object of creating a beach-head for the main invasion in 1943.

Churchill and his Chiefs of Staff were faced at the time with other grave problems. The Prime Minister had expressed the view that it was essential to defend India and the Middle East in order to guard against the possibility of the Germans and the Japanese joining hands. His Chiefs of Staff had come to the conclusion that the focal point, strategically, lay in the Persian Gulf and the oilfields in its vicinity. They were therefore disinclined to commit any forces at all for a landing operation in 1943, which in their opinion was in any case foredoomed to end in catastrophe. The capture of Tobruk by Rommel in June, the headlong retreat of the Eighth Army to the Nile valley and the unexpected success with which the Germans came through the merciless Russian winter and were now thrusting towards the Caucasus were proof enough of the correctness of their views regarding the strategic importance of the Middle East. It certainly seemed as though Hitler intended to envelop the Middle East by means of a pincer operation on a gigantic scale. Here, however, he was threatening the vital artery of the British Empire.

In July, the British refused to consider Operation 'Sledgehammer' (the preliminary landing in France, 1942) and put forward an alternative suggestion of their own—a landing in French North Africa. By a thrust here in Rommel's rear they hoped to put an end to the danger threatening the Middle East. The British Chiefs of Staff had the very greatest difficulty in persuading their American colleagues to agree, for the President himself was adhering rigidly to the decision: 'Germany first.'*

In this way, in the autumn of 1942, the Western powers temporarily transferred their major attention from north-western Europe to the Mediterranean, but without for a moment losing sight of their ultimate strategic objective, the invasion of France. At the beginning of 1943, however, when victory in North Africa was all but in their grasp, when the Middle East no longer stood in any danger and on the Russian front the scales of war had begun to tilt decisively in Stalin's favour, the Allies found themselves faced once again with the question: What next? Should they leap against the European mainland from North Africa, or should they, after all, launch their offensive against the northern coasts of France? They decided in favour of 'Overlord' and imposed strict limitations on operations in the Mediterranean theatre, which were to be confined to Sicily alone. In addition, the Combined Chiefs of Staff were instructed to draw up plans and make the necessary preparations 'for the recapture of Burma (Anakim), beginning in 1943, and for operations against the Marshalls and Carolines, if time and resources allow, without prejudice to "Anakim".'†

The offensive in Burma was to begin on 15 November 1943, while in May attacks with limited objectives were to be launched in Assam, for the purpose of securing suitable bases for the air-bridge to China. These plans for Burma and the Pacific had been forced upon the British much against their will by the American Chiefs of Staff. In conjunction with the obstinate adherence to Overlord, they were destined to become a merciless drag and millstone round the neck of subsequent operations in the Mediterranean theatre of war.

* The resistance of the U.S. Chiefs of Staff was so strong that at one time they went as far as recommending to the President that the United States should turn their back on Europe and concentrate the whole of their war effort against Japan in the Pacific.

† Churchill, *The Second World War*, Vol. IV.

At the end of January 1943 Churchill, by no means pleased at the decisions taken at Casablanca, flew on to Turkey to try and persuade this ally at long last to enter the war. But the Turks proved deaf to all his blandishments and thus frustrated the plans which Churchill had been evolving for the further prosecution of the war in the Mediterranean. There remained now but one way open to him—the road to Italy, and, perhaps, by means of a diversion, into the Balkans.

In May 1943 Churchill sailed for the third time across the Atlantic, this time to attend the Trident conference in Washington. The suggestion that a further conference should be held had emanated from the Prime Minister himself. It was essential, he felt, that a clear-cut decision be reached regarding both the future course of operations after Sicily and the approximate date of Overlord.

At the conference a wide divergence of views became at once apparent. Firstly there was the question of south-east Asia. The thrust into Assam had had to be abandoned on account of supply and transport difficulties, and the attack on Akyab planned for May had also failed to materialize. Churchill could not reconcile himself to the idea of initiating operations against Japan while the fruits of victory in the Mediterranean still remained to be plucked. The Americans thought otherwise. Filled with a deep anxiety regarding the position in Burma and the Pacific, they were most reluctant to allow any Mediterranean operations to interfere in any way either with the planned Far Eastern operations or with the preparations for Overlord. Roosevelt supported the views held by his Chiefs of Staff, not only on purely military grounds, but also for political reasons. A bare eighteen months ahead lay the presidential elections, in which he would certainly be opposed by MacArthur, whose Republican Party were loudly demanding reinforcements for the Far East.

On the next point at issue—what were to be the objectives of the Mediterranean campaign after Sicily—the British again lost all along the line. Churchill urged that as soon as Sicily fell an invasion of the mainland should at once be undertaken and Italy be compelled to give up the fight. The defection of one of the Axis partners, he argued, would have incalculable repercussions. He confidently expected that Turkey would soon declare war and that the gates of the Balkans would thus be opened. Finally, once the Italian fleet had been destroyed or neutralized, powerful British naval forces, he said, would become available for service in south-east Asia and the Pacific. And what of the veteran and experienced divisions in the Mediterranean? They could not possibly stand idle for the eight or nine months that would elapse between the fall of Sicily and the mounting of the cross-Channel invasion. What would the Russians, to whom the Western allies were so greatly indebted, have to say? Italy offered a unique opportunity. It would not be necessary, Churchill said, to occupy the whole country. 'If Italy collapsed the United Nations would occupy the ports and airfields needed for further operations into the Balkans and southern Europe.'*

To all this Roosevelt retorted that the forces which would be set free at the end of the Sicilian campaign must first and foremost be held in readiness for Overlord, to which priority had to be accorded over everything else. At the same time he insisted that forces would have to be transferred from the Mediterranean for the reconquest of Burma and the securing of airfields in Assam. Only in this way could help be given to the Chinese, who, in the President's opinion, were a potent factor in the war against Japan. He was not in favour of an occupation of Italy and took care to see that his Chiefs of Staff did not commit themselves to any such operations. Roosevelt's attitude, which was in complete accord with the views of his Chiefs of Staff, is clearly reflected in the official communiqué: 'That the Allied Commander-in-Chief, North Africa, will be instructed, as a matter of urgency, to plan such operations in exploitation of "Husky" as are best calculated to eliminate Italy from the war and to contain the maximum number of German forces. Which of the various specific operations should be adopted and therefore mounted, is a decision which will be reserved to the Combined Chiefs of Staff.'†

At the time the U.S. Chiefs of Staff were only prepared to agree at the most to an attack on Sardinia and, perhaps, Corsica. This, in their opinion, would give them the requisite bases from which to launch a subsidiary operation in the form of a landing in the south of France in support of the main Overlord invasion. The Americans were completely obsessed with the idea of a cross-Channel invasion and were not in the least worried by the strength of the Atlantic Wall. They did not for a moment doubt that the concentrated mass of material power at their disposal would succeed in blasting the essential breach and opening the way into the heart of Germany. With this in view, they proceeded to amass a vast amount of material and immensely powerful forces in Britain, with which quite simply to blast the Germans out of existence. They showed but little appreciation for the art of manœuvre and seemed rather to prefer to run head-on at their objectives.

The British had very different views. The recollections of the Flanders battles of the First War, which had swept away the flower of British youth, were still painfully vivid in their minds. Now they feared that, once they had regained a foothold on the continent, they would again become tied down in trench warfare, unless they first succeeded in splitting up the German forces; and that could only be accomplished by 'manœuvre'.

* Churchill, *The Second World War*, Vol. IV.   † Ibid.

It was with this in mind that Churchill strove so hard to mount subsidiary operations in the Mediterranean, in order to draw German troops away from France and thus make things easier for the cross-Channel invasion. Neither he nor his Chiefs of Staff had ever intended that the major offensive against Germany should be made via southern Europe or the Balkans.

The Americans, on the other hand, rather suspected that Churchill's Balkan plans had been formulated for political reasons; and that was contrary to their fundamental principle that in strategic planning political considerations carried no weight. Adherence to this principle explains why, since Pearl Harbor, Hull, the American Secretary of State, had not been invited to attend a single conference at which military affairs were under discussion. Roosevelt and his Chiefs of Staff felt that, in the eyes of the American people, their only justification for the employment of American troops in Europe would be that they would be used solely for the purpose of the military defeat of Germany.

Truly astonishing is the fact that the U.S. Chiefs of Staff refused even to recognize the importance of Italy as a base for air operations against Germany. Although Marshal of the Royal Air Force Sir Charles Portal, the Chief of the Air Staff, pointed out that from the airfields of southern Italy attacks could be delivered not only against the Ploesti oil wells, but also, and perhaps even more important, against the aircraft factories in southern Germany and Austria, the Americans remained unmoved. Even the alluring prospect of striking a vital blow at the production of German fighter aircraft and thus achieving one of the essential prerequisites to a successful crossing of the Channel failed to persuade them to agree to the invasion of Italy.

Churchill was greatly disappointed that Italy had not been named as the strategic objective for the second half of 1943. It was to achieve this that he had firstly convened the Trident conference and had then gone once again to Washington. The result, as has been seen, had been a vaguely worded directive, which was neither flesh, fowl nor good red herring. Eisenhower had certainly been instructed to prepare plans 'which, it was hoped, would lead to Italy's withdrawal from the war'; but the Combined Chiefs of Staff reserved the right to decide upon both the scale and the objectives of the operations.

Nor was this all. They deprived Eisenhower of much of the arms and equipment he would need to carry out the instructions given to him. He was told that on the completion of Husky four squadrons of heavy bombers and a large proportion of his naval forces and landing craft were to be transferred to the Far East and to England. His land forces, too, were to be very appreciably reduced. Seven divisions—four American and three British—were to be ready to move to Britain by 1 November 1943.

Still Churchill would not admit defeat. His last bet he staked on Eisenhower himself. As has already been mentioned, on the completion of the Trident conference he flew straightway with General Marshall to Algiers. Although at that conference he had expressly stated that he was planning no attack against the Balkans 'in the immediate future', he had, in actual fact, suggested to the President as early as the autumn of 1943 that a thrust should be made via Laibach into the Viennese basin; and he continued stubbornly to woo the Turks, with the primary object of bursting open the door into the Balkans. This he did not solely on military grounds, not on account of Ploesti alone and the number of German divisions he hoped thereby to divert from Overlord. Behind it all lay grave and important political reasons.

Stalin's unprovoked attack on East Poland and Finland and the rape of the Baltic States were unmistakable signs of a recrudescence of Russian imperialism. Churchill felt sure that the countries of western Europe would preserve their democratic forms of government regardless of where the Allies decided to launch their offensive against Fortress Europe; but it seemed to him to be very doubtful whether the Balkan countries, should they be 'liberated' by the Red Army, would be either willing or able to maintain their traditional State structures in the face of Russian pressure. From 1943 onwards, foreseeing all too clearly the calamity that was coming, he persisted with all that stubborn perseverance of which he was so great a master in his efforts to initiate a strategy which would put a stop to Stalin's lust for expansion. The strategy he envisaged should not, he felt, be confined solely to the achievement of victory in the field over Germany, but should aim also at a political victory over the Russian ally. To implement such a strategy, however, proved to be beyond his powers. His American friends thought they detected a *soupçon* of British imperialism in his arguments, and for that they refused absolutely to risk one single G.I.

As a result of the surprising initial success achieved in Sicily, Eisenhower made up his mind, while the campaign was still but a few week's old, to come to grips with the mainland as soon as Sicily had been conquered. On 20 July the U.S. Chiefs of Staff gave their approval, but added a proviso that these further operations must not be allowed to interfere with the agreed transfer of forces to south-east Asia and Britain, and that these transfers should be initiated according to plan as soon as the Sicilian campaign ended. This proviso exasperated the British. Now, when they only had to lift a finger to bring off a brilliant success, their American friends proposed to put a spoke in their wheel! Churchill was furious; this was something 'up with which he would not put'! On 22 July the British Chiefs of Staff, mindful of Churchill's dictum: 'Why crawl up the leg like a harvest bug from the ankle upwards? Let us rather strike at the knee!' proposed a direct attack on Naples, for which a special assignment of transports with aircraft-carriers in support would have to be made. The U.S. Chiefs of Staff approved of the proposal, but refused to place any additional means at Eisenhower's disposal to enable him to put it into practice. Thereupon the British Chiefs of Staff, without further consultation, issued a stand-fast order to all their naval and air formations which had been earmarked for withdrawal from the Mediterranean theatre. Washington's reaction was swift. Marshall and King declared that they must insist on the carrying out of the orders issued in accordance with the Trident conference decisions.

Then came 25 July, and with it the fall of Mussolini. Eisenhower's hands were tied. The transport and landing craft allotted to him were insufficient to allow him to seize this favourable opportunity and mount a large-scale landing. When the Eighth Army had been halted at Catania, it became obvious that no swift end to the Sicilian campaign could be expected; but equally, until it did end, it would not be possible to withdraw any shipping from Sicily for other purposes.

It was not long before Eisenhower's wings were further clipped. On 2 August Marshall confirmed the order that four groups of Liberators were to be transferred at once to Britain. This very materially reduced the chances of being able to disrupt the German lines of communication through the Alpine passes. There was a derisive note of mockery in the directive which Eisenhower received on 18 August from the Quadrant conference in Quebec. It urged him . . . 'to accept the unconditional surrender of Italy and to obtain the greatest possible military advantage from it . . . to seize Sardinia and Corsica and attempt the establishment of air bases in the Rome area and northward, if feasible, maintaining unrelenting pressure on German forces in northern Italy.'*

This, in all conscience, was asking a great deal of a commander who long since had been denied the means of carrying out operations on anything like the scale now envisaged. The picture as seen from Quebec was very different to that seen by the man on the spot. Those on the other side of the Atlantic seemed to think that the Germans were in headlong flight into northern Italy. They had not realized that it was Kesselring's firm intention, if a landing in upper Italy failed to materialize, to organize the defence of the country far to the south of Rome. By the middle of August a large number of American ships had been withdrawn from the Mediterranean and a considerable portion of the British landing craft had been transferred to the Indian Ocean. The only concession made to Eisenhower had been to permit him to postpone the transfer of eighteen tank landing

* Chester Wilmot, *The Struggle for Europe.*

craft to the Indian Ocean until after the Salerno landing. Burma was given priority over Italy, and the Americans were far more anxious about the Pacific than the Mediterranean. They attached far more importance to the reconquest of Burma and the opening of the land route to China than to the occupation of Italy. They were convinced that without Chinese assistance Japan could not be defeated; but they also knew that without American supplies and help the armies of Chiang Kai-shek could not exist.

In midsummer 1943 there were thirteen U.S. divisions in the Pacific, two in Britain and eight in the Mediterranean. Of these eight, four were earmarked for Overlord, and only four were available for Operation 'Avalanche'—the Salerno landing. So great, however, was the dearth of shipping and landing craft that even these four divisions could only be carried in stages. It was this perpetual and acute shortage of landing craft that was the root of all evil as far as the Italian campaign was concerned.

The Italian High Command had never seriously believed that the land war would ever leap across the seas from North Africa to the mainland, and therein lay the reason for the inadequacy of the defensive measures, which had to be improvised at the last moment. The loss of Sicily had a paralysing rather than a rousing effect, and the internal political events were not without influence on the attitude of the army.

All the more paramount, therefore, became the importance of the German forces, on whose shoulders the main burden of the fight would rest in any case. They were scattered all over southern and central Italy, and, until 8 September, the Army Corps of which they were composed was under the command of the Italian Army. Now that a major enemy offensive was imminent, to concentrate them closely under one hand became the order of the day. In this way the German Tenth Army was born, with a staff composed of officers who had been serving as liaison officers with the Italian Army and with Colonel-General von Vietinghoff-Scheel as Commander-in-Chief.

The forces in Calabria were put under the command of the newly constituted Headquarters LXXVI Panzer Corps, and consisted of those divisions which had been withdrawn from Sicily. The XIV Panzer Corps concentrated in the Naples area, had transferred its 29 Panzer Grenadier Division in south Calabria and its 1 Parachute Division in Apulia to LXXVI Corps. In all, Field-Marshal Kesselring had the forces shown on p. 50 at his disposal.

The German High Command in Italy regarded Operation Husky as a clear indication of the subsequent intentions of the Allies. Although their failure to mount a direct landing in Calabria or to conduct an immediate pursuit across the Straits of Messina might have misled Field-Marshal

Commander-in-Chief, South:	Field-Marshal Kesselring
1. The Tenth Army:	Colonel-General von Vietinghoff-Scheel
Chief of Staff:	Major-General Wentzell
XIV Panzer Corps:	General Hube
Chief of Staff:	Colonel von Bonin
15 Panzer Grenadier Division:	Lieutenant-General Rodt
Hermann Göring Panzer Division:	Lieutenant-General Conrath
LXXVI Panzer Corps:	General Herr
Chief of Staff:	Colonel Runkel
26 Panzer Division:	Lieutenant-General Freiherr von Lüttwitz
29 Panzer Grenadier Division:	Lieutenant-General Fries
1 Parachute Division:	Lieutenant-General Heidrich
2. XI Air Corps:	General Student
2 Parachute Division:	Lieutenant-General Ramcke
3 Panzer Grenadier Division:	Lieutenant-General Graeser
3. 90 Panzer Grenadier Division and Fortress Brigade:	General Lungerhausen (in Sardinia)
4. S.S. Reichsführer Brigade:	In Corsica
5. 2 Air Fleet:	Field-Marshal Freiherr von Richthoven
6. Naval Forces, Italy:	Admiral Meendsen-Bohlken

Kesselring into thinking that Eisenhower, with the efficient Sicilian ports at his disposal, was planning an invasion of the Balkans, he nevertheless remained convinced that the next move would be an early invasion of the Italian mainland. But in this case, too, it seemed to him that the Allies would regard it as important to occupy Calabria in order to protect the flank of their main offensive.

If the Allies launched a general offensive against the heart of the Italian mainland, the consequences for Germany might be incalculable. Once the Allies were in possession of upper Italy, the roads both to southern France and to the rear of the German eastern front would be open to them. If they decided on a cross-Channel invasion, they would be spared the necessity of the subsidiary supporting invasion of southern France; if not, they had as an alternative a unique opportunity of launching an offensive against the rear of the German eastern front and causing it to collapse. The divergence of views among the Allies as regards their Mediterranean strategy came as a rare godsend to the Germans and was much to the detriment of the Allied cause.

After the fall of Sicily the most important question the Germans were asking themselves was: Where would Eisenhower strike if he decided to invade Italy? The obvious answer seemed to be—Rome. The political and strategic importance of the capital justified the bold acceptance of risks. An invasion from the sea with Rome as its immediate objective would lead to more rapid success than a land campaign, subsequent to a landing, say, in the vicinity of Naples. If the Allies landed near Rome, the Commander-in-Chief, South, intended to withdraw with the two divisions and the whole of the anti-aircraft artillery stationed there to the Alban hills and to bring up the three mobile armoured divisions from the Naples area to join him. The LXXVI Panzer Corps, together with the strong anti-aircraft formations stationed in Apulia, would also be ordered to withdraw and take up a position in the Alban Hills.

If, on the other hand, the enemy landed in the Naples area, Kesselring saw no reason why he should give up central Italy without a fight. He did, however, feel that in that case he should be reinforced by one or two divisions from Rommel's Army Group, if he wished to bring the enemy to a halt well down in the south.

In the event of an invasion from the Tyrrhenian Sea, he did not consider that it would be possible to hold the islands. In this event, therefore, he decided that the 90 Panzer Grenadier Division and the strong *Luftwaffe* forces would withdraw to the north coast of Sardinia, cross over to Corsica and thence be transferred, together with the forces in Corsica, via the port of Bastia to the mainland in the vicinity of Leghorn.

If Eisenhower decided to attack via Naples, the Bay of Salerno was the obvious place at which to land. There he would find all the conditions necessary for a successful amphibious operation—calm waters, flat, sandy beaches, mountain defiles which could easily be sealed-off and air support from his land-based fighter aircraft. These were the considerations which decided Kesselring, in view of the unreliability of the Italians to entrust the defence of Salerno Bay to the 16 Panzer Division.

The old division had been through all the horrors of the Stalingrad battles, and it was the 4,000 survivors of that débâcle who formed the nucleus of the new 16 Division. During the Sicilian campaign it had been stationed in the northern sector of Calabria and towards the end of August, split into battle groups, it took over the Salerno sector. The Stempel Battle Group, consisting of the 64 Panzer Grenadier Regiment and attached troops, held a series of strongpoints in the sector Picento–Sele, and the von Döring Battle Group (79 Panzer Grenadier Regiment and attached troops) occupied the sector Paestum–Agropoli. Between them lay groups of Italian security troops.

The fine autumn weather greatly facilitated the rapid fortification of the positions, and in a very short space of time extensive barbed-wire entanglements and minefields constituted a formidably effective barrier. The hesitant caution shown by the Allies, the weakening of their forces available for the invasion and the reduction of the number of their landing craft were all of immense assistance to the Germans. It was indeed a slice of luck that Mussolini's downfall had caught the Western powers so completely unprepared.

At the conference in Carthage to which he had summoned his subordinate commanders, Eisenhower realized to his consternation that, thanks to the shortsightedness of the U.S. Chiefs of Staff, the earliest date on which he could hope to invade Italy would be the beginning of September. He decided to launch his main offensive against Naples. Montgomery was instructed to leap across the Straits of Messina as soon as possible after the end of the Sicilian campaign, with the object of drawing German forces from the Naples area to Calabria. Operation Avalanche was to be set in motion by the U.S. Fifth Army, commanded by General Mark Clark and consisting of the U.S. VI and the British X Corps.

Naples, then, the most important port in the 'boot', was to be the great prize. A direct assault on the port itself was not seriously considered. Two courses were open to the Allies—a landing in the Gulf of Gaeta or an attack via Salerno Bay. In favour of Gaeta there was a lot to be said. The terrain was suitable both for rapid movement by armour and for parachute drops; it was relatively close to Rome; and it was on the right side of the Volturno River. Air Chief Marshal Tedder, however, pointed to a number of disadvantages, one of which was of decisive importance—the radius of action of his land-based fighter aircraft, which, from Sicily, would not be able to support a landing there. The navy, too, had certain misgivings and considered that the anchorage in Salerno Bay was very much better. Salerno had but one drawback—it was encircled by a girdle of commanding heights which the Fifth Army would have to seize with great speed, before the Germans could establish themselves on them. This, it was thought, should not prove to be too difficult, provided that the rapid bringing up of German reserves could be prevented.

The plan envisaged a landing along a stretch of coast some twenty miles wide. The U.S. Corps was to land on either side of Paestum, seize the bridge at Sele, east of Eboli, occupy the high ground to the south thereof and seek contact with the British Eighth Army, advancing from Calabria. To the British Corps was given the task of landing astride the mouth of the

Tusciano River, securing Montecorvino, Battipaglia and Monte d'Eboli airfields, capturing Salerno, Vietri and Maiori and blocking the defiles which gave access to the beach-head. The U.S. 82 Airborne Division was ordered to seal off the Volturno crossings. As soon as the beach-head was secure and sufficient reserves had been landed, the Fifth Army was to break out and capture Naples.

The task allotted to the air arm was to deliver attacks on and block the network of roads in the general vicinity of Salerno and thus seriously delay the bringing up of German reserves. The fighter aircraft were to prevent the *Luftwaffe* both from interfering with the landing operation and from intervening in the subsequent battle. It was further stipulated that forty aircraft would be permanently on patrol over the landing area—a demand almost impossible to fulfil, in view of the distance from Sicily which allowed a twin-engined fighter to remain one hour and a single-engined fighter a mere twenty minutes over the area of operations. To reinforce the fighter umbrella the Admiralty contributed the five escort-carriers *Unicorn, Hunter, Stalker, Attacker*, and *Battler*, grouped together as V Squadron under the command of Rear-Admiral Sir Philip Vian. It was anticipated that from invasion day+2 the Montecorvino airfield would be available for use by Allied aircraft.

The whole of the naval side of the operation was under the command of U.S. Admiral Hewitt. The beach officers in charge of the landing operations were Commodore G. N. Oliver, R.N., in the British sector and Rear-Admiral J. L. Hall in the American. H Squadron (Vice-Admiral Willis), with the battleships *Nelson* and *Rodney*, was to provide overall protection and also to protect the aircraft-carriers *Illustrious* and *Formidable* against attack from the air.

So much for the plan. On 17 August Eisenhower held a further conference with his Commanders and fixed 9 September as the date for the Salerno landings. The attack across the Straits of Messina was to open on 3 September.

Montgomery's preparations to meet this dateline were already in full progress. The attack was to be led by XIII Corps, the British 5 Division being allotted the east coast of Calabria and the Canadian 1 Division the west coast. Both divisions were to cross the straits simultaneously, and strong air formations, light and heavy naval forces were to provide close support.

Behind Messina were 600 guns, forty-eight of them of the heaviest calibre, which Montgomery had borrowed from Patton. In the early hours of 3 September the tempest broke, enveloping the Calabrian coast from Reggio to San Giovanni in a sea of fire and smoke. At regular intervals the fire moved inland and then back to the beaches. With the flickering, rumbling tattoo of the barrage mingled the roar of the fourteen-inch turrets of the battleships; and cruisers, destroyers, gunboats and monitors lobbed their shells into the seething foreground. As daylight broke the air arm joined in, attacking those targets on which the artillery could not bring fire to bear. Montgomery had arranged a firework display reminiscent of El Alamein, as though he were softening-up some mighty fortress preparatory to assaulting it. Little did he know that his guns were firing hundreds of tons of shells at nothing. For, across the straits, in the immediate coastal area, there was not one single enemy. The 29 Panzer Grenadier Division had no intention of allowing itself to be shot to bits on the beaches. It could not, in any case have prevented the crossing, and the task allotted to it was rather to fight delaying actions further inland and hold up the advance of XIII Corps.

The 13 and 17 Brigades of 5 Division and the Canadian 3 Brigade—the leading wave of the attack—had no difficulty, therefore, in getting ashore and forming a beach-head. After the capture of Reggio and San Giovanni, where the Allied troops were greeted with jubilation by the Italians, the British formations wheeled northwards and the Canadians southwards. During the night of 3/4 September a British Commando landed at Bagnare and captured it. Under the protection of the naval forces accompanying it the 15 Brigade advanced steadily without meeting any opposition and was leap-frogged by the 13 Brigade which came ashore ahead of it and fell upon the flank of the German rear-guard to the south of Gioia Tauro and then assumed the role of spearhead of the attack.

On 8 September Montgomery delivered a further blow. In the early hours of the morning he threw the 231 Infantry Brigade ashore at Pizzo, with the object of cutting off the 29 Panzer Grenadier Division. But in vain. The Brigade had the misfortune to run straight into the 3rd Battalion, 4 Parachute Regiment, and Captain Grassmehl kept it pinned down on the beaches throughout the day, until the rear-guard of Fries's Division had passed through the bottle-neck.

The Canadians, too, made rapid progress. On the left flank they advanced with some difficulty through the mountains, but along the coastal road they stormed forward so swiftly that by 10 September they had reached Catanzaro, at the narrowest strip of Calabria.

By this time the British 1 Airborne Division with a bold stroke, delivered not from the air but from the sea, had seized the town and port of Tarento. Having landed thus successfully on the 'toe', Eisenhower decided to strike a blow at the 'heel'. All available divisions, however, had already been allotted to Operation Avalanche, and the British paratroops were all that he could lay his hands on. But they, as it happened, had not at their disposal the same generous transport facilities as had been given to

Ridgway's Division in Sicily. When Eisenhower told Cunningham of his intention of taking Tarento and asked him whether he thought the navy could carry out so hazardous an exploit, Sir Andrew answered: 'Sir, His Majesty's Fleet will proceed wherever you send it.' Brave words—particularly in view of the fact that no help could be expected from the Italians.

At noon on the 8 September 6,700 men of the 1 Airborne Division in Bizerta embarked in the cruisers *Abdiel, Aurora, Dido, Penelope, Sirius* and the U.S.S. *Boise.* Under the command of Vice-Admiral Power, the Squadron, to which the battleships *Howe* and *King George V* also belonged, put to sea on the evening of 8 September. The next afternoon it passed the Italian Tarento Squadron sailing towards Malta and internment, and at 5 p.m. steamed into Tarento harbour. So far all had gone well. The first companies were swiftly disembarked, but as *Abdiel* was about to anchor she ran on to a mine and was so severely damaged that she sank in a few minutes, taking 200 paratroops to the bottom with her. This was a grievous misfortune, but Tarento, the gateway to the rear of the Salerno front and the key to the Apulian airfields, was worth the sacrifice.

As for the invasion of Sicily, overall command of the land operations was exercised by Field-Marshal Alexander, the Commander-in-Chief, 15 Army Group, who for this purpose also had the U.S. Fifth Army, stationed in French North Africa, under him.* By the beginning of September the Fifth Army had completed its preparations, and its convoys started sailing from the North African ports on 5 September, the two British divisions from Bizerta and Tripoli and the U.S. divisions from Algiers, Oran and Palermo. Clark himself embarked on U.S.S. *Ancon*, Admiral Hewitt's flagship, on 5 September. As in all amphibious operations, all army troops were under the command of the officer commanding the naval forces from the time of sailing until they set foot ashore. Hewitt concentrated his four squadrons, H and V Squadrons and the convoys under Admiral Hall and Commodore Oliver, in the southern area of the Tyrrhenian Sea on 8 September. In all, apart from assault craft, there were 450 ships, carrying 169,000 men and 20,000 vehicles.

---

* The Fifth Army Order of Battle for the Salerno landing was:

American VI Corps	*British X Corps*
(Major-General Dawley)	(Lieutenant-General McCreery)
U.S. 3 Inf. Div. (Truscott)	Brit. 46 Inf. Div. (Hawkesworth)
34 ,, ,, (Ryder)	56 ,, ,, (Templer)
36 ,, ,, (Walker)	7 Armd. Div. (Erskine)
45 ,, ,, (Middleton)	Nos. 2 & 3 Commandos
82 Airb. ,, (Ridgway)	U.S. 1st, 3rd & 4th Ranger
13 Field Art. Brigade	Battalions

Air support
    British 1 Tactical Air Fleet: Air Marshal Sir A. Coningham
    U.S. 12 Tactical Air Fleet: Major-General Cannon

The concentration of this gigantic armada could not be kept hidden from the eyes of the German *Luftwaffe*. Air reconnaissance had discovered the convoy of U.S. 36 Infantry Division as soon as it set sail from Oran on 5 September, and the transports carrying the British 46 Infantry Division from Bizerta was picked up on 8 September and attacked twice, losing one landing ship. When the invasion fleet reached the sea area in the vicinity of Naples, the Commander-in-Chief, South, knew that a landing was imminent and issued the code signal 'Alarm Stage II', which brought all German forces to a state of instant readiness.

It was not until the night of 8/9 September, when the invasion fleet was approaching the Italian coast, that the troops were told by their officers of the Italian capitulation. This news put the men in high spirits, and they saw themselves landing in comfort and without opposition on the Italian coast. Subsequent events, however, by no means came up to their expectations! The attack on the coast turned out to be anything but a promenade, and the march to Naples became a dramatic and bloody struggle.

Strong German forces very quickly appeared on the scene, and for days on end the fate of the Fifth Army was balanced on a knife-edge. Only by a hair's breadth did the Allied divisions escape being flung back into the sea; 'Furthermore, we knew that in command of these forces was Field-Marshal Albert Kesselring, one of the ablest officers in the Hitler armies. . . . Kesselring was well qualified both as a commander and as an administrator.'*

The invasion caught 16 Panzer Division while it was still fully occupied in disarming the Italians. Even so, when the first assault boats approached the beaches at 3.30 a.m., they were met everywhere with a tornado of fire. The U.S. 36 Division launched its attack without any covering fire, and it was only in the British sector that the guns of the fleet did their best to pave the way for the assaulting troops. The Americans attacked with the utmost determination. In his first wave Walker sent in the 141 and 142 Infantry Regiments near Paestum, and by 6 a.m. he also had two sections of light artillery ashore and in action. Bulldozers were carving roads through the low-lying dunes, and on the beaches the pioneers were busy preparing for the arrival of supplies, reinforcements and reserves.

The first objective of the British X Corps was the eagerly sought airfield of Montecorvino. To capture it swiftly General McCreery launched his 56 Division against the Tusciano estuary, where Templer had had great difficulty in gaining a foothold in the face of stubborn opposition from 64 Panzer Grenadier Regiment. To his north the 46 Division fought its way ashore; its right wing was also aiming at the airfield, while its left was wheeled by Hawkesworth in the direction of Salerno. During the morning

* Mark Clark, *Calculated Risk*.

the British Commando had taken both the town and the port and were now pressing northwards to secure the Nocera Pass. Salerno harbour, however, was still under heavy fire from the German artillery and could not at once be taken into use by X Corps. The U.S. Rangers, too, had met with success. They had captured Maiori and then blocked the Tramonti Pass.

Despite these initial successes, Avalanche proved to be a hard nut and 'very nearly a disaster' (Mark Clark). The first counter-stroke was delivered by von Döring's Battle Group, the 64 Panzer Grenadier Regiment and attached units. At 8 a.m. he launched a counter-attack against the British who had landed at the mouth of the Tusciano, and after heavy fighting the German forces reached the vicinity of the beaches at 1 p.m. But there the effort ended. The guns of the fleet poured a merciless and devastating fire on the Panzer Grenadiers and drove them back. 56 Division pursued close on the heels of the retreating Germans, and by the evening Templer was close to the airfield and on the outskirts of Battipaglia.

Further south, Stempel's Battle Group, the 79 Panzer Grenadier Regiment and attached troops, had succeeded in bringing the American attack to a standstill. The Battle Group had the inexperienced 36 Division in dire difficulty and kept it pinned down to the beaches throughout 9 September.

By the evening of the first day, the Fifth Army was clinging fast to its hold in all sectors. But the next morning the storm burst—the German counter-offensive, which was to bring Clark's army to the very brink of destruction.

Since early dawn a powerful column had been worming its way through the Calabrian Mountains—the 26 Panzer Division and the main body of 29 Panzer Grenadier Division. These two divisions had been in position a good 125 miles and more away from Salerno, and their object now was to reach the beach-head as quickly as possible. Their march was being constantly held up by obstructions, bomb craters and lack of fuel. But, contrary to their expectations, they were left unmolested all day by the enemy air arm. Tedder had concentrated his forces over the invasion area.

From the north the 15 Panzer Grenadier Division and the Hermann Göring Panzer Division were advancing against the northern wing of the beach-head. In spite of all Kesselring's efforts to clear up the situation in Rome as speedily as possible, the first elements of 3 Panzer Grenadier Division, the Reconnaissance Section, could not be set in motion until 10 September, and it was not until 13 September that the rest of the division was able to join in the battle for the beach-head. The struggle for the mastery of Rome had given the Allies a welcome respite.

Why the O.K.W. did not lift a finger to help the Commander-in-Chief, South, in his life-and-death struggle is a complete mystery. In upper Italy Rommel's Army Group was somewhat futilely wasting its time disarming the Italian troops, while the fate of the Tenth Army in the south hung by a thread. In the Mantua–Modena area were two very efficient Panzer divisions, and Kesselring had asked for them to be transferred forthwith to Salerno. But Hitler refused, without giving a thought to the fact that in southern Italy a battle of vital importance was being fought. Westphal affirms: 'If these high-quality troops had been set in motion towards the front on 9 September—wheeled vehicles by road, tracked vehicles by rail— they would in all probability have arrived to throw their weight into the battle which reached its crisis on 13 September.'* Once the Salerno battle had been lost and the Allies were firmly established on the European mainland, the fact that Jodl himself admitted that this shortsightedness had been a serious mistake was not of much help.

In spite of the very great air superiority enjoyed by the Allies and the murderous supporting fire afforded by their naval forces, by 10 September the first German successes were beginning to materialize. On 9 September the 1st Battalion, 3 Parachute Regiment, which until then had been under the command of 26 Panzer Division, advancing rapidly ahead of the Division, reached Eboli, where on the afternoon of 10 September it received orders from 16 Panzer Division forthwith to attack and recapture Battipaglia. On the previous night the place had been occupied by the Royal Fusiliers of the 201 Guards Brigade. By the evening of 10 September it was once more in German hands. Four hundred and fifty British troops had surrendered to a hundred German paratroops and the company of the 2 Panzer Regiment supporting them! This counter-attack, delivered without any preliminary artillery bombardment, came as a shock to 56 Division, which interpreted it as the opening move of a major counter-move. Templer withdrew his brigades a mile and a half. He still held Montecorvino airfield, which his 169 Infantry Brigade had captured the previous day; but the fire of the German artillery prevented the British from using it right up to 17 September, when Kesselring broke off the engagement.

The U.S. 36 Division was by no means content to rest on the laurels of its initial success. On 10 September it had succeeded in increasing the size of its slender beach-head, and by the evening of the same day its left wing was in the immediate vicinity of Altavilla, high up in the hills, and the commanding Height 424. The floating reserve of VI Corps, the 45 Division, had landed and was pressing forward towards Persano and its final objective, the Sele bridge, the nerve-centre in rear of the German defensive position.

The next four days were full of dramatic events which came within an ace of sealing the fate of the Fifth Army. It was thanks solely and wholly to Tedder's air arm and Cunningham's naval guns that the German Tenth

* *The German Army in the West.*

Army was prevented from inflicting a second 'Dunkirk' on the enemy. On 11 September Kesselring's counter-measures began to take effect. On the right flank of the beach head, such elements of the 15 Panzer Grenadier Division and the Hermann Göring Division as had arrived, went into battle, while on the southern flank the leading elements of 29 Panzer Grenadier Division also joined in.

Since 9 September the invasion fleet had been the target of 2 Air Fleet. During the first two days the latter had achieved nothing worth mentioning; but 11 September brought an important success. During the air attack on the morning of that day the U.S. cruiser *Philadelphia* was severely damaged by a near miss from a radar-controlled bomb. A few minutes later a similar bomb scored a hit on the U.S. cruiser *Savannah*. It pierced the cruiser's forward turret and exploded in the body of the ship, killing 100 seamen. With great difficulty the *Savannah* was kept afloat and eventually managed to limp painfully into Malta.

On land the U.S. VI Corps (General Dawley) made further progress and by 11 September it had pushed the 79 Regiment of the 45 Division back into the vicinity of the Sele bridge. The 36 Division took Altavilla and Height 424. But the German counter-stroke came swiftly. Tanks and pioneers of 29 Panzer Grenadier Division hurled themselves at the 179 Infantry Regiment south of Sele bridge and drove it pell-mell back into the coastal plain. This was the turning point of the battle. The German spear-head was directed against the most sensitive spot in the Allied beach-head, the yawning ten-mile gap between the U.S. and the British Corps. The Fifth Army was in dire peril, and General Clark was compelled to put in the whole of his reserve to plug the gap.

German pressure was now increasing both in the Salerno area and on Battipaglia as well. It was with the greatest difficulty that British X Corps beat off the German counter-attacks. For General Clark the only ray of sunshine on this gloomy 11 September was a signal from Alexander, telling him that the 82 Airborne Division was once more at his disposal and under his command.

The next day the Fifth Army's position became even more critical. The German resistance on the southern flank had, it is true, ceased as the result of the withdrawal of 79 Panzer Grenadier Regiment to the area east of Eboli; but now the 26 Panzer Division had also appeared on the scene. It went into action against the left Flank of the U.S. VI Corps, and on 12 September, together with elements of 29 Panzer Grenadier Division, it advanced as far as Persano. The 4 Parachute Regiment, under command of 29 Division, stormed and retook Altavilla and Height 424 and side by side with the Panzer Grenadiers drove the Americans back into the plains below.

These were shrewd blows. Clark, who in the morning had transferred his command post from U.S.S. *Ancon* to the shore, was not sure that he would not be forced to go back on board. His whole hope was pinned on Ridgway, who had been ordered to land elements of his division in the beach-head that night and form a Combat Group to block the road junctions in the Avellino area. Help for British X Corps was on its way in the shape of 1,500 men aboard the cruisers *Euryalus*, *Scylla* and *Charybdis*, steaming at full speed from Tunisia.

Throughout 13 September the Tenth Army maintained its heavy pressure. Advancing from Persano, the LXXVI Panzer Corps thrust further southwards, and by 6.30 p.m. the 79 Panzer Grenadier Regiment had reached the confluence of the Sele and Calore Rivers. But farther than that they could not go. Under the withering fire of the 158 and 189 Artillery Regiments of the 45 Division the German attack petered out, and the Americans were saved at the moment of their direst peril. For neither Dawley nor Clark himself had any reserves in hand, and the Germans were within little more than two and a half miles from the beaches!

Clark viewed the prospect of the next day or two with grave anxiety. He and Hewitt were now seriously considering re-embarking Fifth Army Headquarters aboard the *Ancon*, while the American commanders of the formations engaged were preparing plans either to evacuate VI Corps beach-head or to stabilize it with the help of reinforcements drawn from British X Corps. As early as 13 September no further reinforcements were available for the American sector.

In this critical situation Eisenhower reported to Washington: 'Our worst problem is Avalanche itself. We have been unable to advance and the enemy is preparing a major counter-attack. The 45 Division is largely in the area now and I am using everything we have bigger than a rowboat to get the 3 Division in to Clark quickly. In the present situation our great hope is the air force.'* During the first four days of the invasion Tedder's airmen had dropped 3,100 tons of bombs on the German encircling girdle— 1,300 tons on 13 September alone. Then on 14 September he received orders to use his strategic forces as well as his tactical squadrons. Every available aircraft of every kind was to go into action at this crucial stage in the battle.

The fleet, too, was ordered to give the maximum support of which it was capable. At Hewitt's urgent request Cunningham sent *Warspite* and *Valiant* from Malta to Salerno and ordered *Nelson* and *Rodney* to proceed to Augusta, in case further help should be needed.

During the night of 13/14 September the first gleam of light pierced the sinister clouds enveloping the Fifth Army. The 82 Airborne Division was on its way. Marshall reports:

* *The War Reports of General Marshall.*

On the morning of September 13 the commanders of our airborne troops were notified that air reinforcements were required by the U.S. Fifth Army within twenty-four hours. At 2045 hours on the same day pathfinder units of the airborne task force took off from their Sicilian base, reaching the drop zone prepared by the Fifth Army on the Salerno beach-head at 2314. Twenty-four minutes later the first elements of the paratroopers arrived. In one and a half hours ninety aircraft dropped 1,300 paratroopers and equipment in an area approximately 1,200 by 800 yards. By 0200 hours, 14 September, these paratroopers were completely organized and marching into position on the front line. Many of the units had had less than two hours to give their planes a final servicing, arrange take-off plans and to load men and equipment. On 14 September the operation was repeated, this time with 131 C-47's dropping 1,900 paratroopers in the same zone while forty C-47's carried a battalion of infantry and a company of engineers to a zone five miles south-east of Avellino, behind the enemy lines.*

Once again the situation changed, and this time the fortune of war swung finally in favour of the Fifth Army. From 14 September onwards it slowly gained the upper hand. From early dawn on that day Tedder's great bombers roared in ever-increasing numbers over the beach-head. Battipaglia and Persano and the defiles in the Salerno area were their principal targets. Squadron after squadron of heavy four-engined bombers continued to pound the German positions and lines of communication until twilight set in; and when darkness fell, innumerable 'illuminated Christmas trees' guided the night bombers to their targets. The next day Tedder repeated the performance, and now the fourteen-inch turrets of *Warspite* and *Valiant* joined in the thunderous concert. By evening the towns and villages in the beach-head and its vicinity were all reduced to smouldering heaps of ruins.

From the south, too, another storm was approaching. Montgomery was getting nearer and nearer to the beach-head. The Eighth Army advance had been very considerably impeded by the rearguards of the 29 Panzer Grenadier and 1 Parachute Divisions, and progress through Calabria had been slow and difficult. In Apulia, too, Heidrich's Division had delayed the advance of the British paratroops with great skill. Despite this, the British 5 and the U.S. 36 Divisions joined hands to the south of the beach-head on 16 September. The spearheads of the Eighth Army offensive had reached Vallo, to the south of Potenza.

On the same day *Warspite* met her fate. In the early afternoon she fell victim to an air attack. A radar-controlled bomb crashed through her forward armoured deck and caused severe damage below. Shortly afterwards a near-miss tore a gaping hole in the ship's side. *Warspite* immediately began to lose way; by 3 p.m. the sea had swamped the last of

* *The War Reports of General Marshall.*

her boilers, but the stout ship remained afloat. Tugs took her safely to Malta, and from there she proceeded first to Gibraltar and then to England. The most famous ship of the Mediterranean fleet which, in spite of her thirty years, had rendered so much signal service, had at long last been driven from the waters she knew so well. After taking part in the attack on the Dutch island of Walcheren in the autumn of 1944, *Warspite* retired honourably from the Service.

Despite the loss of *Warspite*, Clark still remained master of the situation. By the evening of 16 September the British 7 Armoured Division, Erskine's famous Desert Rats, had landed, reinforcements for X Corps had arrived from Tunisia and the U.S. 3 Division was on its way from Sicily.

The German Tenth Army made one last attempt to turn the tide. On 17 September the LXXVI Panzer Corps from Battipaglia launched an attack in the direction of Salerno and XIV Panzer Corps advanced from the north-west in an effort to encircle the British X Corps in a pincer movement, but in vain. After a good start the attacks of both the German thrusts were dispersed by a devastating hail of bombs and the fire from the naval guns. This was the signal for Field-Marshal Kesselring to break off the engagement. As early as 10 September, at a conference with Colonel-General von Vietinghoff, he had decided upon the next line of defence, if south Italy had to be evacuated. At first sight it appeared as though a great deal of territory would have to be surrendered; even so, in view of the mountainous character of southern Italy and the advanced season of the year, there was every justification for hoping that the 15 Army Group could be brought to a standstill south of Rome. Kesselring had already been considering the possibility of being able to stand and fight on either side of the Mignano or the Cassino line, using the Tenth Army to fight a series of delaying actions until construction of the requisite defences in these lines had been completed. Accordingly, on 17 September, the day on which he was compelled to break off the Salerno battle, he gave orders that Tenth Army was not to retire from the Volturno line before 15 October.

After nine days of bloody fighting, a battle in which both sides had suffered heavy casualties came to an end. General Clark puts Allied losses at 5,674 killed, wounded and missing. The salient feature of the operation was the attempt by Kesselring to throw the invaders back into the sea. But, as had happened in Sicily, the army, for all its gallantry and with all the skill of leadership, was not able alone to prevail against an enemy who was able almost unchallenged to throw the whole weight of his naval and air superiority into the scales. It was not only the troops who suffered severely from bomb and shell in the very rocky terrain; the directing staffs were also greatly handicapped. The enemy, protected by his air arm, was able to operate at will both by day and by night; but the German counter-moves had to be restricted to the hours of darkness and were for the most part unable to keep pace with events on the field of battle. The fact that LXXVI Corps had been able to hasten to battle by day and unmolested by the enemy air arm was the one, solitary exception, and this was due simply to the schematic manner in which Tedder controlled the sorties of his air forces.

Despite the disappointing result of the Salerno battle, the Germans could be content with the way things in general were going. The situation in Rome had been very quickly stabilized; the feared landing in the vicinity of the capital had not taken place; Montgomery had failed to seal off Calabria sufficiently far to the north to enable him to catch LXXVI Corps in his trap; the weakened 1 Parachute Division—more than half of its infantry had been committed to the Salerno battle—had given a good account of itself in Apulia, though Kesselring had for a long time been fearful regarding its fate; and the disarming of the Italian forces had been accomplished with comparative ease. Everything could have turned out a great deal worse.

On 18 September General Heidrich at last had his division once more concentrated and under his own command—for the first time since 12 July! At that time some units had been detained in Rome, but had then been gradually transferred to Apulia. There the division had succeeded in fulfilling the task allotted to it. It had blocked the roads leading out of the mountains and considerably delayed the advance of the Canadians debouching from them; it had disarmed a large number of Italian units and had contested possession of the port of Bari until 20 September. In short, the division had held the ring well and truly in the rear of the Salerno battle.

On 22 and 23 September the British 78 Division, an armoured brigade and the headquarters of V Corps, landed at Bari. The Canadians had taken Potenza on 20 September and were pressing on to Melfi. With great skill Heidrich withdrew behind the Ofanto sector. There was much fierce fighting for the possession of the Foggia air base, which fell to the Allies on 27 September. In this instance, too, the O.K.W. had refused the divisions for which the Commander-in-Chief, South, had asked and thus irresponsibly had allowed this important base to pass into enemy hands. For three weeks 1 Parachute Division had maintained its positions against greatly superior enemy forces. Leaders and men alike, the weak elements of the Division engaged in Apulia deserve the highest praise, and one cannot but agree with a British writer's criticism, when he asks: Why take a sledge-hammer to crack a nut?

No less worthy of praise were the divisions of XIV Panzer Corps, which for more than a week held the Salerno passes against all the onslaughts of the British X Corps. It was not until 28 September that McCreery's leading elements reached the Sarno and 1 October that the 'Desert Rats' and Ridgway's paratroops at last marched into Naples.

The next day Churchill telegraphed to Alexander that the end of the month 'will see us in Rome', and on 4 October Roosevelt in a telegram to Stalin expressed his confidence that Allied troops would be marching into the capital in the very near future. Vain dreams! Four weeks were to be turned into nine months before Alexander could hold a victory parade in Rome; and, thanks to the stubbornness with which the German forces opposed the 15 Army Group at Cassino, what was to have been a victorious route march was transformed into a painful and costly inch-by-inch advance.

On 5 October the Fifth Army reached the Volturno and thus completed the first phase of the operations against the Italian capital. It had taken the Americans a whole month to advance from Salerno to the banks of the Volturno; a further four weeks were to elapse before they had broken into the first, outer girdle of defences before Cassino.

From the first moment that the Fifth Army set foot on the European mainland it had had a foretaste of the battles that awaited it at Cassino. It was opposed by *élite* German divisions, and Alexander, too, had contributed the best that he had. Side by side with the Anglo-American forces were the troops of the British Empire—Canadians, New Zealanders, Gurkhas, Rajputs and Maoris. The French, the Moroccans, the Algerians and the Tunisians were there; and then there were also the Poles, who in the end planted their flag on the ruins of Monte Cassino. It was a true battle of all nations.

The bloody battles for Cassino were the salient feature of the first year of the Italian campaign. On Rome the God of War placed a high price in sweat and blood. And Rome was, and remained, the glittering prize, though Eisenhower seems rather to deny this when he says: 'With the establishment of this base [Naples] and with Foggia firmly in our grasp, we had accomplished the first major objectives of the Italian campaign. All later fighting in that area would have as its principal objective the pinning down of German forces far from the region of the major assault that was to take place the following year across the English Channel.'* And Churchill, in turn, held very different views. As will soon be seen, he strove resolutely and spared no effort to hasten the capture of Rome. Nor was Rome the ultimate objective, as he saw it, of the Italian campaign. His eyes were turned rather towards the Balkans, and Italy was to be his spring-board for an invasion of the Viennese basin.

* Eisenhower, *Crusade in Europe.*

Chapter 4

Kesselring or Rommel?
Cassino or Florence?

Hitler was fully aware of the dangers which threatened his position, not only in Italy but also in the Aegean and the Balkans after the defeat in North Africa. Once again there arose the spectre of a possible Allied landing in south-eastern Europe and a repetition of the Balkan campaign of the First World War. This would inevitably have placed Germany at a grave disadvantage. Once the Allies had established themselves in the Balkans and the Aegean Islands, the entry of Turkey into the war would only be a question of time. Germany would then not only lose the vital chromium deliveries from Turkey, but would also be compelled, sooner or later, to write off the Rumanian oil-fields; and an opening of the Dardanelles and a direct sea-route of communication between the Western powers and Russia would constitute a deadly threat to the German eastern front.

Hitler therefore took the possibility of an amphibious attack against Greece and the Aegean very seriously. His fears seemed to be further justified by certain indications which, to his mind, pointed to an operation of this nature. Not the least important of these indications was that mysterious British courier, whose body was washed up on the Spanish coast before the invasion of Sicily began. He was carrying documents which spoke of an imminent landing of strong Anglo-American forces in Greece.

This was sufficient to cause the dispatch, under conditions of considerable difficulty, of German troops, including a Panzer division, to southern Greece. As later transpired, the German High Command had been the victims of a skilful ruse of the Allied intelligence service.

The broken, mountainous terrain of Greece and the confused mass of the Aegean Islands certainly constituted a defensive position organized in depth, which any enemy would be diffident of trying to capture. But if Italy were to defect, as Hitler had been convinced ever since Tunis that she would, the position could change instantaneously. If the Italian garrisons of the islands surrendered, they would be giving the Allies the opening on which Churchill had set his heart: 'If we could gain Turkey it would be possible . . . to dominate the Black Sea . . . and to give a right hand to Russia and carry supplies to her armies. . . .'*

To prevent this handclasp between West and East, Hitler sent Field-Marshal Rommel to Greece as Commander-in-Chief. But scarcely had he unpacked his bags in Salonica than he received telephonic orders on the evening of 25 July to report at once to Führer Headquarters. Mussolini's downfall put the whole world on the *qui vive*, and nowhere more so than in Berlin and Rastenberg, where the 'Brains Trust' reacted in a quite alarming fashion.

At about noon the next day Rommel arrived at Führer Headquarters, to find most of the Big Guns—Doenitz, von Kluge, Ribbentrop, Goebbels and Gauleiter Hofer from Innsbruck—already gathered there. Small wonder that the atmosphere was pretty electric, for Farinacci had reached the goal of his flight and had startled the whole headquarters with the news that the new Italian Government intended in eight or ten days' time to conclude an armistice with the Allies and to guarantee them free access to the mainland at Leghorn and Genoa. This seemed to confirm Hitler's worst fears. There can be little doubt that in his mind's eye he was already seeing the Allies on the march into upper Italy, and he was quite convinced of the existence of a clear-cut understanding between Badoglio and the Western powers. It was hardly to be expected that the Allies would not make immediate military capital out of Mussolini's downfall.

In Hitler's eyes, the paramount importance of northern Italy justified the recall of Rommel from Greece. On 26 July the Field-Marshal assumed command of the forces which in the course of the next few days were to secure the Po valley. For political reasons his headquarters remained for the time being in Munich and did not move to Lake Garda after the Italians had gone over to the Allies.

Rommel seemed to be the right man, should Italy defect, to save the Germans from a St Bartholomew's Eve and to talk to the Italians in

* Churchill, *The Second World War*, Vol. V.

language more usual between enemies than between allies. He could also be confidently relied upon to show no undue 'softness', towards the Italians, to act with vigour and to bring the 'traitors' to book. Kesselring was quite different. Was not his blind confidence partly responsible for the fact that the King and Badoglio had succeeded thus in cunningly hoodwinking the Germans? Did not his affection for the country and its people justify the fear that clemency rather than just punishment would prevail if the Italians, at the end of their resources, abandoned the sinking ship? These were the considerations which led to Hitler's decision that Kesselring must make way for Rommel and the Tenth Army be placed under the command of Army Group B, provided always that von Vietinghoff succeeded in slipping out of the trap in southern Italy. Kesselring in that case would leave the Italian theatre, and the first idea was that he might later be employed in Norway.

These differences of outlook between the two Field-Marshals did not constitute the sole reason why Hitler favoured placing Rommel in command of the operations in Italy. No less contributory was Rommel's strategic conception, the basis of which was to withdraw from southern and central Italy and give battle in the Apennines, between Pisa and Rimini. Hitler's 'almost slavish' adherence to Rommel's ideas led him to opt for this strategy and from 8 September onwards to be inclined to abandon Kesselring's divisions to their fate, as he had abandoned the Sixth Army at Stalingrad, rather than invest even one more soldier in the 'hazardous' enterprises of the Commander-in-Chief, South.

Kesselring himself held very different views. He had good reasons for advocating that the decisive battle should be fought far to the south of Rome and that the possession by the enemy of southern and central Italy should be contested for as long as the strength and resources of the German divisions permitted.

During the retreat through Tripolitania at the turn of the year 1942/3 Rommel had given much earnest consideration to the idea of evacuating North Africa in good time and, instead of attempting to defend Tunisia, of concentrating all efforts on withdrawing the German forces to Italy. They could then either defend the Italian peninsula from the Etruscan Apennines or, should the need arise, abandon Italy and occupy the prepared Alpine defensive positions. This idea had so gripped his imagination during the Tunisian campaign that there may well have been some little justification for the assertion that the Field-Marshal's efforts therein were only half-hearted.

Rommel, brought up in the army school of thought, judged the situation purely from the point of view of operations on land. The decisive factor, as he saw it, was the selection of a position that favoured the defence. He feared the long sea flanks, which would be difficult to defend, and he saw no urgent necessity to deny the enemy possession of the 'leg of the boot'. His primary object was to keep the enemy land forces away from the frontiers of the Reich, and other strategic considerations carried but little weight with him.

Kesselring saw things from a different angle. He viewed them with the eye of an airman. To him, the Allied superiority in the air was the decisive factor, not only in any review of the operational possibilities open to him, but also in the whole of his strategic conception. His mind was dominated by the thought of the strategic advantages in the air which possession of Italy would inevitably confer upon the Western powers. Italy, he felt, would constitute an extremely valuable complement to England, the great parent-ship of the strategic air offensive against Germany. Hitherto, with but few exceptions, the Anglo-American air attacks had been confined to the western territories of the Reich. But once the extensive airfields in southern Italy—Foggia on the Adriatic side and Naples to the west— were in Allied hands, the whole situation would be instantly and radically changed. Southern Germany, which had so far remained almost completely unmolested, would then be within the range of Allied heavy bombers; Austria with her aircraft factories, the bauxite mines in Hungary, the Rumanian oilfields, the great waterway of the Danube—all these would be at the mercy of the Allied air forces. The German High Command had therefore to do its utmost to prevent at all costs the full exploitation of southern Italy by the Allies as a base for their strategic air offensive. This could be accomplished only by ensuring that the airfields there remained under constant threat of German attack and by the ability of the German forces in upper Italy to challenge the Allies to tactical air combat. If that could be done, there was a probability that the threatened Allied air offensive would be dissipated, rather than concentrated on the Reich itself. All this, however, could be accomplished only if the Germans were able to hold the area south of Rome. From the strategic point of view, possession of the Italian capital by the Allies would result in a serious deterioration of Germany's position in the war in the air, which would become untenable, when once the struggle for the Apennines and the Alps began and the Allies were able to employ their light and medium aircraft against southern Germany. These were the considerations which formed the basis of Kesselring's appreciation of the situation.

But apart from this strategic aspect of the war in the air, it also seemed obvious to him that, with upper Italy in their possession, the Allies would have a base from which they would be able to exercise a decisive influence on the German operations on land. If the German forces withdrew to the Alpine positions, the gates to the Balkans and southern France would be thrown open to the Allies, there would at once be a danger of an Allied thrust against the rear of the German eastern front, and any subsidiary amphibious invasion of southern France, in the event of a major cross-Channel offensive, would become superfluous. Furthermore, the long-term exploitation of industrial northern Italy by the German High Command could be ensured only if German forces held a position organized in considerable depth well to the south of the Apennines, and for political reasons it was desirable that the Republic of Saló should embrace as large an area as possible.

Experience in the war had already shown that a defensive position could not be held for any length of time against an enemy with a numerical and material superiority such as that enjoyed by the Allies. For this reason Kesselring very early on defined the successive lines at which the Allied advance, first on Rome and then on the Apennines, was to be halted.

The first of these lines was that of the Volturno River, prolonged on the Adriatic side by the Biferno sector. The implementation of the Field-Marshal's order that this line would in no circumstances be given up before 15 October was facilitated by the delay in the Fifth Army's attack, which, held up by rain and mud, could not be launched until 12 October.

Kesselring's intention was to hold up Alexander's advance for a prolonged period at the narrowest point of the peninsula, the 'waist' of Italy. There, on the Gustav Line, he hoped to pin down the 15 Army Group in a battle of attrition until at least the spring of 1944. This line followed the courses of the rivers Garigliano, Gari and Rapido. From the upper reaches of the Rapido it passed over the Abruzzi Mountains to Castel di Sangro and rested, on the Adriatic side, on the mighty Maiella massif and the lower reaches of the Sangro. The kernel of the Gustav Line was the six-mile wide Liri valley, with its two pivots, the 1,600-foot Monte Cassino in the north and Monte Maio in the south, which towers some 3,000 feet above the valley. In these two solid masses were the hinges of the gateway to Rome, through which winds Highway No. 6, the Via Casilina, directly commanded by the Mount of St Benedict.

In front of the Gustav Line was the Reinhard Line, sometimes called the Bernhard Line and christened the 'Winter Line' by the Allies. In its most important sector it was based on the Mignano defile and its key points Hill 1170, Monte Camino and Monte Sammucro. Like two menacing watch towers, these bare, steep mountains barred the way to Cassino and into the Liri valley.

These naturally strong positions were to be further strengthened very considerably by the swift and intensive construction of defensive localities. The focal point of the whole complex was, in the nature of things, the Gustav Line, and in particular the sector on each side of Cassino.

During the autumn army construction units, the Todt Organization, Italian auxiliaries and labour battalions, under the direction of Pioneer General Bessell, to whom the ever-prying eye of Field-Marshal Kesselring must have been a sore trial, created a strong network of modern defensive localities. The villages in the forward area were transformed into massive strongpoints with bomb-proof shelters; pneumatic drills carved out caverns in the precipitous mountainsides; mine-fields protected easily approachable sectors, and the upper Rapido and the lower reaches of the Garigliano were used to flood certain areas. In short, Bessell transformed the Gustav Line into a position upon which the enemy might well break his teeth, provided that it was defended by even moderately good troops.

In contrast to the construction of these defences, in which considerable assistance had been afforded by the O.K.W., the task of strengthening the Reinhard Line devolved upon the troops themselves. They naturally had less time, less means and only a fraction of the labour which General Bessell had had at his disposal. And it is greatly to the credit of these young German divisions that they nevertheless were able to withstand the onslaughts of the Fifth Army for weeks, until the defences of the Gustav Line were more or less completed. There were two divisions which covered themselves with glory—the 29 Panzer Grenadier Division and the 26 Panzer Division.

The strengthening of the Gustav and Reinhard Lines was the most urgent of the constructional tasks; but behind them lay a further chain of individual positions: on the high ground at Aquino the Adolf Hitler Line (later renamed the Senger Line) barred the way into the Liri valley; immediately south of Rome and running diagonally across the peninsula was the 'C' Line; far away to the north was the Green Line, Pisa–Florence–Pesaro, called the 'Gothic Line' by the Allies, the initial strengthening of which was entrusted to Rommel; and finally there were the Alpine positions, the last barrier before the frontiers of the Reich.

Originally Hitler had accepted the Rommel solution in its entirety. But when, contrary to all prophesy, the catastrophe expected after 8 September in the Commander-in-Chief, South's, area did not occur and the hesitant advance of the Allies in southern Italy precluded any likelihood of a blitzkrieg, the Kesselring conception found more and more favour in his eyes. For a long time he could not make up his mind—even when it was pointed out to him that the Cassino position could be held with half the number of troops that would be required for the Apennine concept. Should he accept the risks inherent in the long sea flanks? Would not a premature surrender of Rome and almost the whole of the peninsula result in a grave loss of political and military prestige? In Russia, as it was, the past few months had brought great losses of territory. In July the Kursk offensive had failed; on 23 August Kharkov had fallen into Soviet hands; on 25 September Smolensk and on 25 October Dniepropetrovsk; and when Kiev fell on 6 November the Germans had been thrown back 250 miles since the summer.

This was a grim balance sheet. Perhaps it could be made to look a little brighter if it were possible to hold Italy? But still Hitler hesitated. If he decided in favour of fighting south of Rome, then Rommel was psychologically not the right man to be Commander-in-Chief in Italy. But he had before made up his mind to appoint him as Supreme Commander in the Italian theatre and to place Kesselring's forces under him from the middle of November. On the other hand, Kesselring had performed the remarkable feat not only of manœuvring his way unscathed out of the deadly dangers resultant upon the Italian surrender, but also of fighting at the same time another battle into the bargain, which had all but ended in a catastrophe for the Allies. And now this 'Air Marshal' was asserting that he could hold southern Italy against the Allied material juggernaut.

Nevertheless, he decided in Rommel's favour. Then, literally at the last moment, he changed his mind. While the order appointing Rommel was being dictated in the teleprinter office, he suddenly decided to appoint Kesselring instead. On 21 November he formally appointed him Commander-in-Chief of all forces in the Italian theatre of war, with the designation 'Commander-in-Chief, South-West (Army Group C)', in order to prevent any repetition of the confusion that had already occurred with the Army Group, South, on the Russian front. Rommel was transferred to France, to take charge of and accelerate the construction of the Atlantic Wall, and later, as Commander-in-Chief, Army Group B, to assume command of the German Seventh and Fifteenth Armies in northern France and Belgium.

Now at last the position in Italy had been clarified and the unfortunate period of duality in the High Command was at an end. It had certainly not helped the German cause, as the first month's fighting had clearly proved. It was immaterial who the Commander was, Rommel or Kesselring; but that there should have been one or the other was essential. As it was, Kesselring had to rely solely on his own divisions, while Rommel's forces were gaining a cheap victory over the Italian formations. Kesselring said: . . . 'Field-Marshal Rommel would have been better advised to have disbanded the Italian divisions and allowed the troops to go free, rather than to have employed his own forces on so sterile a task, which resulted in the flight of large numbers of Italian soldiers, who later formed the hard core of the partisan movement.'*

Nor was that the only or the most damaging result of this divided

* *Soldat bis zum letzten Tag.*

responsibility of command. During the critical period in Rome, the advent of one additional division, had Kesselring been able to call on it, would have led to a much more rapid clearing up of the confused situation. Of even more importance had been the effect on the Salerno battle. Had Kesselring been in sole command, the field of possibilities open to him would have been greatly widened. He would have had very different resources at his disposal with which to contest the possession of the sea and air bases of Naples and the extremely important airfields at Foggia. In all probability he would have succeeded at least in keeping the Neapolitan and Apulian airfields 'in constant danger of German attack' and of thus impeding the full development of the Allied air offensive.

It had taken the Americans long enough in all conscience to appreciate the importance of Italy as a base for the Allied strategic air offensive against Germany. But the shortsightedness of the O.K.W., which had turned a deaf ear to his appeals for reinforcements in the battle for Foggia, had forced Kesselring prematurely to abandon just those tactical objectives which had eventually led the Americans to decide on an invasion of the Italian mainland. In his message to Congress on 17 September Roosevelt said: 'We now intend to establish bases from which our bombers can reach south and east Germany. . . . We shall extend our attacks to the whole of the Reich and its satellites. . . . With Italy in our hands, the distances which we shall have to cover will be far less and our risks will be proportionately reduced.'*

Hitherto three separate headquarters had directed the air operations in the Mediterranean theatre—Tedder's Strategic Bomber Command, under the American Major-General James H. Doolittle, operating from Tripolitania; the U.S. 9 Air Fleet, under Major-General Lewis H. Brerton, operating from North Africa; and the Royal Air Force Middle East Command, under Air Marshal Sir Sholto Douglas, operating from the Near East. With the conquest of southern Italy, however, important changes in the organization were introduced.†

While 15 Army Group was getting its second wind after the capture of Naples and preparatory to the decisive advance on Rome, General Doolittle, at the insistence of the Combined Chiefs of Staff, moved his strategic bomber force from Tripoli to Apulia. In a very short time the Americans, using a vast amount of material, created a network of technically perfect airfields, equipped with the most modern storage tanks, workshops

---

* Roosevelt in his Message to Congress, 17.9.43
† Organization of the Allied air arm, Mediterranean, September 1943: Mediterranean Allied Air Force (Marshal of the Royal Air Force Sir Arthur Tedder).

Tactical Air Force	Strategic Bomber Command
1 Tactical Air Fleet, R.A.F.	15 Strategic Air Fleet
	12 Tactical Air Fleet U.S.A.F.

and barracks, and with runways covered with steel matting. But 'this build-up of air power consumed approximately 300,000 tons of shipping during the most critical months of the Italian campaign. So heavy were the shipping requirements of 15 Strategic Air Force, activated 1 November 1943 under General Doolittle, that the build-up of our ground forces in Italy was considerably delayed.'*

This, of course, did not fit in at all with Churchill's concept. On 17 November through General Ismay he addressed the Chiefs of Staff Committee: 'It is surely altogether wrong to build up the Strategic Air Force in Italy at the expense of the battle for Rome. The strategic bombing of Germany, however important, cannot take precedence over the battle, which must ever rank first in our thoughts. . . . I was not aware until recently that the build-up of the army had been obstructed by the forward move of a mass of strategic air not connected with the battle. This is in fact a departure from all orthodox military doctrine, as well as seeming wrong from the point of view of common sense.'†

But by this time Doolittle's preparations were well advanced. On 1 November he delivered his first attack against the Messerschmitt works in Wiener-Neustadt. This was followed by attacks on the ball-bearing factories in Turin, the railway networks in Genoa, Bologna and Innsbruck, and the oil refineries in Ploesti. Next on the list were the Messerschmitt works in Regensburg and Augsburg, bridges and railways in the Balkans, the Alpine passes and, later, the Po bridges and the Danube, which was continually mined.

With the approach of spring the 15 Strategic Air Force increased its attacks on the Rumanian oilfields. Before the first American attack, delivered from North Africa in September 1943, Germany was obtaining some 220,000 tons of oil per month from Rumania and Hungary. In February 1944 the monthly delivery still topped 200,000 tons, but sank in June to 40,000 tons and in August to a miserable 11,000. This was the work of the 15 Strategic Air Force. At the end of May it had 850 heavy bombers with the appropriate long-distance fighter escort, and in the twelve months from 1 November 1943 to 31 October 1944 flew 150,000,000 air miles, attacking 620 targets in twelve different countries and dropping 192,000 tons of bombs. As against the loss of 2,247 aircraft, the bombers and their escorts shot down 3,653 German planes and destroyed a further 2,016 on the ground. These figures are taken from the War Reports of General Marshall, who goes on to say: 'In the spring campaign the ball-bearing industry in Austria was all but wiped out by our heavy bombers, adding a further bottleneck to German aircraft production. Heavy attacks

* *The War Reports of General Marshall.*
† Churchill, *The Second World War,* Vol. V.

against aircraft factories in south Germany, Austria, Hungary and northern Italy, and particularly round Vienna and Budapest, were estimated to have cut planned monthly production in this area in half by May 1944.'

In this way, when the Germans lost the air bases in southern Italy, the bomber ring was mercilessly closed round the Reich. For the Allies this was a great benefit, which was of direct advantage to Operation Overlord, for the hazards of a cross-Channel invasion could not be accepted until the German fighter aircraft force had been decisively weakened.

In actual fact, the campaign in southern Italy caused both Churchill and Alexander grave anxiety. On 24 October, at Eisenhower's request, Alexander submitted to the conference of Mediterranean Commanders-in-Chief a memorandum in which he summarized the points that were worrying him. Surprised by the German strength in Italy, he frankly admitted that it had been a mistake to have presumed '. . . that some [of the German divisions] would be engaged in northern Italy to deal with the internal situation, which was expected to cause them considerable embarrassment. . . .' The reduction in craft, already decreased by wear and tear, has been so serious as to preclude us from taking advantage, other than with minor forces, of the enemy's inherent weakness, which is the exposure of his two flanks to turning movements from the sea. . . . A stabilized front south of Rome cannot be accepted, for the capital has a significance far greater than its strategic location, and sufficient depth must be gained before the Foggia airfields and the port of Naples can be regarded as secure.'*

Churchill and Eisenhower were held fast in the shackles of the Quebec conference decisions. Since August, landing craft, freighters and transport had continued to leave the Mediterranean, as though the war had for the time being paused to gather fresh strength. Churchill was deeply distressed and in Washington did his best to prevent the withdrawal of further shipping and of the British 50 and 51 Divisions. But the Americans remained obdurate, although Churchill pleaded with Roosevelt that 'Rome and the airfields to the north of it must be taken, cost what it may'. In response to his demand that Eisenhower and Alexander should be given 'everything they required to achieve victory in Italy, regardless of the effect on later operations', the Americans agreed to allow Eisenhower to retain until 15 December the sixty-eight tank landing craft due for immediate transfer to the United Kingdom.

The Americans had set their hearts and minds on Overlord to the exclusion of everything else, and they missed a golden opportunity to reap the harvest of victory in Italy. And the harvest was there, waiting to

* The whole of General Alexander's report is contained in Churchill, *The Second World War*, Vol. V.

be reaped, not only in Italy itself, but also in the Aegean. Once again Washington closed its eyes in almost criminal fashion to the rich spoils which the Aegean offered. The Italians had let it be known that as soon as Italy capitulated they would be willing to make common cause with the Allies, provided that the latter would protect them from being overwhelmed by the Germans. The British, without doubt, had their eye on the island fortresses of Leros, Kos and Rhodes, the airfields on the last named of which would have been of particular value to them; but when 8 September came, General Maitland Wilson, the Commander-in-Chief, Near East, had but meagre forces with which to initiate any operations in the Aegean. He, too, had suffered at the hands of the Quebec 'Lawyer's Agreement'.* He had detailed and trained his Indian 8 Division for the attack on Leros. but on 26 August the ships that were to carry it to the island were withdrawn by the Combined Chiefs of Staff for operations against the Burmese coast. The Division itself was placed under Eisenhower's command and transferred to the central Mediterranean. Wilson was then left with one solitary infantry brigade and a partially equipped Indian division.

Any attack on Rhodes therefore was out of the question, and the Italian garrison surrendered to the Germans. But, with the help of requisitioned coastal craft, sailing vessels and some small tugs, Wilson succeeded in gaining footholds on Kos, Leros and Samos. Of these, Kos, with its airfields, was the most important, and for this reason became the primary objective of the German counter-stroke. On 3 October German paratroops, supported by a simultaneous landing of army units from the sea, dropped on the island and overwhelmed the small garrison, consisting of one British battalion. Six weeks later it was the turn of Leros. On 12 November the Germans launched their attack, again in the form of a combined air and amphibious operation, and on 16 November the last remnant of the British garrison surrendered. In these circumstances, and with Rhodes still in German hands, Samos became untenable and was evacuated.

Churchill had pressed the Americans with the utmost persistence to seize the gateway into the Aegean, but had met with a sharp rebuff. The U.S. Chiefs of Staff, secure in the knowledge that the President was behind them, would not allot one single aircraft, let alone the tank landing crafts he had asked for. The Prime Minister had obstinately bombarded Washington and Algiers with telegrams in the hope of gaining the support of Roosevelt and Eisenhower. On 25 September he had telegraphed to Eisenhower: . . . Rhodes is the key both to the eastern Mediterranean and the Aegean. It will be a great disaster if the Germans are able to consolidate

* Winston Churchill to Eden, 26 October: 'This is what happens when battles are governed by lawyers' agreements made in all good faith months before, and persisted in without regard to the ever-changing fortunes of war.' *The Second World War*, Vol. V.

there' (*The Second World War*, Vol. V), and to Roosevelt on 8 October: '. . . I am sure that the omission to take Rhodes at this stage . . . would constitute a cardinal error in strategy' (*op. cit.*, Vol. V).

Churchill still did not give up hope. He suggested that a conference of Mediterranean Commanders-in-Chief should be held under his chairmanship, and invited Roosevelt to send a representative. But this, too, the President refused to do. And when the conference, attended by Eisenhower, Wilson, Alexander, Cunningham and Tedder (but without Churchill), finally met in Tunis on October 9, it was too late. The Allies had just been forced to realize that Kesselring had decided to fight south of Rome—a fact which Eisenhower described as 'a drastic change in the situation during the last forty-eight hours'. (It may well be that the counter-attack of the 16 Panzer Division at Termoli had been responsible for this point of view.) This change, however, was not altogether unwelcome to the Americans. Eisenhower, now supported by the British Commanders-in-Chief, refused without further ado to consider any attack on Rhodes. '. . . I announced the decision I had reached. . . . Its purport was that detachments from the Italian Command were not warranted and that we could and would do nothing about the islands.'*

'Nevertheless with one of the sharpest pangs I suffered in the war I submitted' is how Churchill describes his acceptance of Eisenhower's decision (*The Second World War*, Vol. V). Although he had given repeated assurances that he had no intention whatever of investing an army in the Balkans, Roosevelt and his Chiefs of Staff remained full of mistrust. The thought that, having once opened the way through the Aegean, Churchill might repeat his ill-fated Gallipoli enterprise, that American G.I.s might become involved in a military adventure which they would be unable to justify in the eyes of the American people and that the latter might then refuse to re-elect Roosevelt in the coming November, was a constant nightmare to them.

The situation would be very different in 1944, when Operation Overlord had brought Hitler to his knees—and that it would Washington was firmly convinced—and reinforcements to the Pacific had taken the wind out of MacArthur's sails. All these decisions were taken, inevitably, at the direct expense of the Mediterranean theatre, though in the long run at the expense of free Europe.

These sins of omission in the Aegean were not, of course, without their political repercussions. First and foremost they had a great effect on Turkey's attitude. At the Foreign Ministers conference in Moscow (19 October–3 November) Molotov unexpectedly urged that Turkey must be persuaded to declare war and open the Narrows to the Russians. Eden

* Eisenhower, *Crusade in Europe.*

promised to approach the Turks again on his way back to London. But the latter proved even less susceptible than ever to British blandishments. They pointed to Germany's unassailable position in the Aegean and in Greece which, they maintained, made it highly inadvisable for Turkey to declare war at this juncture.

The man who had the last laugh was, of course, Hitler. Once more 'he had been proved right'. At the Führer Headquarters situation conference on 24 September, both the army and the navy had urgently pressed for the evacuation of the Aegean and Crete, arguing that these strong-points had been occupied as bases for further offensive operations, but that in the meanwhile the situation had completely altered. Hitler had rejected this advice out of hand, pointing out the political effects such a withdrawal would have on Turkey and the Balkan States.

Although the Western powers had lost the first game in the Aegean, they levelled the rubber with the next deal by occupying the islands in the Tyrrhenian Sea. Here they scored a notable dual success—the conquest of Corsica and Sardinia at the cost of very little effort. Kesselring evacuated both islands voluntarily, as he had made up his mind to do in the event of an Allied invasion of the mainland. The evacuation of Sardinia began on 9 September, under the skilful direction of General Lungerhausen, the G.O.C. 90 Panzer Grenadier Division. Unmolested by the enemy, his division and the strong air force elements were trans-shipped across the Straits of Bonifacio to Corsica. Initially the Italians remained passive and it was only when General von Senger-Etterlin began to transfer the whole German force to the mainland that the Italians, under General Magli, a former colleague of Marshal Cavallero, began to show signs of animation.

The entire operation was executed through the port of Bastia, which was protected to the end by a small bridge-head. In addition to the small naval craft, it was the aircraft of 2 Air Fleet which made possible the transportation of nearly 40,000 German troops to Leghorn and Elba. By the end of September the entire garrisons of the two islands, together with all weapons, vehicles and most of their stores, had been successfully evacuated. 'Field-Marshal von Richthoven's airmen, the enterprise and skill of Captain Engelhardt of the navy and the unceasing and heroic efforts of the naval crews deserve special commendation' (Kesselring, *Soldat bis zum letzten Tag*).

The absence of any activity on the part of the enemy air and naval forces was surprising. It was only during the last few days of the operation that they intervened at all and caused a few casualties. But these were insignificant in comparison with the fact that troops almost to the strength of an Army Corps were brought safely to the mainland. Just as in Sicily, four *élite* German divisions had been allowed to slip away thanks to this 'lawyer's strategy', so now there escaped from Sardinia and Corsica a body of men destined to give the Allies endless trouble on the mainland—the 90 Panzer Grenadier Division. It was the 90, together with two others, which eight weeks later brought Montgomery to a standstill on the Adria, which in the first Cassino battle saved the left hinge of the gateway from destruction and which in future was to be met everywhere, where the Allies initiated some fresh move.

When the final, clear-cut decision regarding command in the Italian theatre was at last taken on 21 November, it seemed as though it had come too late. Side by side with other uncertainties, it was an open question whether the German troops after a retreat of twelve months' duration and involving a distance of over 2,000 miles would still possess the inner fortitude to defend a position in a manner worthy of their traditions. The retreat, which began at El Alamein at the beginning of November 1942 and which continued through Cyrenaica and Tripolitania to Tunis, had by no means come to an end there in May 1943. Sicily, Calabria, Salerno, Apulia were all merely a continuation. Repeated attempts, certainly, had been made to offer serious and organized resistance, indeed, to initiate counter-attacks in an effort to regain the initiative; but for the most part it was numerical and material inferiority that compelled the German forces to continue to retire and confine themselves to delaying actions. Would the new German divisions in Italy now have the strength to fight in earnest for every yard of ground? It must be remembered that a constant feeling of inferiority can in time undermine the morale of the best troops and that a continuous retreat must inevitably give rise to an inferiority complex. That the German troops were able, in spite of it all, to find the strength and courage to resist for months on end the assaults of the finest Allied divisions on the Gustav Line, that they stood fast in the hell of Cassino in spite of overwhelming odds is a very great tribute to the outstanding personality of Field-Marshal Kesselring, 'a proven, bold and capable Commander' (Roosevelt). Like Rommel, he had the gift of winning and retaining the confidence of his subordinates and in particular of the ordinary rank and file. He was 'their' Field-Marshal, and if he said that Rome must be defended, they were quite sure he had excellent reasons for saying so.

As in days gone by, when whole French and German divisions fought and died for their country at Verdun, so now whole companies of Germans fighting at Cassino laid down their lives, faithfully serving their hard-pressed land. No less gallant were the G.I.s, the Tommies, the 'poilus' and the Poles; and every true soldier will appreciate the sacrifice they made.

Chapter 5

In the Rain and the Mud

On 1 October the Fifth Army marched into Naples. By 4 October the first lighters were lying in the badly damaged harbour, and one day later the first of the Liberty ships was unloading at the quay side. From that day onwards the stream of stores and supplies flowed freely through the streets cleared of débris into the vast supply dumps that were springing up everywhere. This was the result of the work of the U.S. Pioneers who, with immense energy and the help of the very latest equipment, had in a fortnight performed the remarkable feat of raising the capacity of the completely demolished port to 20,000 tons per day.

The German Tenth Army and the Italian Navy had done their job very thoroughly, when the important base was evacuated. The entrance to the port and the harbour itself had been blocked with sunken ships, and what had been left of the quays, cranes and warehouses by Tedder's bombers had been blown up. The Allied air raids had caused heavy damage in both port and town, and the streets in the vicinity of the harbour had been blocked with débris. The water and electricity supplies had been put out of action, the railways and stations destroyed and the whole of Naples bore the scars of a major catastrophe.

Here the U.S. Brigadier-General Spence found plenty to do. He had been in charge of the pioneer and technical side of the lines of communication during the Tunisian campaign; and now in Naples he was faced with

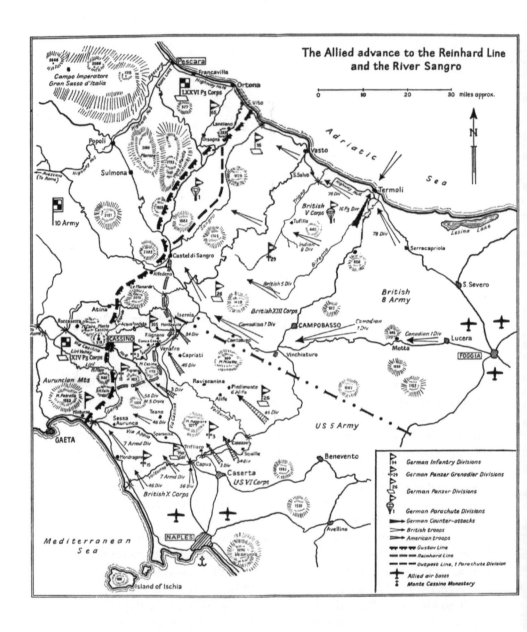

The Allied advance to the Reinhard Line and the River Sangro

a task which made the greatest possible demands on his pioneers. Once again the superb technical and mechanical equipment of the U.S. Army and the ingenuity of the pioneers combined to achieve a truly remarkable feat in a very short space of time. Cranes and grabs cleared the harbour basin, bulldozers and an endless stream of lorries cleared the streets of the débris under which they had been buried. Railway pioneers worked feverishly to repair the lines along which supplies and reinforcements would flow to the front. The 100,000 men who had reached the Volturno by about 10 October consumed enormous quantities of stores.* In addition, there were the requirements of the air force, which had at once set about the task of putting the Neapolitan airfields in order—to say nothing of the heavy equipment required by the engineers for the repair of roads, bridges and railways.

Clark had originally fixed 9 October for his first attack on the Volturno but had been compelled to postpone it; for the day after Naples fell it began to pour with rain. So far Eisenhower's operations had been favoured with brilliant summer weather. Tedder's meteorologists had seemed redundant, and cloudless blue skies and clear nights had allowed his airmen complete liberty of action. Alexander's armour had rolled across the parched plains and the dried-up river beds for all the world as though these had been specially constructed for it. Since Tunisia, the infantry had had no need of any shelter, and though their uniforms may have been clammy with sweat, they had never been drenched by rain. But now, suddenly, the 'sunny South' took on a very different appearance. For days on end the rain poured down in torrents on the bare, steep slopes of the Abruzzi Mountains, over hill and dale and fertile coastal countryside. Small wonder that the men, with the travel agency's picture of 'sun-drenched Italy' in their mind's eye, cursed heartily when some innocent little stream suddenly swelled and swept away the bridges they had so laboriously constructed. They cursed this much advertised land when their feet stuck fast in the cloying mud and no tent could shelter them from the torrential rain. Tanks, lorries and jeeps were bogged down in the morass as soon as they ventured off the metalled road.

The British X Corps, on the coastal plain between Capua and the sea, was all but buried beneath the mud. The fields were one vast yellowish-brown morass, into which the vehicles dared not venture. The U.S. VI Corps under General Lucas, who had relieved Dawley after the Salerno battle, fared a little better. Its assembly area was on slightly higher ground and not quite so muddy. But even there plenty of mud-laden water overflowed the banks of the Volturno.

---

* Eisenhower puts the daily requirements of a U.S. division in the field at 600–700 tons, inclusive of ammunition for heavy artillery and pioneer equipment.

The Volturno flows in very much the same manner as most of the other Italian rivers. From its source high up in the Abruzzi Mountains it flows for a considerable distance southwards through a broad, flat bed, winds south-eastwards till it joins the River Calore and then turns sharply westwards. In the battles that followed, the VI Corps crossed it three times, until the G.I.s began to think that every darn river in Italy was called the Volturno.

Clark planned to cross the river on a broad front. Middleton's 45 Division had made a wide detour via Benevento and was already in position to the north of the lower reaches of the Calore. On its right was Ryder's 34 Division, while Truscott's 3 Division stood in readiness to the south of the Triflisco defile. McCreery set his 56 Division (Templer) straight at Capua, Erskine's Desert Rats were to the south of Grazzanise, and Hawkesworth's 46 Division was in the coastal sector, preparing to attack.

The German shield was formed of General Hube's XIV Panzer Corps. The western coastal plain was defended by Rodt's 15 Panzer Grenadier Division, the Hermann Göring Panzer Division (Conrath) was in position on either side of Capua, with the 3 Panzer Grenadier Division (Graeser) on its left and von Lüttwitz's 26 Panzer Grenadier Division east of the Volturno itself.

The German commander expected the main assault to be launched along Highway No. 7, the Via Appia. North of Capua the highway bifurcates, and the other branch, Highway No. 6, the Via Casilina, also led to Rome. The question was—which of these two would the Allies select after having crossed the Volturno? There was a good deal to be said in favour of the Via Appia. Running, as it did, close to the coast, it almost begged the Fifth Army to use it and thus enjoy the support of the fleet on its flank. Furthermore, it contained fewer defiles than the Via Casilina. On the other hand, long stretches of it had been hewn from the coastal cliffs of the southern slopes of the Auruncian Mountains, where it was very vulnerable and where any deployment of mechanized and armoured forces would be impossible. Finally it was also vulnerable to extensive flooding from the lower Garigliano and from Mussolini's reclaimed Pontian marshes.

The Via Casilina was quite different. It is true that to the south-east of Cassino it squeezed its way for some twelve miles through steep, bare hills, past the 3,500-ft. Monte Cesima, through the Mignani defile, flanked by the mighty massifs of Monte Camino and Monte Sammucro. But beyond that lay the Liri valley and open country ideal for armour all the way to Rome. It thus offered the Fifth Army ample opportunity to exploit to the best advantage its motorized divisions and their modern armament. But before it could do so, it had to break open the 'gateway to Rome' and capture its pillars, Monte Cassino and Monte Maio.

Monte Cassino is not the highest feature on the north side of the Liri valley. But for the best part of two miles the Via Casilina winds its way immediately round the foot of the mountain. The Fifth Army could advance along it only after it had succeeded in neutralizing the monastery hill, particularly as from it the German troops could command the whole breadth of the Liri valley. This fact, perhaps, may have prematurely misled the Allies to the false and momentous assumption that not only the mountain itself, but also the monastery, would be occupied by artillery observation posts. It requires but little military knowledge to realize that a conspicuous building such as this, plainly visible from every direction, would be the last place that anyone would choose as an observation post— if only for reasons of self-preservation. Furthermore, ordinary common-sense should tell anyone that, if the monastery had been incorporated in the German defensive system, it would have drawn the Allied fire like a magnet, and the Germans would certainly have lost their 'eyes' as soon as the offensive opened. Be that as it may, had Alexander and Clark had any inkling of the unpleasant surprise that Kesselring had in store for them at Monte Cassino, they might well have chosen the Via Appia instead of the Via Casilina.

To return, however, to Clark, in position south of the Volturno. He proposed to launch his attack on the night of 12/13 October. The weather had improved, the ground had become reasonably dry, though the Volturno was still tumbling riotously in its over-filled bed. Both Allied corps were to cross the river simultaneously on a broad front, and the 45 Division was given the task of exerting heavy pressure on the German flank with the object of compelling Hube to withdraw his forces in good time from their positions on the river.

Clark's plan for a simultaneous attack was opposed by McCreery, who wished to hold back until the day after the Americans had launched their attack. His object here was to concentrate the German attention on the American sector and thus facilitate the advance of the British Corps over the very exposed ground of the coastal plain which faced them. And, indeed, the British were to run into a very solid wall. On the coast they were faced with the sprawling heights of the 2,500-foot Monte Massico; to the north they were threatened by the mighty massif of Monte Santa Croce; while from the north-east the Germans occupying the 3,000-foot Monte Maggiore dominated the whole of the coastal plain north of Capua. McCreery's wish that the Americans should lead the way was therefore readily understandable. Clark argued that only by a simultaneous attack along the whole front could the German defence be tied down and von Vietinghoff and Hube prevented from moving their reserves at will. He was therefore unwilling to accede to McCreery's request.

General Cannon, the commander of the 12 Tactical Air Fleet, had already moved the majority of his formations from Sicily to the Tyrrhenian Sea side of southern Italy; and now, with the improvement in the flying weather, he was in a position to support the Fifth Army's offensive with the whole of his force.

During the night of 12/13 October, in bright moonlight, the Volturno battle opened with the roar of 600 guns and innumerable mortars and the staccato crackle of machine-gun fire. Behind a wall of fire and smoke, the rafts and assault craft, packed with pioneers and infantry, slipped across the river. Not everywhere did they succeed in reaching the further bank. The first attack on the Triflisco defile, a joint operation executed by the Scots Guards of the 56 Division and the 30 Infantry Regiment of the U.S. 3 Division, failed, as did a second attempt in the same sector. It was only after the two other regiments of Truscott's division had gained a foothold on the north bank to the east of Triflisco and from there threatened the high ground north of the defile, that the German defence gave way, and the 3 Division was able to cross the river.

The attack of the 56 Division, which directed its main assault against the demolished bridge on the western edge of Capua, ran into very serious trouble. Every attempt to cross the river collapsed in the face of the concentrated fire of the Hermann Göring Panzer Division. Rodt's 15 Panzer Grenadier Division, too, fought in a manner worthy of its traditions. In a counter-attack against Santa Maria la Fossa and Grazzanise, it drove back the spearhead of the British 7 Armoured Division, but for all that was unable to prevent the 45 Division from getting three batteries across the river during the first night. Shortly afterwards. Hawkesworth brought up his artillery and transferred it by landing craft to the north side of the Volturno estuary.

With the U.S. Corps everything went according to plan. The 34 Division crossed the river without much difficulty at Squille and Caiazzo and advanced swiftly northwards. To the east of the Volturno the 45 Division stormed unimpeded north-westwards, and the 3 Division, having captured Monticello, reached the commanding heights of Monte Maiulo, some four miles north of the Volturno, on 14 October.

By the evening of the same day the Fifth Army was firmly established along the whole of its front on the north bank of the Volturno. The British 56 Division, using the bridge thrown across by the U.S. 3 Division at Triflisco, had crossed the river and captured Capua. The Desert Rats had got across at Grazzanise. The next day VI Corps continued its advance. In the face of sporadic resistance from the 3 Panzer Grenadier Division, the 45 Division on the right flank reached Piedimonte d'Alife on 19 October, the next day the 34 Division took Alife, and on 21 October

Truscott's troops clambered up Monte Monaco, twelve miles north of Capua. McCreery's divisions, on the other hand, had been able to advance only very much more slowly. In a series of stubborn attacks, the 56 Division fought its way over the thickly cultivated slopes of Monte Maggiore. In the close, equally thickly cultivated terrain of the coastal plain, the 7 Armoured Division seemed to have completely lost that legendary offensive *élan* which had made it so famous in North Africa. It was not until 27 October that the Division reached Spalanise and Francolise. The 46 Division fared even worse and had with difficulty got no further than the other side of the Agnena Canal.

On 25 October Clark halted his offensive on the line Monte Monaco–Visciano–Francolise–north bank of the Agnena estuary, in order to reorganize for the assault on the Reinhard Line. The sinister massifs of Monte Cesima and Monte Santa Croce, the precipitous mountains in the upper Volturno valley, and the bastions of Monte Camino, Monte Maggiore and Monte Sammucro promised hard fighting ahead. The Fifth Army was still nearly thirty miles from Cassino—the thirty most terrible miles that the U.S. Army has ever been called upon to traverse. Torrential rain, icy mountain storms, shelters that were shot to pieces, inadequate winter equipment and, last but not least, the *élite* German divisions turned the battle into a veritable inferno for the G.I.s and Tommies.

The Fifth Army used the time until 31 October, the date of the start of the assault on the Reinhard Line, to regroup within its own Army Corps. The 7 Armoured Division changed places with the 46 Division and took over the coastal sector, while 46 Division was withdrawn into close support behind the 34 Division. Preparatory moves were also in hand on the German side. The position was being further strengthened, and two fresh divisions, the 94 and 305 Infantry Divisions, were brought up and placed under the command of XIV Corps, and the Hermann Göring Panzer Division was withdrawn from the line.

The 94 Division was a 'Stalingrad Division'. From March 1943 onwards it had been slowly rebuilt in France on the remnants of the old division, and in the middle of August it had marched via Mont Cenis into upper Italy under the command of General Pfeffer, who had been in command since the autumn of 1940. The sector which Pfeffer now took over on the lower Garigliano and in the Gulf of Gaeta was not an easy one to defend. The high Monte Maio massif constituted a great menace in that the division would be split into two if it did not succeed in halting the enemy in front of, or at the latest on, the main defensive line. Equipped as it was with horse-drawn transport, the division had no mountain guns, and its artillery was therefore tied to the Ausente valley, which meant that it would be very difficult for the infantry to re-form round the artillery positions once the enemy had broken through the main line of defence. A further source of weakness was the fact that the division was also responsible for the defence of the coast at Terracina. It thus had one eye cocked at its sea flank and the other watching the land front, and in neither sector was it strong enough.

The old Baden-Wuertemburg 305 Infantry Division had also been at Stalingrad and had now been re-raised under its new commander, Lieutenant-General Hauck. Like the 94, the 305 was still an unknown quantity. On 26 July it had marched via the Brenner Pass into Italy and had at once been employed by Rommel in disarming the Italian forces. General Hauck was also faced with considerable difficulties in his sector. His division, now called upon to operate in mountains of over 6,000 feet, had been neither trained nor equipped for mountain warfare. Its comparative lack of mobility and the inadequacy of its anti-tank equipment were further severe handicaps.

The German High Command did not seriously anticipate any attack in the mountainous sectors, but for obvious reasons expected the offensive to develop astride the Via Casilina, for the defence of which 3 Panzer Grenadier Division was responsible. Its commander, Lieutenant-General Graeser, was a first-class soldier who had lost a leg in the First World War—a grave personal handicap in the rugged mountains. There was one novel aspect about this division which gave rise to grave doubts about its reliability. It was composed to a large extent of men of 'Volksliste 3', i.e. of eastern Europeans, in whose ancestry ingenious investigators claimed to have found some traces of Germanic descent. These men could hardly be regarded as fervent patriots, particularly as they were not even citizens of the German Reich, though they could win German nationality by showing conspicuous gallantry in the face of the enemy. At the Salerno and Volturno battles the number of 'missing' in the division was shockingly high, and this had been attributed to the 'pseudo-Germanism' of its composition.

To waste too many words over the magnificent 15 Panzer Grenadier Division and its outstanding commander, Lieutenant-General Rodt, would be like taking coals to Newcastle. The division was holding the line from Monte Faito northwards in the sector common to both Reinhard and Gustav Lines. Its sector then turned eastwards as far as Monte Camino (inclusive), in the defence of which Rodt's men fought with conspicuous gallantry.

The Reinhard Line had been reconnoitred and chosen by General Hube. It was a naturally stronger defensive position than the Gustav Line in rear of it, since the latter had had to surrender to it the two formidable bastions of Monte Camino and Monte Sammucro. But in the Reinhard Line, too, there were weak points. Apart from the poor defensive quality of the lower Garigliano sector, it was overlooked by Monte Croce in the Camino sector and in its key position, the Mignano defile, its main bastion, Monte Cesima, was vulnerable from three sides.

The main object of fighting a defensive battle on the Reinhard Line was, of course, to gain time for the completion of the main defensive position on the Gustav Line. The German forces had been ordered not to retire to the Reinhard Line before 15 November and to hold it until the middle of December. In actual fact, the battle for the Reinhard Line dragged on until the middle of January.

On 31 October the Fifth Army resumed its offensive and had little difficulty in pushing back the weak German rear-guards. On 1 November the U.S. 30 Division took Capriati, east of the Volturno. A Combat Group of the 45 Division crossed the river at Sesto Campana, and the 3 Division following it pressed swiftly along the Via Casilina. The British 50 Division in a rapid advance reached Conca and Roccamonfina. Having captured Mondragone on the coast, the Desert Rats took Monte Cicoli and were advancing astride the Via Appia towards the Garigliano. After a brief period of inactivity the Fifth Army then sprang a disagreeable surprise on the Germans by extending its offensive into the high mountain regions. The 45 Division captured Venafro and the 34 Division broke into the German positions at Pozzilli and Santa Maria Oliveto, and the fate of Monte Cesima hung by a thread. The mountain position had been constructed by pioneers of XIV Panzer Corps and was held by one company of the 3 Panzer Grenadier Division. On 4 November the U.S. 3 Division surrounded the defenders. An attempt by the 3rd Battalion, 6 Parachute Regiment to break the ring from the outside failed and, as no further reserves were available, the mountain was finally lost on 5 November. This, however, did not prove decisive, and the way into the Liri valley was not yet open. Immediately in rear of the Mignano defile were two fresh obstacles, Monte Lungro and Monte Rotondo, and as long as Monte Sammucro and Monte Camino remained in German hands, the way to Cassino was barred.

Clark had had good reasons for concentrating the British X Corps in the Camino massif area. It was here, once the Mignano defile had been opened, that the second key to the Liri valley lay. Templer's 56 Division delivered a determined assault on the bare mountain from the south, but without at first achieving any great success. On 7 November it captured Calabritto and Height 727, to the south of Monte Camino, but there its advance was brought to a halt by a German counter-attack.

By this time a critical situation had arisen in the sectors held by 3 Panzer Grenadier and 305 Infantry Divisions. After the capture of Venafro the U.S. VI Corps pressed forward along the pass in the direction of San

Pietro Infine, with the object of taking the Mignano defile in rear. On 8 November Truscott's 3 Division took Monte Rotondo; further north Middleton's 45 Division gained a firm foothold on Monte Corno and at the same time advanced northwards and north-westwards from Pozzilli. The 305 Division was fighting a fluctuating battle with Ryder's 34 Division, which had advanced into the mountain regions to the north of Middleton. On 8 November General Hauck was no longer able to maintain his position in the face of heavy American pressure and was obliged to withdraw his Division from the salient between Pozzilli and Montaquila to a shorter line on either side of Monte Pantano. Thus the Fifth Army had succeeded, in both the central and left sectors of XIV Panzer Corps, in breaking into the Reinhard Line. The German Corps, however, quickly stabilized the situation by putting in two first-class divisions—the 26 Panzer and 29 Panzer Grenadier Divisions. On 8 November Freiherr von Lüttwitz took over the sector between the completely exhausted 3 Panzer Grenadier Division and the 305 Division and barred U.S. 45 Division's way to Aquafondata, the northern gateway into the Liri valley. On 11 November 3 Panzer Grenadier Division was relieved in the central sector by 29 Panzer Grenadier Division. Monte Rotondo had been recaptured the day before. On 12 November the Americans resumed their attack on the Venafro–San Pietro Infine pass and the next day were in rear of the Mignano defile. Still the German front held. Fries's Division hung grimly to its position. By 16 November it was firmly established in its sector, and Clark had to admit that there was nothing much more that he could do.

At Monte Cassino the prize was still far beyond the reach of the British 56 Division. In spite of three assaults supported by heavy artillery fire, the mountain remained in the hands of the 15 Panzer Grenadier Division. By this time both infantry divisions of X Corps, the 46 and 56, were showing visible signs of exhaustion; from the moment they had landed at Salerno they had been continuously engaged with a foe worthy of their steel; according to Linklater they had suffered forty per cent casualties and had so far lost 197 officers and 3,987 men. The U.S. 3 Division, too, was exhausted and the 34 and 45 Divisions had suffered equally severely. For weeks, in the mud and the icy rain of the Abruzzi Mountains, they had been fighting a series of bloody engagements in which their casualties from sickness had been even higher than their losses in battle. The exhaustion of the troops and the torrential rain that had again started persuaded Clark to suggest to General Alexander that the offensive should be temporarily halted and should not be renewed until Montgomery launched his planned offensive on the lower Sangro on 20 November. So, after a fortnight of bitter fighting, peace descended once more on XIV Panzer Corps' front.

The series of engagements, which were to culminate in the three great Cassino battles, had begun. Despite the material superiority of the Fifth Army, despite the cold, rain and mud, the newly raised German, Italian divisions had prevented the enemy from breaking through into the Liri valley. A few miles behind their main defensive position they had firmly established themselves in new, albeit less favourable positions. The intervention of the 26 and 29 Panzer Grenadier Divisions had exercised a vital influence on the whole of XIV Corps' front. As a breakwater on the Venafro–Aquafondata road, the 26 Division had put fresh stiffening into the 3 Panzer Grenadier and 305 Infantry Divisions and had robbed the U.S. 45 Division of what might have been a walk-over. The 29 Division had added further laurels to its fame. Having relieved Graeser's division, it took the whole burden of the fight for the Mignano defile on its shoulders. It had given its old acquaintances of the Sicilian campaign, the men of the U.S. 3 Division, a further proof of the toughness of its Hessian and Thuringian grenadiers; and the 15 Panzer Grenadier Division had flatly refused to surrender 'their' Monte Cassino. In the end, however, the German forces were too weak to be able indefinitely to face the onslaughts of the Fifth Army without losing ground. In the alpine climate of the Abruzzi the loss of a few positions was of less importance than was the resultant deprivation of shelter for the troops, which became a problem very difficult to solve. The Reinhard Line consisted of a chain of individual strongpoints, built for the most part round the Abruzzi villages, which stood like watch towers on the crests of the hills. When one of these strongpoints was captured by the enemy, the defenders were left exposed to wind and weather, to the storms and rain that lashed the mountains, the rocky ground of which offered no shelter of any kind.

Clark's hopes of seizing Rome by a swift *coup de main* were doomed to disappointment. Montgomery, too, found himself compelled to modify very considerably the more distant objectives he had had in view. On 5 October he telegraphed to Churchill: 'When I have got the lateral Termoli-Campobasso I will have to halt my main bodies for a short period and operate in advance of that lateral only with light forces, while I get my administration on a sound basis during the period of halt. . . . After the halt I will advance with my whole strength on Pescara and Ancona. I shall look forward to meeting you in Rome.'* But it was not until the summer of the following year that the troops of the Eighth Army marched into Pescara and Ancona, at the same time that Montgomery was blasting the vital breach in the walls of Fortress Europe in Normandy; and his meeting with Churchill never took place.

For the time being Montgomery remained in southern Italy, anxiously

* Churchill, *The Second World War*, Vol. V.

observing the bad weather which chose that moment to sweep over Termoli and wondering what was happening 'on the other side of the hill'.

After the loss of Foggia the German 1 Parachute Division was left entirely alone in Apulia and was more than fully occupied in stopping the enemy from entering into the mountains. The 29 Panzer Grenadier Division was moving to its aid, but its progress through the broken mountain country was very slow, and for some time Heidrich's division had to fight alone on a front of wellnigh thirty miles against the whole of the British XIII Corps.

Having captured Foggia, the British Corps advanced in two columns against the German divisional front, its 78 Division moving on Termoli via San Severo and its Canadian 1 Division via Lucera on Vinchiatro, to the south of Campobasso. On 1 October it took Serracapriola on the west bank of the Fortore, and the next day the Canadians broke through the stubbornly defended positions of 4 Parachute Regiment at Motta and pressed on into the mountains. Heidrich had started to withdraw with great skill behind the Biferno when the Termoli disaster occurred, before ever the whole Division had reached its new sector.

From the outset Heidrich had regarded Termoli as a vulnerable spot. As a precautionary measure he had therefore sent ahead a Battle Group of light infantry, pioneers and artillery under the command of his enterprising adjutant. Then what Heidrich had feared, happened. On the night of 2/3 October a British Commando, the 2 Special Service Brigade, made a surprise landing, disembarking at the port and capturing the German staff. They then established contact with the 78 Division's bridge-head near the mouth of the Biferno. These evil tidings reached Tenth Army Head-quarters while Field-Marshal Kesselring happened to be there. The Field-Marshal ordered the immediate withdrawal of the 14 Panzer Grenadier Division from the Volturno sector and launched it against Termoli, with orders to throw the invading forces back into the sea. His primary object was to secure the stability of the Adriatic sector—and, of course, at the same time remove this thorn from the flesh of the 1 Parachute Division. Things did not, however, go as he had anticipated: Kesselring wrote: 'The orders were issued in good time. I was therefore extremely surprised when, between 2200 and 2300 hours, at a time, that is, when I presumed that the division was hastening at full speed towards Termoli, Westphal, my Chief of Staff, reported that Headquarters, Tenth Army had expressed certain misgivings. These I could not share, and I directed that my orders should be carried out forthwith. As a result of the delay and the arrival of the Division in driblets and its subsequent piecemeal commitment into battle, Tenth Army missed the opportunity of achieving a certain success.'*

* *Soldat bis zum letzten Tag.*

Nevertheless, the Grenadiers of 16 Division had advanced to the outskirts of Termoli and on 5 October were actually fighting in the town itself. But the next night the 36 Brigade of 78 Division landed. At the same time the British threw a Bailey bridge across the Biferno and on the morning of 7 October with superior forces fell upon the 16 Division, whose role now changed from pursuer to that of pursued.

Montgomery followed General Herr's slowly withdrawing LXVI Panzer Corps step by step. The time had now come for him to set his lines of communication in order, and he did not feel that he was in a position 'to pursue the enemy with strong forces until the lines of communication had been improved'. Montgomery, of course, did not, on principle allow himself to become involved in a major engagement unless his supply dumps were fully stocked with everything he required. On this occasion Eighth Army's administrative services had not been able to keep pace with the rapid advance through Calabria and Apulia to the line Termoli–Campobasso. In this respect Montgomery was not in the same happy position as Clark, who had a supply base of the capacity of Naples in the immediate proximity of his front.

Although Montgomery had not lost sight of the 'Rome Line'—the diagonal Pescara–Avezzano–Rome road—as his tactical objective, he knew that if the Germans decided to stand and fight south of Rome, he would have great difficulty in reaching it. The approach of winter also caused him grave anxiety. Looking back in retrospect, he says: 'Administration had not been able to keep pace with operational planning, and this was now to have serious consequences, for the winter was beginning. Obviously our difficulties were going to be greatly increased when winter set in, because the "leg" of Italy is essentially ideal defensive country, and when climatic conditions operated in the enemy's favour, it might become almost impregnable . . . on land progress would become impossible off the main roads owing to snow and mud; mountain torrents subject to violent fluctuations would create great bridging difficulties, and flying would be constantly restricted by low cloud and mist.'* And that, indeed, is exactly what happened. While the battle for Termoli was still in progress, heavy rain began to fall, and by the end of the year the Eighth Army had been reduced to a state of immobility by the snow in the Abruzzi Mountains.

Montgomery used the time required for the replenishment of his supplies to regroup his formations. He handed over the coastal sector to V Corps, which he reinforced with the newly arrived Indian 8 Division. XIII Corps moved completely into the mountains and, in addition to the Canadian 1 Division, now had under its command the British 5 Division, which was on the Canadian north.

* Montgomery, *From El Alamein to the Sangro.*

At the end of October, General Herr's Panzer Corps was holding the Trigno sector, with 16 Panzer Division on the coast, the 29 Panzer Grenadier Division further south and the 26 Division astride the Vinchiaturo–Isernia road.

By this time Montgomery's preparations for the Trigno battle had been completed. General Leese, now in command of XIII Corps, was to deliver a strong attack on the southern flank with the object of engaging General Herr's attention, while V Corps proposed to cross the lower reaches of the Trigno, where 78 Division had already established a small bridgehead. To enlarge this and take San Salvo 78 Division launched an attack on 27 October. But despite artillery preparation on the Montgomery scale, the attack failed in the face of the opposition offered by 16 Panzer Division, to whom rain and mud proved valuable allies. The bad weather also led to the postponement of XIII Corps' thrust against the 26 Panzer Division. As there appeared to be no prospect of any improvement in the weather, on the night of 29/30 October General Leese put in the Canadians, who captured Cantalupo two days later.

Once again heavy rain caused the resumption of the British offensive in the coastal sector to be postponed until 2 November. On the night of 2/3 November the 78 Division, with strong support from both artillery and the naval guns, again attacked San Salvo and this time with success. At the same time the Indian 8 Division attacked 29 Panzer Grenadier Division on either side of Montefalcone, but suffered a severe reverse at the hands of 3 Parachute Regiment. In spite of a desperate stand by 16 Panzer Division San Salvo was lost on 4 November, and on 5 November the British took Vasto, the Indians Palmoli and Torrebruno and the Canadians Isernia.

These successes were the signal for General Herr to withdraw his forces to the line of the Sangro, the lower reaches of which had been reached by 78 Division on 8 November. Montgomery's right wing was now face to face with the Gustav Line, and now a new Montgomery set-piece began to take shape. Formations were regrouped, artillery of every calibre was brought up, ammunition dumps rose sky-high and along the roads in the rear areas moved an endless chain of vehicles laden with fuel and munitions. Montgomery was preparing for a decisive victory, the wings of which would carry him to Rome.

It seemed as though the German Tenth Army was doing its best to help him. It withdrew first the 26 Panzer and then the 29 Panzer Grenadier Divisions to the Via Casilina, where the battle for the Reinhard Line was raging. The Eighth Army was left therefore facing only two divisions— the 65 Infantry Division in the Gustav Line on the lower Sangro, and the 1 Parachute Division, which was holding an outpost on the middle and upper Sangro.

By the middle of November both wings of 15 Army Group had reached that bulwark of the German defences which was to resist its every effort until May of the following year—the Gustav Line. The key to the whole defensive system was Monte Cassino, which in the months to follow drew to itself the best troops that Kesselring and Alexander had to offer. But the Reinhard Line, too, still remained unbroken, and for the possession of it and of the Rome Line there was to be much hard fighting in the weeks ahead.

The high hopes of the Allies had been submerged in a sea of rain and mud; even Churchill himself had to resign himself and admit that 'there now remained no hope of marching into Rome this year'.

On 12 November the British Prime Minister had left England on board H.M.S. *Renown* and at about the same time Roosevelt set sail in the new battleship *Iowa*. Both were making for Cairo, the first halt on their way to Teheran, where the Big Three were to meet for the first time. In Cairo, Western ideas were to be co-ordinated in preparation for the Teheran meeting, for it seemed advisable to have ready cut-and-dried proposals to put to Stalin upon the realization of which British and Americans were agreed. Such agreement had by no means existed before Cairo, and the Teheran conference promised to develop into a long tug-of-war between Churchill and Stalin, with Roosevelt as referee. Churchill was not in the least pleased to see Chiang Kai-shek in Cairo, and even the charm of Madame Chiang Kai-shek failed to restore him to good humour.

The Generalissimo urged that this fobbing-off of China with fine phrases and empty words should now cease and that his country should be given concrete help at once. In other words, that the Allies should implement their promises, mount Operation 'Anakim', the invasion of Burma, and get on with the construction of the Burma road into Yunnan, along which the vital help to China could be sent. Roosevelt listened with a sympathetic ear to these requests and discountenanced Churchill with a firm promise that a blow against the Japanese would be launched in the next few months—probably in March.

Churchill regarded this promise as a serious threat to his Mediterranean plans. He could now hardly hope to get back a single assault craft from Admiral Lord Mountbatten, with which to augment Eisenhower's amphibious resources. During 1943/44 the question of landing craft, and in particular of tank landing ships, was one of the most irksome problems facing the Allies. The demands of Overlord, to say nothing of Anakim, had denuded the Mediterranean to an ever-increasing degree, robbed the Allies of the means of exploiting the Italian surrender and forced Alexander to fight his way painfully up the 'shaft of the boot' in the hope—some time or other—of reaching Rome, but with his armies bled white and battle-weary. Landing craft were not required solely for the purpose of turning

Kesselring's flanks from the sea and delivering a deadly 'swipe' at his lines of communication. There were other and equally alluring prospects— the Aegean islands, the Balkan partisans, who, despite the opening of the Adriatic, had been so deplorably left in the lurch, and Turkey, awaiting the chance to open the Narrows and place the Anatolian airfields at the Allies' disposal. In short, the Mediterranean was shouting to high heaven for action—and for landing craft. The Americans guessed that Churchill would once again vigorously develop these arguments in Cairo and Teheran in a final endeavour to persuade Roosevelt and his advisers to accept the Mediterranean strategy he advocated. 'It was their experience that, while the Prime Minister gave the most enthusiastic and eloquent approval to Overlord in principle, he steadfastly refused to accept it as a scheduled fact, preferring to believe that German power could be worn down by attrition to the point of collapse, whereupon the Anglo-American forces in the United Kingdom could perform a triumphant march from the Channel to Berlin with no more than a few snipers' bullets to annoy them.'*

On the other hand, Churchill had repeatedly assured them that it had never been his intention to thwart Overlord, and in Teheran he admitted to Stalin 'it is our duty and obligation to use every ounce of our strength against the Germans on the other side of the Channel'. Be that as it may, the Americans—except in so far as the strategic bombing offensive was concerned—were not prepared to agree to a war of attrition. They were determined, to use Chester Wilmot's phrase, 'not to out-manœuvre Hitler but to out-produce him'; and the only place where it would be possible and advantageous to throw the whole weight of their vast production of armaments into the scale seemed to them to be the plains of France.

The U.S. Chiefs of Staff were therefore taken aback when in Cairo Churchill raised the question whether, after reaching the line Pisa–Rimini, the Allied forces should wheel left against southern France or right into the Balkans. 'They felt certain that whenever the persistent Prime Minister started talking about Rhodes, or veering towards "the right" from northern Italy, he was resuming the advocacy of strategic diversions in south-eastern Europe and away from northern France. They prepared themselves for a battle in Teheran, in which the Americans and Russians would form a united front.'† Nevertheless, the Americans could see no way of avoiding consulting Stalin as to which of these operations, from the Russian point of view, should be given priority.

On the opening day of the Teheran conference, the chair was taken by Roosevelt. He caused no small surprise by speaking of the possibility of landing on the other side of the Adriatic and, with the assistance of the

* Sherwood, *The White House Papers of Harry Hopkins*, Vol. II.   † Ibid.

Tito partisans, invading Rumania and then thrusting at the rear of the German eastern front and linking up with the Russian forces advancing from Odessa. Hopkins, obsessed with the idea of the cross-Channel invasion, was horrified by these new ideas expressed by the President and hastily scribbled a note to Admiral King: 'Who's promoting that Adriatic idea that the President continually returns to?' To which King replied: 'As far as I know, it's his own.'

Any such ideas were frightening in the extreme to the U.S. Chiefs of Staff. But for Churchill they were grist to his Balkan mill; and to Stalin they were a signal to 'clear decks for action.' From that moment he used every means he could to frustrate any such plans. Welcome though the tying down of strong German forces in Italy was to him, he sensed the danger which from this direction might threaten his own future intentions. But on the question of future operations in Italy he came into sharp conflict with Churchill.

The Prime Minister in an eloquent speech painted a rosy picture of the advantages that would accrue from a vigorous exploitation of the situation in the Mediterranean generally and first and foremost in Italy. Alexander, he said, intended to capture Rome in January, and the operations he envisaged stood a good chance of destroying some ten German divisions— they might even lead to a miniature Stalingrad, he asserted. With great enthusiasm he took up Roosevelt's Balkan idea and himself proposed a landing at the head of the Adriatic and a thrust into the strategic centre of Europe, the Viennese basin. Sherwood noted: 'He then reverted to the desirability of getting Turkey into the war, as he did over and over again with a persistence that was both admirable and monotonous.'*

Stalin was not interested in either of these suggestions. It was obvious that he had changed his mind, particularly as regards the entry of Turkey into the war. He repeatedly expressed his conviction that Turkey would not in any circumstances allow herself to be drawn into a war against the Axis partners. This made strange hearing, when it is remembered that in Moscow a few weeks previously he had urged Eden to make renewed representations to Ankara on his way home. But it was not only as regards the Balkans alone, but also as regards Italy that Stalin raised objections, though his object in both cases was the same, namely, to keep the Western powers out of the Balkans. An Allied landing at the head of the Adriatic threatened to frustrate Russian plans in the Balkans, and to that he was determined to put a stop at all costs. It was for this reason that he strove so persistently to ensure that future operations in Italy should be of a completely secondary nature and that the spear which the Allies were threatening to hurl against the Balkans should be aimed at southern

* *The White House Papers of Harry Hopkins.*

France instead. Not only did he demand that an Allied landing on the French Riviera should be mounted two months before the start of the cross-Channel invasion, but went so far as to insist that Alexander should halt his offensive in Italy, give up any idea of capturing Rome and confine himself to defending what he already held with a force of ten divisions! The forces that Alexander would then be able to release should be used, he said, for the invasion of southern France. Once again the Italian campaign constituted the point at issue, and once again, indirectly, the fate of Monte Cassino hung in the balance.

It may well be argued that the Trident conference decisions robbed Eisenhower of the means with which to exploit Mussolini's downfall, achieve a resounding success and deny Hitler any chance of defending the Italian peninsula; or that it was the failure of the Italian General Staff to fulfil its obligations which led to the abandonment of a landing near Rome; or that it was the lack of shipping resulting from the Quebec 'lawyers' agreement' that prevented Eisenhower from using the long sea flanks and made him decide on the Salerno landing. But in the final analysis, all these decisions and errors of judgement had a vital bearing on the fate of the Monte Cassino monastery. A concatenation of somewhat incomprehensible decisions led ultimately to the bloody battles of St Benedict's Mount and the destruction of his superb monastery. But— had the Western powers agreed to the Russian proposals, it would, ironically enough, have been Stalin of all people, who had saved the monastery at the last moment!

As it was, the extravagant demands of the Red dictator went too far, of course. Stalin's proposal was a direct challenge to Churchill, who was not prepared, at this juncture, when all England was waiting for the fall of Rome, to abandon an objective for the attainment of which so much British blood had already been shed. Any such thought was quite intolerable, and on this issue he was determined to have his own way. But although he succeeded, it was Stalin who was in reality the ultimate victor. He did not mind very much whether the Western allies took Rome or not; but he had got what he wanted—an undertaking that they would invade southern France. With plausible military arguments, with 'well-meaning' advice and with a half-promise that Overlord would be supported by a general offensive on the Eastern Front, he disguised his real intentions and succeeded in diverting the Western powers from the Balkans and the eastern Mediterranean. Having thus neutralized the potential menace to his plans from Italy and chained the Allies to 'the Anvil', he was quite certain which flag would be hoisted in the Balkan countries once final victory had been achieved.

Churchill, however, was by no means content to accept the Teheran decisions—priority for Overlord and Anvil as the major operations for 1944—without further ado. As will later be seen, in the summer of 1944, after the capture of Rome, he again made strenuous efforts to persuade the Americans to 'wheel right' into the Balkans. Although Alexander had been compelled to advance painfully and inch by inch through southern Italy, and although the 15 Army Group took five months to burst asunder the hinges of the gateway at Cassino, it was still by no means too late to advance from the capture of Rome to victory in the Balkans. But once again it was the U.S. Chiefs of Staff, strongly supported this time by Eisenhower, who threw away a chance of victory 'offered to them on a silver salver'.

In contrast, Churchill, after the Teheran conference, was more concerned than ever regarding future developments in Italy, as became evident when the British and American leaders met in Cairo to decide the personal appointment changes to the various high commands necessitated by the Teheran decisions. The most important of these was the appointment of a Commander-in-Chief for Overlord. At the Cairo conference the U.S. Chiefs of Staff suggested the appointment of a single Commander-in-Chief, vested with plenipotentiary powers for the whole of the European theatre of war in north-west Europe and the Mediterranean. Among other things, he would have authority to move troops, landing craft and shipping from one theatre to another without, as before, having to obtain the prior sanction of the Combined Chiefs of Staff Committee. This proposal failed in the face of strong British opposition. To Churchill, the idea of being deprived of any control in 'his' Mediterranean theatre was quite unacceptable. He therefore strongly advocated that there should be an American Commander-in-Chief for Overlord and that a British General should be appointed as overall commander of the whole Mediterranean area, combining, that is, the commands exercised at the time by Eisenhower and Wilson.

For a long while Roosevelt had hesitated between Marshall and Eisenhower as Commander-in-Chief, Overlord. The decision in favour of Eisenhower was taken '. . . against the almost impassioned advice of Hopkins and Stimson, against the known preference of both Stalin and Churchill, against his own proclaimed inclination to give George Marshall the historic opportunity he so greatly desired and so richly deserved'.* How strongly Roosevelt felt that he could not spare his Chief of Staff is clearly shown by his remark to him: 'With you out of the country, I don't think I'd get a single night's sleep.'

The appointment of Eisenhower necessitated a complete reorganization of command in the Mediterranean theatre, to take effect from 1 January

* Sherwood, *The White House Papers of Harry Hopkins*, Vol. II.

1944. From that date General Sir Henry Maitland Wilson was to take over from Eisenhower and at the same time retain his appointment as Commander-in-Chief, Near East. Tedder was to go to London as Eisenhower's deputy. The navy had already got a new Commander-in-Chief in Sir John Cunningham, who had taken over from Sir Andrew Cunningham in October, when the latter had been appointed to succeed the late Admiral Pound as First Sea Lord. Tedder's place in the Mediterranean was to be taken by the U.S. General Ira C. Eaker, who until then had been commanding the U.S. 8 Strategic Air Fleet and been responsible for the daylight raids on Germany and the western occupied territories. His place in England was to be taken by General Doolittle who was to be succeeded as Commander, 15 Strategic Air Fleet in Italy, by the U.S. General Twining. A new appointment was that of General Spaatz, who was recalled to London to assume overall direction of the whole of the American bomber offensive against Germany and her satellites. Another noteworthy innovation was the placing, with effect from 5 December 1943, of Middle East Command, R.A.F., under the command of the Allied Commander-in-Chief, who then became responsible 'for all operations in the Mediterranean, with the exception of the conduct of strategic bombing'.

For Montgomery, the day of parting had arrived. To command the land forces in the initial phases of Operation Overlord, Churchill, contrary to the expectations and wishes of the Americans, chose not Alexander but Montgomery. Eisenhower himself, speaking of Alexander, describes him as 'Britain's most outstanding strategist . . . a friendly and pleasant type . . . whom the Americans could not help liking'. Churchill, of course, knew this and, with the Mediterranean in his mind's eye, he was hoping to make capital out of the high esteem in which Alexander was held by the Americans. Montgomery, on the other hand, was not nearly so popular with them. They certainly had a high opinion of his capabilities and the successes he had achieved, but they found it hard to stomach the tight rein on which he held his subordinates. Of this, too, Churchill was well aware, particularly as Eisenhower, on appointment as Commander-in-Chief, had let it be known that he would prefer Alexander to Montgomery. But Churchill deliberately left Alexander in Italy, simply because of the affection he enjoyed among Americans. By so doing, he believed he would stand the best chance of gaining the American support which he needed so urgently for the coming offensive against Rome.

Churchill was now determined to take matters into his own hands. On the conclusion of the second Cairo conference he hastened to Tunis to co-ordinate the threads for the final blow against Rome. To him, the eye of the needle was Anzio, just south of the capital; and it was through there that he intended to pass the thread with the object of throttling von Vietinghoff on the Cassino front and placing a deadly halter round the neck of Rome. But it was not until the late spring, after the inferno of Cassino had at last died down, that Alexander was able to pull the threads together.

All this, however, was still a long way ahead. At the moment the Allies were far away on the outskirts of Cassino. Rain and mud made their lives a misery, and the German defenders had no intention of yielding an inch of ground without a fight.

Chapter 6

German Troops Rescue the Monastery Treasures*

Among the officers bending over the maps in the battle headquarters of the Hermann Göring Panzer Division was a middle-aged staff officer, Viennese by birth, named Lieutenant-Colonel Julius Schlegel, the commander of the Divisional Maintenance Section. It was October 1943. The Division was in Capua, and the Fifth Army onslaught on the Volturno had already begun. The staff conference was concerned not so much with the withdrawal which the Division was about to make as with the further conduct of operations, as outlined by Field-Marshal Kesselring. General Conrath spoke in considerable detail about the Reinhard Line and in even greater detail about the Gustav Line, then in the initial stages of construction. It was on the latter, the General explained, that the enemy offensive was to be brought to a final halt. The fiercest fighting, he said, was expected to take place in the Liri valley and on the high ground on either side of it, and he was at pains to make clear to his officers the very great tactical importance of Monte Cassino. At the mention of this latter, Schlegel pricked up his ears.

* This chapter is based on a series of articles written by Lieutenant-Colonel Julius Schlegel, the initiator and organizer of the operation, which appeared in *Die Oesterreichische Furche* (Nos. 45–50, 1951) and which Colonel Schlegel placed at the author's disposal; and also on the article '*Der Untergang von Montecassino*', by Father Emmanuel Munding.

A lover of the arts and a zealous visitor to the museums and galleries of Italy, Schlegel was filled with foreboding at the thought that the decisive action of the coming battle was to be fought at the foot of a mountain which was crowned with an artistic jewel of unique beauty. He knew how easily in the heat of battle all other considerations were swept aside, how little mercy had been shown in this war to civilian property and works of art; he knew that in the air raid on Rome on 19 July the famous church of San Lorenzo had been severely damaged; he had seen in Sicily whole towns and villages blown out of existence by Allied bombers. Would they hold their hands at Monte Cassino? Would they respect its sanctity and cultural significance?

Schlegel did not believe they would. The proximity of the town of Monte Cassino, through which ran the Via Casilina, the road to Rome, was alone enough to make it certain that further air attacks would be made upon it. In that case, how easily a bomb released too early or too late might land on the House of St Benedict itself. And what of artillery fire? Did not the same apply to that too? German or enemy shells, a little too low in their trajectory, might easily strike the summit of the mountain and discharge their explosive wrath among the architectural beauties and works of art of the monastery. Schlegel himself had been both a gunner and an airman, so he was well qualified to assess the dangers that threatened the venerable abbey.

These torturing thoughts gave him no rest. He knew all about the treasures of Monte Cassino, their glory and their immense value. An inner voice urged him to do something about it. But what could he do? Who would give him authority to do anything? What would a court martial verdict be, if on his own authority he neglected his duty and used men, vehicles and precious petrol and oil for an enterprise that had no military purpose and was not of the slightest importance to the prosecution of the war? And suppose, after all, that the monastery was not bombed, that the battle took some other course or that the Allies respected the immunity of the monastery? What then? No one would be able to defend his actions, and things would go badly with him. Yet the small inner voice persisted: 'You must do it!' He remembered the Bishop's Palace in Monte Cassino town, which had been destroyed by bombs, and the Serpentina Road, winding up the mountain from town to monastery, which was also disfigured by a number of gaping craters. The war was indeed creeping closer and closer.

The 14 October saw Schlegel in his car, with a South Tyrolean to act as interpreter, on his way to call on the Bishop and Abbot of the monastery.

'The Lord Bishop and Abbot of Monte Cassino, Gregorio Diamare, a venerable old gentleman of eighty, was waiting for me in the reception hall. With modest dignity, humbly, yet with an air of awareness of his high office as the successor of St Benedict, he advanced to meet me. There was nothing either of the aesthete or of the lord and master about him; very simply, he exuded infinite goodness. That was the first impression I got, an impression of the innate sanctity of the man, which shone through his eyes as the salient characteristic of his personality and which seemed to envelop his whole person like a cloak of soft and silken material.' These are the words with which Schlegel describes his first glimpse of the Lord Bishop.

Schlegel found it by no means easy to persuade him that the monastery was in grave danger. He simply would not believe that any such danger existed or that the Allies would not show the same consideration for the disciples of St Benedict as had been accorded to them by the Germans. German troops had, of course, been permitted to visit the monastery, but without arms and escorted always by one of the monks. In things of this sort, Kesselring would tolerate no nonsense! Up till now there had been no incidents of any kind, and it was obvious that the German troops had received very strict and detailed orders.

The very fact that the Bishop had offered asylum to thousands of Italian civilians and that no attempt had been made to evacuate the monastery is in itself eloquent proof of the absolute conviction of the people of Monte Cassino, clergy and laity alike, that the monastery was in no danger of succumbing under the hammer-blows of war. It is true that war had left its scars on the town below, which had suffered considerable damage. But then the town was in an important defile, easy to block, through which flowed all the German reinforcements and supplies to the Volturno front.

Schlegel set about the task of explaining to the Bishop as gently as he could that he was making a grave mistake if he thought that the monastery could not possibly be endangered. He was at pains to try and shake the venerable old gentleman's misplaced confidence, without going too bluntly into details. For one thing, he had to be extremely careful not to give any hint of the German High Command's intention of fighting the main defensive battle on the Rapido–Garigliano line or to suggest in any way that the forward Cassino position would only be held for a limited period. Cautiously he developed his arguments, and in this he was greatly helped by Father Emmanuel Munding, a German monk, who had been 'seconded' for five years from his own monastery to Monte Cassino and who had accompanied the Bishop as interpreter. When Schlegel pointed out that bombs had already fallen close to the monastery, the Bishop had replied that the airmen would never deliberately destroy it; but, said Schlegel it was quite possible that stray bombs might fall and cause incalculable havoc among the refugees and the treasures. To this the Bishop retorted that the monastery did not contain as many treasures as the German Colonel seemed to think. It was obvious that he did not quite trust Schlegel and suspected that the Germans were trying to get hold of the works of art and, perhaps, take them off to Germany. Allied propaganda may well have been partly responsible for thus awakening the old gentleman's suspicions.

Don Mauro, the librarian, who had joined the conference, regarded the uninvited guest with even more suspicion. His thoughts, too, were running along the same lines, and to him Schlegel was suspiciously like the fairy-tale wolf in sheep's clothing. But he could not refuse when the Bishop gave Schlegel permission to visit the library. There the German Colonel had his first glimpse of the priceless treasures which for centuries had been housed and cherished within the walls of Monte Cassino and the most valuable portions of which he and his troops were destined to rescue and preserve for posterity. Here, in the archives section, slumbered the old parchments, codices and incunabula which set forth *in toto* the great story of the monastery. Schlegel was enthralled, and Don Mauro became very much more approachable when he saw the obviously genuine interest his visitor was displaying.

This first visit to the Bishop did not, however, accomplish very much and certainly did not come up to Schlegel's expectations. There was no doubt that he had failed to shake the Bishop's confidence, who simply refused to believe that any harm could come to the House of St Benedict. This, after all, was the twentieth century; he was living among civilized people, not wild barbarians like the Goths and Saracens of old.

But one thing Schlegel had achieved—he had won the confidence of Father Emmanuel. Speaking to him in German, he had been able to give a few concrete hints, and as he took his leave the German monk asked him to come again and to warn them if it became dangerous to delay. This Schlegel promised to do, and at the same time he asked Father Emmanuel in the meanwhile to have another talk with the Bishop and try to make him understand the very real dangers threatening the monastery.

Schlegel wasted no time. The very next day he again called on the Bishop. This time, in addition to Father Emmanuel and Don Mauro, the Prior of the monastery, a man of striking appearance, with the head of a scholar, was also present. The atmosphere was already more cordial, and Schlegel's first visit had obviously had some effect. Above all it was Father Emmanuel and the Prior who gave Schlegel the courage to put his point of view more urgently. The Bishop's confidence obviously began to waver as the German Colonel painted the picture of the military situation in sombre colours and suggested that he should drive a representative of the monastery to the Vatican to request the help of the Pope. But Gregorio

Diamare retorted that little help could be expected from that quarter. Had he, Schlegel wondered, been in touch with Rome in the meanwhile? Or had he, after all, realized the danger?

Schlegel decided to speak more plainly. Although he did not specifically mention the imminent struggle for the Gustav Line, he gave his listeners to understand that Monte Cassino might well become the focal point of the battle, if the Allies used the sea flank and effected a landing in its vicinity. That settled the issue. The Bishop, who up till then had been so full of confidence, was now suddenly shocked and filled with trembling anxiety.

Schlegel hastened to offer his help, although he had not the slightest idea how he would be able to implement his promise. Had he perhaps bitten off more than he could chew? How would he be able to transport this mass of treasures to safety? He possessed neither the vehicles nor the inexhaustible supply of petrol that would be required. Without the concurrence of General Conrath he could hardly embark on so large and important an enterprise. In these circumstances, to act too hastily, he felt, would be unwise. He therefore advised the Bishop to call his monks together in conference. He, Schlegel, would return in two days' time to learn their decision. As he was leaving, Father Emmanuel begged him to keep his promise and return. He himself would do all he could to persuade the monks to Schlegel's way of thinking.

Meanwhile the Fifth Army had crossed the Volturno and were approaching Cassino in their advance on Rome. General Clark's success had certainly influenced the monks' conference, for when Schlegel returned two days later, the die had already been cast. The Bishop had decided that not only would he grasp the helping hand that Schlegel had offered, but he would also ask Schlegel to take the House of St Benedict under his wing; for his part, he promised to assist in the rescue work with every means at his disposal.

Schlegel's first suggestion was that a lorry, which he promised to send the same day, should be loaded with such articles as the Bishop chose and, accompanied by two monks, should then be driven to Rome. After the lorry had been unloaded, the two monks should give the driver a receipt which he, Schlegel, would then bring to the Bishop. Gregorio Diamare gratefully accepted the suggestion; and when Schlegel handed him the receipt the next day, the ice was finally broken. Now all the Bishop's misgivings had been dissipated. He urged Schlegel to get on with the work as quickly as possible and assured him that any orders he chose to give would be faithfully observed by the monastery. Schlegel, however, to whose tact and moderation all concerned pay tribute, did not avail himself of this right to give orders. Before taking any action, he always consulted the Bishop or his immediate advisers.

Colonel Schlegel had taken upon himself a heavy responsibility. When he had made his initial offer of help he certainly had no means of forming a clear idea of what the offer involved; and he most certainly had not realized that 120 lorry-loads would barely suffice to move even the more valuable treasures of the monastery. There was another point. Rome was nearly one hundred long miles away—and the skies between belonged to the other side. Could he be sure that enemy fighter-bombers would not dive down on the lorries and destroy them and their priceless contents—at a time, too, when the question of whether or not the Allies might after all spare the monastery itself was still very much in the hands of the gods? These were indeed anxious days for the enterprising Schlegel, particularly as none of his superiors knew anything of the arrangements he had made. Even General Conrath had no idea of what was going on at Monte Cassino—and Conrath was a most rigid disciplinarian!

Now Schlegel found himself confronted with an obstacle which at first sight seemed insuperable—the vast number of refugees to whom the Bishop, faithful to the tenets of Benedictine hospitality, had given asylum, even to the extent of feeding them from monastery resources. In the courtyards, the apartments of the college and the seminary, which were separated from the rest of the convent by a wall, were something like 1,100 people, among them whole families who had brought their goods and chattels with them. The monks had closed their gates to no one, although the monastery was not in any way equipped to cope with such a mass of people. These refugees were now very much in the way. They had, Schlegel felt, to be moved—and for two reasons: firstly, for their own safety, and secondly, because it would be asking for trouble to attempt to move, in the presence of such a concourse, the valuable articles of gold and silver work, the intrinsic value of which alone was very great indeed.

He realized, of course, that the Bishop could not turn them out without further ado, so he had no option but to resort to a subterfuge. He called all the refugees together in one of the courtyards and told them that he was well aware of the many things lacking for their comfort in the monastery; but, he said, to befoul the abbey in the way they had done—and not only the courtyards, but all the rooms as well—was a poor way of showing their gratitude for the monks' hospitality. Apart from that, he continued, in view of the inadequate sanitary arrangements there was a very grave risk of serious epidemic. He called upon them, therefore, to set to at once and clean the whole place properly.

This, of course, was not to the liking of his audience, and what Schlegel hoped for actually happened—most of the refugees packed up and departed. Whether they were prompted by the fear of possible epidemic, whether they were simply lacking in any elementary sense of sanitation, or whether they were simply work-shy, was of no importance. They had gone, and the small handful that remained were respectable people with a proper appreciation of cleanliness; later they were to be of great assistance in packing and loading the treasures, and not one single article was stolen by them.

At first the lorries which Schlegel sent were loaded indiscriminately. As with the first consignment, each convoy was accompanied by two monks, who then remained in Rome, but faithfully sent back the receipts notifying safe arrival. The monks were very impressed by the orderly and reliable manner in which everything was done and were highly appreciative of the organizational ability displayed by the Germans. Now that all was going so well, they urged that the archives and library, the pride of the monastery should also be conveyed to safety.

This was easier said than done. Certain preparatory measures had to be taken, which Schlegel already had in hand. The valuable parchments and ancient documents could not be just dumped 'naked' into a lorry, for they could so easily have been damaged by the bumping and friction inevitable during the long journey. Packing cases, obviously, were essential. Schlegel was not defeated. In the monastery he set up a complete packing-case factory. The wood he obtained from a small factory he had found between Cassino and Teano. The necessary tools and a team of carpenters were provided by his own Maintenance Section. Any further assistance he required he recruited from the civilians who had remained in the monastery. With the Bishop he arranged for the monastery to provide them with food, and from his own quartermaster's stores he managed to get them a small daily ration of cigarettes. These little benefits acted as a great spur to the Italian helpers, and in a few days his factory had turned out some hundreds of packing cases. In addition he had to find wrappings for the pictures and a number of special chests for the more valuable articles.

Everything now was running like clockwork. As soon as a case was ready, off it went either to the archives or to the library, to be filled with valuables and loaded on the lorries waiting in the courtyard. As soon as a lorry was fully laden, it set off for Rome. Even so, Schlegel felt he would be able to save only a fraction of the books and archives. As time passed, however, and there seemed to be good prospects of moving the less valuable contents, he found that the supply of packing cases was not keeping pace with the demand, and many volumes of manuscript had to be loaded, wrapped simply in protective cloth. All nevertheless reached their destination undamaged. Schlegel wrote: 'In this way something like 70,000 volumes were safely transported from the archives and the library. The original documents—some 1,200 in all—many of them hundreds of years old, of priceless historical value and bearing the seals of Robert Guiscard, Roger of Sicily and many distinguished Popes and rulers, were brought to a place of safety.'*

But this was by no means the end of Schlegel's labours. There were still masses of things of inestimable value waiting to be carried to safety. Schlegel did his best to ensure that every lorry was fully laden and that every nook and cranny in it had been used to the full. He had to ensure that there was no wasteful use of this transport which, in the ultimate analysis, he had withdrawn from the front—and a front which, since Sicily, had been shouting for lorries and fuel. Thus, together with all the other treasures of gold, silver, books and documents, room was found, among many other things, for a collection of fine paintings. Often the necessary packing was lacking, and he had no option but to place the pictures face to face, with such protective material between them as he could lay his hands on. The lorries were driven by specially selected men, on whom the priceless value of their cargoes had been impressed. To avoid possible loss through air attack they had strict orders to maintain an interval of at least three hundred yards between lorries; and in actual fact, not a single lorry was hit. A fine record, when it is remembered that there were in all 120 lorry loads, packed with treasures, monks, nuns and orphaned children. Only once was there a narrow escape, when some outside lorry squeezed in between two of Schlegel's lorries and was promptly caught by a burst of machine-gun fire; Schlegel's lorries escaped unscathed.

So far all had gone well. Innumerable loads had already reached their destination safely, no one had interfered with the good work and all was going according to plan. Then, in a flash, the whole situation changed and disaster threatened. An Allied broadcasting station suddenly announced: 'The Hermann Göring Panzer Division is busily engaged in looting the monastery of Monte Cassino!' That was a bad business. Now the whole thing would be blazoned abroad, albeit in a distorted form. No one paused to ask whether the statement was true or whether perhaps the Germans were acting with the consent of the monks. Without further ado everyone believed what the enemy propaganda told them—German troops had disturbed the peace of the monastery and were looting its contents. A formation had been mentioned by name, so you could bet on it, people said, that the Divisional Commander had had a hand in the game as well! Potent poison indeed for the witches' broth in the propaganda kitchen!

Schlegel found himself in a most unenviable position. It certainly seemed as though things had gone beyond his control. Initially he had sent one lorry, then a few more, and only thereafter, at the urgent request of the Bishop, had he organized column after column. From the military point of

* In *Die Oesterreichische Furche.*

view he had, of course, far exceeded his authority. How could he justify having given priority over his important military duties to private possessions, however valuable, and what right had he to employ German troops for a purpose which had nothing whatsoever to do with the prosecution of the war? For days on end he had been busily at work, without even having told his General what he was about. The latter would be furious when he heard about it; nor was he likely to confine himself merely to an expression of his fury. Unauthorized use of lorries and petrol . . . ? obviously a case for a court martial, and the verdict could hardly be anything but guilty. Now the bombshell had burst, the Division had been mentioned by name. He was in for a rough passage, even though his conscience was clear as far as the 'looting' was concerned.

The first unpleasant repercussions were not long in coming. A staff colonel from 'up top' arrived, charged with the job of 'investigating the truth of the Allied allegations and taking such steps as he deemed necessary'. What he saw on arrival seemed at first sight to justify the Allied accusations. The courtyard of the monastery was full of German soldiers, busily engaged in loading up German lorries. The Staff Colonel questioned Schlegel closely—was he acting under orders, had the matter been reported to the Commander-in-Chief, South, who had provided the lorries and fatigue parties, had the Bishop specifically asked for German help and, finally, was he, Schlegel, anything of an art expert?

Under this bombardment of questions Schlegel took evasive action and did not, perhaps, adhere very rigidly to the truth. But his answers at least satisfied the Staff officer on the major issue—the charge of looting—and he also appreciated the point when Schlegel stressed the need for immediate action if the treasures were to be saved from the disaster that threatened them. It so happened that while they were talking a fresh air raid descended upon the town of Cassino, pointedly underlining the cogency of Schlegel's arguments. The Staff Colonel took another swift look round the basilica and departed, without, however, interrupting the salvage work or ordering that it should cease.

Scarcely had he left than a posse of military police arrived! Now the fat was properly in the fire! Twenty men under the command of an officer entered the monastery at the double. Schlegel asked them what had brought them there, to which the officer replied that he had been ordered by the Commander-in-Chief, South, to find out whether the monastery was being looted and if so to arrest those responsible. Schlegel referred him to the monks, who, of course, told him the truth about what was happening. He had therefore no option but to express his regret and depart.

Leccisotti, who, incidentally, is full of praise for the tactful way in which Schlegel had conducted the whole affair, referring to this incident, says that

Schlegel 'stood no nonsense and peremptorily turned an S.S. group out of the monastery, when they intruded in search of prey and booty'.* Good Dom Tomasco Leccisotti was a witness of this scene, but as he spoke no German he did not know what passed between Schlegel and the military police officer. When the military police departed, he presumed that Schlegel had sent them about their business. He could not imagine that they had hastened up the mountain to protect the monastery, but imputed more sinister motives; and since Allied propaganda had always depicted the S.S. as the arch-perpetrators of looting and murder, he jumped to conclusions and turned perfectly honest military police into marauding S.S. men. 'I never had occasion to throw S.S. men out of the monastery, since none ever intruded,' wrote Schlegel in a letter to the author. It is interesting to note what a great influence Allied propaganda had on the monks. On the other hand it must be remembered that Leccisotti wrote his book immediately after the war, before the events of it had had time to fall into perspective.

In view of what had happened, Schlegel felt that he could no longer delay reporting to the Divisional Commander. It was high time to inform General Conrath, before the story reached him from some third party. Schlegel was very uneasy about the outcome. He did not quite know how he could justify his high-handed action or whether he would be able to enlist the General's sympathy for the salvage work he had undertaken.

It was Lieutenant-Colonel Bobrovsky, the D.Q.M.G. of the Hermann Göring Division, who proved to be a friend in need. He and Schlegel were intimate friends, and Bobrovsky himself was *persona grata* with General Conrath and might well succeed in acting as mediator between Schlegel and the General. When Schlegel and Bobrovsky reported to him, General Conrath had heard nothing of the Allied broadcast. Vividly the two officers described the importance of the monastery and its treasures, which Schlegel had begun to bring to safety. Admittedly they were careful to avoid telling the General at once how much had already been done; better, they thought, to break it to him gently—there were all those lorries and the petrol and the fatigues and—well—better play for safety!

To their great relief, the General did not turn out to be the wild man that Schlegel's guilty conscience had expected. Very much the reverse—not only did he unreservedly approve everything that Schlegel had done and order him to carry on, but he also directed that further means should be placed at his disposal. This was indeed a great triumph. Relieved of his burdensome responsibility, Schlegel could now extend his activities and do everything the Bishop and monks had begged him to do. But time pressed. The Fifth Army was advancing, very soon Cassino would be

* *La distruzione di Montecassino.*

involved in the turmoil of battle, and disaster might come to the monastery overnight; and by no means all the movable treasures had already been removed.

It was then that Schlegel came across a new treasure-trove, the existence of which the Bishop had kept hidden from him. Among the refugees he had noticed two men dressed in the grey uniforms of Italy's corps of museum attendants. One day he questioned them and learnt to his surprise that they were, indeed, members of that corps and were on duty as such in the monastery.

But there was no museum there, Schlegel argued, and surely the monks themselves were the guardians of their own treasures? True, replied the men, but there was also a very great secret which they could not divulge. With the aid of a little persuasion and a few cigarettes the secret diminished in stature. Bit by bit the men lifted the veil. The monastery, it seemed, had a proper picture gallery, containing priceless paintings by all the most famous Italian masters!

The details of how this unique collection had come to the monastery Schlegel now learnt from the two attendants and Father Emmanuel. In Naples an art exhibition had been organized, for which all the most important galleries in Italy had loaned their masterpieces. This was just before the war came to the mainland itself. When Naples was hit by the first air raid, the exhibits were packed up and, at the request of the Italian Government, sent to the monastery for safe custody. The Bishop had remained silent about these masterpieces, because he had felt that he had no authority to take any decision as to what should be done with them. He had been by no means eager to accept the responsibility of being the custodian of such treasures in the first instance, but since the monastery was in receipt of an annual grant from the Government for the upkeep of its archives— which, since 1868 had become the property of the Government and not of the monastery—he felt that he could hardly refuse.

For Schlegel the question now was—should he undertake to transport these pictures, too, which in reality had nothing to do with the monastery? He would be taking a big risk if he did. They might so easily be damaged or destroyed in transit, and at the back of his mind was always the thought that the monastery after all might not be bombarded at all. What, then, if it remained unscathed and some of these irreplaceable treasures were destroyed in transit as a result of his own over-hasty action? In spite of his misgivings, he decided to risk it. But again—where should he take them? The paintings were the property of the Italian State and could not, like the treasures of the monastery, be taken to the Vatican. Obviously there would have to be consultations with some State officials, but—with whom? Mussolini had been back in office a bare month, the machinery of his new régime was still all too inadequate and was in any case far too busy with other worries to bother about the safety of an exhibition of paintings. In the end he decided to take the paintings to a castle in Spoleto, in which his Maintenance Section had established a store depot, under military guard. There they would at least be well guarded.

His lorries were still busy, carrying the contents of the monastery archives to Rome. Each lorry was still being accompanied by two monks and was being unloaded in San Paolo or San Anselmo, the seat of the supreme head of the Benedictine Order. There were a large number of Mass vessels, each one of which was a masterpiece of the goldsmith's art, and of reliquaries, that were of great importance to the whole Catholic world. There was also an old, worm-eaten cross, so large that it could only be carried diagonally across a lorry. This venerable crucifix, which was of the thirteenth-century Siena school, could not be left behind. There were numerous other treasures—ornate Mass vestments, antique holy books, valuable paintings, the rich carpets from the church, five gold lamps from the sacrament altar and many other things besides.

With complete confidence the monks gave into the safe keeping of the German troops the earthly remains of the holy saints of Cassino—of Desiderius, of Bertharius, who was put to death by the Saracens in the eighth century, and others. With solemn ceremony the greatest treasure of all, one of the greatest holy relics of the Catholic world, the reliquary of St Benedict himself, was handed over. With infinite care it was lowered into a specially constructed case, and monks and soldiers alike stood respectfully by, while the Bishop blessed it before it set out for Rome. For the old Bishop himself it was a bitter moment, filled with the painful thought that now at last the House of St Benedict was no more. For thirty years the 297th successor of the Patriarch had ruled in peace over the monastery; but now the founder of the Order had forsaken it and his protecting hand had been taken away from the monastery.

By the beginning of November Schlegel's task was nearing completion. From Monte Cassino the noise of battle was already audible. The time had come to leave the monastery hill. When the Bishop heard from Rome that the reliquary of St Benedict had arrived safely, he told Schlegel: 'You have earned our undying thanks,' and he pressed him to say how he could give some concrete expression to his gratitude. But all that Schlegel modestly asked was that the Bishop should hold a Mass for him and his men.

The Mass, attended by all the remaining monks and the German soldiers engaged on the rescue work, was an impressive ceremony. The Bishop himself conducted the service, visibly moved, as though he realized that this was the last Mass he would celebrate in the superb basilica. After the service the Bishop beckoned to Schlegel to come to the high altar and there, with many expressions of gratitude, handed him a parchment manuscript, drawn up in the style of the ancient codices and embellished with the seal of Monte Cassino on an orange tassel, the text of which read:*

In nomine Domini nostri Jesu Christi—Illustri ac dilecto viro tribuno militum Julio Schlegel—qui servandis monachis rebusque sacri Coenobii Casinensis amico animo, sollerti studio ac labore operam dederit, ex corde gratias agentes, fausta quaeque a Deo suppliciter Casinenses adprecantur.

Monticasini Kal. Nov. MCMXLIII.

Gregorius Diamare

Episcopus et Abbas

Monticasini.

These men had not only saved the world-famous collection of books, the priceless archives, reliquaries and sacred vessels from destruction; they had also saved the lives of monks, nuns and orphaned children and had brought to a place of safety the masterpieces of the Naples Art Exhibition. Among these were three Titians, two Raphaels, some Tintorettos, Ghirlandaios, Brueghels and many others besides. Of the works of Leonardo da Vinci only a few have been preserved for posterity. His *Leda* was saved by Schlegel's men and has long since been restored to its rightful place in Naples. And it is these same men that the world has to thank for the preservation of vases and sculptures from ancient Pompeii. Thanks to them these fine examples of Roman art escaped the bombs of 15 February and still grace the museums of the world.

On 3 November the work came to an end. Schlegel offered to take the Bishop to Rome in his car, but the latter refused, saying that he could not desert his diocese now, in its moment of dire peril. (The Bishop was also Bishop of the diocese of Monte Cassino, the *Terra sancti Benedicti*.) So this venerable man, who had ruled over the monastery since 1912, remained there with five of his own priests, one priest of the diocesan administration, and five monks. They remained at their posts to the bitter end and they all came out of the inferno of 15 February alive.

The time had now come for Schlegel, too, to say good-bye. On 3 November he left the place which owed so much to his endeavours, taking the aged Prior and Father Emmanuel with him.

While the last cases were being hastily packed in Monte Cassino, negotiations were being conducted between the Italian Ministry of Educa-

---

* In the name of our Lord, Jesus Christ, to the illustrious and beloved Tribune, Julius Schlegel, who saved the monks and possessions of the holy monastery of Monte Cassino, these monks of Cassino give their heartfelt thanks and pray to God for his future well-being.

Monte Cassino. In the month of November 1943.

Gregorius Diamare

Bishop and Abbot of Monte Cassino.

tion, the Vatican and the Commander-in-Chief, South, regarding the handing over of the treasures stored in Spoleto. Kesselring suggested that the archives and the pictures from the Naples exhibition should be transferred to the neutral territory of the Vatican and that the Cassino monks who had previously had charge of them should go with them. In this way, thanks to Kesselring, all these great treasures were finally brought to rest in a place of absolute safety. On the evening of 8 December the last lorry-loads from Spoleto were safely delivered in Rome. In the presence of the German Town Commandant, high officials of the Curia and the Italian State, they were formally handed over, and the Bishop of San Paolo thanked the German authorities, and in particular Lieutenant-Colonel Schlegel, for what they had done.

The manner in which these treasures had been brought to safety was an act of exemplary military discipline and civic consideration. The German soldier had shown that he was capable not only of fighting cleanly against his enemies, but also, when appealed to, of doing what he could to help his fellow men. Rarely, if ever before in the annals of war, can troops have been diverted from their lawful occasions or an officer have disinterestedly risked severe punishment in a more worthy cause.

Nevertheless, it was a long time before the world condescended to recognize and pay tribute to the work that had been done. It was not until Schlegel's articles appeared, supported by irrefutable proofs in the form of documents, photographs and letters of gratitude, that public interest was aroused; and then at last the truth, for so long buried beneath a mass of lies, distortions and calumnies, began slowly to emerge. In a series of Press articles—*The Times* published an article by Schlegel on 8 November 1951—and lectures by Schlegel himself, the truth about Cassino and the behaviour of the German troops became known throughout the world.

It was certainly high time that those malicious tongues should be silenced which, during and after the war, had deliberately and completely misrepresented and distorted the facts about Monte Cassino. Wartime propaganda is about as dirty a business as there is, and it is therefore no wonder that it seized upon Monte Cassino with eager avidity. Its object, of course, was to expunge the devastating effect that the destruction of the monastery had had on world opinion. The poison pens of the propagandists were by no means content with merely declaring that the Germans had misused the monastery for military purposes; they went a step further and asserted that Kesselring's troops had occupied and plundered the place with the thoroughness of the Huns of old. There must have been a number of guilty consciences, for it was not only the Press and radio which broadcast these untruths to the world; Allied military historians joined in the witch hunt. Norman Macmillan, the chronicler of the Royal Air Force, says: 'German propaganda asserts that the treasures of the monastery were saved and handed over to the Vatican authorities. But one statue was stolen from the altar and handed over to Göring, and of the 187 cases taken from the monastery fifteen were later missing, and a number of other valuable articles were stolen.'*

The same tune was played by the director of the Naples Museum who, in a broadcast in October 1943, trumpeted that the Naples collection of paintings, taken for safety to Monte Cassino, was now being looted by the German barbarians. Yet he is the one man above all others who can testify that not one of the paintings fell into unlawful hands and that all had been returned to adorn the galleries from which they had been loaned to Naples. But what, one may well ask, would have happened to these jewels of European culture had not the Germans saved them from the bombs that descended on their asylum?

It was, however, not only our enemies, but also some of our own people who slung mud at the rescuers of the Cassino treasures. Some boast that it was thanks to them alone that they had not been smuggled into Germany, others pointed the finger of scorn at the 'looters' and joined the ranks of those who libelled the defenders of Cassino. In the notorious London District Cage—the interrogation camp for German 'war criminals'— officers of the 1 Parachute Regiment were accused by their own countrymen of having looted Monte Cassino. These calumnies continued until Field-Marshal Alexander himself intervened and asserted that the Cassino treasures had been rescued and not looted by German troops.

The monks themselves had, of course, from the very outset borne witness to Schlegel's good work; and when he revisited the monastery for the first time in 1952 he was given an enthusiastic welcome. In Rome, too, he was received as an honoured guest by the Head of the Benedictine Order. It sounds like a malicious joke that this man who had done such splendid work should have been kept under lock and key for seven months as a suspected war criminal. Nor is that the end of the story. For years on end his property and possessions remained sequestrated, and a Communist, of all people, settled comfortably into Schlegel's house.

Thus we see a representative of the very Power, which we with justice regard as the arch-enemy of our European civilization, throwing out of his own home the man who saved some of the most cherished emblems of our Western culture. An injustice of this nature is food for thought. It is a symbol of how far this continent of ours is from achieving any semblance of solidarity. Surely it is time we realized that without Western solidarity our civilization stands in grave danger of destruction; and it is, perhaps, not too much to hope that the tragedy of Monte Cassino will remain as a warning of this danger and a mute appeal on behalf of reconciliation and peace.

* *The Royal Air Force in the World War*, Vol. 3.

Chapter 7

Monte Cassino—the Prologue

On 8 November, while the U.S. Fifth Army was assaulting the Reinhard Line, Alexander, at a conference at his headquarters, accepted Montgomery's plan for a break-through on the Adriatic sector. While the Fifth Army maintained its strong pressure on its own front, Montgomery intended to drive a deep wedge into the northern sector of the Gustav Line on a narrow front, break through to the 'Rome Line' and on to Pescara and Chieti. From there he proposed to wheel left along the Via Tiburtina (Highway No. 5) to Avezzano, in rear of the Cassino front, and threaten and perhaps capture Rome itself. Clark meanwhile would advance in the general direction of Frosinone, an important road junction some thirty miles behind the Gustav Line.

Montgomery proposed launching his attack on 20 November. But heavy rain, which brought snow in the Abruzzi Mountains, forced him to postpone the operation repeatedly, until at the end of the month the weather god relented and the Eighth Army was able to advance. It was nevertheless doubtful whether at this season of the year the favourable weather would last very long. This uncertainty had a very direct influence on Montgomery's plan, and his insistence on secure lines of supply greatly curtailed the scope of his operations. He himself says: '. . . the weather forced me to adopt a policy of advancing by short, methodical

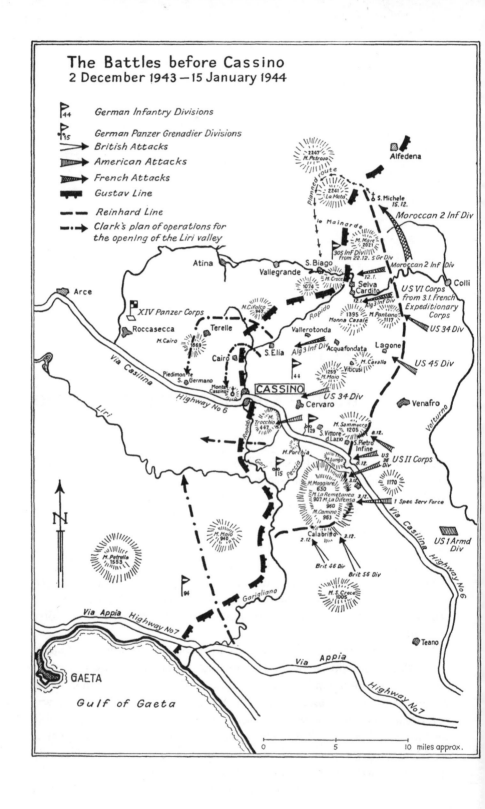

The Battles before Cassino
2 December 1943 — 15 January 1944

Legend:
- German Infantry Divisions
- German Panzer Grenadier Divisions
- British Attacks
- American Attacks
- French Attacks
- Gustav Line
- Reinhard Line
- Clark's plan of operations for the opening of the Liri valley

Alfedena

2247 M.Petroso

planned route

2241 La Meta

S. Michele 15.12.

Moroccan 2 Inf Div

le Mainarde

M. Mare 2021

305 Inf Div III from 22.12. 5 Gr Div

Moroccan 2 Inf Div

Colli

S. Biago

Atina

Vallegrande

M.Croce 1074

Selva Cardito

US VI Corps from 3.1. French Expeditionary Corps

Arce

XIV Panzer Corps

M.Cifalco

Rapido

12.1.

Alg 3 Inf Div

12.1.

M.Pantano 1117

US 34 Div

Roccasecca

Terelle

M.Cairo 1669

S. Elia

Vallerotonda

1395 Monna Casale

Acquafondata

Lagone

US 45 Div

Cairo

Alg 3 Inf Div

M. Cavallo

Viticusi

Piedimonte S. Germano

1259 M.Maio

US 34 Div

Venafro

Via Casilina

Highway No 6

Monte Cassino

44

CASSINO

Cervaro

M. Sammucro 1205

8.12.

Liri

M. Trocchio 447

Rapido

129

S.Vittore d.Lazio

S. Pietro Infine

US II Corps

Gari

15

Peccia

M.Porchia

US 36 Inf Div

8.12.

Volturno

M.Lungo

3.12.

1170

M.Maggiore 630 M.La Remetanea 907 M.La Difensa 960 M.Camino 963

3.12.

1 Spec Serv Force

US 1 Armd Div

N

M. Maio 940

Calabritto

2.12.

3.12.

M. Petrella 1553

Brit 46 Div

Brit 56 Div

94

Garigliana

M. S. Croce 1005

Teano

Via Appia   Highway No 7

GAETA

Via   Appia

Highway No 7

Gulf of Gaeta

0   5   10   miles approx.

stages, between which communications could be established and demolitions and obstacles overcome.'*

The attack against the lower Sangro was to be delivered by V Corps. The 78 and the Indian 8 Division were given the task of breaking into the Gustav Line on a narrow front and gaining possession of the Sangro heights. The focal points in this first phase would be the attack on the strongly fortified strongpoints of Mozzagrogno and Fossacesia. The second objective allotted to these divisions was the line Ortona–Lanciano, and their final objective was Pescara. On the Corps' left flank was the New Zealand 2 Division, which had arrived in October. Its task was to thrust towards Orsogna and Guardiagrele, drive back the right wing of the German 65 Infantry Division and then break through to Chieti and advance on Avezzano. As a subsidiary part of the plan, the XIII Corps was ordered to attack Alfedena and Castel del Sangro with the object of drawing and pinning down enemy forces, before the main attack on the lower Sangro was delivered.

Between the 9 and 15 November 78 Division had succeeded in establishing a narrow bridge-head across the lower Sangro, which, by 24 November, had enlarged to a width of some five and a half miles and a depth of one mile and a half. About the middle of the month XII Corps on the left flank delivered its subsidiary attack, capturing Alfedena on 24 November and holding it against numerous counter-attacks. By this time 4 Armoured Brigade had got about a hundred tanks across the river and installed them in 78 Division's bridge-head, into which the leading elements of the Indian 8 Division's attack now also moved. During the next few days, the weather cleared, and Montgomery fixed 28 November for the launching of the main attack. Nine regiments of light and three of medium artillery had been concentrated on the lower Sangro, and Coningham's bombers and fighters were standing ready to go into action.

As has been already mentioned, the defence of the Adriatic sector of the Gustav Line had been entrusted to the 65 Infantry Division. It was a newly raised division, equipped with horse-drawn transport and devoid of any experience of major operations. From the great Maiella massif to the coast it had a front of well over fifteen miles to defend. The right and middle sectors were in a good state of defence, but the coastal sector was less well found. Here the position was not organized in any great depth, and there were gaps in it which afforded excellent observation posts both up and down the river. Two days before the start of the British offensive Field-Marshal Kesselring had visited the division and had been very worried about this weakness on its left flank. By that time, however, it was too late to hand over the sector to the experienced 1 Parachute

* *El Alamein to the River Sangro.*

Division, as it had been the Field-Marshal's intention to do. The 20 Panzer Division, which was in position behind Ziehlberg's 65 Division, was also not yet available. General von Ziehlberg, however, was full of confidence about the future, but unfortunately the very first day of the battle was to show that his optimism had been misplaced.

On 27 November Air Marshal Coningham delivered his first air attack and gave 65 Division a severe hammering. His principal targets were the fortified localities and the artillery positions. All day long the inferno continued, giving Ziehlberg's troops their first taste of Montgomery's 'eggs'. The next day the air attack was resumed, supported this time by an artillery bombardment of a ferocity that these German troops had never experienced in their lives and left them breathless.

At 9.30 p.m. the first wave of the assault went in. The Indians captured Mozzagrogna in their initial onslaught, but were driven out again by a counter-attack. During the night they once again captured the village and held it. The 78 Division broke into the German position at Fossacesia, and by the morning of 29 November the New Zealanders had established a strong bridge-head north-west of the Sangro. The 78 Division mopped-up Fossacesia and was then ordered to advance on San Vito.

By the evening of 30 November the V Corps had reached the first of its objectives and the whole hogsback of the Sangro heights was in British hands. The German 65 Division had been completely shattered. More than a thousand of its men had been taken prisoner; General von Ziehlberg and the officer commanding the regiment on its left flank had both been severely wounded in the opening stages and had taken no further part in the battle. A huge gap had been blown in the German line, and the way to Pescara lay open.

Montgomery does not appear to have realized the chance that was being offered to him; in any case, he did not grasp it. He contented himself with ordering the 78 Division and the 4 Armoured Brigade to attack and capture San Vito and 'to send light forces towards Ortona'. When the Eighth Army Commander spoke of 'light forces' it was a sure sign that he had turned his attention from the front to his lines of communication. Two divisions had burst open the door to Pescara, and only the New Zealanders had as yet failed to reach their objectives, Orsogna and Guardiagrele. Yet, before even thinking of exploiting these unexpectedly great initial successes, Montgomery first ordered that bridges be built across the Sangro and then that the badly damaged roads be repaired and made passable for his supply columns, and by the time these tasks had been completed it was too late.

In the meanwhile the counter-measures taken by Tenth Army and the Commander-in-Chief, South, were in full swing. On 29 November the trusty 29 Panzer Division was withdrawn from its position in the Reinhard Line, where all was momentarily quiet, and put into the Adriatic sector. Despite the heavy attacks delivered against it as it hastened along the steep mountain roads, the Division's leading elements went into action against the Indian 8 Division on November 30 and drove the leading Gurkha battalion of the 17 Brigade back to Mozzagrogna. In this way the Germans were able to establish a strong position on the line Lanciano–Guardiagrele, which for weeks held the New Zealanders at bay.

A second barrier, held by the 90 Panzer Grenadier Division, which had reached the front from Sardinia via Corsica, was thrust forward in the coastal sector. It was only with considerable hesitation that the O.K.W. had released the Division, which had been in the Venice area and was being retained by Führer Headquarters as a general reserve. Its début was anything but fortunate. Initially it was sent into action piecemeal and far too hastily and achieved nothing. Nevertheless it succeeded in holding the sector until the middle of December, and it was not until then that the British X Corps broke through to Ortona. Then command was assumed by Colonel Baade, who had made a name for himself at the storming of Bir Hachim during the battle for Tobruk in the summer of 1942. 'He was an exceptionally capable commander,' comments Kesselring, 'who, like General Heidrich, proved equal to all the demands made of him.'

Finally, the southern flank of the German position was covered by two mountain battalions, which occupied the Maiella massif. The 3rd Battalion, 4 Parachute Regiment, reinforced the garrison of Ortona and greatly strengthened the German defences there. All was now ready for the second round.

Montgomery, however, made no move until 4 December. On that day the 78 Division and the 4 Armoured Brigade took San Vito, and the Indian Division captured Lanciano. But once again Montgomery halted the advance, this time on the Moro sector. He found himself faced with a compact, continuous front, which forced him to regroup the whole of his forces. He withdrew the 78 Division from the line and sent it into the mountains. The coastal sector was taken over by the Canadian 1 Division, and to the south of the Indian 8 Division he put in the 5 Division, together with Headquarters, XIII Corps, under whose orders the New Zealanders and the 5 Division were now placed.

As before, Montgomery's objectives were Pescara and Avezzano. The Canadians and 5 Division were ordered to establish a bridge-head across the River Pescara, while the New Zealanders were to take Chieti and from there advance against the rear of the Gustav Line. Montgomery was on tenterhooks. He had only a few weeks in which to attain his object before he was due to return to the United Kingdom at the end of the year. It is

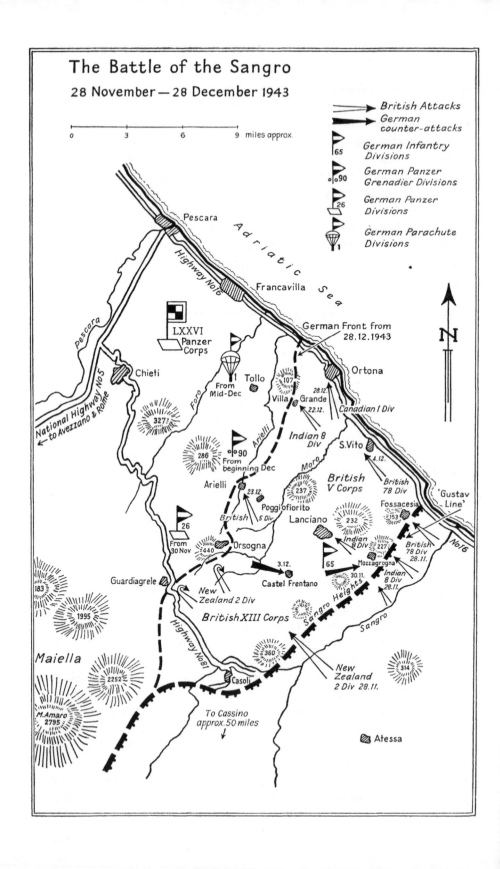

The Battle of the Sangro
28 November — 28 December 1943

British Attacks

German counter-attacks

65 — German Infantry Divisions

90 — German Panzer Grenadier Divisions

26 — German Panzer Divisions

1 — German Parachute Divisions

0   3   6   9 miles approx.

Adriatic Sea

Pescara

Highway No 16

Francavilla

Pescara

LXXVI Panzer Corps

German Front from 28.12.1943

Chieti

National Highway No 5 to Avezzano & Rome

Foro

1 From Mid-Dec

Tollo

Villa Grande

107

28.12.

22.12.

Ortona

Canadian I Div

327

Arielli

286

90 From beginning Dec

Indian 8 Div

S.Vito

4.12.

'Gustav Line'

Arielli

Moro

British V Corps

British 78 Div

26 From 30 Nov

23.12.

British 5 Div

Poggiofiorito

237

Lanciano

232

Fossacesia

153

Orsogna

440

65

Indian 8 Div

227

British 78 Div 28.11.

Guardiagrele

3.12.

Castel Frentano

Mozzagrogna

30.11.

Indian 8 Div 28.11.

No 16

183

New Zealand 2 Div

British XIII Corps

Sangro Heights

Sangro

1995

Highway No 81

360

Maiella

314

2252

Casoli

To Cassino approx. 50 miles

New Zealand 2 Div 28.11.

M.Amaro 2795

Atessa

N

said that at the beginning of the offensive he had promised his troops that they would celebrate Christmas in Rome. Now it was high time for him to keep his promise.

The third phase of the offensive was to be opened in the coastal sector by V Corps, which was ordered to threaten 26 Panzer Division's lines of communication and then help XIII Corps to capture Orsogna and Guardiagrele. The first objective was Ortona. Montgomery launched the Canadians against the town, situated close to the sea, and ordered the Indians to by-pass it to the south and seize Tollo.

On 10 December the Canadians at last crossed the River Moro. They heavily attacked 90 Panzer Grenadier Division, driving it back northwestwards and finally breaking into the German northern flank on 14 December. The 90 Division had been severely mauled and was no longer capable of holding the gap in the Adriatic sector. These were confused and turbulent days, when even Headquarters, LXXVI Corps, often did not know exactly where friend and foe stood. The fate of the German front was once more hanging by the proverbial thread, and there seemed to be no further possibility of quenching the fire at Ortona.

But the 'fire brigade' was on its way—the 3 Parachute Regiment, under its commander, Colonel Heilmann, who had been awarded the Oak Leaves to his Knight's Cross for gallantry in Sicily.

General Herr himself personally briefed Heilmann at Corps Battle Headquarters, but was not able to tell him whether the Canadians had yet captured Ortona or not. Battle Headquarters of 90 Division was in a worried state of mind, and the situation on its front seemed to be in a pretty average mess. At length, however, Heilmann received definite information that Ortona was still free of enemy, that the pioneers were busy constructing obstacles and that he would find the battle headquarters one of 90 Division's battalions south-west of the town.

Heilmann decided to make a personal reconnaissance and found that the information given to him by divisional headquarters had been correct. But for the battalion headquarters he searched in vain and eventually learnt that the battalion commander had been severely wounded and had been captured by the Canadians. While on reconnaissance Heilmann had suddenly found himself in the midst of a group of enemy tanks, which chased him all the way back to Ortona, but failed to put an unpleasant end to his 'Sunday picnic'. (This happened on Sunday, 15 December.) Heilmann's report to Panzer Corps Headquarters cleared up the situation. The left wing of 90 Division had ceased to exist, and Ortona lay unprotected at the Canadians' mercy.

Speed was now of primary importance. But General Vokes, the Canadian commander, was kind enough to do nothing for the next twenty-four hours, and during the night of 15/16 December the 2nd Battalion, 3 Parachute Regiment, commanded by Captain Liebscher, was able, under cover of darkness, to slip quietly into the sector of the lost position, into which no Canadian troops had penetrated. The next night the experiment was successfully repeated on the right flank, where Heilmann's 1st Battalion occupied the Villa Grande.

The paratroops arrived just in time, for on 18 December General Vokes set his Canadians in motion again with a concentrated attack on Ortona. Nine light and three medium regiments of artillery supported the assaulting brigades, which, reinforced by the Canadian 12 Armoured Regiment, fell upon the German paratroops. There followed two days of bitter and fluctuating fighting before the Canadians gained a foothold in the suburbs of Ortona on 20 December; but some considerable time was still to elapse before they captured the rest of the city.

Gradually, as its units were withdrawn and emerged battalion by battalion from the mountain sector, the whole of the 1 Parachute Division was advancing; and as each successive battalion arrived it at once went into action in 3 Parachute Regiment's sector.

The Indian 8 Division worked its way forward to the Villa Grande which barred the way to Tollo and in a furious onslaught overran this stubbornly defended strongpoint. But it was not until 23 December that the Essex Regiment of the Indian 17 Brigade forced its way into Tollo; even then the 1st Battalion of the 3 Parachute Regiment clung obstinately to the northern portion of the town, which by now was in complete ruins.

At Orsogna Montgomery was even less fortunate. Both this village on its high perch and the fiercely contested Guardiagrele remained firmly in German hands. Montgomery wrote: 'The opposition at Orsogna and Guardiagrele was still very sticky, for the two villages had been converted into major strongpoints, and their location on dominating ground made them very difficult to approach. The ground floors and cellars of the houses had been strengthened, and in them the enemy garrison withstood repeated air attacks.'* Four times the New Zealanders had advanced to the capture of Orsogna, and four times had they been bloodily repulsed. On 3 December they were thrown back as far as Castel Frentano by 26 Panzer Division's counter-attack. The second attempt on 7 December, supported by strong artillery and air forces, failed, as did also the third, the net result of which had been the capture of Poggiofiorito by the 5 Division, attacking on the New Zealanders' right. Despite these failures, XIII did not give up. On 23 December, supported by the whole of its own artillery and five of 5 Division's artillery regiments, it delivered its fourth attack against

* *El Alamein to the River Sangro.*

Orsogna and the German positions to the north of it, but yet again with very little success. Five Division captured Arielli, but Orsogna remained firmly in General von Lüttwitz's hands. It was only to the north-east of the town that the New Zealand 5 Brigade succeeded in penetrating into the German position; but to break through it proved beyond its powers. In these engagements the 26 Panzer Division fought magnificently and in a manner worthy of its high traditions.

The New Zealand 2 Division's offensive had been blessed with but little fortune. Since crossing the Sangro it had lost more than 1,600 men. The 26 Panzer Division had given the New Zealanders a sharp lesson and had left them in no doubt that in Italy the laurels of victory were far harder to gain than they had been in North Africa, where from El Alamein onwards the Germans had been facing hopeless odds. For these young men from the New Zealand farmsteads and for their commander, General Freyberg, Orsogna was a foretaste of what the German paratroops had in store for them at Cassino.

Ortona, the other tough nut, had also not been cracked, and the battle for it reached its climax on Christmas Eve. General Vokes, it seemed, was anxious to make Eighth Army Commander a present of the place for Christmas. During the afternoon of 24 December the German defenders were subjected to the heaviest artillery bombardment they had yet experienced. Instead of decorating their Christmas trees, they had to rush to arms, and they returned in good measure all the Christmas gifts that the Allied gunners loaded upon them.

At Villa Grande the 1st Battalion of the 3 Parachute Regiment bloodily repulsed the Indian 8 Division's attacks, but at Ortona the Canadians, after a bitter struggle through the ruined streets, succeeded in fighting their way step by step into the centre of the town. There the German pioneers had left innumerable cunningly designed booby-traps; the German artillery did its share in making things unpleasant, and what the pioneers and artillery failed to do was well and faithfully done by the 2nd Battalion of the 3 Parachute Regiment. Liebscher's battalion had served its apprenticeship in the house-to-house fighting in Centuripe; at Ortona it qualified as a master of its craft and was destined, twelve weeks later at Cassino, to pass its final examination *summa cum laude*.

The Canadians had been extremely surprised by the bitter resistance they had encountered at Ortona. Linklater says:

The noise of extensive demolitions in Ortona was heard by the Canadians as they approached the town, and the Loyal Edmonton and, later, the Seaforth of Canada were gravely obstructed by the high piles of debris that confronted them when they advanced on the only line that topography permitted. The outlying houses were strongly defended, and the solitary avenue of approach, deliberately left open, led to the main square of the town, into which a great number of automatic weapons, well sited in concealed and protected positions in the surrounding buildings, poured their fire. Anti-tank guns from positions close behind the barricades of rubble could fire at the bellies of the tanks climbing over the obstacles, and unoccupied houses had been cunningly prepared as booby-traps.

The two Canadian battalions, each on a front of about 1,250 yards, sought limited objectives and made slow progress from house to house. The fighting was particularly savage. On one occasion a whole platoon was killed when the house it occupied blew up; and immediately the Canadians withdrew from another house, which they had prepared with explosives and timed fuses, and a score of Germans, lured into it, lost their lives in a loud reprisal. For seven days there was bitter fighting for possession of the town, and not until 28 December did a patrol of Princess Patricia's Light Infantry break out of the ruins and move northwards on the coast road to make contact with the 48 Highlanders, who had been fighting across country west of the town.*

'It was our first big street-fighting battle,' comments Churchill, 'and from it many lessons were learned.'† But to judge from the subsequent Cassino battles, these lessons do not appear to have been assimilated, for with the great air attack of 15 March the Allies themselves barred their own way to Cassino and created there a heap of ruins very different to those at Ortona.

After evacuating the coastal town, the 1 Parachute Division retired to a previously prepared position some two miles in rear, at the same time setting about the task of re-forming its units, which had become confused and intermingled during the recent fighting. This it succeeded in doing, despite the proximity of the enemy, though one sector of the new position remained unoccupied for the whole of one day.

The Canadians had had enough. Their rifle companies had been reduced to a mere twenty or thirty men apiece, and they could do no more. The Indians and the New Zealanders had also fought themselves to a standstill, and Montgomery therefore had no option but to call off the attack.

Perilously and with a great deal of good fortune, LXXVI Panzer Corps had survived the first round, for at the decisive moment Montgomery had not the requisite forces available with which to complete its destruction. He had failed to crown his outstanding Mediterranean successes with the capture of Rome. In spite of his lavish material expenditure, his victorious Eighth Army had suffered a rebuff and had not succeeded in breaking the German front. In a month of hard fighting it had been able to advance a bare dozen miles—and its left wing, indeed, less than seven miles—from the Sangro; and Pescara, Avezzano and Rome seemed farther away than ever.

* *The Campaign in Italy.*   † *The Second World War*, Vol. V.

On 30 December Montgomery handed over command of the proud Eighth Army to Lieutenant-General Sir Oliver Leese. From the landing-strip on the Sangro 'Monty' set out on his flight to the United Kingdom, where, as Commander-in-Chief of 21 Army Group, he was to play a vital part in the preparation and carrying-out of the cross-Channel invasion.

Sir Oliver Leese showed no interest in Pescara and Avezzano, but turned towards Monte Cassino, the irresistible magnet of the Italian theatre of war. Consequently it was not the U.S. Fifth Army but the British Eighth—though not British or Commonwealth troops—that eventually completed the capture of St Benedict's Mount. It was finally captured by General Anders and his Poles; and how shabbily did Great Britain reward their feat of arms!

Scarcely had Montgomery made his first move across the lower Sangro than Clark struck once again against the Reinhard Line. During the two weeks' pause since the previous assault, his army had been considerably reinforced. He had, it is true, been forced to surrender the British 7 Armoured Brigade and the U.S. 82 Airborne Division (less the 504 Regiment) to Overlord, but replacements had more than filled the gap. The U.S. Corps under General Keyes, who had made a name for himself in western Sicily, had been brought across, and from overseas had come the 1 Special Service Force, consisting of three mixed Canadian and American brigades specially trained in mountain warfare, and the U.S. 1 Armoured Division; and at the end of October General Dapino and the Italian 1 Mechanized Brigade, some 5,000 strong, also joined Fifth Army. These were the first Italian troops to go into action against the Germans. In addition Clark had been promised the Moroccan 2 Infantry Division, which was due to arrive early in December and take over a sector of the right wing of the army.

Thus for Operation 'Raincoat', as the operations for the opening-up of the Liri valley had most appropriately been named, Clark had approximately eight divisions at his disposal. The British IX Corps, consisting of the 46 and 56 Divisions under McCreery, was still in the coastal sector. To its north was the U.S. II Corps, Keyes, consisting of 36 Division with 1 Special Service Force under command and the 3 Division. The Army's right sector was formed by U.S. VI Corps made up of 43 and 34 Divisions under General Lucas. The Italian contingent was placed under the command of II Corps.

XIV Panzer Corps was also preparing for battle. It could not hope for very much in the way of reinforcements, and all that General von Senger had in reserve were a few battalions of the Hermann Göring Division, and these could not make good the weakening of the Corps' sector that had resulted from the transfer of 26 Panzer Division to the Adriatic front.

The sector previously held by 26 Division was taken over by the 44 Hoch und Deutschmeister Infantry Division. The old 44th had been decimated at Stalingrad, and the newly raised division had arrived in Italy immediately after Mussolini's fall. Like the 65, 94 and 306 Infantry Divisions, its transport was horse-drawn—a great disadvantage in action against a highly mechanized and well-armed enemy. Furthermore, it had had no training in mountain warfare, an omission which became glaringly apparent in its handling of its artillery and the arrangements it made for getting supplies to its troops in the front line. The task allotted to the Division was no easy one. It had not been in action before and had never had the experience of being subjected either to carpet bombing from the air or a concentrated artillery barrage. The coming battle was certain to be a severe test, for there was little likelihood that the Fifth Army would by-pass the high ground, since the road from Venairo to Santa Elia Fiumerapido, north of Cassino, passed through the middle of the division's sector, and the enemy would certainly wish to secure that important mountain road.

The rugged heights of the Abruzzi Mountains were essentially terrain which demanded the employment of specialized mountain divisions. Such divisions existed, of course, but they were all fighting on the plains of Russia—they could, in any case, hardly have been kept 'in cold storage' until the war had spread to the mountains of southern Italy. But to transfer them now from the eastern front was an almost impossible task. For one thing, available transport was already strained to the limit, and for another, any attempt at large-scale transfer to Italy was tantamount to an invitation to the enemy air arm. As a rule, major movements to the Italian front had to be halted far away in the north, whence the troops proceeded in 'penny packets' southwards and were also generally thrown in penny packets into battle—with disastrous results.

This is exactly what happened to General Ringel's 5 Mountain Division. The Division had for a long time been on the broad plains of the northern sector of the Eastern Front on Lake Ladoga and, as subsequently transpired, had long since forgotten all it had ever known about mountain warfare. It was due to arrive in Italy in the middle of December, and the Corps Commander had decided that it should relieve the 305 Infantry Division on the Corps' left flank. For there, astride the important Colli–Atina road, it would be in real mountain country, a tangle of precipitous, trackless and snow-clad peaks, round which an icy wind whistled. On the extreme left of XIV Panzer Corps' sector, the Abruzzi range was dominated by the 7,000-foot peaks of Monte Petroso and Monte La Meta; to the south was the Mainarde plateau with its commanding peaks, Monte Mare (6,200 feet) and Monte Marone (5,800 feet). Even Monte Pantano, south of the Colli–Atina road, was well over 3,000 feet high. In this sort of country, only specialized troops could hope to stand up to the highly trained and experienced mountain divisions which General Clark would launch against them.

These were the only changes envisaged in the Reinhard Line. On the right flank, as before, was the 94 Infantry Division; the 15 and 29 Panzer Grenadier Divisions still occupied the key positions leading into the Liri valley, against which the main assault would undoubtedly be launched and where Monte Camino, Monte Lingo and Monte Sammucro held the Via Casilina in a tight grip.

The defence of the Monte Camino massif and its subsidiary spurs, Monte La Defensa, La Remantanea and Maggiore, was entrusted to 104 Panzer Grenadier Regiment of the 15 Division; Monte Lungo was held by 15 Panzer Grenadier Regiment, and the lofty San Pietro Infine and the Sammucro massif by the 71 Panzer Grenadier Regiment—both belonging to the 29 Panzer Grenadier Division. The peak itself of Monte Sammucro (3,800 feet) was occupied by 11 Regiment's 2nd Battalion. Here these three regiments fought a series of engagements as hard as any that had preceded them in the Italian campaign, engagements in which the Allied material expenditure reached an unprecedented height and which in bitterness and the demands they made on the troops were in every way comparable to the struggle for Monte Cassino itself. It took the Fifth Army fourteen days to break through the Mignano defile; four further weeks elapsed before it captured Monte Trocchio, the spring-board into the Liri valley; and it was not until 24 January that General Ryder, an old veteran thruster from the First War, was able to knock at the door of Monte Cassino. But the German doorkeepers kept them tightly locked, and even when General Eaker pulverized the little town, they still remained where they were.

Clark's plan of attack envisaged three phases. He intended to deliver his first blow against the Monte Camino massif, employing the British X and the U.S. II Corps. When this barrier had been burst asunder, II Corps were to attack and take Monte Sammucro. In conjunction with this attack the U.S. VI Corps was to thrust westward astride the Colli–Atina road. The third phase was to be a continuation of the advance through the Liri valley and the capture of Frosinone. By that time, it was thought, Montgomery's offensive might perhaps have won the decisive battle for Rome— or that, at least, was what was hoped!

To divert attention from the main attack and draw German troops away from the Via Casilina and into the coastal sector, the Allied fleet was to steam into the Gulf of Gaeta, where the British 23 Armoured Brigade would deliver a feint attack against the lower Garigliano. General von Senger, however, was not taken in by this ruse.

On the night of 1/2 December Clark opened the flood-gates. The first wave surged towards Calabritto, which the British 46 Division captured after a sharp engagement. A few hours later, at 4.30 p.m. on 2 December, a veritable torrent of shells descended on the Monte Camino massif. Nine hundred and twenty-five guns of all calibres up to and including g·4s bombarded the German positions on Monte Camino, La Defensa, La Rementanea and Maggiore. Eight hundred and twenty of them concentrated their fire on the 104 Panzer Grenadier Regiment, holding the slopes of Monte Camino. This was the greatest concentration of artillery fire that had yet been seen in the Italian campaign. For ten hours the Allied gunners threw everything they had at the Germans. In the first two days of the battle they fired 207,000 shells on the Monte Camino massif alone— 4,066 tons of metal or about 270 railway waggon loads, indeed an imposing visiting card from the American armament industry.

In the dark, early hours of 3 December, the whole of the British 56 Division, the 136 Brigade of 46 Division, supported by 40 Armoured Regiment, advanced from the south to the attack on Monte Camino. At the same time the U.S. Rangers and the 1 Special Service Force launched an assault from the east against the massif and before daylight came captured Monte La Defensa and pressed on to Monte Rementanea. To the north of them the U.S. 142 Infantry Regiment of the 36 Division stormed Monte Maggiore. For some days a fluctuating battle raged. Attack and counter-attack followed each other in swift succession. Individual battalions of the Hermann Göring Division tried in vain to drive back the enemy. But they did at least succeed in bringing the spearhead of the attack on Monte Maggiore to a halt.

The summit of Monte Camino was held by a weak battalion of the 104 Panzer Grenadiers. For several days, under continuous and heavy artillery fire, the battalion heroically stood firm and repulsed all attacks until 6 December, when the summit was finally lost. For some hours afterwards, messages from positions on the reverse slopes of the mountain reported that the battalion was still holding the summit. It was only when a patrol went forward that the truth became known. The men visible on the summit were corpses, and not a single Grenadier remained alive.

On December Monte Maggiore at last fell to the Americans, and the defenders retired to the Peccia sector. A thrust by the 46 Division south of Monte Camino, however, placed the left wing of 129 Panzer Grenadier Regiment in deadly danger. An orderly withdrawal across the Garigliano was not possible, for the flood waters had washed away all the bridges. At the last possible moment, however, the O.K.W. gave permission for the regiment to retire, and although it managed to escape, it lost all its heavy weapons. The gentlemen in Rastenberg obviously found it easier than did

General Senger's Battle Headquarters at Rocasecca to decide whether or not an exhausted regiment should be permitted to withdraw a short distance!

Monte Lungo, San Pietro and Monte Sammucro nevertheless remained in German hands. In this sector it was not until 8 December that U.S. II Corps launched its attack. The Italian contingent was detailed to participate in the attack on Monte Lungo. But when its reconnaissance section reached II Corps' assembly area, the G.I.s of the 142 Regiment, who had never before seen an Italian uniform, took them prisoner as a precautionary measure. The Italians' first assault on 8 December was a fiasco and was repulsed by 15 Panzer Grenadiers with heavy casualties. The attack by the U.S. 143 Regiment, delivered the same day against San Pietro also failed to reach its objective. For the moment, at least, the U.S. 36 Division could win no laurels at Monte Lungo. Fifteen Panzer Grenadier Regiment defended stubbornly and its 2nd Battalion was mentioned in dispatches; and it was not until 16 December, after a heavy artillery bombardment, that the Americans and Italians stormed and captured the mountain.

On the same day Monte Sammucro also fell. The 3,800-foot mountain was the key point of the Reinhard Line. Whoever held it had an uninterrupted view to Cassino and into the valleys of the Liri and the Rapido. For days the men of the 141 and 143 Infantry Regiments and the paratroops of 504 Parachute Regiment had stormed against this bulwark, so stubbornly defended by 71 Panzer Grenadier Regiment. The attackers suffered heavy casualties. The 1st Battalion of the 143 Regiment lost two-thirds of its strength, the 2nd Battalion of the 141 could only muster 130 men after its unsuccessful attack on San Pietro. And this was against a German regiment which had been engaged almost without pause since Sicily, which, like the whole of Fries's Division, had always been thrown in where the fighting was fiercest, and the companies of which had been reduced to a handful of emaciated, bearded, but broken men. Great honour is due to them all and to none more than the defenders of the summit of Monte Sammucro.

The following extract from his book reflects the high opinion which Field-Marshal Kesselring held of the fighting qualities of the 29 Panzer Grenadier Division:

I well remember the somewhat apologetic report given to me at his battle headquarters by one of my most able divisional commanders, General Fries of the 29 Panzer Grenadier Division, in which he described his untenable position (which he continued nevertheless most firmly to hold). His exhausted companies, he told me, were facing two enemy divisions, both of which were being frequently relieved; the Allied divisions were nearly twice as strong as ours, while their artillery and its fantastically abundant supply of ammunition was in the ratio of ten to one against us. Getting it frankly off his chest to his Commander-in-Chief was obviously a great relief to Fries. With a smile I told him that though I was only a Bavarian, I would like to remind him, a Prussian, that the Prussians never asked how strong the enemy was, but only where he was to be found. . . . The fact that Army Group in mid-December had entrusted to his division so momentous a task as the holding of Monte Lingo was not only a tribute to the men and their leaders, but also a correct appreciation of the opponents they were facing.*

And, indeed, the 29 Division seemed to be indestructible. Until 11 January it was continuously in the forefront of the Cassino battle; and ten days later it launched a counter-attack which brought British X Corps' offensive on the Garigliano to a halt and put an end to the danger threatening the Cassino front from that direction.

After the loss of Monte Lungo and Monte Sammucro, General von Senger could see no reason for trying to continue to hold San Pietro Infine, where the 71 Regiment had already repulsed three heavy attacks. On the night of 17 December, after a violent counter-attack near San Pietro and directed primarily against the 3rd Battalion of the 143 Regiment, which suffered heavy casualties, Fries's Division disengaged from the enemy.

General Keyes, commanding II Corps, pursued closely on the heels of the Grenadiers. Slowly his divisions fought their way forward to San Vittore del Lazio, to Cervaro and to Monte Trocchio, the last barrier before Cassino.

On the left flank of XIV Panzer Corps the American attack had now also assumed threatening proportions. The battle for the Via Casilina was only one part of the Fifth Army's planned operations. While II Corps was advancing slowly towards Cassino, VI Corps was first to clear the way into the Rapido valley and then exert leverage north of Cassino. An advance of this nature, diagonally through the mountains to the Colli–Atina road would have enabled the Allies to break through the Gustav Line north of Cassino.

It is obvious that VI Corps' offensive had been planned by the Fifth Commander simply as an attack in support of the British Eighth Army and had therefore not been adequately prepared to stand any chance of success. The failure of this enterprise, which was vainly continued in January by the French Expeditionary Corps, had grave consequences. The Fifth Army refrained from turning the flank of XIV Panzer Corps and contented itself with a series of fruitless frontal attacks against Cassino, until Alexander, after the second battle of Cassino, decided after all to prise open the gateway to Rome by means of a turning movement. But it had required two heavy defeats to make the enemy realize that there was no need to

* *Soldat bis zum letzten Tag.*

charge head-on at the wall, when one could get into the house by the side door.

Thus, from the very outset, the operations of VI Corps were under an unlucky star. In the first week in December General Lucas had set his divisions on the move. The 34 Division attacked Monte Pantano, which was held by the 577 Grenadier Regiment of the 305 Infantry Division, but after days of heavy fighting and the loss of 800 men, it had advanced less than two miles. The 46 Division crossed swords with the Hoch und Deutschmeister on Height 769, but without any marked success. The situation changed, however, in the second week of December, when the Moroccan 2 Infantry Division arrived in VI Corps' sector.

The decision that the French Expeditionary Corps should participate in the Italian campaign had been taken before the Salerno landing. But for psychological reasons it had been agreed that the Corps should not be landed until Naples had been taken. In the middle of October General Dody concentrated his 2 Moroccan Infantry Division in the Bizerta–Oran area; the main body of the Division embarked on 17 November and on 25 November disembarkation in Naples began. Two days later General Juin established the headquarters of the Corps Expéditionaire Français in the Institut Français in Naples.

The French Corps was ideally suited for the conditions in the Italian theatre of war. The tough, North African hillmen were always a thorn in the flesh of the German divisions and frequently caused Field-Marshal Kesselring very grave anxiety. In the first battle of Cassino they came within an ace of capturing the monastery; and in May 1944 they it was who in their final assault on the Cassino front reached the goal for which Alexander had been striving for months and for which so much blood had been shed— the Liri valley.

On 7 December the Moroccan 2 Division began to relieve the U.S. 34 Division, and on 12 December General Dody assumed command of the sector astride the Colli–Atino road. Three days later the Moroccans went into action. Their first objective was San Biago Saracinisco, which formed part of the Gustav Line. Experienced mountaineers that they were, the Moroccans had no intention, in this difficult terrain, of running their heads against the wall by delivering a frontal attack, but chose instead to execute an outflanking movement. Attacking northwards the 4 and 8 Moroccan Rifle Regiments broke through to Michele, but a German counter-attack on 16 December drove them back. On 18 December the Goumiers tried their luck again, but their ammunition gave out, and the attack failed.

General Lucas had no use for tactics of this kind. He called off the French turning movement and put in a frontal attack against the 305 Infantry Division. He was encouraged to do this by the fact that on 17

December the 5 Moroccan Rifle Regiment had captured the Pantano massif and advanced as far as the northern slopes on Monte Casale.

At the same time the U.S. 45 Division took the mountain village of Lagone and pressed forward to Monte Cavallo, half-way between Venafro and Sant' Elia. There they encountered the leading companies of the 5 Mountain Division, which was about to take over the sector from the 305 Division.

The 5 Mountain Division under the command of General Ringel, an officer of the old Imperial German Army, had fought side by side with the paratroops in Crete; now they were to renew this old acquaintance at Cassino, but not, this time, in offensive operations, but in defence against an enemy who had long since recovered from the blows suffered during the early years of the war. Even so, the Division, and particularly its 85 Regiment, did not make a very auspicious start in the fighting astride the Colli–Atina road. It had not appreciated the conditions under which it was now being called upon to fight and was unable overnight to readjust itself to them. It had come as an unpleasant surprise to find in the 'sunny South' a climate which, with its snowstorms, its incessant rain and its icy winter nights, was as unpleasant as anything that the eastern Front had had to offer.

It is therefore not surprising that Ringel's Division in its first encounters and in the over-hasty manner in which it was called upon to relieve the 305 Infantry Division suffered a number of sharp reverses. As each battalion arrived it was thrown at once into battle, often without its proper complement of pack animals—a shortsighted policy which had dire consequences.

General Ringel assumed command of his new sector on December 22. Dody, who had been maintaining his pressure on the whole front, increased it very considerably on 26 December, when he sent in the 8 Moroccan Regiment to attack the Mainarde, where the 100 Mountain Regiment just managed to hold on to its position, thanks to a timely counter-attack delivered by the 115 Panzer Grenadier Regiment. The next day, however, the Moroccans again attacked, with strong artillery support, and this time they captured the position. The fighting continued till the end of the month, but still General Dody had not succeeded in breaking through to his objective, San Biago.

The Hoch und Deutschmeister Division had also been roughly handled. The U.S. 45 Division, advancing westwards without pause and driving the Germans before it, captured the commanding height of Monte Cavallo on 22 December and then pressed on towards Viticuso.

At the end of December Middleton's Division was withdrawn from the line, and its place was taken by 30 Division. The 45 Division had been withdrawn to take part in operations designed to bring about the collapse of the Gustav Line and the capture of Rome by the shortest possible route—a landing at Anzio–Nettuno.

On 30 December the British No. 9 Commando landed from the sea in rear of the German outpost line on the lower reaches of the Garigliano, and at the same time the 201 Guards Brigade delivered a frontal attack on the river's mouth. The British took a handful of prisoners, but failed to gain any ground.

A heavy snow storm on New Year's Eve, which cut off the positions and roads in the Abruzzi Mountains from the rest of the world, now brought operations for the time being to a standstill on the whole front.

It was not until the 4 January that the U.S. II Corps—less 3 Division, which had been withdrawn for the Anzio landing—resumed its attack astride the Via Casilina. On the Corps' right flank the 1 Special Service Force advanced to the assault on Viticuso and Monte Maio,* while the 34 Division attacked Cervaro and San Vittore. Behind them was the U.S. 1 Armoured Division ready to break out as soon as the Stars and Stripes were planted on Monte Trocchio.

On 5 January, after heavy fighting, the 29 Panzer Grenadier Division was forced by the 135 Infantry Regiment to vacate San Vittore. The next day an armoured Combat Group broke into the German positions on Monte Porchia, and though a battalion of the Hermann Göring Division drove the Americans out again, it could not prevent the enemy from finally gaining possession of this important feature (7 January).

In the Cervaro area General Ryder made a clean sweep. After the capture of Viticuso the 1 Special Service Force drove the 132 Panzer Grenadier Regiment off Monte Maio and pushed the 'High and Mighties' back to the high ground north of Cervaro. It was only with the greatest difficulty that the greatly weakened 44 Division managed to hold its own in this confused engagement. Ryder pressed on vigorously. His troops drove the Vienna Grenadiers over Monte Aquilone to Monte Capraro and from there back to Cervaro. On 11 January the U.S. 168 Infantry Regiment fought its way into the completely devastated town and established itself in the ruins.

Now the time had come to occupy the Gustav Line, if the Germans were to get there before the Americans. The 29 Panzer Grenadier Division was withdrawn for a long overdue rest and transferred to the coastal sector on either side of Ostia. The Hoch und Deutschmeisters now took over the whole line between the 15 Panzer Grenadier and the 5 Mountain Divisions, and on the 13 January retired to the Gustav Line.

On 15 January the U.S. 135 Infantry Regiment captured the heavily defended Monte Trocchio—the bare, commanding height a mile and a half

* Not to be confused with the mountain of the same name in the Liri valley.

in front of Cassino, on which, in the months ahead, the Forward Observing Officers of the artillery and the Air Force Liaison Officers of the Fifth and, later, the Eighth Armies were to establish their observation posts.

Since the 12 January fighting had again flared up on XIV Corps' northern front, where General Juin was aiming his hammer-blows directly at the Gustav Line. At the end of December the French Corps had been reinforced by the Algerian 3 Infantry Division under General de Monsabert, and on 3 January General Juin had assumed command of the sector previously held by the U.S. II Corps, which was to launch the amphibious attack against the German flank at Anzio.

The battle for the Gustav Line opened with heavy air attacks on the German airfields and lines of communication in central and upper Italy, in the course of which the railway stations of Florence, Pisa, Arezzo and Terni were very severely damaged. The French attack started at 6.30 a.m. on the morning of 12 January. The Moroccan Division, hoping to catch the 85 Mountain Regiment by surprise, launched its attack north of the Colli–Atina road without any preliminary artillery bombardment. The Algerian Division, after a short, intensive artillery barrage of fifteen minutes' duration, advanced against the 4,300-foot Monte Casale, which towering above the upper Rapido valley, dominates Vallerotonda, Aqua-fondata and Santa Elia and gives a clear view of the steeply rising Cairo massif. Juin's main objective was Atina, which he regarded as the key to the whole Cassino problem. The place, admittedly, offered no tactical base for an advance on Rome, but once it was in French hands, the way to the rear of the Cassino front would be open and the scene set for a turning move-ment against the Gustav Line. Firstly, however, Monte Santa Croce to the south of Biago, Monte Casale, Vallerotonda, Aquafondata and Sant' Elia and the entrance into the Belmote valley all had to be captured.

The Moroccan Division took Cardita and Selva, where, according to French reports, the German pioneer officer responsible led them safely through the minefields, but were held up before Monte Santa Croce, which the Moroccan 5 Rifle Regiment then attacked incessantly, in vain and with severe losses, for twelve days on end.

The Algerian Division had an easier passage. At 5 p.m. on 12 January its 7 Rifle Regiment reached the crest of Monte Casale. Its leading battalion, however, suffered such severe casualties in the final assault that it had to be re-lieved forthwith. One after the other Aquafondata and Sant' Elia fell into their hands. The Algerians nevertheless pressed on at the German's heels; and on 16 January they reached the Rapido, which they crossed on 20 January.

The Moroccans meanwhile were still striving hard to capture Monte San Croce. But against the stubborn defence of the 8, 115 and 578 Grena-dier Regiments they failed to achieve their object. Again and again they obtained a foothold on the lower slopes of the mountain, only to be thrown back by counter-attacks. On 24 January the Moroccan Division called off its attack and went over to the defensive, leaving the mountain still firmly in German hands.

Up to 20 January Juin had adhered to his intention of advancing astride the San Biagio–Vallegrande road and breaking through to Atina. But the latest developments now demanded new measures. On the southern flank of XIV Panzer Corps, McCreery had created an extremely dangerous situation, and the Anzio landing had begun. The break-through into the Liri valley nevertheless remained problematical—at least for as long as Monte Cassino remained in German hands. The Fifth Army therefore planned a new manœuvre to get round this bulwark. U.S. 34 Division was ordered to attack north of Cassino and capture the monastery hill from the north. To the French Corps Clark gave the task of wheeling south-westward and capturing Terelle, whence it was to attack Piedimonte San Germano and thus get in rear of Cassino town and the mountain defences. This operation, which was the salient feature of the first Cassino battle, opened on the evening of 17 January with a general offensive by the British X Corps against the 94 Infantry Division.

Notwithstanding the numerical and material superiority it enjoyed, it had taken the Fifth Army two and a half months to break through the Reinhard Line and in eleven weeks it had advanced only twelve miles. Its losses had been heavy. Clark put his casualties at 15,864 dead, wounded and missing. XIV Corps, too, had suffered severely; its divisions had fought on till they were bled white; under the most difficult conditions they had stood firm in the face of every assault that the enemy had launched against them, and in spite of the hitherto unparalleled artillery fire to which they had been subjected, in spite of snow, rain and icy winds; where failures had occurred, they had been due primarily to lack of battle experience, to over-hasty commitment to battle and to unfamiliarity with the conditions prevailing in the Italian theatre of war. But the fighting spirit of the troops had remained excellent. In his New Year Order of the Day Field-Marshal Kesselring pays tribute to this spirit in the following terms:

The fateful year of 1943, the fourth year of war, has ended. Despite his lavish use of American, British and French forces, the enemy has not succeeded in destroying the German armies in the Mediterranean area. Eisenhower's and Montgomery's hopes have been thwarted, because we have survived all the hardships of mountain warfare and have risen superior to both the physical and moral effects of the heaviest possible artillery bombardments and air attacks. For this I give you my thanks. Your soldierly bearing in battle, the stead-fastness of your morale and the skill of your leaders will continue to thwart every enemy attempt to destroy us. . . .

The gallantry displayed by the Allies is worthy of equal praise. The veterans of the British X Corps had fought as they had done in Africa and at Salerno. The new U.S. divisions had put their teething troubles behind them; they were no longer the green G.I.s who had dropped everything and run when Rommel had attacked them at Kasserine. The American troops in the forefront of the Cassino battle had fought with the greatest possible determination and recovered from numerous reverses in a manner that had exceeded all expectation.

It was at this stage of the war that the Germans revised their opinions regarding the American soldier. Hitler's opinion of the United States Army was based on Rommel's first encounter with it in Tunisia:

Both Hitler and the German Command in the West were gravely at fault in their estimate of American strength and skill. The High Command was contemptuous because the American Army had such a small professional core and so little military tradition or experience, but Hitler's scorn had a different source. 'In assessing the military value of the Americans,' says Speer, 'Hitler always argued that they were not a tough people, not a closely-knit nation in the European sense. If put to the test, they would prove to be poor fighters.' Hitler had learnt nothing since the Tunisian campaign, when he readily accepted the report by one of his entourage, Sonderfuehrer von Neurath, that the American troops were 'a shocking crowd.' According to Neurath, who said he had been interrogating hundreds of American prisoners, 'Most of them have come over to make money, or for adventure, or to see something new, to be in something exciting for once. Not one of them has a political opinion or a great ideal. They are "rowdies" who quickly turn and run; they could not stand up to a crisis.' When this was reported to him, Hitler commented: 'America will never become the Rome of the future. Rome was a state of peasants'.

The Americans were not peasants: therefore they could not be tough; their armies could not have that deep, inner fortitude which the dumb but staunch peasantry had always provided in the mass armies of the Continental powers. To Hitler it was as simple as that. He did not realize that America's strength lay in the very absence of the 'peasant mentality', with its narrow horizons, its acceptance of the established order and its ignorance of machines. The basic German miscalculation was the failure to appreciate that America's military prowess was a logical consequence of her industrial power. The Germans learnt by experience that this power had given the Americans boundless equipment, but they did not realize that it had also provided a vast reservoir of manpower skilled in the use of machines.*

It was not for nothing that among the Americans in Italy the saying went round: 'It takes twenty years to make a man and a few hours to make a machine; so—let's get busy on the machines!' In the Abruzzi Mountains,

* Chester Wilmot, *The Struggle for Europe.*

however, machines alone were of little avail; there the most important factor was the infantryman. And in the preliminary battles before Cassino the American infantryman had fought with courage, skill and determination. Bulwarks like Monte Sammucro cannot be captured by artillery alone, and still less with the aid of tanks. Here the issue lay between man and man.

The greatest surprise, however, was the fighting spirit shown by the French Expeditionary Corps. The 1940 campaign had cast a sombre shadow over the French Army, and no one believed that it would ever recover from the devastating defeat that had been inflicted on it. But now General Juin's divisions were proving to be most dangerous customers. Nor was this attributable solely to the Algerians' and Moroccans' experience in mountain warfare. Three factors combined to mould these troops into a dangerously efficient fighting force: the mountain warfare experience of the French colonial troops, the ultra-modern American armaments with which they had been equipped, and the fact that they were led by French officers who were masters of the profession of arms. With these three basic elements Juin had moulded a formidable entity. In the battles that followed, the Corps proved equal to every demand made of it, and Field-Marshal Kesselring himself assured the author that he was always very uneasy about any sector of the front on which the French popped up.

Had Clark given more heed to Juin's views in the Cassino battles and accepted his plan of thrusting via Atina into the Liri valley, the three savage battles of Cassino would probably never have been fought and the venerable House of St Benedict would have been left unscathed. But Juin's contribution to the force was, numerically, comparatively minor, and his influence in the council chamber, during the first few weeks at any rate, was proportionately small. It was only after he had achieved some undeniably great successes that more attention was paid to his views. But by that time the fat was already in the fire; on the evening of 17 January, when the British X Corps crossed the Garigliano, the deadly juggernaut was set in motion against Cassino. This was the beginning of the first Cassino battle.

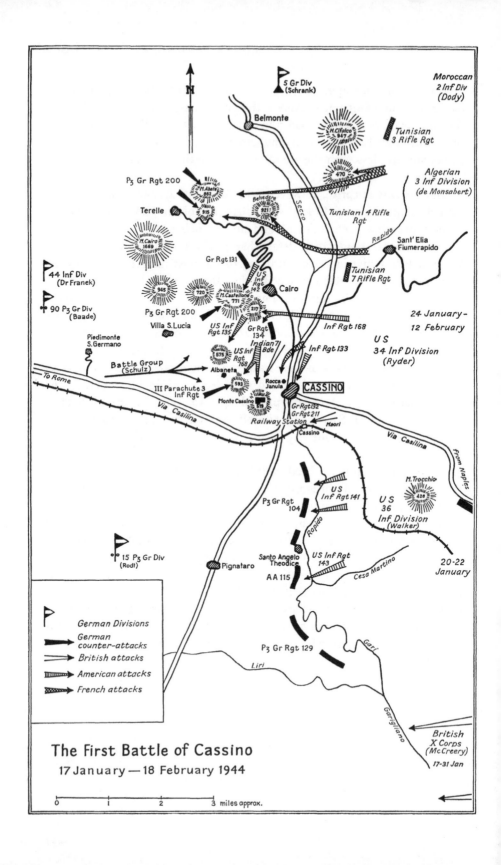

The First Battle of Cassino
17 January — 18 February 1944

German Divisions
German counter-attacks
British attacks
American attacks
French attacks

Chapter 8

The First Cassino Battle

More than four months had passed since the Salerno landing, and there was still no clear indication of when, at long last, the Allies would win the great prize of Rome. In fact, their most formidable task—the breaking of the Gustav Line—still awaited them; and when they decided to make their main effort against the strongest sector of the line, on either side of Cassino, it was obvious that they were about to engage in a battle which would far overshadow all the hard fighting on the Volturno, the Reinhard Line and the Sangro.

The salient feature of these bloody battles was the struggle for the possession of Monte Cassino. Millions of shells, thousands of tons of bombs had to be expended before a breach was blown through which the Allies could stream to the Italian capital. Thousands of German soldiers, whole legions of allied soldiers of some fifteen nations were to lay down their lives in the struggle for the 'gateway to Rome'. Cassino was the Verdun of the Second World War. Mark Clark wrote: 'The battle of Cassino was the most gruelling, the most harrowing, and in one respect perhaps the most tragic, of any phase of the war in Italy. When I think back on the weeks and finally months of searing struggle, the biting cold, the torrents of rain and snow, the lakes of mud that sucked down machines and men, and, most of all, the deeply dug fortifications in which the Germans waited for us in the hills, it seems to me that no soldiers in history were given a more difficult assignment than the Fifth Army in that winter of 1944.'*

Yet the task which confronted the German divisions was even harder. They found themselves face to face with an enemy who lacked for nothing, whose resources were inexhaustible, who had thrown immense material power into the scales and who had undisputed command of the air, not only in the battle area, but in the whole theatre of war. Despite the preceding battles, the Allied forces had by no means been decimated; their formations were constantly being relieved, transferred for a rest to a quieter sector or reinforced by new arrivals. For the majority of the German formations things were very different. No sooner had they quenched the fire on one sector of the front than they were thrown into battle somewhere else; scarcely had they enjoyed a day or so of rest than they were rushed off to oppose some threatened break-through. The 29 and 90 Panzer Grenadier Divisions, the 26 Panzer and the 1 Parachute Divisions were 'fire brigades' in the truest sense of the word. These were the divisions which, decimated and with their battalions reduced to company strength, time and again thwarted the Allied hopes. In Italy, as in Russia, it was not possible regularly to relieve and rest the formations holding the front line, as had been the practice in the First World War. On the Italian front the German forces were so thin on the ground that each and every division was worked to the limit of human endurance. Only the 94 Infantry Division went fresh and at full strength into the decisive Cassino operations.

German and Allied accounts divide the struggle for Monte Cassino into three and four phases respectively. The Germans regard the British X Corps offensive as the start of the Cassino battles; in the Allied concept the first phase was the attack of the French Expeditionary Corps on 12 January, which the Germans regard as an epilogue to the operations on the Reinhard Line, rather than as the prologue to the Cassino battles.

On 15 January the U.S. II Corps had taken Monte Trocchio, and on the 17th McCreery attacked on the Garigliano. Clark was on tenterhooks. On 22 January the U.S. VI Corps was due to land at Anzio, and it was essential that by that time the whole of the Cassino front should be ablaze, that the German reserves should be pinned down and, if in any way possible, that the Liri valley should have been opened. Otherwise the invasion forces would be in dire peril.

A few days before the attack, the X Corps had been reinforced by the 5 Division, which Alexander had transferred from the Adriatic front. The task allotted to it was to cross the Garigliano at its estuary, capture Minturno and the high ground to the north of it and open up the Ausente valley. The main thrust of the attack was to be delivered by the 56 Division

* *Calculated Risk.*

in the Corps' centre; its orders were to take the strongly fortified Castel-forte and break through via Coreno to Ausonia and San Giorgio a Liri. The 46 Division's task was to cross the river on either side of Sant' Ambrogio and from there screen Keyes's (U.S. II Corps) attack against the lower Rapido, fixed for 20 January.

Clark's intention was obviously to pin down German reserves, force his way into the Liri valley and roll up the XIV Corps from the south. It was only after he had failed to do this that he shifted the main weight of the attack farther to the north and tried to shatter the northern hinge of the 'gateway to Rome' by an attack delivered by Juin and Ryder.

On the afternoon of 17 January the usual barrage descended on the 94 Infantry Division, and at 9 p.m. McCreery's divisions advanced to the attack. The 17 Brigade of 5 Division launched itself, without artillery preparation, against 94 Division's outposts occupying the Burkhard Line forward of the Garigliano and drove them back across the river at the first attempt. At the same time the Division landed a Battle Group from the sea behind the German lines in the vicinity of Minturno theatre and Monte d'Argento. The amphibious attack, supported by the cruisers *Orion* and *Sparta* and five destroyers, was only partially successful, because most of the assault boats lost their bearings and landed the troops not behind the German but behind the British lines. Nevertheless the German outpost line was completely overrun—in fact the whole of the 94 Division was taken by surprise by X Corps' attack.

To the north of the great road bridge and close to the railway bridge the 13 Brigade effected a crossing and during 18 January captured Minturno and Tufo, and by the evening the 5 Division was looking down into the Ausente valley, where the divisional artillery of the 94 Division was in position. For General Steinmetz, who had taken over command of 94 Division at the beginning of January, these were anxious hours, particularly as the British 56 Division had broken through on a broad front.

Templer's brigades had crossed the river without any difficulty. The 169 Brigade was directed against Monte Castelluccio and the village of Suio, while 167 Brigade attacked Monte Savatitto. During 18 January both brigades succeeded in penetrating deeply into 276 Grenadier Regiment's positions. By evening Templer had the leading elements of his armour across, in order to have them ready to hand for the assault on Castelforte. But the 46 Division met with a severe rebuff. Nowhere did it succeed in crossing the river, and after suffering severe casualties it had been forced to call off its attack.

In spite of this set-back, the British X Corps succeeded in turning 94 Division out of the positions which it had been building and strengthening for months on the forward slopes of the bare mountain, and the German troops thus found themselves without any cover and at the mercy of heavy artillery fire. This was not the only misfortune on this unhappy 18 January. A far greater danger was threatening—a break-through into the Liri valley and the resultant collapse of the whole Cassino front.

General von Senger telephoned to Field-Marshal Kesselring from Steinmetz's battle headquarters, asking him urgently to send up the Army Group reserves—the 29 and 90 Panzer Grenadier Divisions—to avert the danger that was threatening the whole of XIV Corps. General von Vietinghoff made a similar and urgent request; to him the outlook seemed to be as sombre for the right wing of his army as it did to von Senger for his corps. Only by a counter-attack could the position in the southern sector of the Cassino front be restored, and for that reserves were needed. General von Senger had none and Tenth Army had none. There remained therefore only the general reserve which Kesselring had prudently retained in his own hand.

The Field-Marshal was at that time convinced that the Allies would carry out a tactical landing in rear of the Cassino front—though when and where it would take place he did not know. He was certain that General Alexander would not for long be content painfully and with heavy losses to gain a few miles of ground and that the pinning-down of German forces in Italy was not the sole task given to the powerful forces he commanded. This massive concentration of force before Cassino must be aiming at a greater goal, and that goal could only be Rome. When he then found himself thus bombarded by Tenth Army with urgent requests to put in his general reserve and restore the Cassino situation, he did not find it easy to reach a decision. His own comment is as follows:

If I refused the requests of Tenth Army, its right wing might be pressed back and there would be no knowing where it could be brought to a halt again. At the time I had visions of developments which, in actual fact, occurred in the May offensive. If our retreat coincided with a landing from the sea, the consequences would be incalculable. I did not believe that the U.S. Fifth Army's attack had been launched simply to conceal a landing operation or solely in support of it. It seemed to me that the Allies would not land until the attack in the south had progressed to the point where it would be able not only to facilitate the landing itself, but also to co-operate on the spot with the invading forces in a species of battle of encirclement. However that may be, I felt I was right in assuming that General Clark and Field-Marshal Alexander would have exploited the initial success on the Garigliano to roll up the right wing of Tenth Army, had not the German counter-measures forced them to halt the attack. To avoid a blow which might well decide the whole campaign, something had to be done. The enemy's success had been swift, and half-measures were of no use. I therefore thought it better to clear up the situation at one place, so that I should still have sufficient forces in hand with which to confront any new danger that might arise.*

Kesselring therefore decided to repair the damage on XIV Corps' front. To this end, he sent Headquarters, I Parachute Corps, to the danger spot on the Garigliano and placed 29 and 90 Panzer Grenadier Divisions and 94 Infantry Division under its command. This he did, although his Chief of Staff, General Westphal, was of the opinion 'that . . . the attack and landing in Tenth Army's sector was only a feint, designed to pin down our own forces and denude the Rome area to the greatest extent possible'. At the same time the 3 Panzer Grenadier Division, now in Army Group reserve, was brought forward to Arce.

Realizing that a British advance through the Ausente valley must lead to the overrunning of the 94 Division, General Schlemm ordered the 29 Division to counter-attack via Ausonia–Coreno and placed the greatly depleted 276 Grenadier Regiment and the 194 Artillery Regiment under its command.

On 20 January Fries's Division launched its counter-attack and drove the 56 Division back through Castelforte. By the second day the Division had taken 500 prisoners. The counter-attack had caught Templer's Division just at the moment when the first impetus of its own attack had waned, when the men were tired and the artillery was in process of taking up fresh positions from which to support the next advance. Now, however, appeals for help were coming in from Anzio, where U.S. VI Corps had landed on the morning of 22 January. The main object had been achieved and the threatened break-through into the Liri valley had been averted. The 90 Division had also been in action in the Minturno area. It had not launched any counter-attack, because delays on the line of march had caused it to reach the battle area piecemeal; but as its battalions arrived, they were put into the southern sector of 94 Division to strengthen the defence and placed under 94 Division's command. In this way the second menace against the Ausente was also frustrated.

The Anzio landing now began to cast its sinister shadow equally over both sides on the Cassino front. On 22 January, the same day as the Anzio landing took place, Headquarters, I Parachute Corps, established itself in the area of the beach-head, and the Garigliano sector was handed back to XIV Corps; a week later, just as Templer was about to deliver another attack on Castelforte, his 167 Brigade was withdrawn from the front and transferred to Anzio. Eventually, at the beginning of February, the whole of Templer's 56 Division moved to the Anzio beach-head, and the danger on the Garigliano was thus finally averted.

* *Soldat bis zum letzten Tag.*

Meanwhile X Corps had succeeded, despite German counter-measures, in exploiting its initial success. 5 Division had taken final possession of Monte Natale, north-west of Minturno, on 29 January; 46 Division, using 56 Division's crossings, had captured Monte Juga, from which Baade's Division had tried in vain to dislodge them; and X Corps' latest success had been the capture of the important Monte Faito, the little brother of Monte Maio, the southern pillar of the Cassino gateway.

Although General McCreery had been denied success in the Liri valley, the Allies had nevertheless achieved something by the attack on the Garigliano. At the appropriate moment they had succeeded in drawing the German reserves to the Cassino front and away from Rome. This, however, did not bring them the results for which they were hoping, since General Lucas at Anzio failed to take advantage of the favourable opportunity offered to him and was content for the moment to mark time. Since the German reserves had been committed on the Garigliano he had stood in no danger of being driven back into the sea before he had firmly established himself.

The Garigliano bridge-head later proved to be of great use to the Eighth Army when Alexander was preparing for the spring offensive. Clark packed the bridge-head with twenty assault battalions, American, French, Moroccan and Algerian; and it was from this bridge-head that the decisive blow in the battle for Cassino was struck, when General Juin took Monte Maio, broke through into the Liri valley and thus burst open the gateway to Rome. But before that happened, a lot of water was to flow down the Garigliano.

The attack launched on 20 January by U.S. II Corps against the 15 Panzer Grenadier Division on the Rapido and the Gari had a very different outcome. Here, the 36 (Texas) Division under General Walker met with a severe reverse, losing 1,700 men and failing to reach its objective. With this attack, too, General Clark had hoped to draw German reserves to the Cassino front and ease the task of the Anzio landing forces; at the same time, however, as on the Garigliano, his ultimate object had been to break through the Gustav Line and then advance to join up with the Anzio beach-head. But before II and VI Corps joined hands at Anzio no less than four long months were to elapse.

To have attempted to cross the lower Rapido and the Gari, dominated as they were by the Monte Cassino massif, was from the very outset a daringly hazardous enterprise. The field of view of the German artillery observation officers over the battlefield on both sides of these rivers was so uninterrupted that any attempt to put troops across or to bridge them was inevitably doomed to failure. The Rapido and the Gari on the eastern side of the Liri valley constituted a formidable obstacle. Some ten to fifteen yards wide, they flow in the rainy season in a torrent of flood water which, as we have seen, had proved fatal to one of the regiments of the 15 Panzer Grenadier Division during its withdrawal from the Reinhard Line. The name Rapido itself gives some indication of the speed at which this malevolent little river flows between its perpendicular banks to the sea.

The main defensive line of the Gustav system adhered closely to the course of the river. At this point, in the plains, it was slightly set back from the undergrowth on the river bank and took a zig-zag course, which explains why the Texas Division in its attack was caught in so murderous a cross-fire and suffered such severe losses. The key-point of the sector was the little village of Santo Angelo in Teodice, perched just above the Rapido, which the Allied bombers had destroyed and the German pioneers had built up into a well-fortified and formidable strongpoint. Subsequent events were to show how well they had done their work, for the dugouts proved to be both shell- and bomb-proof and, as later happened at Cassino itself, the débris resultant on each successive bombardment provided fresh and excellent cover for the defenders. The bombardment of towns and villages, as far as the attacker is concerned, often proves to be a two-edged sword and is by no means always to the disadvantage of the defence.

The river sector was held by the 15 Panzer Grenadier Division. The northern sector, up to and inclusive of Santo Angelo, was occupied by 104 Panzer Grenadier Regiment; south of it was the 115 Reconnaissance Section, while the defence of the Gari was entrusted to the 129 Regiment. Behind the Division was massed a formidable array of artillery, consisting of the 51, 602, 988 and 992 sections of the Army Artillery and the 71 Mortar Regiment with its dreaded smoke shells. In addition, the artillery of neighbouring divisions, and particularly the 96 Artillery Regiment of the 44 Infantry Division in the sector on each side of Cassino, could bring fire to bear on 15 Division's front. Here, then, at the entrance to the Liri valley, XIV Panzer Corps was very much better equipped than on the Garigliano, and it is no wonder that the U.S. II Corps came to grief.

Clark planned to send the 36 Division (Walker) across on each side of Santo Angelo, whence it was to push forward as far as Pignataro and pave the way for the advance of 1 Armoured Division into the Liri valley. The attack was to start on the evening of 20 January.

Throughout the whole of 20 January bombers of 12 Tactical Air Fleet dropped their bombs on the positions and the lines of communication of the 15 Division. In the afternoon II Corps Artillery (34 and 36 Divisions) joined in, and at 8 p.m. the 141 Infantry Regiment surged forward to the river bank, whence a heavy artillery barrage was to support its crossing. But the German artillery was very much on the alert. Its fire not only caused severe casualties among the troops, but also destroyed much of the equipment—rafts, assault boats and bridge sections—upon which the troops were relying. Nor was that all; the German fire tore to shreds the tapes with which the U.S. pioneers had so laboriously marked out the lanes cleared through the minefields, and the infantry, hurriedly seeking cover from the German fire, strayed into the middle of minefields, where they suffered further heavy losses.

Despite the fury of the fire it encountered, the 1st Battalion of the 141 Regiment succeeded in reaching the river to the north of Santo Angelo, but could do no more than get two companies across to the west bank. Although the U.S. pioneers set to work at once, behind the two leading companies, to construct pontoon bridges, the remainder of the battalion failed to get across. The two companies which had succeeded were caught in the murderous fire of the 104 Regiment and had no choice but to dig themselves in up to their necks. The rest of the battalion was withdrawn to its assembly area at dawn on 21 January.

South of Santo Angelo in 115 Reconnaissance Section's area, the 1st Battalion, 143 Infantry Regiment, had succeeded in getting across the river. Its attack was brought to a standstill, however, on the west bank itself before ever it had time to develop, and the devastating fire of the defence left the battalion with no option but to retire back across the river.

The results of this first attempt were by no means flattering to the 36 Division. But Walker and Keyes had no intention of giving in. They well knew what was at stake, and Keyes was determined to get to Anzio! On the morning of 21 January, while he was at Walker's battle head-quarters, he decided to make another attempt that same day and as quickly as possible to cross the river to the south of Santo Angelo and relieve the two companies farther to the north.

But the second attempt also brought nothing but more casualties. Towards 6 p.m. on 21 January the 143 Regiment resumed its attack in the southern sector, and its 3rd Battalion crossed the Gari. During the night it even succeeded in getting its 2nd Battalion across and pushing it forward some 500 yards westwards. But there it became stuck and now it was the turn of the 129 Panzer Grenadier Regiment. Brilliantly supported by the artillery, the Regiment drove the Americans back across the Gari, taking a large number of prisoners. The 1st Battalion alone, in masterly co-operation with the 3rd Battalion, the 96 Artillery Regiment, brought in 500 American troops.

In the meanwhile, north of Santo Angelo the 141 Regiment had succeeded in getting two more battalions across the Rapido. But here again, as had happened south of the village, they failed in their attempts to bridge the river and get tanks and heavy weapons across. The German gunners, who from the slopes of Monte Cassino had been able to observe every move, were as alert as gun-dogs. Any movement in the vicinity of the river, anything that looked like an attempt at bridging, drew furious fire, some of it pretty heavy stuff into the bargain. For Section 992 of the Army Artillery was armed with those 8.2 mortars that had been famous during the First War, and where their shells landed it was a waste of time even to try and pick up the pieces.

But the 141 Regiment itself fared no better than the 143rd, and it, too, met with a bad reverse. On the afternoon of 22 January the 104 Panzer Grenadier Regiment brought up its reserves, rose from its fox-holes and drove the Americans back across the Rapido. Once again the 'Texas Boys' came out with a black eye. General Rodt's cautious report estimated 36 Division's losses to date at 400 dead and 500 prisoners. In reality, Walker's Division lost far more. Clark himself put its casualties at 1,681—143 dead, 663 wounded and 875 missing.

The three-day battle had resulted in a brilliant success for the German defence. The 15 Division, which had already distinguished itself in Sicily, at Salerno and on the Volturno, had now performed yet another impressive feat of arms. In co-operation with Colonel von Grundherr, commanding the 414 Artillery Regiment, it had inflicted a severe defeat on the American Division which had fought so well at Salerno, had captured Monte Maggiore and had stormed and taken the hotly contested village of San Pietro Infine.

To throw Rodt's Division out of its strong positions on the river, however, required greater strength than Clark at the time had at his disposal, and it was not until May that the greatly superior forces of the British XIII Corps was able to drive back the 15 Panzer Grenadier Division and cross the Rapido on a broad front.

The heavy defeat suffered by the 36 Division on the Rapido caused a great outcry in the United States. After the end of the war, at a divisional reunion the ex-servicemen passed a resolution, demanding that the Congressional Committee for Military Affairs should hold an inquiry on the failure of the Rapido enterprise. The Committee sought the advice of the Minister for War, and General Clark confirmed that the attack had been 'necessary' and that: 'The heroic enterprise and the sacrifices made by the 36 Division undoubtedly drew the Germans away from our Anzio landing in the first critical hours of our going ashore . . . thus contributing in a major degree to minimizing the casualties in that undertaking and to the firm establishment of the Anzio beach-head.'* But a study of the whole operation, made with the knowledge of the German counter-measures taken, shows beyond any possible doubt that not one single German soldier was withdrawn from the Rome area to the Cassino front

* Mark Clark, *Calculated Risk.*

as a result of 36 Division's attack. It had not even been necessary to call upon the reserves of XIV Panzer Corps, let alone those of Tenth Army, in order to repulse Walker's attacks on the Rapido and the Gari. The 15 Division, supported, naturally, by the Corps Artillery of XIV Corps, crushed the attacks without any extraneous assistance.

The credit for drawing the German tactical reserve to the Cassino front belongs to the British X Corps. But even though the 29 and 90 Panzer Grenadier Divisions had been transferred when the Anzio landing occurred, their absence did not prove to be any great handicap, since General Lucas failed entirely to take advantage of the moment of surprise and made no move until his supply dumps had been replenished. The result was that the 29 Division, which was relieved from the Cassino front on 10 February, arrived back in ample time to prevent a break-through by U.S. II Corps at Anzio. It is true that the 90 Division was withdrawn, when the fighting on the Garigliano subsided, into Army reserve in rear of the Cassino front, but the abortive attack of the Texas Division had no bearing on this move, since by that time Walker had long since been driven back across the Rapido. There is no doubt that Clark hoped with II Corps to break the defensive girdle south of Cassino, as, indeed, he himself admits: 'It was the plan of this attack to penetrate the Gustav Line south of Cassino, open up the Liri valley, outflank the Cassino bastion and thus clear the way for a drive towards Anzio by elements of the 1 Armoured Division.'*

The whole II Corps operation seems from the very outset to have had all the makings of a failure. For either the attack of the British X Corps on the Garigliano would lead to the collapse of the Cassino front, or, if it did not, then the attack of a single U.S. Division would certainly not succeed in opening up the Liri valley—particularly as Clark had chosen, from the point of view of ground, the most unfavourable place at which to launch it.

The Fifth Army Commander, however, was not dismayed. Three days after the Texas Division disaster he launched his third attack, this time to the north of Cassino town.

The third phase of the first Cassino battle was one of the bloodiest fights in the whole struggle for the possession of Monte Cassino. Clark threw everything he could lay his hands on into the battle, and Kesselring, von Vietinghoff and von Senger did likewise. The furious onslaughts of the Americans, French, British, New Zealanders, Indians, Algerians and Tunisians came within a hair's breadth of achieving a decisive victory, and it was only with a last, desperate effort that XIV Corps prevented the capture of the Monastery Mount. The U.S. 34 Division was knocking at the very doors of the cloister, from the heights to the west of Cassino,

* *Calculated Risk.*

Ryder's troops were looking down on to the Via Casilina leading to Anzio and Rome, the whole mountain was ablaze, and it was literally at the very last moment that the 'fire brigade' appeared. This time it was the 1 Parachute Regiment, reinforced by the Machine-gun and 3rd Infantry Battalions of the 3 Parachute Regiment and under the command of Colonel Karl Lothar Schulz, a veteran thruster of the German paratroops, who had been with them at Rotterdam and in Crete.

After the unsatisfactory affairs on the Garigliano and the failure of the Rapido enterprise, Clark set to work methodically to open up the Liri valley from its northern slopes. He put two Army Corps into the battle with the object of finally opening the road to Rome for his armoured forces. On the right flank he put in the French Expeditionary Corps with orders to break through the Gustav Line to the west of Sant' Elia, capture the Cairo massif and cut the Via Casilina, the vital artery of the German defence, in the vicinity of Piedimonte San Germano. Between the town of Cassino and the French the task allotted to U.S. II Corps was to cross the Rapido near Cairo and, having penetrated the Gustav Line, to swing south-wards and fight its way to Monte Cassino. Clark was hoping to defeat his adversary with a right hook, but no blow he could deliver proved powerful enough to knock out his opponent.

Just as the attack was about to begin, General Juin received orders to change the direction of his attack. He was not to bother about Atina, but was to swing south-westwards with Colle Belvedere, Colle Abate and Terelle, situated some 3,000 feet up on the northern slopes of Monte Cairo, as his objectives. The Algerian 3 Infantry Division was detailed to lead the attack, while the Moroccan Division was given the task of tying down the German forces on its front by means of a series of local attacks.

The U.S. II Corps had only the 34 Division and the 756 and 760 Armoured Sections at its disposal. To harmonize with the plan of attack, General Ryder divided his forces into two columns, one of which was to advance towards Terelle in close co-operation with the Algerians, and the other to break through the Gustav Line north of Cassino and then press on to Monte Cassino itself. The French attack was fixed for 2200 hours on 24 January and that of the Americans for the morning of 25th. Before he could reach Terelle, Juin had first to capture Colle Belvedere (2,250 feet) and Colle Abate (3,000 feet)—an extremely difficult task, when it is remembered that the Algerians' assembly area in the vicinity of Sant' Elia were only some 250–300 feet above sea level. The Algerians were being launched against high walls, at the feet of which were deep mine-fields, wire entanglements and a broad stretch of flooded country barring the way to the Gustav Line.

The defence of the Monte Cassino and Monte Cairo massifs had been entrusted to the 44 Infantry Division, command of which had been assumed by General Franck on 10 January. The Hoch und Deutschmeisters were thus holding the most important key positions in the whole of the Cassino front. If the enemy succeeded in breaking through here, the results would be incalculable. In the area from the south of Cassino railway station to the Secco valley* the Division was occupying well-constructed positions in the Gustav Line itself, with strong artillery and the 71 Mortar Regiment in support in the Liri valley behind it. Cassino town was held by the 132 Grenadier Regiment, to the north of which was the 131 Grenadier Regiment; and on the Division's left flank, opposite the Algerians, was the 131 Regiment. The 'High and Mighties' had already been pretty severely mauled in the previous engagements in front of Cassino, and there was little doubt that it would only be able to stand up to further attacks for a strictly limited period.

But at first no reserves were available. The Anzio landing had had an introspective effect, and although the storm clouds were gathering at Cassino, such troops as Tenth Army could spare were being drawn towards the beachhead. It was not until the end of January that the 90 Division could be withdrawn from the Garigliano and plunged into the blood-bath of Cassino.

On the evening of 24 January Juin launched his attack with the Tunisian 4 Rifle Regiment as its spearhead. The capture of Monte Cifalco, which dominated the Secco valley and the Sant' Elia area, was of primary importance, and although the 3rd Battalion of the Tunisian Regiment took the forward positions situated on Height 470, it was unable to dislodge the 5 Mountain Division from the mountain itself. To the end of the battle it remained in German hands and was a thorn in the flesh of the French, for from its slopes the German artillery observation officers had a clear view both of the flanks and rear of the attacking French and of the Americans advancing southwards.

With their left flank protected by the Algerian 7 Rifle Regiment, the Tunisians, who made short work of crossing the Rapido and passing through the German minefields, stormed the steep slopes with incredible dash. The 131 Regiment, obviously knocked off balance, was quite unable to prevent them from gaining a firm foothold on the eastern slopes of Monte Belvedere. The Grenadiers lost heavily, and the commander of the Regiment was killed on the first day of the battle. But the situation in which the Tunisians now found themselves was no sinecure. The German artillery fire directed from Monte Cifalco was devastatingly effective, and in its attack on Monte Belvedere the 1st Battalion of the 4 Rifle Regiment lost its commander, and all its company commanders were either killed or

---

* This Secco is a northern tributary of the Rapido, not to be confused with the Secco which is a tributary of the Liri.

Mussolini, taken immediately after his liberation by the Germans on the Gran' Sasso. Behind him, Skorzeny, who discovered where Mussolini was being held captive.

General Alexander.

Field–Marshal Kesselring.

Lieutenant-Generals Clark and Leese.

Lieutenant-General Richard Heidrich, the G.O.C. 1st Parachute Division.

General Heilmann, the soul of the German defence at Cassino.

The superb basilica of Monte Cassino monastery, before the bombardment.

The departure for Rome of the mortal remains of Saint Benedict (in suitcase). Archbishop Don Gregorio Diamare, with cross, bids farewell to the sacred relics.

Some of the rescued works of art being unloaded at the San Paolo monastery in Rome.

From the portals of the monastery, Archbishop Diamare (with upraised hand) gives his blessing to one of the convoys about to depart for Rome. Extreme left (with outstretched hand), the German monk Father Emmanual Munding; in the background, right, Lieutenant-Colonel Schlegel, the instigator of the rescue operations.

A Thanksgiving Mass held by the Archbishop for the German troops on the successful completion of the rescue operations.

Cassino and Rocca Janula before destruction. In the background, the Santa Elia hills.

Cassino town at the end of January 1944 …

… and two months later, after the second battle of Cassino.

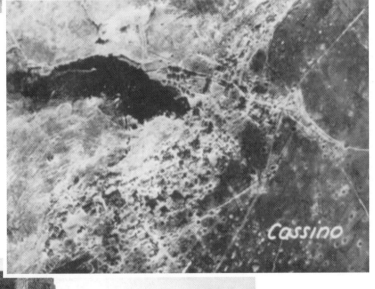

View of the monastery, taken from the ruins of Cassino town.

Allied bombers attacking Cassino town. A photograph taken by a German war correspondent from the ruins of the monastery.

German paratroops in the ruins of the monastery.

General Juin (right) and General de Monsabert watching a French attack in the Monti Arunci area.

Cassino defenders: two German paratroopers in the ruins.

Polish soldiers advancing.

Another building is cleared: New Zealanders at Cassino.

The monastery in ruins.

The rebuilt new monastery, ten years later.

Cassino, May 1960. An international reunion of those who fought at Cassino pay homage to their dead comrades.

wounded. Despite this, the battalion planted its colours on the summit of Belvedere on the afternoon of 25 January.

The next day the Tunisians maintained their heavy pressure on Terelle, and their 2nd Battalion captured Colle Abate and the important Height 862 to the north of it. Terelle now lay at their feet. Yet, despite these impressive successes, they were in a somewhat precarious situation. They were suffering severely from the German artillery fire; they had advanced a long way; reinforcements could not reach them and ammunition and food were running short. Juin had advanced dangerously far into the Gustav Line. The American attack north of Cassino had failed, and Keyes had not, as arranged, pushed his reserves at once into the breach made by the Algerian Division.

It was while they were in this precarious situation that the German counter-stroke on 27 January hit the Tunisians. Under cover of concentrated artillery support—some 5,000 rounds were fired by eighty guns—the 200 Panzer Grenadier Regiment under the command of Colonel Baron Behr launched a counter-attack against Colle Abate and Height 862. In spite of the heavy French artillery fire, the Grenadiers captured both heights, but their subsequent attacks failed in the face of the Tunisians stubborn defence.

On the left flank of 44 Infantry Division elements of the Tunisian 4 Rifle Regiment had pushed forward into the Secco valley, but here, too, the position had been restored by a German counter-attack. South of Monte Belvedere, however, there still yawned a dangerous gap; here the 44 Division stood in deadly peril of being rolled up from the north, and it was essential that something be done quickly to obviate the danger. To their rescue in the hour of need came the 191 Grenadier Regiment of the 71 Division, which succeeded in plugging the gap between Colle Abate and Monte Castellone. Necessity had compelled General von Senger to use the Regiment for this hazardous purpose. His original intention had been to reinforce Rodt's Division with the 71 Division; but when Juin broke fresh ground in the Terelle area and the Secco valley, von Senger's first thought was to use the 71 Division for a counter-attack. But after the surprising successes of the Algerian Division, he could not do so, but had to content himself with using the regiments of the 71 Division to patch up the holes pierced in the forward defensive localities. With the 211 Regiment he bolstered up the thinly held positions in the Cassino town sector—and by so doing, as will soon be seen, he saved Monte Cassino itself. General Raapke, the Commander of the 71 Division, however, played no part in these new moves. All the reinforcements which were hurried to the threatened sectors automatically came under the command of 44 Division.

The fight for Terelle continued. On 28 January the Tunisians on Monte Belvedere were relieved by the Algerian 7 Rifle Regiment, and the next day the Algerians stormed Colle Abate and Height 862. The 200 Grenadiers were hard pressed. The battle continued with fluctuating fortune, the heights changing hands again and again, until on 1 February they finally remained firmly in German hands. Thus the way was barred to the French Corps, and the defence of this threatened sector was entrusted to a man of outstanding merit. Baade, who had been living in spartan simplicity in a smoky dugout near Castro Cielo, had once again justified the confidence that the High Command had placed in him.

In the meantime the situation immediately north of Cassino had also become extremely critical. When Ryder's 34 Division, supported by a mighty artillery barrage, set out to cross the Rapido on the night of 24/25 January, the 133 Infantry Regiment succeeded in getting three battalions across the river in the vicinity of the old Italian barracks and penetrating into the positions of the 134 Grenadier Regiment. Heavy fire from the German artillery, however, made the Americans' position untenable, and they had to be withdrawn again across the river. On 26 January the U.S. 135 Infantry Regiment tried its luck north of the town, but without success. Only one company got across the river, and all the rest became bogged down in the morass, the minefields and the barbed wire, exposed to the heavy fire of the German defence. A further attack delivered by the 100th Japanese-American Battalion suffered a like fate.

Until the 30 January Ryder had met with no success worth mentioning, and it was not until that day that the first of his regiments, the 168 Infantry Regiment, succeeded in crossing the Rapido. On the evening of the same day Colonel Boatner, commanding the 168th, went on to capture the village of Cairo and Heights 56 and 213.

General Keyes now proceeded to strengthen his right flank. He withdrew the 142 Regiment from 34 Division, placed it under Ryder's command and sent it to the Belvedere area. But now, instead of exerting his pressure against Terelle and the gateway to Piedimonte and Roccasecca, from the pillars of which Juin had already drawn the nails, Ryder ordered the 143 Regiment to veer southwards towards Monte Cassino. American attention was fixed wholly and solely on the town and monastery of Monte Cassino. Here they realized, quite rightly, was the key point, but it never seems to have struck them that it was not necessary to take the bull by the horns if the beast was exposing its flank to a lethal blow. Monte Cassino exercised a magnetic influence, and General Keyes was not the only one who succumbed to it. His successors on the field of battle, General Freyberg of the New Zealanders and the Polish General Anders, equally fell victims to its spell.

Ryder now launched four regiments at the hard-pressed 44 Infantry Division in an attempt to give it the *coup de grâce*. General Franck was very worried. It seemed to him that it could only be a matter of time before his division was completely annihilated. His battalions had been reduced to weak companies and were being commanded by platoon commanders, and the prospect was indeed sombre. The 131 Grenadier Regiment, over which the storm of the Algerian onslaught had burst, had had to be completely written off; the 134 Regiment in the centre faced imminent destruction, and in and around Cassino the 132 Regiment was but little better off. The divisional artillery had also suffered severe losses; 2 Section of 96 Artillery Regiment, for example, was in position between the houses of Terelle with its last three remaining guns. It was lucky that the 190 Artillery Regiment (belonging to the 90 Division) was now in position and would provide a little stiffening. As far as the town of Cassino itself was concerned, there seemed to be no cause for undue anxiety; but the situation on the high ground to the north-west was critical in the extreme. It was here that disaster threatened—and here, too, that it occurred.

On 1 February, the ninth day of the offensive, Ryder resumed his hammer-blows against 44 Infantry Division. In the Cairo area, where his previous attacks had penetrated the German lines, he concentrated three regiments for an attack southwards in the direction of Monte Cassino. The 135 and 142 Infantry Regiments were directed against the heights of Monte Castillone and Colle Santo Angelo, and the 168 Regiment against the famous Height 593, the Calvary Mount and tactical centre of the Cairo massif.

In thick fog in the early hours of 1 February Ryder launched his vital attack. In swift succession Monte Castillone and Colle Maiolla fell. After three days of fierce fighting, in which the U.S. 34 Division lost heavily, the 2nd Battalion, 135 Regiment, and the 3rd Battalion, 168 Regiment, were less than two miles from the Via Casilina. Monte Cassino and Highway No. 6 seemed doomed. On 4 February the 135 Regiment made further progress. Colonel Ward captured Colle Santo Angelo, but was thrown out again by a counter-attack. To the south-east Colonel Boatner got within 500 yards of Height 593. One last, short rush, and the Monastery Mount, it seemed, must fall to him.

On 5 February a platoon of the 135 Regiment advanced to beneath the walls of the monastery itself, pressed on to Height 435 and in broad daylight drove a German observation post out of its position. Never again were the Americans to get so close to the monastery. German reinforcements—the 361 Regiment, followed by Heidrich's paratroops—now began to appear on the scene.

Down below in the town itself the battle had been raging since 2 February. Here the U.S. 133 Infantry Regiment under Colonel Marshall captured the barracks and advanced against the northern part of the town and Height 193, the Rocca Janula. Supported by 760 Armoured Section, its 3rd Battalion fought its way into the houses on the outskirts of the town. But Marshall had not reckoned with the enterprise shown by the 211 Grenadier Regiment. Knuth's Grenadiers launched themselves at the Americans and drove them back 1,000 yards northwards. Marshall, however, would not give in. On 3 February he delivered another attack and captured Height 175 and a few houses; but despite strong artillery and air support, the Americans were unable to penetrate into the town. The 211 Grenadiers repulsed every subsequent attack, and its outstanding performance was mentioned in German dispatches.

On 5 February the 1st Battalion of the 133 Regiment attacked the steep slopes of Rocca Janula, but in vain. Here, too, Marshall's troops were knocked back with a black eye by Knuth's Grenadiers. Cassino town was proving to be a hard nut, and not even the heaviest sledge-hammer in Alexander's well-equipped workshop proved powerful enough to crack it.

Up in the mountains a most stubborn battle was in progress. On the night of 5/6 February the 3rd Battalion, 168 Infantry Regiment launched a direct attack on Monastery Mount from Height 445. The monastery at the time was still undamaged and its high walls still towered up into the snow-laden February sky. If the Americans had succeeded in capturing the hill and entering the monastery, then the latter would have been out of danger. But the 168th had no luck. In the deep ravine on the edge of the northern slope of the hill they ran into a murderous crossfire which forced them to retire. The 135 Regiment fared better. On 6 February Ward's 2nd Battalion took the Calvary Mount, Height 593, and the key to Cassino was thus in American hands.

But General Baade, whose sector now extended to the monastery itself, was determined to deny his opposite number, General Ryder, the opportunity of opening the monastery gates. On 7 February the 90 Panzer Grenadier Division, with 361 Regiment attached, delivered its counter-attack. Though they suffered heavy casualties, the Grenadiers drove the Americans off Height 593; but, in spite of all their efforts, by 9 February the Calvary Mount was once again in American hands.

By this time, however, the paratroops, with the 3rd Battalion, 3 Parachute Regiment, under its enterprising commander Major Kratzert, were at hand. Kratzert, an Austrian, was an ex-officer of the old Imperial Army and was therefore by no means a youngster. On 10 February he launched his battalion against the Calvary Mount and captured it the same day; and from then onward, despite the blood shed on its bare slopes by Americans, British, Indians and Poles, it remained firmly in German possession. The Polish cemetery bears eloquent witness to the fierce fighting of which it was the centre.

Schulz's battle group had reached the Monte Cassino massif at a very opportune moment. It had come straight from the other battle-cauldron, the Anzio beach-head, into which it had been thrown, battalion by battalion, as and when it could be released from the Adriatic front. Now its 1st Machine-gun Parachute Battalion took up its position on the slopes of Monte Cassino from Rocca Janula to the Calvary Mount. Kratzert's battalion remained on Height 593, and the high ground to the north as far as Monte Castillone was occupied by the 1 Parachute Regiment. The Schulz Battle Group hung almost literally by its eyebrows on the last precipitous slopes in front of the Via Casilina. Its position had no depth whatever, and a determined onslaught on it might well have sent the defenders hurtling down into the valley below. But not one yard of ground did it surrender. Although it had found no prepared positions awaiting it, although hastily piled heaps of stones afforded the only cover it had, it nevertheless repulsed all the attacks launched by the U.S. II Corps and the Indian 4 Division against it.

Whence this sudden appearance of the Indian troops? At the end of January General Alexander had transferred the New Zealand 2, the British 78 and the Indian 4 Division from the Adriatic sector and formed them into a New Zealand Corps. His object was either to use these *élite* troops to break the Cassino front if Clark's operations then in progress failed to do so, or, if Clark succeeded, to use them in exploitation of his success and push them through to the Anzio beach-head. Command of this corps was given to the famous New Zealander, General Freyberg.

Freyberg had served with distinction in the First War. In 1914 he made his way to the United Kingdom, joined the British forces as a volunteer and during the war rose from 2nd Lieutenant to Brigadier. He had acquired a considerable reputation, particularly as a result of his vigorous intervention at Bailleul, where, during the German summer offensive of 1918, he succeeded in plugging an extremely dangerous hole in the British Line. For this action he had been awarded the Victoria Cross. In 1941 he was commanding the New Zealand 2 Division in Greece, and after the British withdrew from the Balkans he was appointed, on Churchill's recommendation, commander in Crete. But here, too, he had had to retreat in the face of German paratroops.

The New Zealand 2, the Indian 4 and the British 78 Divisions were indeed the finest weapons in the whole of Alexander's armoury. Just how good they were a glance at their records will show.

In their first engagement in Greece the New Zealanders had been forced to give way in the face of greatly superior German weapons, but very shortly afterwards they fought a life-and-death battle with the German paratroops of the 5 Mountain Division in Crete. Names like Malemes, Galatas and Suda are stirring landmarks in the history of this fine division. Re-raised from the remnants that had emerged from Crete, the Division was once more in action in 1941 at Tobruk, where it was the first to re-establish contact with the garrison that had been cut off for many months. When Rommel chased the Eighth Army headlong back into Egypt, the Division became surrounded at Mersa Matruh. But during the night it stormed at the point of the bayonet through the encircling German forces and fought its way back to the Eighth Army at El Alamein. In this daring enterprise Freyberg himself was wounded, and Churchill telegraphed to him: 'Deeply moved to hear of your new wound and new glory. Trust that your injury is not serious and that you will soon be back commanding your splendid division. All good wishes to you and them.'* Referring to this exploit, Rommel remarks: 'Unfortunately the New Zealanders under Freyberg escaped. I would far rather have seen this division, which was one of the best of the British divisions and which we had often met in 1941/42, safely in our prisoner-of-war cages than at the front against us.'

The battle of El Alamein found the New Zealanders in a key position, from which they launched the main attack against the dividing line between the German and Italian forces, broke the Axis front and by 4 November were in full pursuit of their enemy.

For anything in the nature of an outflanking movement Montgomery always preferred to use the New Zealanders, as he did at Agheila and Tripoli, and it was an operation of this kind that led to the swift collapse of the Mareth Line, where Freyberg made a wide détour to the south and then thrust into the rear of the German position. Only Orsogna had been a disappointment to them. It was one of the very few defeats that the New Zealanders had to admit.

The War Diary of the Indian 4 Division speaks for itself. As early as December 1940 it gained great distinction in Wavell's battles against Graziani in the Libyan desert. In March 1941 in the British attack on Abyssinia, it captured the famous Keren Heights on the northern front after twelve days of bitter fighting. Returning to Libya, the Indians were always to be found where the fighting was fiercest. At the battle of El Alamein they fought with great distinction on the Ruweisat Redoubt; in the battle for the Mareth Line they broke through the German front in the all but impassable Matmata Mountains; and in May 1943 Alexander threw them against the vital point, Mejed el Bab, where they burst through

* *The Second World War*, Vol. IV.

the German positions at their first onslaught and paved the way for the Desert Rats to march into Tunis.

The deeds of the 78 Division are well known. Centuripe, Adrano, Termoli, San Salvo and San Vito are battle honours of this famous division, whose men wear a yellow battle-axe as insignia on their arm.

And now these picked men had been brought up to smash the Cassino barrier, for in the meantime Alexander had placed the New Zealand Corps under the Fifth Army; and when all else had failed Clark turned to the New Zealand Corps—not to set them on the road to Anzio (that still lay a long way ahead)—but at long last to wrest Monte Cassino from these stubborn Germans.

On 6 February Freyberg took over from the U.S. 36 Division and on 12th assumed command of the Cassino sector. The Texas Division moved up into the mountains beside the 34 Division, and the 4 Division prepared to continue the attack from the Cairo area. It had been Clark's intention, once 36 Division had captured Monte Cassino, to push the Indian Division on to Piedimonte; but if Ryder's attack failed, then the Indians were themselves to storm and capture the mountain.

On 11 February Keyes struck with both his divisions. The 36 were given the task of taking Massa Albaneta and the Calvary Mount, while 34 Division was to launch a direct attack against the monastery itself from the north.

After a heavy artillery preparation, the Americans advanced to the attack in driving snow; but they did not get far. The 141 Regiment, which had not yet recovered from the wounds it had sustained on the Rapido, was held up before it was within striking distance of Massa Albaneta, and the 142nd were severely mauled on the slopes of the Calvary Mount. The abundant machine-guns of the paratroops gathered a grim harvest. By the evening, the battalions of the 142 Regiment, which had hardly been in action at all on the Rapido and had suffered only a few casualties on Monte Castellone, were all reduced to an average of a hundred men.

The 168 Infantry Regiment fared but little better. Colonel Boatner had seen plenty of hard fighting in his service, but in comparison with this black 11 February, everything before faded into insignificance. As his regiment approached the northern slopes of Monastery Mount in a violent snow storm, it was met with a murderous machine-gun fire. Major Schmidt, the commander of the 1st Parachute Machine-gun Battalion, put in everything he had. The heavy machine-guns wrought terrible havoc in the ranks of the assaulting Americans long before they reached the German positions, the attack collapsed and the G.I.s retired hastily northwards, even abandoning some important high ground which had previously been in their possession.

The fiasco of 11 February was enough to persuade Clark to relieve the 34 Division and put in the Indians. The positions occupied by the U.S. 133 Regiment, which up to 11 February had been able to penetrate no more than a hundred yards into the northern outskirts of Cassino, were taken over by the New Zealand 6 Brigade, and the stage was set for the next act.

Meanwhile, the 90 Panzer Grenadier Division had taken over the whole sector hitherto held by 44 Infantry Division. General Baade, sitting in his fox-hole, need not have worried; the front held. Below, in the town itself, the Grenadiers of 211 Regiment remained unshaken; the paratroops had proved themselves worthy of their reputation; the 191 Grenadier Regiment had done all that had been asked of it in front of Terelle. The left flank was now firmly held in the hands of his own division.

Only at Monte Castellone was the enemy causing him a little anxiety. Here the Americans were in the immediate vicinity of Villa San Lucia and from this mountain eyrie it was but a stone's throw to Piedimonte and the Via Casilina. To avert the danger, Baade launched a counter-attack against Monte Castellone on 12 February, and once again it was the 200 Panzer Grenadier Regiment under Colonel Baron Behr which had been detailed for the operation. There was plenty of artillery support. Colonel von Grundherr, the commander of XIV Corps artillery, made available every gun he had and produced the heaviest concentration of fire that had ever been produced on the German side in Italy.

On the morning of 12 February, under cover of this awe-inspiring barrage, Baron Behr advanced to the attack and at first gained a certain amount of ground; but as soon as the American artillery got wind of the attack, it overwhelmed the Grenadiers with a devastating curtain of fire. In the bare, open country, devoid of all cover, the German casualties were severe, the attack failed, the Regiment lost nearly 150 men and Monte Castellone remained in the hands of the Texas Division. Although the Americans were able to repulse a German counter-attack, they were no longer capable of further offensive action. Linklater wrote: 'The II Corps had broken through the Gustav Line only to be defeated on the last defences of Monte Cassino, where its forward troops were little more than a mile away from Highway 6. Victory had seemed to be within reach, but the closely packed fortifications on the mountains and in the town had been too strong for direct assault, and the extremely efficient movement of German reinforcements and the fanatical bravery of their persistent counter-attacks had reduced the American Division to a battered remnant, incapable of any further offensive. Responsibility for continuing the battle now passed to General Freyberg and his New Zealand Corps.'*

* *The Campaign in Italy.*

The day before this, 11 February, on Alexander's instructions, Clark had ordered Freyberg to attack the Monastery Mount with the Indian 4 Division, and with the New Zealand Division to establish a bridge-head across the Rapido to the south of Cassino town. Heavy snow-drifts, however, had caused the attack to be postponed. In the meantime feverish conferences were in progress on the question of bombarding the monastery itself, for Freyberg, assuming it to be occupied by German troops, was obstinately insisting that a bombardment of it was essential. (The story of how the venerable abbey came to be destroyed is told in the next chapter.)

As the last bomber dropped its deadly load into the smoke and dust enveloping the monastery on that fateful 15 February, one solitary company of the Royal Sussex Regiment (Indian 7 Infantry Brigade) advanced to the attack—but not against the ruins of the monastery, as would have been tactically the correct thing to do, but against the Calvary Mount! The 4 Indian Division, whose Commander, General Tuker, had in the meanwhile been admitted to hospital, was in no position to follow it up with an immediate infantry attack, since the Rajputana Rifles and the Gurkha Rifles, which should have participated in 7 Brigade's attack, were still on the other side of the Rapido! 'For the moment at least, the enemy was jarred off balance, and for a moment, there might have been the chance of a decisive success, if Freyberg had hit him quickly.'*

This omission alone suffices to show how futile, from the military point of view, the bombardment of the monastery had been. Major Schmidt and the German gunners would have had ample time to reoccupy it if, prior to the bombardment, they had, indeed, been abusing the sanctity of the holy building. For Freyberg did not launch his attack against it until eighteen hours after the end of the bombardment, by which time the effects of it had long since evaporated, if, indeed, it can be said to have had any effect at all on the German defence.

On 16 February fighter-bombers again attacked the ruins, and on the evening of the same day the Royal Sussex advanced alone to the assault. The attack was doomed to failure, since no single battalion could possibly have captured the hill. Scarcely had the British troops deployed than they ran into a minefield and there suffered the same fate as overtook the U.S. 168 Regiment. A murderous storm of machine-gun and shell fire tore the Royal Sussex to shreds, and twelve officers and 130 men lay dead and wounded in front of the German position.

Now at last it began to dawn on the Allied command that half-measures against the paratroops would achieve nothing, and decided that the attack planned for the next day should be delivered by five battalions,

* Mark Clark, *Calculated Risk*.

with a sixth in support to act as fatigue parties for the assaulting troops.

But this third and last assault on the monastery also failed. It is true that the Gurkhas pressed forward in battalion strength to Height 444, two hundred yards north-west of the monastery, but on 18 February when daylight came, they found themselves penned in between the monastery and Height 569, wavered and finally withdrew to the position from which they had launched their assault. The attack of the Essex Regiment and the Rajputana Rifles against the Calvary Mount and that of the 1st Battalion, 2 Gurkha Rifles, on Case d'Onfrio also collapsed. That was the miserable net result of a series of badly organized attacks to ensure the success of which the monastery had been sacrificed in a most irresponsible manner.

Down below in the valley, too, Freyberg had missed the bus by the time he at last decided, on 17 February, to strike a blow against the 211 Grenadier Regiment. The result was a complete air-shot. Once more he had attempted something with forces wholly inadequate for the task set them. Freyberg's intention was to cross the Rapido south of Cassino in the vicinity of the demolished railway bridge and capture the railway station. If this succeeded, and if the Indians managed to capture the monastery hill, then, he hoped, the Germans would certainly evacuate the town.

The attack across the river was to be delivered by the New Zealand 5 Brigade; but here again a cheese-paring policy was adopted. Instead of putting the whole brigade into the assault, General Parkinson, commanding the New Zealand 2 Division, decided to use only the 28 Maori Battalion. On 17 February the Maoris assembled north-west of Monte Trocchio, between the Via Casilina and the railway station, with an assault group of the 4 Armoured Division behind them, ready to exploit their success. When darkness fell, the battalion went into the attack, captured the railway station and advanced south-westwards to the Rapido. Success continued to reward their efforts and they crossed the river without much difficulty. But the tanks were unable to follow them into the marshy swamp-land.

The German counter-stroke was delivered on the afternoon of the next day. After most careful preparations, Major Knuth's Grenadiers, effectively supported by armour, bore down upon the Maoris and flung them back across the river. The Grenadiers crossed in pursuit, overran the Maori company holding the railway station and drove the whole of the 28th Battalion back eastwards.

After this reverse Freyberg called a halt, and Alexander decided that he would resume the attack only 'after a bombardment in the real sense of the word and not simply a small demonstration like that of 15 February'.

The attack was scheduled for 24 February. But torrential rain and driving snow led to repeated postponements, until finally on 15 March there descended upon the town of Cassino that terrible deluge of bombs which was the overture to the second act of Alexander's controversial plan of campaign.

The success achieved by the Allies in the first Cassino battle, which started on 17 January and ended on 18 February, were by no means convincing. All they had succeeded in doing was to pierce the right wing of the Gustav Line at a few places and to drive a wedge into the German front north of Cassino. In their main purpose—to break through the Gustav Line and open the gateway to Rome—they had failed completely.

The battle had ended in an undeniable victory for the German defence. Infantrymen, Grenadiers and paratroops had successfully confronted an enemy endowed with inexhaustible material assets, who enjoyed absolute superiority in the air, had thrown his best divisions into the battle and who had now been fought to a standstill. Only the New Zealand Division was still capable of offensive action.

Why General Freyberg set about his task in so hesitant a manner will always remain a mystery. Had he, perhaps, expected from the bombardment an effect so devastating, that no concerted attack by infantry and armour would be necessary? This would seem to be the only possible explanation of his hesitancy. Why had he used only six of the twenty-four battalions under his command? And why did he not launch his assault against the monastery immediately after the air attacks?

The first battle of Cassino ended in a victory for the defence. The Press of the world made no secret of its surprise that, for the first time since El Alamein, German troops had succeeded in resisting the vast material resources of the Allies and in standing their ground in the face of daunting enemy superiority. Disappointment in the various Western headquarters was keen. This time the previous calculations had not worked out and the usual procedure of crushing the enemy with bombs, shells and armour had not brought the anticipated success. Even so, those in the Allied camp persisted in their belief that with a concentration of bombers and artillery unprecedented in the annals of war they would be able to burst asunder the gateway to Rome. But even the 1,250 tons of bombs and the 600,000 shells that crashed down on the defenders of the town and ruins of Cassino in the second Cassino battle did not suffice to break the German resistance.

Chapter 9

The Destruction of the Monastery

Throughout the long years of war the monks of Cassino had lived in peace on their placid hill, without coming into contact with any of the horrors of the struggle. Not until May 1943, when German reinforcements began to march along the Via Casilina, the ancient military highway from Rome to Naples, did the monks realize that the war was now threatening to encroach on their existence. But many months were still to pass before the fury of it descended for the first time upon the world of St Benedict. It occurred on the night of 19/20 July 1943, when Allied bombers attacked the Aquino airfield in the Liri valley below. Up in the monastery excitement and anxiety were intense. The airfield was a sheet of flame, and in the sky above the monastery floated those notorious Christmas-tree lights, the magnesium flares with which the pathfinders guided the bombers behind them to their targets. The monks spent a sleepless night, wandering about the abbey, seeking protection among the many holy relics and praying to God to safeguard their House from damage and destruction.

The next day the airfield was again attacked, and it was not long before the Allied bombers turned their attention to the town of Cassino, without at first, however, causing much destruction. A few bombs hit the Bishop's Palace and caused a certain amount of damage.

It was about this time that the monks suffered an annoying misfortune. A German aircraft struck the cables of the cable railway connecting the monastery with the town below. The cables broke, and communication between town and Abbey became much more difficult. By cable car the journey took a bare eight minutes, but now on foot it took a good hour to get from one to the other.

Cassino town gradually became full of German field hospitals. Initially these were more in the nature of casualty clearing stations, at which the sick and wounded from Sicily were given attention and a rest on their way home to Germany. But with the beginning of the Salerno Battle, the three hospitals which had been established in school buildings and the quarters occupied by the nuns, rapidly filled. The German monk, Father Emmanuel Munding, strode sturdily each day down the hill to visit and comfort his wounded compatriots. Frequently he had hastily to take cover as Allied aircraft roared overhead. The few bombs that had already been dropped on the town served to indicate that some time or other Cassino would be the target of a massed attack, notwithstanding the Red Cross which flew from the hospital roofs. For Cassino was on the important road to Naples and could, at least temporarily, be put out of action by air attack; even so, provided that the Allied aircraft conducted their bombing with reasonable accuracy, the German hospitals did not appear to be in any very great danger.

It was not long before Tedder's bombers arrived. On the 10 September they delivered a heavy attack on the overpopulated little town, and although the hospitals were not hit, casualties among the civilian population were severe. This attack was the signal for the Italians to flee headlong from the town. Nor did it take them long to make up their minds where they would go; up there, in the monastery there was ample room for thousands, and there they would be safe from the wicked bombers. Some crept for safety into the numerous caverns on the slopes of the Monastery Mount; but most of them made straight for the monastery itself, streaming there in hundreds and begging to be allowed to remain there. Magnanimously Bishop Diamare gave them the shelter they sought, and in a very short time there were 1,100 of them in the west wing of the monastery, where they were housed in the college and the episcopal seminary.

The monks, of course, were quite unable to provide for such a concourse of fugitives, and each arrival was expected to bring his own supplies of food with him. The inhabitants of Cassino and the nearby villages therefore started hauling food supplies to the abbey, as though they intended to prepare for a lengthy sojourn there.

At the same time the nuns of the three convents, with orphans in their care, moved up from the town to the monastery. As was related in a previous chapter, a month later they were taken by German troops to safety in Rome.

One night a bomb, dropped most probably in an emergency, fell close to the monastery itself; and though it did no harm, the incident gave rise to the fear that stray bombs might well cause serious damage.

On the night of 10/11 October Cassino town was again the target of an Allied air raid. A number of bombs fell on the slopes of the mountain, but again the monastery itself was not hit. By this time Colonel Schlegel had skilfully arranged for the transfer of the fugitives to a place of greater safety, but when he himself left the abbey on 5 November, there still remained some 150 civilian refugees. As the U.S. Fifth Army approached the abbey, however, more and more Italians fled to the convent, and in no time there were several hundreds claiming shelter and the hospitality of the monks. In some cases fugitives had been advised by German troops to make for the monastery; and on all sides, everyone was quite convinced that the monastery would be spared by the Allies.

Through the medium of the German Ambassador to the Vatican, Pope Pius XII in good time approached Field-Marshal Kesselring with a suggestion that Monte Cassino should be excluded from the battle zone. Kesselring readily expressed his willingness to accept the suggestion, provided that the other side did likewise. Accordingly, at the beginning of December he directed that the area on a 400-yard radius round the monastery should be regarded as a prohibited zone, and on this boundary circle notice boards were prominently placed, forbidding members of the German Armed Forces, regardless of rank, to approach any nearer to the monastery. Not content with that, and to ensure that his orders were obeyed, and at the request of the Bishop, he placed a military police guard at the gates of the monastery, with strict orders to prevent any German troops from entering the precincts.

Kesselring's orders were rigidly respected, even after the military police guard was, for some reason, withdrawn after the Anzio landing. This has been confirmed by Major Werner Schmidt, who, in the first half of February, as already stated, took over the defensive positions on the northern slopes of Monte Cassino and on Rocca Janula. Schmidt issued the strictest orders to his paratroops that in no circumstances were they to set foot in the monastery; and that these orders were rigidly obeyed is confirmed by the Bishop himself. Schmidt set up his battle headquarters in a rain-sodden cave on the forward slopes of the mountain, 400 yards from the monastery.

By the beginning of 1944, the Fifth Army was approaching the foot of the mountain. Disaster was on the march, and the fate of Monte Cassino was to be quickly fulfilled. The first shells, fired by the artillery of U.S. II Corps, which found their way into the monastery area hit the reliquary chapel behind the Sacristy and destroyed it. Thanks to Schlegel and his men, however, the precious reliquaries had been safely transferred to Rome. This was the prologue to further bombardment. The 15 January was a black day. Heavy artillery shells hit the monastery and severely damaged Luca Giordano's great fresco over the portals of the Basilica. From then onwards, the monastery was hit again and again and suffered grave damage.

On the 5 February, following a heavy bombardment, forty women fled to the monastery from the caves and grottoes in which they had taken refuge. Terror-stricken, they surged round the monastery and threatened to burn down the gates unless they were admitted. When the monks opened the gates, in addition to these women a large number of other civilians pushed their way in and once more filled the abbey, creeping into the basements and cellars, where they felt they would be comparatively safe.

On the same day, the refugees in the monastery suffered their first casualties, a man, two women and a boy being killed by the shell fire. On 8 February the monks counted more than one hundred shells which hit the abbey. But worse was to come. On 9 February the superb bronze gates of the main portal of the Basilica, which the Bishop Desiderius (1058–87) had had made in Constantinople, were severely damaged. The next day there was great excitement in the monastery. In the afternoon some Italian boys brought to the Bishop some leaflets, which they had just picked up in the garden and which in the name of the Fifth Army called upon the monks to vacate the monastery:

Italian friends, beware! We have so far carefully avoided bombarding the monastery of Monte Cassino. The Germans have not hesitated to take advantage of the fact. But now the battle is approaching the precincts of the holy place. The time has now come when we must turn our weapons against the monastery itself. We warn you, so that you may seek safety elsewhere. This is a most urgent warning! Leave the monastery at once! Take heed of this warning! It is issued for your own benefit.

THE FIFTH ARMY

It was not clear, however, what the U.S. Fifth Army proposed to turn against the monastery. The wording '*siamo costretti a puntare le nostre armi in tutti i modi di civitare il bombardamento del monastero di Montecassino*' gave no clear indication of Allied intentions, particularly as in Italian the word '*bombardamento*' can be applied equally to artillery fire or air attack.

The leaflet naturally caused panic among the refugees. Many dashed out at once to seek shelter in the near-by caverns and caves; others crept into the deepest cellars they could find, and many sought refuge in the

Basilica, convinced that God would not permit the superb church which contained the grave of St Benedict to be destroyed. During the morning the Bishop and his monks had joined the refugees in the college, which Schlegel had recommended to them as being the safest place. Here they were thirty feet underground, and above them was the sixty-foot tower which contained the meteorological office.

At first the Bishop could not make up his mind what was the best thing to do. Initially, he told the monks that each was at liberty to seek shelter as he deemed best. But finally he decided to ask the appropriate German military authority for help to move the monks and refugees to safety during the night of 15/16 February. But preparations had to be made and agreement reached with the relevant German staff, before the evacuation could take place. This took time, since no one dared to show his face outside the precincts during daylight and contact with the Germans could only be made during the hours of darkness. To evacuate the monastery the very next night seemed impossible, for 'the leaflets calling upon the fugitives to leave the monastery had been dropped late in the afternoon of 14 February, and to accomplish the difficult task of organizing the civilian evacuation by the morning of 15 February was not possible. It was decided that the organized evacuation should take place on the night of 15/16 February; but anyone who so desired was at liberty to leave at once. Apart from this, at the time the leaflets had been dropped, the monastery had already been hit several hundred times—perhaps even a thousand—and those who knew that there were no soldiers or military installations of any kind within the confines of the monastery refused absolutely to believe that it would be deliberately bombarded and razed to the ground by massed and concentrated air attack.'*

Then, unexpectedly, two young Italians volunteered to go out at once to try and contact the German troops in position at Massa Albaneta. They had not gone far, however, when rifle and machine-gun fire drove them back. A second attempt, this time under the protection of a white flag, also failed. This created great despondency among the inmates of the monastery, who felt that they were held captive within the mighty walls, unable to do anything to help themselves and at the mercy of such fate as the Fifth Army had in store for them.

That evening, the Sacristan, Don Agostino, made his way to a German officer who had been observed in a place where, it was thought, it might be possible to get to him. The officer in question was Lieutenant Deiber, who was in command of two tanks of the 90 Panzer Grenadier Division. To him Don Agostino, who spoke German, gave the Bishop's message, asking the German authorities for assistance in the evacuation of the monastery

* La Distruzione di Montecassino—Documenti e Testimonianze.

and for a lorry to be sent for the conveyance of those unable to walk. The Bishop intended to proceed with his monks direct to the Allied lines and to send the refugees in the reverse direction into the German-held area.

That same evening Deiber reported to Schmidt for orders. For obvious military reasons Schmidt had no option but to refuse permission for the monks to pass through the German lines. The Serpentina, the only road from the monastery to the town, had for days been under fire, bomb and shell craters had made it all but impassable for vehicles, and it was thus impossible, in any case, to send a lorry. Schmidt directed that both monks and refugees should leave the monastery and take the mountain track leading to Piedimonte, though he did not fix any specific time for them to do so.

This message was passed on to the Bishop by Deiber at five o'clock the next morning, four and a half hours, that is, before the beginning of the air attack.

Leccisotti's assertions that the Germans ordered the monastery to be evacuated during the night of 15/16 February and stated that anyone attempting to approach Cassino town would be fired upon are both inaccurate. In reality Schmidt left the Bishop complete liberty of action and did no more than suggest that he should take the path to Piedimonte, since it was freer of artillery fire than any other. More than that, Schmidt, who was expecting to be attacked at any moment, could not do; of necessity he had to leave it to the inmates of the monastery to work out their own salvation. Their request to be allowed to go across to the Allied lines Schmidt could not in any circumstances grant. In the valley below were the American tanks, watching like hawks for the slightest sign of movement on the mountain slopes. The ground was, in any case, so uneven that the monks could only have reached the American lines by daylight; in the process the German positions would inevitably have been disclosed, and it is not difficult to guess what then would have happened—the tanks and the artillery would at last have found the targets for which they had been seeking for days. That was a risk which Schmidt could not possibly accept.

Although Schmidt had given him a free hand, the old Bishop could not bring himself to abandon the monastery at once. It may be that he under-estimated the dangers that were threatening, or he may have thought that to move out by daylight was too risky. In the end he adhered to his resolve to leave during the night of 15/16 February.

At about the same time, the fitters and mechanics of the Allied air fleets were checking the bombers which were to bring death and destruction to Monte Cassino. On the morning of 15 February, in clear flying weather, the first wave of 142 Flying Fortresses took off from the Apulian airfields and set course for St Benedict's Mount. Shortly before ten o'clock they sighted the mountain on which the mighty building peacefully rested.

The monks still had no idea that the rumble of heavy bombers which they could hear approaching from the north concerned them in any way. Prayers were just being said in the Bishop's small room. The monks were praying to the Mother of God to protect them, and when they reached the words '*pro nobis Christum exora*', a terrific explosion shattered the peace. The first bombs were bursting. It was nine forty-five.

The bombers dropped their deadly loads in two waves: '142 Flying Fortresses dropped 287 tons of 500-lb. explosive bombs and 66½ tons of 100-lb. incendiaries; they were followed by forty-seven B-25s and forty B-26s, which dropped a further hundred tons of high-explosive bombs. The buildings of the monastery were destroyed and breaches were blown in the walls; but thanks to their great strength, these walls were not split from top to bottom.'* The effect, nevertheless, was completely devastating. Monks and civilians alike were terrified; all went down on their knees or flung themselves to the ground. The Bishop himself gave absolution to those around him. Terrible explosions rent the air and filled the rooms with dust and acrid smoke. Not only the monastery, but the whole mountain quaked as though it were being shaken by some giant hand. Suddenly, after half an hour, there was silence again, and the inferno seemed to be over. Then a deaf and dumb man, who for many years had been in the service of the Sacristan, burst in upon the monks and with signs and gestures indicated that the Basilica, in which he had taken refuge, had been reduced to a heap of ruins. The very heart of the whole monastery, the most precious treasure of Monte Cassino, had been the first to be destroyed.

The Bishop now hastened out into the open, to be confronted with a truly terrifying spectacle. Where once the superb Basilica had risen proudly heavenwards, there now remained only the stumps of shattered pillars; where once the roof had spread its shelter over treasures of inestimable beauty, was now only the blue vault of heaven; and over the whole of the shattered monastery swept thick, dark clouds of smoke. Only the lower terraces remained intact, and rubble and débris were everywhere piled sky-high. It was a horrible picture of desolation, into the midst of which the American artillery now began to direct a furious bombardment.

The terror among the refugees was indescribable. Many forsook their places of refuge, fled out into the open and were at once caught in the midst of the murderous artillery fire. Others ran panic-stricken to the portals of the monastery to seek shelter and safety outside the doomed building; but they, too, were caught by the shells and laid low. Hundreds

* General Sir Henry Maitland Wilson in Report to the Combined Chiefs of Staff, 8 January–10 May, 1944.

were buried beneath the débris in the Priory courtyard. Some of them may have still been alive; but when some stout-hearted souls went out to their assistance, the storm broke out afresh, and they too, were caught and killed while on their errand of mercy.

Once again the fury of the bombs wrought their terrible work. The apartments in which the Bishop, the monks and three families of refugees had sought shelter were partly destroyed, but by great good fortune no one was hurt. From the cellars below the anguished cries of terror from the women and children penetrated into the room above; and all the time shower after shower of bombs came crashing down. It seemed as though the end of the world had come.

At last, in the afternoon, the hell came to an end. Covered in dust, his garments in shreds, the aged Bishop, who had been temporarily cut off by the collapse of a ceiling, crept out into the open. His heart bled as he gazed on this picture of terrible and senseless destruction. In the middle of the Priory courtyard gaped a huge crater, the cloisters had collapsed and the roof over the Torretta had been blown to pieces. The palm trees which had for so long graced the courtyard had been reduced to pitiful stumps. The central courtyard, attributed to Bramante, had been completely shattered, its beautiful pillars and the superb Loggia del Paradiso had collapsed and were lost for ever. Great sections of quarried masonry, torn from their places by the fury of the bombs, lay scattered about the courtyards like so many lumps of sugar. The statue of St Scholastica had disappeared and that of St Benedict had been decapitated. On all sides a picture of nothing but ghastly destruction, a picture that proclaimed more eloquently then any words the futility of war.

The strong, fortress-like outer walls of the college had remained intact, but the font in the central courtyard, a perfect example of Renaissance art, had collapsed; the marble staircase leading up to the Basilica and into the Courtyard of the Benefactors had been shattered and buried beneath a heap of rubble. The Courtyard of the Benefactors itself was a deplorable sight. The numerous statues of the men of both the laity and the Church who in the course of centuries had made the monastery the object of their special care, had been hurled from their pedestals, buried beneath the rubble or completely destroyed. And the Basilica! Rubble and débris were piled fifteen feet high in the aisles and all that remained of the pillars were a few pitiful stumps, mutely rising in accusation to heaven. Everything else had been destroyed—the frescoes, the magnificent choir, the wonderful organ. But, as was later found, the grave of the founder had suffered no damage; neither shell nor bomb had been able to disturb the resting place of St Benedict and St Scholastica. The Sacristy, too, with its beautiful murals and carvings had been levelled to the ground. Only the entrances to the crypt had remained unscathed, though the crypt itself had been partially destroyed. In the Torretta a few objects had survived, among them the *'cella'* in which, according to tradition, St Benedict had written the Rules of his Order.

The magnitude of the destruction and the shattering impression which the sight of the ruined abbey made on the minds of men are well reflected in a remark made by General Juin, when he revisited the monastery in the spring of 1947: 'It weighed on my conscience,' he said, 'to know that I had been involved, even if only at a distance—but without any feeling of compunction—in the attack which had caused all this havoc. I hastened away from the scene of destruction, to turn my eyes to something durable and living.'

The work of destruction was complete, in spite of Churchill's assertion: 'On February 15, therefore, after the monks had been given full warning, over 450 tons of bombs were dropped, and heavy damage was done. The great outer walls and gateway still stood. The result was not good.'* To this it is the author's duty to retort that only the strong outer walls of the western transept, the staircase leading to the entrance and part of the Torretta escaped undamaged by the bombs. The whole of the rest of the monastery was one vast heap of rubble. From the point of view of the attack, it could certainly be said that the result had been 'good'.

It was not irreplaceable works of art alone that had fallen victim to this attack; a large number of civilians had perished under the hail of bombs and beneath the collapsing buildings and falling roofs. Some of the aircraft, taking them to be German soldiers, had opened fire with their machine-guns on the refugees fleeing pell-mell from the doomed buildings. The most careful estimates place the number of killed at approximately 250, and this is probably correct, though the precise number will never be known.

Of the monks themselves, none had been seriously injured. A few had been buried under the ruins, but all had managed to free themselves and reach safety. But among the refugees there were heart-rending scenes. Parents abandoned their shrieking children and fled to safety; sons fled, leaving their aged parents to their fate; one woman had both her feet blown off, many lay dying, and agonizing shrieks rose from the buildings, the corridors and—the heaps of rubble. It was a scene of human misery, despair and desperate need.

When the bombing came to an end, the artillery fire also ceased for the time being. A few of the monks and the majority of the civilians took advantage of the pause to leave the monastery and make their way into the valley in the direction of Piedimonte. There remained behind the Bishop,

* *The Second World War*, Vol. V.

six priests and lay preachers and a few hundred refugees, who clustered together on the staircase to the entrance. The Bishop and his monks made their way to the Capella della Pietà in the Torretta, where they were comparatively safe.

At about 8 p.m. Lieutenant Deiber reappeared and is said to have stated that negotiations with the Americans had already been initiated for an armistice to enable the survivors to be taken to a place of safety. No such negotiations, however, took place. Field-Marshal Kesselring certainly gave an order that the inmates were to be rescued forthwith and the Bishop and monks sent to Rome.

At the end of his conversation with the Bishop, Deiber asked him whether he was prepared to state in writing that no German soldier had been asked into the monastery before the attack began. Bishop Diamare, using the altar of the Pietà as a desk, at once drafted (in Italian) and signed the following declaration:

I solemnly declare that no German soldier has ever been stationed within the precincts of the monastery of Monte Cassino; that for a while three military police were on duty, with the sole object of ensuring that the neutral zone round the monastery was being respected. But these latter were withdrawn twenty days ago.

> signed Gregorio Diamare
> Bishop and Abbot of Monte Cassino.
> Deiber, Lieutenant.
> Monte Cassino, 15 February 1944

And in German was added:

I confirm, as requested, that there has never been and there is now no German soldier in the Monte Cassino monastery.

> (*signed*) Gregorio Diamare
> Deiber.
> 15 February 1944.

The hope that an armistice would be arranged and that they would be rescued by the Germans persuaded the Bishop and his monks to remain in the ruins until the morning of 17 February. They did not know that just as they were leaving the monastery, German soldiers were on their way to fetch them and conduct them to Rome.

By 17 February the majority of the refugees had departed of their own free will. Except for the monks, all that remained were three families, a few abandoned children, some old people and half a dozen able-bodied men. The greatest problems were care of the wounded and water shortage, until one of the monks discovered that the small cistern in the kitchen was undamaged. Water supply was, later, one of the great problems which faced the defenders of the ruins.

Still there was no peace for the survivors. Mercilessly the Allied artillery poured its shells into the ruins, roofs continued to collapse under the weight of the rubble heaped upon them, and the hard-pressed people did not know from one moment to the next when they might be buried under the ruins. On the morning of 17 February the last of the inmates set out on the hazardous journey to Piedimonte.

The woman who had lost both her feet, and a sick child, were put on improvised stretchers, one of the lay brothers carried a lamed infant in his arms, and the monks helped the aged Bishop along. In this way the pitiful little handful set forth on its twenty-five mile march. Before leaving the monastery the Bishop gave absolution to them all and then, grasping a large wooden cross, he resolutely set forth. Fortunately, the artillery had ceased fire, and the little band reached the chapel of San Rachiso unharmed. When they reached the plain below, it was found that the maimed woman was missing. The eighty-year-old lay brother, Carlomanno Pelagalli, had been seen coming down the final slope and approaching the Via Casilina, but after that all trace of him disappeared. It was later learned that he had turned back, to die in the monastery in which he had served for fifty years. He was found by men of the 1st Battalion, 3 Parachute Regiment, when they occupied the ruins on 20 February, wandering round with a flickering candle in his hand, searching for rooms which no longer existed. The Battalion medical officer took him in his care until he died.

When they reached the valley below, the monks and refugees came across a German field dressing station, where they were advised, in view of the increasing artillery fire, to continue their journey in small groups. Here the Sacristan, Don Agostino, and a German soldier who was guiding the party to Piedimonte were wounded, but fortunately not badly. The Bishop was completely exhausted. The long march over the shell-torn tracks and rugged slopes had brought the venerable old man to the verge of a physical breakdown.

The German medical orderlies at once took charge of him and applied restoratives, and while they were doing so, a German soldier arrived with the news that the High Command were searching urgently for the Bishop and monks and that Schulz's Battle Group had been ordered to find them and escort them to safety; and at about 4.30 p.m. an ambulance arrived to fetch the Bishop. 'The N.C.O. was most kind. He said there was no time to lose, but he gave us oranges, saw to it that the maimed child was comfortably settled on a stretcher, got the three women in and finally helped the

Bishop and his secretary into the ambulance. He started his engine and apologized in advance for the shaking we were about to receive, explaining that the continuous artillery fire would compel him to drive at high speed.'* The ambulance took them to Castellmassimo, the battle head-quarters of XIV Corps, where a reporter from the broadcasting service was waiting, and to him the Bishop gave an interview. In this way the German High Command intended that the whole world should be told from authoritative lips that the monastery had not been misused by the Germans for military purposes, as the enemy propaganda had been asserting for days. In Castellmassimo Bishop Diamare was treated with great courtesy. General von Senger did his best to provide him with comfortable quarters and to try to help him forget the experiences of the past few days. As soon as the Bishop felt strong enough, the General proposed to send him to Santo Anselmo to stay with the Head of the Order, who was a compatriot of von Senger's.

When the car in which von Senger's A.D.C. was taking them to Santa Anselmo reached the outskirts of Rome, however, it was stopped, and the Bishop was invited to go to the broadcasting station. Here a prepared statement, setting forth the truth about the destruction of the monastery was submitted to him, with a request that, if he approved of the text, he would broadcast it. As the contents were correct in every detail, the Bishop had no hesitation in acceding to the German request.

In Santo Anselmo he met all his sons once again, who had preceded him to Rome. Most of them, of course, had been spared the horrors of 15 February, which had witnessed chronologically the latest, but in magnitude the most complete, destruction of the ancient monastery.

How did it come about that the monastery was destroyed in this way? Who gave the order that it should be bombarded? Who bears the responsibility for the downfall of Monte Cassino?

The Allied propaganda machine started in good time to work at full speed, and Press and radio trumpeted to the world at large that the Germans had turned the monastery into a fortress bristling with guns, and that it was for this reason that the Allies had so far failed to gain a decisive victory at Cassino. In these circumstances, there was no alternative but to bring weapons to bear against it.

German propaganda did not fail to reply. It issued a categorical declaration that not one single German soldier was in the monastery or in its immediate vicinity and a solemn warning against the use of arms against this venerable and holy place.

But by 12 February the air attack had already been decided upon, despite the fact that the orders for it were based solely on the unsubstantiated

* Leccisotti, *Monte Cassino*.

assumption that the monastery constituted the keypoint of the whole defensive system.

It was not until after the Commander-in-Chief, Mediterranean, General Sir Henry Maitland Wilson, together with the American General Jacob Devers, had made a personal reconnaissance by helicopter over the monastery and had reported that they had seen wireless antennae inside the monastery and observed German soldiers moving about inside and immediately outside the buildings, that the Allied High Command felt that it now had proof that the monastery had been occupied by the Germans; and since the reconnaissance had been carried out at a height of under 250 feet, the proof seemed to be both concrete and irrefutable.

The Mediterranean High Command, which was predominantly British, hesitated no longer. Maitland Wilson summarized his appreciation of the situation in a telegram addressed to the British Chiefs of Staff, assuring them that the abbey formed an important part of the German defensive system, that their artillery was using it as an observation post, that snipers were already installed there and that in the immediate vicinity there were guns, dug-outs and ammunition dumps. London, disinclined from the outset to veto the bombardment, now agreed that the monastery must be destroyed, and General Eaker, the Commander-in-Chief, Allied Air Forces, Mediterranean, received orders from Maitland Wilson to prepare an immediate and massive attack.

Churchill attributes the responsibility for the destruction of Monte Cassino to Alexander: 'The Army Commander, General Mark Clark, unwillingly sought and obtained permission from General Alexander, who accepted the responsibility.'

There is no justification for the assertion. As Commander-in-Chief, 15 Army Group, Alexander had not under his command the requisite forces to carry out such an operation. He was in command of the land forces only, and had no authority to issue orders to the air arm as a whole or any part of it. The latter, in so far as the tactical air arm was concerned, came under the sole command of General Maitland Wilson. But he, too, had no four-engined bombers which he could send against Monte Cassino. General Eaker, his Air Commander, had at his disposal only light and medium bombers and no Flying Fortresses. The latter belonged exclusively to the U.S. 15 Strategic Air Fleet, and that was commanded not by Wilson or Eaker, but by General Spaatz, who from London was directing the American war in the air against Germany and her allies. It is therefore not unreasonable to assume that Spaatz must have released Flying Fortresses for the attack at the request of the highest British authorities.

Alexander may well have said that he would accept the responsibility. But in the final instance the ultimate responsibility rested, surely, with the highest authority, both political and military, in Britain. For the destruction of Monte Cassino was not a purely military decision; there was also an important political aspect involved.

Through the diplomatic representatives accredited to the Holy See, the Vatican, too, had approached the Western powers in an attempt to ensure that the monastery would not become involved in the fighting and that its sanctity would be respected. The Allies, however, would do no more than promise that they would try to avoid destroying the monastery. But when the Allied High Command in Italy demanded the bombardment of the abbey, a political problem at once arose. The governments concerned, however, seem complacently to have brushed aside this awkward aspect. It is therefore not surprising that the Vatican regarded this repellent piece of destruction as a very unfriendly act. Its official newspaper, the *Osservatore Romano*, wrote: 'The Vatican has seen no evidence to show that the monastery was being used by the Germans as a strongpoint'. . . and went on to say that the tragic end of Monte Cassino had evoked lively indignation throughout the world and had been an unforgivable insult.

The western powers were prepared to risk a deterioration of their relations with the Vatican in order to safeguard the lives of Allied soldiers.

As early as 11 February Allied Headquarters in Italy announced: 'The reports that the Germans were using the monastery of Monte Cassino as a strongpoint have in the meanwhile been confirmed. Reports from authoritative observers show that not only a large number of machine-guns, but also artillery have been placed in positions dominating the crest of the mountain.' (*Neue Zuericher Zeitung*, No. 245/44.) And on 13 February, the day after Freyberg made his demand, the United Press issued the following report: 'Although it was initially announced that the Benedictine monastery on Monte Cassino, which the Germans have fortified, would be spared in deference to representations made by the Vatican, it has now been officially stated that the Fifth Army will perhaps be unable "to continue to avoid this issue".' (*Neue Zuericher Zeitung*, No. 260/44.) More brazen still, however, was the Allied communiqué of 15 February: 'Pilots of the medium bombers report that numbers of German soldiers were observed fleeing out of the monastery, but that no monks or civilians were seen. During the first attack in the morning, pilots of the Flying Fortresses counted about one hundred German soldiers fleeing from the monastery. . .' (*Neue Zuericher Zeitung*, No. 2672/44.)

On the other hand the German Supreme Headquarters communiqué of 16 February stated: 'The venerable building of Monte Cassino monastery which, as was reported yesterday, was attacked by the enemy air arm, though no German troops were in it, has been almost completely destroyed and burnt out. . . .'

Since then, of course, the whole world has recognized that the holy place had been most scrupulously respected by the German troops and that all assertions to the contrary had borne no relation to the facts.

After Field-Marshal Kesselring had ordered his proscribed zone round the monastery, the only Germans to visit Monte Cassino were: General von Senger und Etterlin, Commander XIV Panzer Corps, on Christmas Day to attend Divine Service in the crypt; Dr Poppel, the medical officer of the 1st Parachute Machine-gun Battalion and two medical orderlies between the 10 and 14 February, at the request of the monks, to treat wounded civilians. The last German soldier to cross the threshold had been Lieutenant Deiber; but he, too, had been asked to come by the monks. There were no others, and all assertions to the contrary are either genuine errors or wicked lies. There is today ample evidence—much of it emanating from Allied sources—to prove conclusively that the monastery was at no time ever used by any member of the German armed forces for any military purpose whatsoever. Before it was destroyed, it had never been occupied by German troops, and no observation post, weapon or store depot of any sort was ever established there. The immediate vicinity of the abbey was also deliberately avoided by all German troops. All weapons and all positions were outside the radius prescribed by the Commander-in-Chief, South West. The nearest troops to the monastery were two tanks of 90 Division, which were in position 450 yards south-west of it. Four hundred and fifty yards south of it were four mortars, and 450 yards to the south-east 71 Mortar Regiment had established an observation post.

In spite of this, it is to this day still being asserted that German positions, with fortified emplacements and dug-in tanks, were in the immediate vicinity of the abbey. Churchill himself says: '. . . the enemy fortifications were hardly separate from the building itself.' (*The Second World War*, Vol. V.) In actual fact, neither in the vicinity of the monastery nor on the slopes of the mountain had any fortifications been constructed; the only fortifications were those of the Gustav Line on the eastern edge of Cassino and to the north of the town. In any case, those north of the town had been captured by the Americans long before the question of the bombardment of the monastery came up. There were a few positions and ammunition dumps, but these were as far removed from the 400-yard zone as were the fortified emplacements which Churchill's imagination put inside it.

The following are some examples of the evidence, to which reference was made above. On 18 February Field-Marshal Kesselring issued the following official statement:

1. . . . .

2. The enemy High Command has stated that the attack was delivered with the object of destroying the German forces occupying the monastery and the fortified emplacements they had constructed there. This I emphatically reject.

A few months ago, the Vatican approached me through the medium of the German Ambassador to the Holy See with a request that I would refrain from incorporating the monastery in the battle area. To this request I at once acceded, provided that the other side agreed to do so as well. I thereupon issued orders forbidding any member of the German armed forces to enter the monastery or to approach its immediate vicinity. Strict adherence to these orders was ensured by the appropriate military authorities and in particular by the establishment of pickets of military police round the immediate vicinity of the monastery. Until after the bombardment, use was not even made of permission, in case of necessity, to convey badly wounded into the monastery. On the other hand, Italian refugees were freely allowed to take shelter in the monastery if they so desired. On the day of the attack there were several hundred such refugees in the monastery, who, confident that the sanctity of the holy place would be respected, had sought refuge there. In order to ensure the safety of the irreplaceable treasures and library, I had long before approved of their removal by German troops, who handed them over to the Vatican State.

3. The assertion that the monastery had been transformed into 'the strongest artillery fortress in the world' is a wicked lie.

4. The further assertions that the building and its grounds had been used for the establishment of other military installations—machine-gun nests, observation posts, etc.—are pure fabrications. Once the treasures had been moved to safety, no German soldier set foot in the abbey again. The bombardment by the American artillery on 15 February and subsequent air attacks therefore caused no damage of a military character, and no member of the German Armed Forces was even wounded. The monks who had remained there and the Italian refugees alone suffered as a result of this enemy action.

5. My assertion that no member of the German Armed Forces had ever been stationed in the monastery is confirmed by the following statements:

(a) By the Abbot of Monte Cassino Monastery, Bishop Gregorio Diamare:
'As requested, I hereby declare that there neither is nor ever has been any member of the German Armed forces in the Monte Cassino monastery'.
(signed) Gregorio Diamare
Ciscovo Abate di Montecassino
15. 2. 1944

(b) By the Monastery Administrator, Don Nicola Clementi, and the Episcopal Delegate of the Administrative Department of the diocese of Monte Cassino, Don Francisco Salconio:
'I, Don Nicola Clementi, Administrator of the monastery of Monte Cassino, and I Don Francesco Salconio, Episcopal Delegate of the Administrative Department of the diocese of Monte Cassino, who survived the

bombardment and destruction, declare that there were no German defensive installations or military material of any sort either in the monastery itself or in its immediate vicinity.'

(*signed*) Don Nicola Clementi
Don Francisco Salconio.
15. 2. 1944.

6. Consequent upon the destruction of the monastery, the incorporation of the ruins into the German defensive system followed as a military matter of course.

7. The Papal residence of Castell Gandolfo, also severely damaged by an Allied air attack, in which more than 500 persons, including fifteen nuns, were killed, was also never occupied by German troops. The extraterritoriality of the estate was rigidly respected.

(*signed*) Kesselring
Field-Marshal.

The news of the destruction of the monastery naturally created a great stir throughout the world. Goebbels, of course, made the most masterly use of this grist brought thus fortuitously to his mill, and for days on end the 'Monte Cassino Story' filled the columns of the German Press and became a major feature of the broadcasting service. For their part, the Allies were doing their best to justify their action and to portray it as a lesson that the Germans would do well to take to heart. The *Neue Zuericher Zeitung* (No. 275/44) for example, contained the following report of a Press conference given by President Roosevelt:

The decision (to bomb the monastery) is of fundamental significance regarding the Allied attitude towards the question of the protection of historical and cultural monuments in the theatres of war. Roosevelt clearly defined this attitude at his recent Press conference. For as long as 'no military necessity existed', he said, such objects should be spared—but no longer. It was of greater importance to safeguard the lives of Allied soldiers. If the Allies were confronted with the choice of saving either cultural monuments or human lives, there would be no doubt as to their decision, the President declared.

And the Archbishop of Canterbury stated in the House of Lords:

Some people ask scornfully what is the worth of a few dead stones in comparison with the life of one single soldier? But they forget that these things belong to the very civilization for which we are fighting against barbarism. On the other hand, others, in their zeal for history and art, entirely overlook the merciless demands of war. In the interest of the enslaved and oppressed countries we must not let ourselves be deterred by anything which will lead to the swift defeat of our enemies. The enemy must not be allowed to think that, if he uses cultural or historical establishments as military positions, he will remain immune from attack (*Neue Zuericher Zeitung*, No. 278/44).

The *Basler Nachrichten*, however, expressed a different point of view:

We cannot accept as an answer that these were merely inanimate objects and that a human life is of more value than the venerable monastery (Quotation published in the *Deutsche Allgemeine Zeitung*, No. 51/44).

Be that as it may, the Allied High Command certainly believed it had ample proof that Monte Cassino had been transformed into a fortress and been occupied by German troops. In view of the Allied attitude described above,- however, towards the preservation of cultural monuments, their decision to raze the monastery to the ground should cause no surprise.

It is, nevertheless, difficult to avoid gaining the impression that the proofs were slender in the extreme. General Maitland Wilson, it is true, did not hesitate, at no small personal risk, to go out and convince himself of the correctness or otherwise of the troops' reports, but what he can have taken to be wireless antennae remains a complete mystery. Did he seriously believe that German troops would move about freely, either in or outside the abbey, while an enemy reconnaissance aircraft was flying over them? It is axiomatic that all movement 'freezes' in such circumstances, and if German troops had, indeed, occupied the monastery, then they would have had the best of reasons for 'making themselves scarce'.

The question, then, inevitably arises—was the destruction really necessary, even if the Germans had not respected the inviolability of the monastery? And the answer is: It was not!

To many this may sound nonsense. But consideration of the following aspects may, perhaps, cause them to change their minds. From the very outset it was a grave tactical blunder to attempt to capture so naturally strong a position by means of a frontal attack. Established practice has proved the wisdom of attacking an obstacle of this nature by indirect means. With the attack of the British X Corps on the Garigliano, the thrust of the Texas Division on the Rapido and the French Corps' offensive, General Clark had, of course, been making strenuous endeavours to bring about the fall of Monte Cassino by means of a turning movement. But, as has already been mentioned, the monastery hill was like a magnet exercising a quite incredible fascination, against which Clark's perception was completely powerless.

It must be remembered that Colonel Schulz's paratroops were hanging by their eyebrows to literally the last slopes before the Via Casilina. Had

the Allies dropped their bombs on these positions instead of on the monastery, they could have by-passed the monastery without a qualm, particularly as it was completely dominated by the height to the north-west of it.
A thrust over the mountains and down to the Via Casilina would have put
them in possession of Monte Cassino without even breaking a window in
the monastery.

Furthermore, it may well be asked again why the Allies did not seize the
chance offered to them by Juin's capture of Monte Belvedere. The Via
Terelle also led to the Via Casilina, and the German gunners assumed to be
in the monastery would have been powerless to intervene in such an
operation.

The Allies themselves furnish the answer. When in the second battle of
Cassino they were making no progress and this time really were suffering
from the effects of German artillery fire directed from the monastery,
day after day they put a smoke screen round the monastery and blinded the
gunners. That they nevertheless failed to break through is due to the facts
that their infantry had already reached the limits of human endurance
and that by this time the German defence in the town of Cassino had been
strengthened to such a degree that it was quite capable of resisting any
pressure that the enemy could bring to bear on it.

If the Allies were convinced that the monastery had been transformed
into 'the strongest artillery fortress in the world', they could have neutralized the effectiveness of this 'fortress' to a very large degree by a continuous
use of smoke, and there then would have been no need to make the Germans
a present of a ready-made fortress by bombarding it. For this indeed was
the sole result achieved by the destruction of the monastery. Now the
German paratroops occupied the ruins and entrenched themselves, well
protected in the innumerable underground cellars and corridors, the floors
of which were covered with a mattress of dust several feet thick. Now the
Germans had every right to occupy it and to turn it truly into the lynch-pin
of their whole defensive system; and now Freyberg himself was to feel
the weight of the boomerang which, at his insistence, the Allied High
Command had hurled at Monte Cassino.

No matter how one twists and turns the facts, there is no justification for
this senseless piece of destruction. Nor was it only a tactical and political
blunder. The destruction was an irreplaceable loss to the whole of the
Christian world. In this connexion, General von Senger und Etterlin
says: 'Up to a point the Allies' decision to destroy the monastery is
understandable. . . . Anyone who has led troops in battle appreciates
the feelings of the private soldier of whatever nationality, when face to face
with an obstacle. He does not wish to see his comrades killed, to be killed
or wounded himself, or to be robbed of victory simply because some

building or other must be spared. But where lies the boundary of the liberty of action of a military commander, in whose hands lies not only the safety of the men entrusted to him, but also the decision regarding the value or otherwise of "buildings"?'

The verdicts of authoritative critics and experts, many of them from the Allied camp, are nearly all devastatingly condemnatory. Great tribute must be paid to General Clark for his courage, in the interests of historic truth, in taking the following objective viewpoint:

I say the bombardment of the abbey was a mistake, and I say this with a full knowledge of the controversy which has arisen over this episode. The official attitude is perhaps best summarized by the State Department's memorandum of 16 October 1945 to the Under Secretary of State of the Vatican, which says that 'the Allied commanders at the front had irrefutable proof that the abbey of Monte Cassino formed part of the German defensive system'.

I was one of the Allied commanders at the front and I was in command at Cassino, and I say there was no proof that the abbey was being used by the Germans for military purposes. I affirm that no German soldier was ever in the abbey for any purpose other than to tend the sick or to visit the cloister—and after the beginning of the battle they had no chance of visiting it. The bombardment of the abbey was not only a superfluous mistake from the propaganda point of view, it was also a tactical mistake of the first order. It greatly enhanced the difficulties of our endeavours and increased our losses in men, machines and time.*

Fuller, too, in the conclusions he reaches, is very much the reverse of complimentary to the Allied headquarters:

The blame for the failure was debited to the abbey, instead of to the hill upon which it stood; therefore it was decided to destroy the building. . . . Because the abbey was so obviously a bomb-trap and because Monastery Hill provided the Germans with innumerable observation posts, it is highly improbable that Kesselring—an able soldier—would occupy the abbey itself, and since then it has been stated by the monks who lived there that it was never used as an observation post. . . . But all that this destructive bombing did was to turn the abbey from a building into a fortress, because the defence of a rubble heap mixed with ruins is an easier and more comfortable operation than the defence of a building. Not only is material at hand to construct strongpoints with, but there are no roofs and floors to fall upon the defenders. Therefore, the bombing of the abbey was not so much a piece of vandalism as an act of sheer tactical stupidity.†

General Maitland Wilson, no doubt for good reasons, remains reticent.

* *Calculated Risk.*   † *The Second World War.*

All he says is:

On the main front our attacks were repulsed, thanks to our inability to take possession of the mountain on which the Cistercian abbey stood, and this in spite of the heavy bombers we had sent against the monastery.*

And so, Monte Cassino fell victim to human inefficiency, political considerations and the brutalizing influences of war. Many of Europe's cultural monuments had died before it, many more were to suffer a like fate after it. But still—Monte Cassino lives! Where before there was nothing but a mountain of ruins and rubble, the walls and roofs of the immortal House of St Benedict have today been resurrected. Unbroken in spirit and full of courage, the Benedictines have rebuilt their monastery; fresh branches are growing from the evergreen tree-trunk that is the ancient symbol of Monte Cassino, and once more the time-honoured motto resumes its age-old significance: *Succisa virescit!*

* Field-Marshal Lord Wilson, *Eight Years Overseas.*

Chapter 10

Anzio–Nettuno—A Miscalculation

So far the course of the Italian campaign had been a deep disappointment to the Allies. Rome, the great prize, had receded further than ever from their grasp, the German resistance had grown steadily stronger and the calculations of the military planners that the enemy forces would be annihilated by the use of overwhelming air power and artillery had been proved wrong. Churchill himself growled: 'This stagnation of the Italian campaign is becoming a veritable scandal.' He did all he could to put an end to the 'scandal' and concentrated his efforts on trying to get the campaign moving again. To capture Rome and then march on into the Balkans—that was the ultimate object of all his thinking and scheming.

But in the late autumn of 1943, the attempt to break the German defensive system by means of a frontal attack had, in reality, stood little or no chance of success. The struggle for the Reinhard Line, which had been so costly for the Allies, had been a clear indication of what Alexander's divisions could expect in their onward march on Rome. There is nothing that the Allies would have liked better than to have prised open the German position by means of an amphibious attack directed against its flank and rear. Eisenhower had planned to put a division ashore near the mouth of the Tiber and at the same time break through with both Armies. But the defence of the Reinhard Line had proved to be so stubborn, that he feared that a single division would be too weak to survive south of Rome

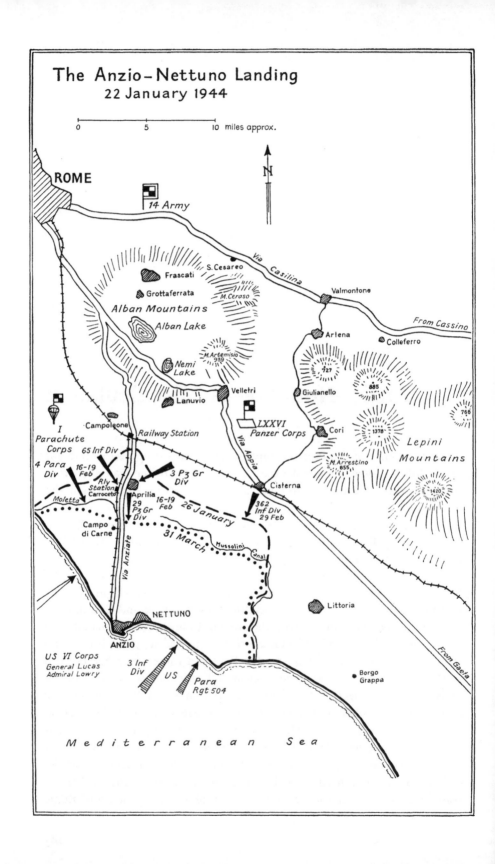

The Anzio–Nettuno Landing
22 January 1944

until such time as the Fifth Army could advance and reach it. Actually, the Volturno and the Reinhard Line were merely the prologue; the scene for the first act of the play proper was the Gustav Line.

But Eisenhower was suffering from the same old trouble. He certainly had sufficient transport and landing craft for a single division, but if he wanted to land in greater strength—and his appreciation of the situation led him to believe it was essential that he should do so—then the means at his disposal were inadequate. The most important of these means was, of course, the tank landing ships, which were used not only for the transportation of armour, but also of the very great number of vehicles which the assaulting divisions would require. In the Mediterranean area in the autumn of 1943 there were still 104 of these ships of special design, the salient feature of which was their shallow draught, and these would have been ample for the transportation of two divisions.

But Operation Overlord had been granted dictatorial priority over everything, including the sinews of war in the Mediterranean area. In accordance with a programme drawn up by the Combined Chiefs of Staff, most of the L.S.T.s in the Mediterranean were to return to the United Kingdom during the course of the winter for overhaul, to allow crews to be trained in handling them in tidal waters and to be ready in good time for the cross-Channel invasion. By the middle of January 1944 there would remain only thirty-four L.S.T.s in the Mediterranean, and of these some were due to return to England in February. For one thing, thirty-four L.S.T.s were, of course, wholly inadequate for the landing of forces of the requisite strength at the mouth of the Tiber, and for another, Eisenhower, who in the meantime had been appointed Supreme Commander for Overlord, was now far more interested in a landing in southern France. As far as he was concerned, the Italian theatre of war in the immediate future was only of secondary importance.

Once again it was Churchill who took matters into his own hands, as he had done in May in Algiers, and tried to break the deadlock. After the second Cairo conference it had been his intention to visit Alexander and Montgomery in Italy. But when he landed in Tunis on 11 December he was stricken with pneumonia, which put him completely out of action for a week. But by 19 December, when General Alan Brooke, the Chief of the Imperial General Staff, on his way back to London broke his journey at Carthage to visit him, the irrepressible Winston was up and about again. General Brooke gave his fullest support to Churchill's plan that sufficient landing-craft should be allowed to remain in the Mediterranean for a landing south of Rome, and on the same day Churchill sent a telegram to the British Chiefs of Staff Committee, demanding an immediate report on how many landing craft still remained in the Mediterranean theatre. This information he had to have, if he were to succeed in persuading the Combined Chiefs of Staff Committee, in which the Americans had the last say, to postpone any further withdrawals.

On 24 and 25 December Churchill was in conference in Algiers with Eisenhower, Bedell-Smith, Alexander, Tedder, John Cunningham and Maitland Wilson, successor elect to Eisenhower. Only one, albeit important man was missing—General Mark Clark, who would be commanding the landing south of Rome. Someone had omitted to send word to the man on whose shoulders the responsibility for the whole of the proposed enterprise would rest.

The results which emerged from the conference were a decision to land two divisions at Anzio–Nettuno, to entrust the carrying out of the operation to the Fifth Army and to seek the concurrence of Washington to the retention of fifty-six British L.S.T.s in the Mediterranean. Together with the thirty-four which were in any case not due to leave until March, this would give a total of ninety L.S.T.s—provided the Americans concurred. Churchill and the Commander-in-Chief, Mediterranean, were convinced that they could bring the battle for Rome to a successful conclusion in seven to ten days and would then be able to return the L.S.T.s for the purposes of Overlord.

Things, however, did not work out that way at all. Instead of the end of January, it was the beginning of June before the Allies marched into Rome; instead of ten days, they were to take more than a hundred before they had finished with the hell of Anzio.

On 28 December Roosevelt's reply reached Marrakesh, where Churchill in the meanwhile had gone to recuperate. It confirmed that the Prime Minister had won a complete victory. The President signified his concurrence to the retention of the fifty-six L.S.T.s until 15 February, provided that Overlord remained the accepted major operation and that the grand invasion would not in any way be prejudiced. But Churchill did not worry unduly about that aspect. Once American troops had been landed side by side with the British at Anzio–Nettuno, he was certain that the Americans would do everything they could to ensure Clark's victory, even if it meant postponing the despatch of the L.S.T.s till a little later.

Churchill was highly delighted and telegraphed to the President: 'I thank God for this fine decision, which engages us once again in whole-hearted unity upon a great enterprise.'* He invited the Commanders-in-Chief to a further conference on 7 January, this time in Marrakesh. There now only remained technical details to be settled. The main obstacle, the lack of landing craft, had been overcome. It was decided to place General Lucas, the Commander of U.S. VI Corps, in command

* *The Second World War*, Vol. V.

of the operation and to give him one British and one American division. Support troops—armour, Commandos, airborne and the like—were to be supplied in equal proportions by the British and the Americans. The date of the landing was fixed for 20 January. Clark was directed to deliver strong attacks along the Cassino front before the landing took place, with the object of drawing reserves from the Rome area and pinning them down on the main front. Clark succeeded in doing so. Nevertheless the landing developed into a failure, thanks to the inordinate caution displayed by the U.S. General in command.

The German High Command had, of course, for a long time been expecting a landing of this nature. The staff at Frascati could not believe that the Allies would be content to continue for very long to inch their way forward to Rome, when the sea was theirs and the *Luftwaffe* had to all intents and purposes been swept from the sky. Kesselring's Army Group thought that Naples would be the base for a fresh amphibious operation, but it was only very rarely that German reconnaissance aircraft were able to penetrate to the Naples area. Reports from agents were also few in number and too vague in content to give any clear picture. But at the beginning of January, the High Command had received information that 350,000 tons of shipping had been concentrated in Naples harbour. The final indication that amphibious operations were imminent however would, it was felt, be a concentration of strong forces of warships; and for information on this score the High Command hoped to get some indication from the German Central Contre-Espionage Service. Writes Westphal: 'When the chief of the German Contre-Espionage, Admiral Canaris, paid a visit to the Army Group on 21 January, his opinion of the enemy's amphibious intentions was urgently sought. Above all we wanted to know the number and whereabouts of warships, aircraft-carriers and landing vessels. Canaris was unable to give figures in detail, but firmly believed that there was in any case no landing to be feared in the near future. It is evident that it was not only our aerial reconnaissance that was practically paralysed, but the counter-espionage system as well. The enemy landed at Anzio and Nettuno a few hours after Canaris's departure.'*

Kesselring, however, was quite convinced that a landing was imminent. For some time immediately preceding the invasion he had placed both the staffs and the troops in Italy on an alarm footing. It was on 21 January, in response to the urgent representations of his staff that this continuous day and night state of instant alarm was exhausting the troops, that he cancelled the order; and it was on the very next night that U.S. VI Corps landed. That no immediate harm resulted was due to other causes.

In December 1943 Army Group C had issued Alarm Orders for the

* *The German Army in the West.*

whole of Italy. These orders laid down in detail what staffs and formations had to do in the event of any one of a variety of landings occurring and by what roads and time formations were to proceed to the scene of the landing. In short, there existed a General Staff plan, in which provision had been made to meet every possible contingency and to ensure, at least, that the enemy would not gain any swift initial advantage. But the troops available were far too few to allow an immediate large-scale counter-attack with the object of driving the enemy back into the sea. Kesselring had nevertheless withdrawn two Panzer Grenadier divisions from the front. The 29 Division was already concentrated on each side of Rome, and the 90 Division was on the way there when Clark attacked on the Garigliano. Once these reserves had been withdrawn, Lucas seemed to have an easy task, for there had remained only two battalions in the vicinity of the Eternal City. The first round might well have given VI Corps a decisive victory, if Lucas had made proper use of his opportunities.

The invasion began at five o'clock on the morning of 21 January when the invasion fleet, consisting of 243 ships of all descriptions—warships, transports and landing craft—set sail from Naples and its adjacent anchorages. This imposing armada, under the command of the U.S. Rear Admiral Lowry, had 50,000 assault troops and 5,000 vehicles aboard.

During the previous few days the 12 Tactical Air Fleet had been bombing the German rear lines of communication, the airfields in Rome and the German air bases in central Italy. Now twenty-eight fighter and thirty-two bomber squadrons were standing by, ready to break the German resistance south of Rome and pave the way for VI Corps to the capital.

The final objective was Rome itself. This was specifically stated in the Fifth Army's Operation Order, which directed that, having consolidated his beach-head, Lucas was forthwith to secure the Alban Mountains and march on Rome.

On the moonless night of 21/22 January, in impenetrable darkness the invasion fleet approached the coast on each side of Anzio. As it was hoped to take the Germans by surprise, there was no preliminary bombardment by the fleet, and only one British warship fired about 800 rockets. On shore, however, everything was suspiciously quiet; no searchlight flashed into life, there was no fire from any coastal battery. The Germans obviously seemed to have been taken completely by surprise, and this was confirmed when, at 2 a.m. the leading assault boats reached the shore and the L.S.T.s opened their cavernous jaws, and still not a shot was fired. The beaches were deserted and open to the incoming flood.

The landing in the American sector went like clockwork. Under Truscott, their trusty commander in Sicily, the 3 Division went ashore immediately east of Anzio, and three battalions of Rangers and the 504

Parachute Regiment landed to the north-east of it. In the British sector, too, the landing took place without incident. Here, north of Anzio, the 1 Division, which had not been in action since the capture of Pantelleria, was disembarked, and with it landed three Commandos, one Special Service Brigade and one armoured regiment. By eight o'clock, the Americans were masters of Anzio and Nettuno, and the British were firmly established on the Anzio–Rome road. Of German opposition there was still not a sign, and only a few aircraft of 2 Air Fleet swept surreptitiously through the sky.

Out at sea, protected by a balloon barrage, sprawled the mass of the invasion fleet, and round it fussed a number of destroyers, like sheep-dogs guarding their flock. The number of warships protecting the operation was remarkably small. Admiral Lowry who, in addition to being responsible for the entire naval side of the enterprise, was also in charge of the disembarkation of the American troops, had only the cruisers *Brooklyn* and *Penelope* and five destroyers at his disposal. There were neither battleships nor aircraft-carriers present.

Behind the first wave, a second assault wave, consisting of the U.S. 1 Armoured, and 45 Infantry, Divisions and three sections of Corps artillery, was ready, waiting in Naples. In all, General Alexander had detailed 109,000 men, of whom 50,000 constituted the first wave.

By midnight on 22 January, no less than 36,000 men and 3,100 vehicles had been disembarked. Despite this, the Allied troops advanced slowly and with hesitant caution; they lacked that boldness which would have enabled them to go on and seize Rome by a *coup de main*. Yet all the time the road to Rome was open to them, even though Kesselring was making frantic efforts to block it. German counter-measures were being pressed forward at full speed, and for the time being there was no sleep for staffs and troops alike. At the outset there had been nothing available but the two battalions previously mentioned and a few coastal batteries, with which to oppose Lucas. But Operation 'Richard'—the alarm plan drawn up in December—was swiftly put into operation. General Ritter von Pohl was ordered to set up south of Rome as strong an anti-tank barrier as he could with his anti-aircraft units and to hold it until such a time as the first oncoming troops were able to reach the battle area. Very soon troops were on the march from every direction. Despite the critical situation on the Cassino front, Tenth Army, too, managed to make the contribution expected of it, and no one, of course, was more directly concerned than Tenth Army in eliminating this threat to its rear.

As the battalions reached the beach-head area, they were placed under the command of General Schlemmer, who had been ordered by Kesselring to take up a position as far to the south of Rome as he could. Every yard, the Field-Marshal emphasized, was of importance; the farther southward

Schlemmer pushed now, he said, the less ground would he later be called upon to capture in battle, probably with heavy losses.

In this way a ring was gradually being built up round the invading forces. Panzer Grenadiers, paratroops, infantry, anti-tank units, artillery and armour combined to form an unbroken front. They came from almost every division in the country—the 3 and 90 Panzer Grenadier, the 26 and Hermann Göring Panzer, the 1 and 4 Parachute Divisions. It was a veritable tower of Babel, in which units 'fought side by side and all mixed up in a heap'; and it was General Schlemmer, commanding the 1 Parachute Corps who performed the remarkable feat of welding this heterogenous mass of fighting men into a corporate, coherent military entity.

From the Adriatic Kesselring had brought across the LXXVI Panzer Corps, and from North Italy he sent for the headquarters and staff of the Fourteenth Army. When General von Mackensen, commanding the Fourteenth Army, reported to the newly established Army Group Headquarters on Monte Soratti on 23 January, Field-Marshal Kesselring knew that the immediate danger had been averted and that von Mackensen's next task would be to consolidate his defensive front and initiate measures for a counter-attack.

The Battle Group Gericke* affords a typical example of the extent to which lack of reserves compelled the Germans to improvise, and of the heterogeneous composition of the troops which formed this first, hasty barrier. The 4 Parachute Division was raised in Perugia in January 1944. Veteran parachute formations, like the famous Assault Regiment† formed the nucleus, and the majority of the men had been transferred from the ill-starred Air Force Field Divisions and the *Luftwaffe* ground organizations. The Division, commanded by Colonel Trettner, was still in the process of being raised when, on 18 January, it received orders to form one battalion, composed primarily of experienced paratroops and trained infantrymen, from each of the regiments already raised. The resultant three battalions were then formed into a battle group under Major Gericke as a swiftly available reserve in the event of any enemy landing. By 19 January Gericke's command was ready to go into action, but its transport was sufficient for only one battalion and it had only half of its authorized scale of ammunition. When Gericke received General Schlemmer's order: 'Send one battalion forthwith to Albano' at 5 a.m. on 22 January, he had to withdraw the transport from the other two battalions in order to comply. This was truly a poor man's war! Gericke himself hastened to

---

* Gericke, it will be remembered, commanded the attack on the Italian General Headquarters on 9 September 1943.

† The Assault Regiment achieved fame in 1940 by capturing Fort Eben Emael and the bridge over the Albert Canal.

Schlemmer's battle headquarters at Grottaferrata, and the latter was relieved to have now a regimental staff which would be able to take further units under its wing. Accordingly, he pressed upon Gericke the 2nd Battalion, 300 Panzer Grenadier Regiment, the 9th Battalion, 361 Panzer Grenadier Regiment (both of 90 Division), Schmidt's Assault Artillery Section (I Parachute Corps) which was armed with Italian guns, and one company of Tiger tanks. During the afternoon two battalions of Gericke's Battle Group arrived from the Perugia area—Hauber's battalion, drawn from the Assault Regiment, and Kleye's battalion, drawn from 11 Parachute Regiment. More and more troops were placed under Gericke's command: the anti-aircraft platoon of the 14th Battalion, the 200 Panzer Grenadier Regiment; the heavy artillery section of the 13th Battalion, 191 Grenadier Regiment (71 Division); the guards and duties platoon of the Commander-in-Chief, South-West; a battery from 307 Army Anti-Aircraft Artillery (without guns); and in the evening the commander of 677 Section, Coastal Artillery reported for duty, followed during the night by 2nd Battalion, 71 Panzer Grenadier Regiment (29 Division), and, on the morning of 23rd, the Reconnaissance Section of 26 Panzer Division; and the last to join him were the 241 Mixed Anti-Aircraft Section and the 94 Light Anti-Aircraft Section.

Gericke's Battle Group thus consisted of men drawn from a good dozen units, from battalions to platoons, representing every available arm of the Service to be found in the country. Only the navy was missing!

The situation was much the same on the eastern sector of the beach-head. It was only gradually that some sort of order was introduced. In the western sector, General Graeser, 3 Panzer Division, was in command; on 26 January 4 Parachute Division was put into the coastal sector; on 28th the 65 Infantry Division took over the sector to the west of the Anzio–Albano road, the 715 Infantry Regiment took up a position covering the Alban Hills and the 367 Infantry Division was put in on either side of Cisterna.

Thus, by the end of January, the position round the beach-head had been consolidated and a strong defensive front had been formed. The High Command, however, was by no means content to remain on the defensive, but was determined to drive the enemy back into the sea.

The order to counter-attack came from Hitler himself, and the O.K.W. did all in its power to help Army Group C; from Germany it sent troops of the Reserve Army like the Lehr Infantry and Artillery Regiments, the 1027 and 1028 Panzer Grenadier Regiments; from France came the 715 Infantry Division, and from Yugoslavia the 114 Rifle Division; medium and heavy artillery, among them a few railway batteries, and about 200 tanks, some of them Tigers, were among the reinforcements sent, and from what had formerly been the Fourteenth Army came the 65 and 362 Infantry Divisions. This time the navy did not mean to be left out of it. U-boats and frogmen arrived with plans to attack the heavy warships and the great concourse of transports and freighters.

Hitler was in urgent need of a success—and not only in order to restore to some extent his waning prestige; he had very real reasons which made it imperative that this 'abscess' south of Rome should be cut out. If he succeeded in throwing the enemy at Anzio back into the sea, such a success would certainly have repercussions on the Allied plans for the invasion of France. The hope that it might compel the Allies to revise and increase the scope of their preparations to an extent which would preclude the possibility of any cross-Channel invasion in 1944, was justified. That would gain most valuable time, and time was what Hitler urgently wanted, if only from the point of view of the development of his 'secret weapons', which were beginning to play a prominent part in Goebbels' propaganda.

Clark and Alexander at once visited the beach-head on the first day of the invasion. On board Admiral Lowry's flagship, the U.S.S. *Biscayne* from which General Lucas was conducting the enterprise, Clark had an excellent view of the land operations in progress and was greatly surprised to see how smoothly everything ashore was going. Alexander reported to Churchill that on the same day he had impressed upon Lucas the importance of advancing immediately inland with strong reconnaissance forces. This, he had said, might well be decisive, since there seemed to be a good chance, thanks to the failure of the Germans to organize any defence, of gaining a lot of ground very quickly and without undue casualties.

Despite this, Lucas still hesitated. When Clark revisited the beach-head on 25 January, the U.S. 3 Division was still about four miles south of Cisterna, and the British 1 Division had halted about a mile and a half in front of Campoleone. And by this time the German defences had grown so strong that Lucas now had no chance whatever of breaking through to the Alban Hills, the tactical centre of the coastal sector. Nearly twenty miles stood between him and Rome and the Via Casilina, and there remained no prospect of his being able to cut the vital artery of the Cassino front.

Clark was disappointed at the dilatory manner in which the situation in the beach-head was being developed. Even at Salerno during the first few days things had moved more quickly, and there he had had first to fight for a foothold on the beaches before being able to push on to the Sele bridge and Altavilla. So, on 28 January the Commander-in-Chief, Fifth Army, set off once more for Anzio to see for himself what was happening. On this trip he had a very narrow escape when an American mine-sweeper opened fire on his launch and killed several of those accompanying him. At VI Corps battle headquarters he impressed urgently on

Lucas that it was high time he advanced and took Cisterna and Campoleone, the two key-points.

At Cassino the battle was approaching its dramatic climax, when Lucas at last launched his offensive on 30 January. On that day Truscott's 3 Division, with strong artillery support, attacked Cisterna. But it had no luck. The two battalions of Rangers taking part were cut off and taken prisoner, only six men succeeding in getting back to the American lines. The whole attack was repulsed with heavy loss, and the Combat Group of 1 Armoured Division, which was supporting General Penney's attack on Campoleone, reported that it had been held up by extensive minefields and stubborn resistance. Here, too, Lucas suffered a sharp reverse, and Campoleone remained firmly in German hands. On 2 February the attack on both places was called off, and Lucas had to admit defeat.

The next day, General von Mackensen struck back. South of Campoleone the Germans attacked Penney's Division and drove the British back to Aprilia and Carroceto. The German defence was growing appreciably stronger in every way. The 'Anzio Express', as the Allied troops had named the German railway artillery, went most vigorously into action against Anzio harbour and the shipping anchored there. Heavy artillery dominated the landing zones on the open beaches, and the *Luftwaffe* displayed unwonted activity. The O.K.W. communiqué for 24 January had announced that aircraft had sunk four landing ships with a total tonnage of 12,000 tons, and on the 30th that four freighters and three further landing ships had been damaged. On 23 January the destroyer *Janus* and on 29th the cruiser *Penelope*, two famous ships of the British Mediterranean Fleet, were sunk.

These losses were no encouragement to General Lucas to launch a major offensive before the anticipated German counter-attack had taken place and been repulsed. The *Deutsche Allgemeine Zeitung* hit the nail pretty squarely on the head when it stated on 31 January: 'It is obvious that, after his experience at Salerno, the enemy is determined this time to delay the decisive battle until he is quite certain that the forces at his disposal outnumber the Germans many times over.'

In London and Washington disappointment at the slow progress was profound. On 6 February Churchill impatiently asked Maitland Wilson why the U.S. 504 Parachute Regiment had not been used in the manner appropriate to its composition and why, during the first twenty-four hours, no attempt had been made to seize the Alban Hills, Velletri, Cisterna and Campoleone by means of a swift surprise attack? Maitland Wilson replied apologetically that at the last moment Clark had ordered that the paratroops should not be dropped, but should be landed from the sea; and he added that both Clark and Alexander had urged Lucas on the first day of the invasion to press forward inland. To which Churchill, with every justification, retorted that it was not the duty of a commander to 'urge', but to 'order'.

To use the American paratroops as infantry was undoubtedly a mistake. Had Clark decided to drop the 504 Regiment inland, somewhere in the vicinity, say, of the Alban Hills, he would have forced Lucas to make a swift push forward in order, if for no other reason, to establish contact with it. As it was, VI Corps messed about until the end of the month, and by the time Clark took matters into his own hands, the game had already been lost.

Maitland Wilson ascribed Lucas's hesitancy to his 'Salerno complex'— a complex from which the VI Corps Commander was understandably suffering. Lucas felt that he must ensure that he was sufficiently well equipped to deal with the German counter-attack that was bound to come, before himself advancing to an all-out attack. This 'Salerno complex' might well find justification in many situations, but at Anzio, where 'no one could have prevented a boldly executed thrust from reaching Rome' (Westphal), it was very much out of place.

On the other hand, it must not be forgotten that Lucas's predecessor, General Dawley, had had to go because at Salerno he had failed to halt VI Corps, which had been pushed rapidly forward to the Sele bridge and Altavilla, when the Germans launched their counter-attack against it. At Anzio, Lucas was determined to avoid any repetition of the danger, but did not seem to realize that by so doing he was throwing away an easy victory and ruining the whole operation. For, as long as VI Corps was not in a position to block the Via Casilina and cut through the German lines of communication network round Rome, there was no reason why the German High Command should contemplate evacuating the Gustav Line. But the whole object and purpose of the Anzio landing had been to compel the Germans to do just that!

As it was, by 28 January Lucas had contented himself with pushing his troops a mere ten miles inland—just far enough, that is, to place the beaches and the little fishing-port of Anzio beyond the reach of the German field artillery. Thus the advantage gained by the surprise landing was sacrificed, Kesselring was given time to move his pieces into place on the chessboard, and Churchill was forced ruefully to admit: 'As I said at the time, I had hoped that we were hurling a wild cat on to the shore, but all we got was a stranded whale.'*

Churchill was determined to get to the bottom of this wretched affair. On receipt of Maitland Wilson's reply, he asked Admiral John Cunningham to give him precise details of the number of vehicles so far put ashore. 'The reply was both prompt and startling. By the seventh day 12,350

* *The Second World War*, Vol. V.

vehicles had been landed, including 356 tanks; by the fourteenth day 21,940 vehicles, including 380 tanks. This represented a total of 315 L.S.T. shipments. It was interesting to notice that, apart from 4,000 trucks which went to and fro in the ships, nearly 18,000 vehicles were landed in the Anzio beach-head by the fourteenth day to serve a total force of 70,000 men, including, of course, the drivers and those who did the repair and maintenance of the vehicles.'*

This—one vehicle for every four men—was in all conscience a quite intolerable ratio. Furthermore, when it is remembered that VI Corps had accumulated mountains of stores on much the same scale, it became clear why the initial success achieved by the landing had been so meagre; and even this success had been gained at the price of severe losses. Alexander puts British casualties up to 6 February at 2,704 and American losses up to 9 February at 4,219—a total of 6,923. This was the bill presented to General Lucas, the price he had had to pay for all his mistakes. Later, as had happened to his predecessor, he was sent into the wilderness, and General Truscott mounted the charger that was to lead the Allies into battle.

General von Mackensen realized that before he launched a general attack he would have to secure Aprilia, to the north of Anzio, as his starting line. Here, however, he came up against one of the strongest shields with which the Allies were protecting the Anzio beach-head. Nevertheless the German attack against it succeeded. After two days of heavy fighting, Aprilia fell on 9 February, and on the next day Carroceto also passed into German hands. But the capture of Carroceto had been achieved at heavy cost as it was only after the most bitter fighting that the place, defended by the Scots Guards, fell. For three days the 145 and 147 Grenadier Regiments of the 65 Infantry Division and the Gericke Battle Group attacked the British positions to the north-west and west of Carroceto and very slowly and with severe losses to both sides forced the Scots Guards to retire.

The attack had begun on the night of 7/8 February, and during the 9th the 147 Regiment succeeded in advancing to the Anzio road, south of Carroceto. Then General Penney the commander of the 1 British Division, threw his last reserves, the 3 Infantry Brigade, into battle. But it, too, was unable to stem the German onslaught. It was only when General Lucas sent the U.S. 45 Division and the 504 Parachute Regiment to help that the most serious danger, south of Carroceto, was averted. Even so, the fate of the place itself still hung in the balance. The Scots Guards were under a hail of fire from three sides. From the east came an attack by the 26 Panzer Reconnaissance Section, from the north a battle group of the 3 Panzer Grenadier Division, and from the west Gericke's Battle Group. Throughout

* Churchill, *The Second World War*, Vol. V.

the whole of 9 February the paratroops were pinned down before Height 80 and Carroceto railway station, where the Scots Guards were prepared to fight to the death.

General Schlemmer now went forward to Gericke's battle headquarters, whence he intended to direct the attack in person. But it was not until the morning of 10 February, when Gericke ordered No. 2 Company of Kleye's battalion to make a detour northwards and attack the enemy from the flank, that things began to move; and then, when Kleye launched his concentric attacks, he stormed and captured Height 80.

Meanwhile, the report had come in that the 3 Division had thrust its way into Carroceto. General Schlemmer at once issued orders that every available means was to be used to establish contact with it. Lieutenant Weiss, who had assumed command after Kleye had been killed in the attack on Height 80, collected a small force of some sixty men from his greatly weakened battalion and with them stormed and captured the key group of houses north-west of the railway station, taking eighty-one prisoners; he then went on to the station itself, taking the Scots Guards in possession completely by surprise and gathering in about a hundred more prisoners. The enemy defeat seemed to be complete; but the British recovered swiftly and, supported by tanks, launched a counter-attack against the station. Weiss's assault group was split asunder, and the gallant Lieutenant found himself with only twelve men under his immediate command. Some thirty of the prisoners he had taken escaped; but he kept a sharp eye on the remainder, whom he had locked in the station cellar. With his twelve paratroops Weiss successfully held on to the railway station, and even when a Sherman tank clambered up on to the platform, he still stood his ground. But when he saw another tank knocked out by paratroops of the 11 Regiment just south of the station, he thought it time to beat a retreat.

Weiss did not remain idle for long. North-east of the station was some rising ground, occupied by the Scots Guards. The British artillery, which presumed that this position, too, had been lost, suddenly opened fire on it. The Guards, not unnaturally, resented this unfriendly act, abandoned their position and made for the railway station. Just as they were reaching it, Weiss dashed out with his remaining nine men, firing with everything they had. Taken utterly aback at finding the Germans in possession, the Guards laid down their arms and surrendered.

That finally disposed of the railway station. Meanwhile, the place itself had fallen, and 26 Panzer Reconnaissance Section was in firm possession. But this success at Height 80 and the station had been dearly bought. When the Kleye Battalion was withdrawn from the line on 13 February, it had been reduced to a strength of six officers and 259 N.C.O.s and men.

Four officers and 287 men had been killed and wounded by the furious artillery fire and the determined resistance of the Scots Guards.

But the milestone still showed ten miles to Anzio. Aprilia and Carroceto had been only the curtain-raiser; the main battle was still to come, and the overwhelming material superiority of the enemy and the determination of his troops left no room for optimism. The German attacking divisions had a hard task before them. The Allied High Command had correctly interpreted the actions at Aprilia and Carroceto as the opening moves of an impending general offensive. VI Corps, for its part, abandoned all idea of attack and passed over to the defensive. Its strength was such that it was able to take up a strong position, organized in depth, on which it was confident that it could hold any German counter-attack directed against the beach-head. In this, its confidence was justified by subsequent events.

Thus the first phase of the battle for the Anzio beach-head came to an end on 11 February, while in the Cassino area the struggle continued with undiminished fury. The Allied High Command's calculations had not worked out. Its forces had not succeeded either in breaking through the Gustav Line or in involving Army Group C in a 'miniature Stalingrad'. On the Allied side, disappointment was great. It had not for a moment been thought that Kesselring would be able to master the dangers crowding in upon him in so confident a manner. Churchill himself says: 'The ease with which they moved their pieces about the board and the rapidity with which they adjusted the perilous gaps they had to make on their southern front was most impressive. It all seemed to give us very adverse data for Overlord.'*

Kesselring was most anxious to launch his decisive counter-stroke at the earliest possible moment. Every day that passed was to the enemy's advantage. It was important that the Allies should be prevented from making good the heavy losses they had suffered at Aprilia and Carroceto and organizing a defensive system which would be difficult to overcome. On the other hand, he had to bear in mind that most of the German formations taking part in the offensive had had but little experience of large-scale operations and would require some time to become familiar with them. On the question of where the enemy should be attacked Kesselring and von Mackensen were in complete agreement. The idea of cutting off the Anzio beach-head by a flank attack delivered from the coastal sector held by 4 Parachute Division was attractive, but there was a danger that such an attack might well be stifled at the outset, or at least be brought to a standstill before it could develop, by the guns of the Allied warships. It is true that the thickly wooded country would afford excellent cover to the advancing infantry, but the effectiveness of strong armoured forces

* *The Second World War*, Vol. V.

would be severely restricted. On the southern flank of the beach-head, quite apart from the danger of naval intervention, the swampy nature of the ground and the numberless ditches which intersected it precluded the possibility of any attack in that sector.

There remained, therefore, the area between Aprilia and Cisterna; and it was here, on each side of Aprilia, that von Mackensen proposed to deliver his main attack, with two subsidiary attacks in support. With this Kesselring agreed, but then Hitler himself decided to intervene and called for details of von Mackensen's intentions. Hitler ordered that the attack be delivered on a very narrow front, in order to make the best use of the very strong German artillery forces engaged, and, with von Mackensen's concurrence, directed that the Lehr Infantry Regiment should lead the attack. The results of these two orders were catastrophic. The German assault units, jammed in a long and narrow strip, were easy meat for the enemy artillery and air arm. The Lehr Regiment failed completely to make any progress. This unit, created primarily for instructional purposes, had been praised to high heaven, but—and this was certainly not the Regiment's fault—it lacked experience of major operations, and its men proved quite incapable of standing up to the heavy weight of metal hurled at them. The fact that the Regiment was on unfamiliar ground and could not therefore attack by night was a further grave disadvantage. The attack thus had to be launched at dawn, which gave the enemy artillery and air arm the best possible chances of retaliation.

On 16 February, at 6.30 a.m. after an imposing artillery barrage, the Lehr Regiment advanced to the attack. At the same time the 65 Infantry and 4 Parachute Divisions attacked from the north-west. The U.S. 45 Division defended itself desperately. Its artillery fire tore gaping holes in the ranks of the slowly advancing Germans. By midday of 17 February the attack had penetrated the American positions east of the Anzio–Albano road to a depth of a little more than 2,000 yards on a front of two and a half miles. Despite the intervention of German fighter-bombers, despite the heavy artillery fire directed on the Allied positions, lines of communication and beach zones, the attack progressed with painful slowness, step by step. The enemy artillery fire and his carpet-bombing were devastatingly effective; on 17 February alone Eaker's bombers flew 700 sorties, primarily against Aprilia and the Anzio–Albano road.

Notwithstanding the enormous material support given to it, the U.S. 45 Division had the utmost difficulty in holding its positions. Thanks to the intervention of the British 1 Division, which joined in during the night of 17/18 February, it succeeded in stabilizing its front, but its losses had been heavy.

The Lehr Regiment had suffered no less heavily, and by the 17 February it could do no more. The 65 Infantry and 4 Parachute Divisions had also been badly mauled. But on 18 February the 29 Panzer Grenadier Division brought fresh impetus to the attack. In a difficult situation and without any hope of achieving surprise, it launched itself against the enemy and drove him back to the vicinity of Campo di Carne. Two of its battalions, the 1st and 3rd Battalions, 3 Panzer Grenadier Regiment, penetrated even further, but were surrounded and mopped up.

The counter-attack had now reached the U.S. positions taken up on the first day of the invasion, the 'initial line', and VI Corps' situation was critical in the extreme. Mark Clark complained: 'We were back to a line that had nothing much behind it except the beaches and the sea. We were obviously going to take it on the chin with everything Mackensen could throw at us the next morning.'* But the Germans, of course, could not know that. The attack had cost severe casualties, which bore no relation to the small amount of ground gained; the Allied superiority in artillery and air power was overwhelming; there seemed to be no chance of advancing the remaining seven and a half miles to Anzio, and Kesselring therefore decided to stop the attack.

Hitler was bitterly disappointed. He stood in urgent need of a success. Lack of the necessary forces, if nothing else, had prevented him from achieving it in Russia; but here at Anzio there had been at least a good chance of success. Accordingly he ordered that the offensive be resumed at the end of February, this time at a different place—Cisterna.

Although Kesselring did not expect this attack to achieve any decisive results, he hoped that it might at least succeed in compressing the beach-head and reducing it to its original proportions. This would have resulted in a considerable saving of forces for the Fourteenth Army. Three weak divisions were detailed for the attack on the veteran U.S. 3 Division. But once again they were massed on a narrow front, and there was no chance of achieving surprise.

The attack was fixed for 25 February, but heavy rain caused the final decision to be postponed until 28th. On that day the rain was still pouring down, and Kesselring was quite prepared to order a further postponement. At the request of the troops themselves, however, he refrained from doing so. The LXXVI Panzer Corps launched its attack on 29 February. By this time the weather had cleared, and the Allied naval guns and air forces were able to operate without restriction. The U.S. 3 Division—old acquaintances from the days of Sicily and the Reinhard Line—defended their positions stubbornly and gave no ground at all. The attack came to a standstill, and on 1 March Kesselring decided finally to break off the offensive. Clark, on the other hand, having repulsed the attack, decided to withdraw some five

* *Calculated Risk.*

miles from the Cisterna area and take up a position which corresponded roughly with the 'initial line'.

Although the beach-head had now been reduced very considerably in size, the German counter-offensive, the objective of which had been the Anzio beaches, had palpably been a failure. Why?

General Westphal's answer to that question is as follows:

There were a number of reasons for their failure. The north-to-south direction of the attack did not come as a surprise. The quantity of ammunition available was inadequate to silence the much greater fire power of the enemy artillery. The numerous armoured formations could not operate effectively, because the muddy ground compelled them to remain on the roads and causeways, where they presented excellent targets. The Allied air supremacy could not be broken even for a few hours, and it was not even possible to drive away their artillery spotters which hovered constantly over the front. Finally, the concentration of troops prescribed by the O.K.W. proved disadvantageous. Thus failed an undertaking which was launched with great hopes and an abundance of resources unknown on the German side since the capture of Sebastopol. . . . Our strength was no longer adequate; we were not capable of aggressive action.*

Kesselring regarded it as his duty to bring these facts to Hitler's personal notice. As a dispatch would probably have been pitched unread into the waste-paper basket, he sent Westphal to Berchtesgaden. At first, Jodl refused to admit Kesselring's Chief of Staff, but after he himself had spoken to Hitler, the latter demanded furiously to see 'the man who had slandered his troops'. The only tangible result of Westphal's three-hour interview with Hitler was a demand from the latter that twenty officers should be sent from the Italian theatre of war to Führer Headquarters to report to the Supreme Commander on the conditions under which they were fighting. 'He would have done better still,' remarks Westphal drily but with justice, 'if he had visited the front in person and convinced himself of our artillery and air inferiority on the spot.'

Although the Allies had maintained the upper hand in the February battles for the beach-head, their success had not been easily achieved. For the period 16–20 February Clark himself puts their casualties at 404 dead, 1,637 wounded and 1,025 missing; and to these must be added the naval losses. On 18 February alone the 2 Air Fleet sank 16,000 tons of shipping, including two L.S.T.s; and on the same day Lieutenant-Commander Fensky torpedoed and sank the British 5,000-ton cruiser *Sparta* in the Gulf of Gaeta.

The repulse of the last German counter-attack in the Cisterna area by no means meant that the Allied troops could now enjoy a period of

* *The German Army in the West.*

comparative quiet. The whole beach-head lay, as before, well within the range of the German heavy artillery, whose shells reached the British and American troops even in those places where they were entitled to expect a little peace; and the 'Anzio Express' continued to send its greetings to Nettuno, to Anzio and to the great supply dumps piled high on the beaches and in the neighbouring woods.

As the year progressed, conditions in the beach-head became more and more unhealthy. The flooded Pontine Marshes were an ideal breeding-ground for myriads of mosquitoes, and malaria took a heavy toll among the troops. Neverthless the beach-head remained a thorn in the flesh of Tenth Army. There was now no hope of removing it, and its threat to the Cassino front remained constant.

It was not until the French victory on the Garigliano that the struggle for the beach-head came to an end. It had lasted for 135 days, had consumed 523,358 tons of supplies, and 18,000 Italian refugees and 33,000 sick and wounded Allied soldiers were evacuated from it. Anzio had not only sapped the strength of the German divisions; it had also taken very heavy toll of the Allies.

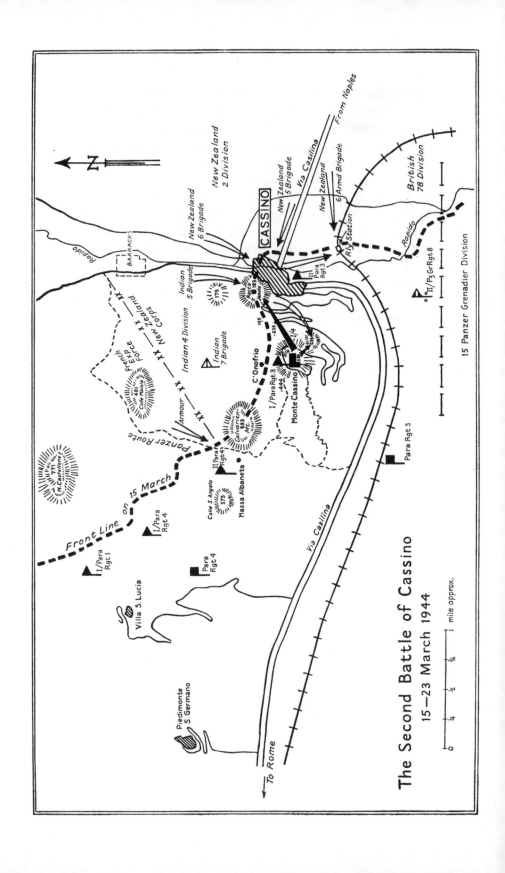

The Second Battle of Cassino
15–23 March 1944

Chapter 11

The Second Cassino Battle

Compared with the strenuous efforts they had made, their five weeks of severe fighting had brought but little gain to the Allies. It is true that the U.S. Fifth Army had broken through the German lines north of Cassino and that its left wing had reached the west bank of the Garigliano. But its main objective, the break-through into the Liri valley, had not been reached; and the landing at Anzio had not achieved the success expected of it. The town of Cassino and the monastery were still firmly in German hands; and for as long as Kesselring could keep the gates barred and locked and the German flag flying over Cassino, Alexander had no chance of making full use of his superiority in armour. Before the Allied divisions could set out on the march to Rome, either the monastery hill or Monte Maio to the south of it had to be captured.

Although the previous frontal attacks had brought nothing but defeat and disappointment, Alexander decided on 23 February once again to storm this seemingly unconquerable bastion by means of a direct assault. But this time a concentration of artillery and air power unmatched in the annals of war was to pave the way for the assaulting troops. The German defenders were to be 'neutralized' by a tremendous storm of shells and bombs, so that all Freyberg's infantry would have to do would be to occupy a silent and pitiful heap of ruins.

General Alexander seems not to have appreciated the chance offered to him by the Garigliano bridge-head; or perhaps he was wary of trying to lever the Cassino bulwark out of the line by means of a flank attack via Terelle and the rugged, very broken ground of the snow-covered Monte Cairo massif, despite the fact that up in the mountains the French Expeditionary Corps had already carved out a considerable piece of the Gustav Line. Instead, he elected once more to hammer away at the town of Cassino and the monastery hill, confident that the Germans would be unable to withstand the tremendous material blows he was preparing and that Freyberg's *élite* divisions would succeed in bursting asunder the barrier and achieving the desired break-through.

Had the Allied High Command listened more closely to General Juin and accepted his advice, Freyberg would probably have been spared the severe defeat which he had to admit in the second Cassino battle, and in that case there might well have been no need for the vast spring offensive which ultimately broke the Cassino barrier. Juin still regarded an attack against Atina as the solution to the Cassino problem and still believed that his Corps was capable of carrying such an attack to a successful conclusion. He again invited the High Command's attention to Atina and requested in vain to be entrusted with this task. After the disaster of the March battle, the French General declared: 'In view of the defensive measures taken by the enemy, too little importance is being attached, in my opinion, to the Atina area. The country there consists of a large basin, through the rear areas of which it is possible to reach Rome by circuitous routes; these routes are not being threatened at all by Fifth Army's attacks. For this reason, it is essential to take Atina, and only the French Expeditionary Corps is in a position to do so.

'I gather that the possibility of such an operation by the C.E.F. has been duly considered, but is regarded as a deviation from the main line of attack selected. The operation may well appear to constitute a deviation; but the decisive factor is the success ultimately achieved.'*

Subsequent events proved the correctness of General Juin's appreciation. But Alexander, like so many others, had fallen victim to the seeming magnetic attraction of Monte Cassino. There may perhaps have existed a certain reluctance to see the French gain the ultimate victory, or alternatively a firm conviction that Freyberg, notwithstanding his initial reverses, would be able, with the support of heavy artillery preparation, to overcome the town and mountain. Or it may be that the Allied High Command, with the destruction of the monastery on its conscience, was unwilling to deviate from the course it had selected and shrank from admitting that the monastery hill could have been captured without the destruction of the abbey. Be that as it may, Juin's suggestion bore fruit two months later,

* Jacques Mordal, *Cassino.*

though not at Atina, but south of Cassino in the Auruncian Mountains. Here at last the French Corps was given the opportunity of executing the manœuvre which its commander had advocated from the beginning and which ultimately led to the evacuation of Monte Cassino.

For some weeks after the end of the first Cassino battle the front remained quiet, for once again winter intervened and crippled both sides. Up in the Abruzzi Mountains it snowed day after day and all day long, and in the valleys below rain fell with a persistence reminiscent of an Eastern monsoon. The valleys of the Rapido, the Liri and the Garigliano were transformed into glutinous morasses, the positions and dug-outs were flooded, and the slimy roads became as slippery as ice. Not an aircraft was to be seen in the sky, and only the artillery, firing perfunctorily, showed any signs of activity.

But what would happen when winter gave way to spring and the weather became dry and clear? That was the question which primarily exercised the minds of the German High Command. Would the Allies resume their direct attacks on Cassino, or would they attempt a movement of encirclement, either north or south of the town? The fact that the French Corps was north of the town boded no good. On the other hand, the mentality of the Allied High Command, which manifested itself in a preference for the use of overwhelming material, did not preclude the possibility of a repetition of the previous frontal attacks.

The Germans were not idle during these long weeks of rain. The 90 Panzer Grenadier Division, which had suffered severe casualties during the February fighting, was in urgent need of rest; and, since only a division of equal quality and experience could be relied upon to withstand the attacks anticipated in the Cassino sector, Kesselring chose the 1 Parachute Division to relieve it. The division was held in considerable respect by the enemy, and it quickly proved that Kesselring's choice had been a good one.

Baade's Division was relieved on 20 February, when the town and hill were taken over by 3 Parachute Regiment, under the command of which was also placed the 2nd Battalion, 8 Panzer Grenadier Regiment (3 Panzer Grenadier Division), on the right flank. To the north-west of it were the 4 and 1 Parachute Regiments, and the defence of Monte Cairo was entrusted to the 4th Mountain Battalion. The 2nd Battalion, 3 Parachute Regiment, with attached troops, relieved the 211 Grenadier Regiment in the town; the 1st Parachute Machine-gun Battalion handed over Rocca Janula and the monastery hill to the 1st Battalion, 3 Parachute Regiment, whose 3rd Battalion positions on the Calvary Mount were taken over by 2nd Battalion, 4 Parachute Regiment.

The 15 Panzer Grenadier Division, now on the right of Heidrich's Division, was to remain until further orders in its positions on the Rapido, but was eventually to be relieved by 71 Infantry Division. But as the regiments of 71 Division became available they were put in between the 16 and 94 Divisions instead. Of Rodt's 15 Division only one regiment was withdrawn from the front. To the north of Heidrich's Division was the battle-weary 44 Hoch und Deutschland Infantry Division, holding the keypoint, Terelle, and further north still, in the mountains, was the 5 Mountain Division, under its new commander, General Schrank.

On 26 February General Heidrich assumed command of the eight-mile-wide sector held by the 1 Parachute Division. The Order of Battle was as under:

DIVISIONAL HEADQUARTERS

G.O.C. Division	General Heidrich
G.S.O.I	Major Heckel
G.S.O.II	Captain Stangenberg
G.S.O.III	Lieutenant Treiber
A.D.M.S.	Colonel Dr Eiben
D.Q.M.G.	Colonel Dr Ehlers

1 PARACHUTE RECONNAISSANCE SECTION — Captain Hauptmann Graf
   No. 1 Coy.—Wireless Coy.
   No. 2 Coy.—Telephone Coy.

1 PARACHUTE REGIMENT — Colonel Karl Schultz
   Staff & Reconnaissance Section
   Pioneer platoon
   Cycle platoon
   No. 13 Coy.—Mortar Coy.
   No. 14 Coy.—Anti-tank Coy.
   1st Battalion — Major Werner Graf von der Schulenburg
   Staff and Reconnaissance Section
   Nos. 1, 2, 3, Coys.—Rifle Coys.
   No. 4 Coy.—Machine-gun Coy.
   2nd Battalion — Major Gröschke
   same as 1st Battalion
   3rd Battalion — Major Becker
   same as 1st Battalion

3 PARACHUTE REGIMENT — Colonel Heilmann
   1st Battalion — Major Böhmler
   2nd Battalion — Captain Foltin
   3rd Battalion — Major Kratzert

4 PARACHUTE REGIMENT — Major Grassmehl
   1st Battalion — Captain Beyer
   2nd Battalion — Captain Hübner
   3rd Battalion — Captain Maier

(Composition of 3 and 4 Regiments as for 1 Regiment.)

I PARACHUTE ARTILLERY REGIMENT	Major Schramm
Staff and Reconnaissance Section	
No. 1 Section	Captain Scheller
Nos. 1, 2, 3, batteries—7.5 cm. mountain guns	
No. 3 Section	Captain Tappe
Nos. 7, 8, 9, Batteries—10cm. light gun (special type for paratroops)	
I PARACHUTE PIONEER BATTALION	Captain Frömming
Battalion Staff and Reconnaissance Section	
Nos. 1, 2, 3, Coys. Pioneers	
No. 4 Coy.—Machine-gun Coy.	
I PARACHUTE ANTI-TANK SECTION	Major Brückner
Staff and Reconnaissance Section	
Nos. 1, 2, 3, 4 Coys.—7.5 cm. anti-tank guns, motorized	
No. 5 Coy.—7.5cm. anti-tank guns, self-propelled	
I PARACHUTE MACHINE-GUN BATTALION	Major Schmidt
Three machine-gun companies	
PARACHUTE MEDICAL SECTION	Colonel Dr Eiben
Two companies	

As a result of the heavy losses in men and material suffered by the Division at Ortona, the strength and armament varied from unit to unit.

To hold an eight-mile front was asking a good deal of the Division, when it is remembered that it had suffered heavy casualties at Ortona, that the fighting strength of its battalions averaged 200 men and that its companies muster more than thirty or forty men apiece. The division had been in action without respite since Salerno and it was overtired before ever it took up its positions in the Cassino sector.

On 23 February the 1st Battalion, 3 Parachute Regiment, occupied the ruins of the monastery. Its innumerable cellars and subterranean passages afforded ample cover for the eighty odd paratroops, certainly as far as artillery fire was concerned. But on top of the cellars rubble and debris were piled yards high, and it seemed highly improbable that they would be able to withstand another air attack. The artillery nevertheless remained a constant source of burdensome irritation. It was shooting at the abbey from three sides, and its fire made use of the main entrance impossible, both by day and night. It was only after they had knocked a hole in the massive west wall of the Torreta that the defenders were able to come and go more or less unmolested by gunfire.

During the lull before the next general offensive, the Division was feverishly employed on the construction of defensive emplacements—a truly thankless task on the bare, chalk slopes of Monte Cassino and Monte

Castellone! Fatigue parties and mules humped supplies of food and ammunition up the mountains, which, despite their minor height, possessed all the characteristics of major mountain ranges. Again and again the working parties were forced to fling themselves to the ground by the searching fire of the enemy guns, which probed every ravine and searched every footpath. By day the enemy would open battery fire on any single man who poked his nose into the open, and concealed tanks were quick to open up on any movement observed in Cassino or on the slopes of the hill. By day, therefore, the terrain around the battlefield was like a dead wilderness. But at night the Via Casilina, the ravines and the mountain paths sprang into life, with lorries hastening forward to the front and fatigue parties panting their way to the crests of the hills.

It was not until the beginning of March that the weather started to improve and blue skies returned once more to southern Italy. The peaks of the mighty Abruzzi Mountains still wore their white caps, but down in the valleys the first tender shoots of green were beginning to burgeon, and the air was sweet with the fragrant breath of approaching spring. Very soon it would become known where the Allies intended to strike their next blow. It was now good flying weather, in the valleys of the Liri and the Rapido the softened earth was drying rapidly; and good weather for armour, too, was at hand. At first, however, all remained quiet—until 15 March, when the storm broke with tremendous fury over Cassino.

This heavy blow had been well prepared at leisure and was based directly on Alexander's own plan. As early as 24 February Fifth Army, in accordance with 16 Army Group directive, had issued its Operation Order No. 16, the gist of which was as follows:

I. The employment of the New Zealand Corps on the Cassino front necessitates a regrouping of the Fifth Army forces on the Rapido Garigliano, with the object of forming a new reserve. . . .

(b) During this process formations will ensure that pressure on the enemy is maintained, that preparations for the offensive are taken in hand and that an attitude of truculent defence is adopted, in order to secure the sectors already reached, to pin down the enemy and facilitate the resumption of the offensive. New Zealand Corps will prepare plans to enable it to take immediate advantage of any enemy movement to the rear.

(c) On the Anzio front the defensive positions will be strengthened, and no opportunity will be lost to resume the offensive.

II. TASKS. . . .

(c) The New Zealand Corps will continue its attack and capture the high ground in the Cassino area and establish a bridge-head across the Rapido. . . . In accordance with army instructions, plans will be prepared for a continuation of the attack from this bridge-head in a north-western direction.

In accordance with these orders, U.S. II Corps was withdrawn from the front and, reinforced by the 88 Division newly arrived from the United States, was transferred as army reserve to the Alifi area. II Corps positions on Monte Castellone were taken over by the French Corps, which had been reinforced by Moroccan 4 Mountain Division. The New Zealand Corps took over the whole sector from the Calvary Mount to the confluence of the Liri and the Gari.

After Alexander had issued orders on 11 February that all available means were to be concentrated in support of the New Zealand Corps and Freyberg's demands had been passed on to the air force to ensure that he was given the maximum possible support from the air, some little time elapsed while all these preparations were being meticulously carried out. The air support which Freyberg had been given when the monastery was destroyed had obviously been a waste of time and effort. Now, however, preparations were taken in hand for a far greater blow, directed this time against the town itself. General Eaker was directed to concentrate every available bomber; and Fifth Army Ordnance set about the task of amassing a dump of 600,000 rounds of artillery ammunition, no less than a third of which was to be fired on the first day of the attack. All this took time, and it was mid-March before the preparations were completed and, with the return of fair weather, the attack could be launched.

Impressed by the failure of the Indians and the Maoris in February, Freyberg decided that the whole Corps should this time participate in the attack. His plan was that the New Zealanders should take Cassino and Rocca Janula, and that the Indians, debouching from these captured positions, should storm and take the monastery hill itself, while the New Zealanders completed the mopping-up operations in the town. Once the town and hill had been taken, the British 78 Division was to thrust across the Rapido on both sides of Santo Angelo in Tedice, where the U.S. 36 Division had suffered so severe a mauling. The focal point of the new attack, therefore was Cassino itself. It was hoped that here, where the German paratroops had established themselves in the houses and cellars, an air attack of unprecedented proportions would blast them out of existence and that anything that might still remain alive would then be finished off with a few thousand rounds of gunfire.

The 15 March came. The almost oppressive quiet of the previous night came to a sudden and violent end. At first the monotonous drone of aircraft approaching the town from the north did not seem to denote anything unusual. Most of the defenders were 'old hands', who had become quite accustomed to the Allied 'air traffic' during their long sojourn in the front line. But when the leading bombers opened their bomb-hatches punctually at 8.30 a.m. and the first carpet descended upon Cassino, everyone in the town knew that this was 'it'—the expected major offensive had started. The bombers came on in an endless stream. The first wave was followed ten minutes later by the second, and from then onwards for hours wave followed wave at intervals of ten or fifteen minutes, adding their quota to a drama that must rank as one of the most terrifying spectacles in the annals of war. The very first wave had enveloped Cassino in a pall of dark grey dust, hiding from view the horror below, where men, houses and machines were being blown to pieces.

In this hell it seemed as though all will to resist must be quenched, the very breath of life be choked and all life be brought to an end. As wave succeeded deadly wave, the inferno seemed endless. Ruins were ploughed up and ploughed again; bombs tore gaping craters in gardens, fields, and meadows; whole streets collapsed suddenly into a mountain of rubble; trees flew through the air, as though hurled by some giant hand; the Day of Judgement seemed to have dawned. Among the crashing colonnades and collapsing roofs death reaped its grim harvest. There was no escape. Every man died, crouching where he was—or lived with a faint and desperate hope that this terrible slaughter, against which there was no defence, might at last come to an end. But for four hours the bombs continued to rain down on the ranks of the 3 Parachute Regiment. Until midday, agony and death alone held sway in the doomed town, and many men, maimed, shattered or suffocated, now lay beneath the ruins of Cassino. Here is an account by one who survived to tell the tale, Lieutenant Schuster, commanding No. 7 Company:

Tensely we waited in our holes for the bombs to drop. Then they came. The whining scream of their approach, the roar of their explosions and the noise of the aircraft themselves mingled with echoes flung back from the hills to produce an indescribable and infernal bedlam of noise. The whole earth quaked and shuddered under the impact. Then—a sudden silence. Hardly had the dust settled a little than I dashed out to visit the other two strongpoints. I stumbled blindly about in a welter of craters. From somewhere a voice shouted: 'All's well!' and then the next great wave of air hulks loomed into view above me.

I could not go back. I remained where I was, and the flood-gates of hell opened once again. We could no longer see each other; all we could do was to touch and feel the next man. The blackness of night enveloped us, and on our tongues was the taste of burnt earth. 'I'll come again,' I said, felt my way towards the exit and rolled out into a crater. I had to grope my way forward as though in a dense fog, crawling, falling, leaping; as I reached my post, another wave was on the way in. The men pulled me head over heels into our hole. Then down came the bombs again. A pause, and once more I groped my way across the tortured earth. Direct hits—here, here and here; a hand sticking out of the débris told me what had happened. When I got back, the men read in my eyes what I had seen. The same, unspoken thought was in all our minds—when would it be our turn? The crash of bursting bombs increased in intensity. We clung to each other, instinctively keeping our mouths open. It went on and on. Time no longer existed, everything was unreal. We shifted our positions and, well, we thought, if we can still move, we're still alive—sixteen of us.

Rubble and dust came pouring down into our hole. Breathing became a desperate and urgent business. At all costs we had to avoid being suffocated, buried alive. Crouching in silence, we waited for the pitiless hail to end.

Lieutenant Jamrowski, an imperturbable Prussian, commanding Nos. 6 and 8 Companies, says:

Thunderous explosions brought me leaping from my bed. At the dugout entrance stood a runner, who shouted that fifty or sixty Lightnings had dropped bombs. The thought flashed through my mind: 'This is it!' As I was about to jump out of our cellar, the runner yelled: 'Look out! More of them!' and as he yelled the first bombs began to fall. Outside it must have been absolute hell. The bombing went on and on. There was nothing we could do but crouch, tense and expectant, where we were. Then came a brief pause . . . or could it, we wondered, be the end of this inferno? Corporal Kübrich, commanding a mortar section, jumped down into my cellar. He had streaked here like a hare—but he was only just in time. The whole town had been completely obliterated, he reported. Instead of having to make the usual detour, he had been able to make a bee-line for my battle headquarters. He was anxious to go on to his own section's position, but that, for the time being, was quite impossible. Bombs were now falling like rain, and in our underground shelter the thought struck me that we were just like a submarine crew whose U-boat was being pursued by depth-charges.

Then came a longer pause. 'Two volunteers to go to X and Y positions!' I shouted. At once my trusty lance-corporal, Jansen, and a runner from No. 8 Company sprang towards the exit. Jansen had just got clear away, when another explosion blew the other runner back into the cellar. In rapid succession a number of bombs fell very close, and one scored a direct hit on the forward exit of the cellar. Luckily the front of the building collapsed slowly, and we were able to escape into the rear part of the cellar; but a good number of our weapons and some of our ammunition were buried under the débris.

The entrance to the cellar was completely blocked, and we were cut off. By the light of a flickering candle we sat among the ruins and glumly took stock of the situation. After a while the explosions seemed to be a little more distant. 'Let's get cracking,' I shouted, 'and clear the entrance! We must get out of here!' We set to work, clawing at the mass of rubble and earth. We lost all sense of time, and how long we worked I don't know; but we seemed to be making no impression, and it looked as though we should never get out; some of the men began to lose heart, and I, too, was hard put to it to overcome an inner feeling of helplessness. At last we seemed to be making progress, and then the rubble and earth outside came sliding down and undid all that we had done. 'Never mind—stick it!' I shouted. 'We're not going to die here, like rats in a sewer!' Once again we started to claw away, and after hours of labour we cleared a small cleft. But here, solid masses of masonry, beyond our strength to shift, barred further progress. We shouted to attract attention, and our shouts were heard by two runners from Battalion Headquarters, who were out looking for us. With their help, we cleared the entrance, and after being buried alive for twelve hours, we squeezed our way out into the open. Darkness had now fallen. Cassino was unrecognizable in the tangled mass of ruins and rubble that confronted us. . . .

But the Allies had not come out of it unscathed. The bombing had been pretty poor. Some of the aircraft dropped their bombs far behind their own front line—on the battle headquarters of the French Corps, on Eighth Army Headquarters and on the New Zealand artillery—killing seventy-five and wounding 250, exclusive of the high casualties suffered by the Italian civilian population.

For this attack General Eaker had gathered together the strongest force of aircraft that had ever been concentrated in the Mediterranean theatre. Seven hundred and seventy-five aircraft—575 heavy and medium bombers and 200 fighter-bombers and fighters—had taken part. On Cassino and Rocca Janula, an area 1,500 by 500 yards, 260 Flying Fortresses Mk. B 17, 220 Mitchells and Marauders, forty-five A-20s and fifty A-36s had dropped 1,250 tons of bombs.* Fighter-bombers and fighters attacked the German artillery, the Liri bridges, the Aquino airfield, the amphitheatre and railway station in Cassino, and the supply dumps in Pignataro, San Giorgio, Ponte Corvo and Ceprano.

To the astonishment—and relief—of the garrison, the abbey itself was not bombed. This was a bad blunder, since the roofs and cloisters that had remained undamaged would hardly have stood up to another heavy bombardment. The defence would have been largely neutralized, and the Indians would have been able to capture the hill without much difficulty.

Eaker lost only six aircraft, and the bombers, flying in close formation and unharassed by any German fighters, were able to return unscathed to their bases.

The last bomb fell at twelve-thirty p.m. At that precise moment, the artillery opened fire. The curtain was rising on the second act. The artillery of three corps—the New Zealand, the U.S. II and the French—joined by Eighth Army artillery and the batteries of the British X Corps set about the task of crushing the last shreds of German resistance. By three-thirty, zero-hour for the combined infantry and armour attack, 746 guns had fired nearly 200,000 shells on the town and hill, a weight of metal corresponding roughly to 1,300 lorry-loads. Once again the ruins of Cassino were being churned up, and once again death reaped its harvest. The paratroops had experienced many artillery bombardments in the past, but this tornado of

* A conservative estimate. Some accounts put the figure as high as 2,500 tons.

shells far surpassed anything they had faced in Sicily, at Salerno or at Ortona. General Heidrich and Colonel Heilmann were extremely worried; they were convinced that nothing could survive.

The Allies were of the same opinion. Six senior generals, among them Alexander, Eaker and Clark, had watched the whole fearsome spectacle from Cervaro. To them it was obvious that the New Zealanders and Indians were bound to capture their objectives. Of the six, the most excited was the man primarily responsible, General Eaker, the commander of the M.A.A.F. (Mediterranean Allied Air Force). When the air attack came to an end, he rushed to a short-wave transmitter and announced that 2,500 tons of bombs had just been dropped, far exceeding anything that had ever been dropped on Berlin. And he added: 'The Germans would do well to bear in mind that what we have done to Fortress Cassino on the Ides of March, we will do to every other position they decide to hold' (*Daily Mail*, 16.3.'44).

But one of the places the Germans decided to hold, and to go on holding, was—Cassino, in spite of the devastating tornado which had laid the whole town in ruins. To the disagreeable surprise of the Allied High Command, Eaker had failed to break the backbone of the defence. The measure of their surprise is reflected in the following letter written to Washington by General Devers, Maitland Wilson's deputy:

On March 15 I thought we were going to lick it by the attack on Cassino and advance up the Liri valley. We used air, artillery and tanks, followed closely by infantry. I witnessed the attack from across the valley. It got off to a start with excellent weather. The bombing was excellent and severe, and the artillery barrage which followed it and lasted two hours was even more accurate and severe, with 900 guns participating. Two groups of medium bombers, followed by eleven groups of heavies, followed by three groups of mediums, started on the minute at 8.30 a.m. and closed at twelve noon, the groups coming over every ten minutes up to nine o'clock and thereafter every fifteen minutes. In spite of all this excellent support all afternoon with dive bombers and artillery fire, the ground forces have not yet attained their first objective. . . . These results were a sobering shock to me. The infantry had been withdrawn in the early morning hours five miles to the north of Cassino. When they arrived back in the town of Cassino at approx. one o'clock close behind the barrage, the Germans were still there, were able to slow up their advance and were to reinforce themselves during the night by some unaccountable means. . . .*

In this, Freyberg had adhered strictly to his plan of attack. While the barrage was still raging over Cassino, the New Zealand and Indian infantry, strongly supported by armour, advanced against the town and Rocca

* The War Reports of General Marshall, General Arnold, Admiral King.

Janula. One hundred and forty-four guns of the New Zealand Corps were operating in close support, covering them with a creeping barrage as they moved forward in leaps of 150 yards. Full of optimism the infantry approached their objectives. But when they reached the northern sector of the town, they were astounded to be met with machine-gun and rifle fire, and they thence proceeded with extreme caution to the task which, despite the bombs, they were not destined to accomplish.

And, indeed, no one could have believed that after such a tornado there would still remain one single German soldier capable of offering resistance. By all human standards, the fighting spirit of such paratroops as had not been buried beneath the ruins must surely have been shattered to a degree that would render them incapable of any further endeavour. Cassino itself was completely unrecognizable. Where houses and lines of streets had stood there was now only one vast mound of rubble, interspersed with yawning craters. The Rapido, dammed in many places by the masses of fallen masonry, overflowed its banks and filled the craters with water. It was a picture as gruesome as any that the fields of Flanders had had to offer in the First World War.

Men had died everywhere, and the attack had wrought terrible havoc in the ranks of the 2nd Battalion, 3 Parachute Regiment. The day before the attack it had mustered about 300 men and five guns; now at least 160 men and four assault guns lay buried beneath the ruins. Worst hit of all had been No. 7 Company. Only a mere handful had survived the onslaught of guns and bombs, only then to find themselves cut off; and a few indeed succeeded in fighting their way back to their own lines. The other companies had been reduced to fifteen or twenty men apiece, and only No. 6 Company had escaped without loss. At the beginning of the air attack, it had been with the battle headquarters, in reserve in the cellars of a large business house. In the pause that had followed the first wave, Captain Foltin had transferred his staff and No. 6 Company to a rock cavern at the foot of the monastery hill—a move that spelled salvation for him and defeat for the New Zealanders!

The latter had advanced gaily and for the most part in close formation to the outskirts of the town; the tank commanders were standing upright in their turrets as though on a ceremonial parade. They were the first targets of the German snipers, and over many a tank commander his turret crashed closed for the last time in his life.

As the last shells burst and the barrage passed on to search the depth of the German position, the paratroops, gaunt-looking, in tatters and covered with dust, crept out of their holes and took post behind the nearest remnant of wall they could find. Of their prepared positions no vestige remained.

Only very slowly did the enemy gain ground. By the time darkness fell, the New Zealand 6 Infantry Brigade,* advancing from the north with the 25th Battalion leading, had penetrated some two hundred yards into the devastated town. After a hard fight the New Zealanders had overwhelmed the decimated garrison of Rocca Janula and from there were in a position to dominate the whole of Cassino. But the attempt of the 26th Battalion to cross the Via Casilina inside the town and advance southwards had failed when it reached the Hotel Continentale, where Sergeant-Major Neuhoff, one of the outstanding platoon commanders of the 2nd Parachute Battalion, refused to yield an inch. The New Zealand 24 Battalion, moving up in support of the 26th, also failed to make any impression.

One thing the New Zealanders quickly found out: The U.S. Air Force had presented the Germans with a first-class tank obstacle: The towering piles of rubble, the torn and débris-strewn streets, the innumerable deep bomb craters made it quite impossible for the New Zealand 4 Armoured Brigade to penetrate into the town and support the infantry. Its tanks had to halt on the edge and leave the infantry to its own devices as soon as the latter penetrated into the zone of ruin and rubble. The most strenuous efforts to clear a way for the tanks with bulldozers made painfully slow progress. It took the pioneers thirty-six hours to clear a narrow corridor to the centre of the town; and through a narrow gap of that nature it was quite impossible to launch a tank attack.

At the battle headquarters of the 3 Parachute Regiment, where, by chance, General Heidrich had been since early morning, nothing was known until the evening regarding the tragedy that had befallen the 2nd Battalion. Since mid-morning, all wireless and telephone communication had been disrupted, runners could not get through the heavy fire, and contact with XIV Corps had been lost. General Heidrich knew that he could give his men in the forward areas no assistance by day. It was therefore doubly important to support them with artillery fire, and it was this that the General regarded as his primary task. By evening, he felt, he would have a clearer idea of how things were in Cassino and whether he could then intervene with his reserves. In fact, during the afternoon he succeeded in concentrating the mass of his artillery fire on Cassino and in breaking up enemy concentrations both outside and in the northern sector of the town. This undoubtedly robbed the New Zealand attack of much of its impetus.

* The New Zealand 2 Division consisted of:
4 ARMOURED BRIGADE
    18, 19, 20 Armoured Regiments and 22 Motorized Battalion
5 INFANTRY BRIGADE
    21 and 23 N.Z. and 28 Maori Battalions
6 INFANTRY BRIGADE
    N.Z. 24, 25, and 26th Battalions
Divisional artillery, engineers, admin. and staff.

The 71 Mortar Regiment, under the command of Lieutenant-Colonel Andrae, was extremely effective. Its shrieking salvoes and plunging fire had the same effect as carpet-bombing and brought the enemy to a complete standstill, and from the Aquina airfield fire from a heavy anti-aircraft section also descended on them. All weapons combined in helping to break the tip of Freyberg's spearhead and to support the paratroops in desperate battle; and by evening it became clear that this support had enabled the 3 Parachute Regiment to score an undisputable defensive success. The engagement is mentioned in the O.K.W. communiqué in the following terms: 'On the southern front, after an exceptionally heavy air attack, the enemy, strongly supported by tanks and artillery, attacked Cassino. The attack failed in the face of the heroic resistance of the 3 Parachute Regiment under Colonel Heilmann and the effective support afforded to him by 71 Mortar Regiment under Colonel Andrae.'

But despite all the efforts of the paratroops and the concentrated fire of guns, mortars and anti-aircraft artillery, by the evening of 15 March two-thirds of the town was in Allied hands. But this did not by any means signify that the way through Cassino to the Via Casilina was now open. For as long as the Germans held the centre of the town and the railway station, Cassino remained unconquered.

Disappointed though they were at the results of the first day's fighting, the Allies were still optimistic. Heavy harassing fire was being laid on to prevent the bringing up of German reserves, and they felt justified in hoping that the next day would see the whole town in their possession. As night fell, it began to rain heavily. An impenetrable darkness spread itself like a protective mantle over the reserves, who were now hastening towards Cassino, and the artillery being sent up from other sectors to reinforce the defence.

Colonel Heilmann pushed the last of his reserves into the hard-pressed town and appointed a staff officer, Captain Rennecke, to command them. During the next few days a stream of reinforcements poured in—elements of the 2nd Battalion, 1 Parachute Regiment, and the pioneer battalion and motor-cycle rifle company of the Division. Cassino had become the symbol of the German paratroops' will to resist.

After the New Zealanders had taken the northern sector of the town and Rocca Janula, Freyberg at once extended the attack to embrace the monastery itself. At 9 p.m. an intense barrage, that was to continue for eight hours, was directed against town and hill. Dense clouds of chalk dust and the sickly-sweet smell of corpses from the victims of the 15 February attack penetrated into the deepest cellars of the abbey. Anxious glances were cast at the roofs over the underground passages, which shuddered under the impact of the heavy shells. But when the storm eased, there had been no casualties in the monastery.

Just before midnight the Essex Regiment of the Indian 5 Brigade had relieved the New Zealanders on Rocca Janula and had gone forward as far as Height 165. The whole sector of No. 2 Company of the 3 Parachute Regiment was now in enemy hands and the company itself had ceased to exist. Only one survivor succeeded in making his way to the monastery with news of the disaster that had overtaken them.

Now the way to the abbey lay open. But when the Rajputana Rifles advanced towards Height 236 they were held up by the right wing of No. 3 Company. Furthermore, they came under fire from their own artillery, and after losing all their officers, they abandoned the attack and withdrew back to the Rocca Janula. The next attempt was made by the 1st Battalion, 9 Gurkha Rifles. The Gurkhas advanced southwards, by-passed Height 236 and assaulted Height 435. The ruins of the abbey were still under heavy and continuous artillery fire which did not slacken until dawn was beginning to break. Then, as it became lighter, the defenders caught sight of the little Gurkhas clambering their way up the rugged slopes of Height 435—'Hangman's Hill'. The machine-guns leapt into action. From all the holes and windows of the ruined abbey a furious fire was opened on the Gurkhas and swept them from the hillside. In a flash the spectre had disappeared from the summit of Height 435.

After their heavy losses, the Gurkhas were in no state to launch a further attack. To escape from the direct fire from the monastery they took cover on the reverse slopes, but there artillery fire pinned them down to the barren rocks and cut them off from their base. They had advanced too far, and now it was going to be very difficult to reach them with the supplies they required. At dawn on 17 March an assault platoon of the 1st Battalion, 3 Parachute Regiment, under Sergeant-Major Steinmueller stormed and recaptured the crest of Height 435. But the Gurkhas launched an immediate counter-attack and flung the paratroops back into the monastery, and the Germans lacked the requisite reserves with which to organize a counter-stroke and destroy them.

This penetration by the Gurkhas had caused headquarters of both XIV Corps and Tenth Army grave anxiety. The abbey was now being surrounded from both south and west. Both headquarters urged that the situation be immediately restored. But General Heidrich preferred to destroy the enemy by fire, rather than to risk heavy casualties in an assault; and, as later transpired, this fire proved extremely effective. Not only did it compel Freyberg to arrange to supply the Gurkhas from the air, but it also caused heavy casualties.*

For both these reasons Freyberg was most anxious to bring relief to the

---

* A patrol on 29 March found 165 dead Gurkhas, twenty machine-guns, 103 rifles, thirty-six tommy-guns and four wireless sets on Height 435.

hard-pressed Gurkhas. But on the night of 16/17 measures were in hand on the German side to surround them and thus put a final end to the danger which their presence constituted, not only to the monastery, but also to Cassino itself.

On 16 March the New Zealanders in Cassino shifted the main thrust of their attack to the eastern sector of the town, concentrating primarily on the area where the Via Casilina entered the town. After a heavy artillery preparation, the 26th Battalion advanced to attack the botanical gardens and the Hotel Continentale, but was repulsed. The next day the Battalion attacked again, supported this time by a number of tanks, which advanced from the east. After heavy hand-to-hand fighting the New Zealanders occupied the botanical Gardens, but failed to capture the hotel. With the utmost determination, and securely screened by the tanks, the New Zealanders advanced southwards towards the railway station and captured that important strongpoint.

Cassino was now under fire from two directions and was, indeed, all but surrounded. Only 1,200 yards separated the New Zealanders at the station from the Gurkhas on Height 435. To the south of the town, the Via Casilina was under small-arms fire, and during the night the Gurkhas slipped singly through to the station. Just one more, minor push, and the trap would have been closed. Victory was beckoning to Freyberg, but he failed to seize the unique opportunity given to him.

To recapture the railway station the motor-cycle company of Heidrich's division launched an attack across the Rapido at 4 a.m. on 18 March. Unfortunately, during the advance to the river it was caught by a sudden burst of fire from the German mortars and suffered heavy casualties. As they had no boats, the men had to wade across, up to their necks in the icy water. But by four-thirty they had reached the vicinity of the locomotive sheds, which formed the keypoint of the defences. With dug-in tanks, locomotives and waggons protected by sandbags the New Zealanders had transformed the sheds into a formidable strongpoint, against which the attackers could make no progress.

For twenty-four hours the fight raged to and fro, but the station remained in enemy hands; and when the motor-cycle company had finally to be withdrawn across the river, it totalled nineteen men.

The New Zealanders remained at the station, only 300 yards from the Via Casilina. But Freyberg refrained from exploiting this success; on 18 March he renewed his attack on the town itself, determined once and for all to drive the Germans out of the ruins. But the paratroops stood resolutely firm.

The position of the Gurkhas on Height 435, however, was now very precarious. On 19 March at 5.30 a.m. the 1st Battalion, 4 Parachute

Regiment delivered a counter-attack from the abbey on Rocca Janula. The leading assault elements broke into the castle, but had to withdraw in the face of superior numbers. But the Indian 5 Brigade was not to be shifted, and the German attack came to a halt at Height 165, only a short distance from Rocca Janula. A second attempt, made by the pioneer battalion, was repulsed with heavy losses. The pioneers succeeded in blowing a large breach in the outer walls, but were unable to penetrate into the castle itself.

Nevertheless the attack of the 1st Battalion had achieved its main purpose, and the Gurkhas were cut off. There was, indeed, a 200-yard gap between Height 165 and the left wing of the Cassino defences, but this was effectively covered by fire. The Gurkhas were in an unenviable position. They were being grievously harassed by shell fire, their rations were all but exhausted, and they had no water. The attempts to drop supplies to them had been of little or no help, since most of the loads had fallen in the German lines, much to the joy and comfort of the paratroops. The German artillery fire, searching every nook and cranny, suddenly intensified, for after the last failure against Rocca Janula General Heidrich decided not to launch any further attack either against the Gurkhas or the castle. Instead he gave the artillery the congenial task of knocking out the Gurkhas and shooting the castle to bits. For this purpose a 21 cm. battery of French mortars was brought up to 'Dead Man's Gully', but its efforts were of no avail and all its shells came down in the northern sector of Cassino.

The 1st Battalion's counter-attack had caught the Indian 5 Brigade just at the moment when the Essex Regiment was advancing to reinforce the Gurkhas on Height 435, and the British troops at once became involved in the fight for Rocca Janula. The 4/6 Rajputana Rifles also found their way to Height 435 barred. The Essex and the Rajputs had been ordered, together with the Gurkhas, to storm and capture the monastery on 19 March, and it had been Freyberg's intention to supplement this attack with a thrust by armour from the north-west. With this pincer movement he hoped at last to crack the nut.

On the morning of 19 March, with no knowledge, presumably, of the events at Rocca Janula and without suspecting that 4 Brigade's plans had gone completely awry, a company of the New Zealand 20 Armoured Regiment attacked Massa Albaneta, where, according to plan, it was to link up with the Gurkha and Rajputana Rifles and with them to advance to the capture of the monastery. The armoured attack came as a complete surprise to the paratroops. No one had for a moment expected to see tanks operating in this wild and broken hill country. What the Germans had failed to spot had been the enemy engineers, who for weeks past had been preparing a path viable for tanks towards Albaneta. Now, suddenly, seventeen light tanks appeared, advancing against the 2nd Battalion, 4 Parachute Regiment. Not one of them, however, got far. Some were destroyed by the fire of the artillery, others were knocked out by the paratroops themselves at close range, and the remainder were blown up after their crews had abandoned them in panic. The repulse of the armoured thrust removed a serious threat to the monastery. But the news of the failure must have filtered through very slowly to the Allied High Command, for in its communiqué of 20 March it announced that the armoured unit (which had ceased to exist) had thrust down into the Liri valley and was now in position 500 yards from the Via Casilina.

On that same 19 March, however, a desperate struggle was, in fact, in progress for the possession of the Via Casilina. The Maoris had pushed forward into Cassino town to that corner where the Via Casilina takes a sharp turn to the south. But they could get no further than the Hotel Continentale. In the north-west sector of the town the 25th Battalion had been equally unsuccessful in its attacks on the paratroops' positions. Here, where Cassino nestles on the lower slopes of Height 193 (on the crest of which stood Rocca Janula) Lieutenant Jamrowski was the soul of the defence. With a handful of haggard, exhausted men he had not only re-pulsed every attack delivered against him, but had also launched a number of counter-attacks and dealt the New Zealanders some shrewd blows.

The fighting on both sides was exceptionally grim. Hidden from view amongst the chaotic masses of rubble, man fought man in single combat, until one or the other could fight no more. Quarter was neither asked nor given, and though the fighting was perhaps the bitterest yet seen in the Italian campaign and every yard was contested to the end, both sides observed the decencies of war. The Allied communiqué of 19 March states: 'The severity of the fighting is shown by the small number of prisoners taken during the past few days—only fifty-one Germans have been reported by the Allies. . . .' (*Neue Zuericher Zeitung*, No. 476/44.) These figures speak for themselves, and it can safely be assumed that the number of New Zealanders and Indians taken up to 19 March was much the same.

So far Freyberg's success had not been very convincing. In the northern sector of the town the New Zealanders had pressed forward to the Via Casilina, in the eastern sector they had pushed the paratroops back to the Rapido, and the railway station and Height 453 were in Allied hands. Measured against the immense amount of material expended and the severe losses suffered, this did not amount to a great deal. The Germans still held the heart of the town, they still held the abbey, and the attack was making no progress. But according to Alexander's plan, Allied armour should by this time have been well along the road to Rome.

Once again Churchill became impatient. The date fixed for Overlord was drawing nearer, and it was most desirable that a decisive victory should be gained in Italy before Eisenhower's divisions were launched across the Channel. With these thoughts in his mind, the Prime Minister telegraphed to Alexander on 20 March: 'I wish you would explain to me why this passage by Cassino Monastery Hill, etc., all on a front of two or three miles, is the only place which you keep butting at. About five or six divisions have been worn out going into these jaws. Of course I do not know the ground or the battle conditions, but, looking at it from afar, it is puzzling why, if the enemy can be held and dominated at this point, no attacks can be made on the flanks. It is very hard to understand why this most strongly defended point is the only passage forward or why . . . ground cannot be gained on one side or the other.'*

In his reply, Alexander, after pointing out the tactical significance of the Liri valley and Monte Cassino, expressed the opinion that, in view of the extremely difficult nature of the ground and, in the higher regions, the depth of the snow, an outflanking movement via the high ground north-west of Cassino or via the Monte Cairo massif offered no prospect of success. To attempt to capture Cassino from the south, as the U.S. 36 Division had already tried to do, was inadvisable, he said, owing to the swampy nature of the ground in the vicinity of the Rapido, the lack of roads and the strength of the enemy fortified positions. Alexander continued:

Freyberg's attack was designed as a direct assault on this bastion, success depending on crushing enemy resistance by surprise and an overwhelming concentration of fire-power. The plan was to rush Cassino town and then to flow round the east and southern slopes of Monastery Hill and take the bastion by storm from a direction where the enemy's artillery could not seriously interfere with our movement. It very nearly succeeded in its initial stages, with negligible losses to us. . . .

The destruction caused in Cassino to roads and movement by bombing was so terrific that the employment of tanks or any other fighting vehicles has been seriously impeded. The tenacity of these German paratroops is quite remarkable, considering that they were subjected to the whole of the Mediterranean Air Force plus the better part of 800 guns under the greatest concentration of fire-power which has ever been put down and lasting six hours. I doubt if there are any other troops in the world who could have stood up to it and then gone on fighting with the ferocity they have. . . . The plan must envisage an attack on a wider front and with greater forces than Freyberg has been able to have for this operation.†

* Churchill, *The Second World War*, Vol. V.
† *The Second World War*, Vol. V.

In reality, Alexander had realized that the battle had already been lost, and he had decided to transfer the British Eighth Army to the Cassino front to deliver the decisive blow. On 21 March he discussed with his commanders in the field whether the battle should not be broken off forthwith. But Freyberg vowed that with a final effort he would achieve the desired break-through. Alexander decided to give him the chance, but once again, on 22 March, the New Zealand Corps hurled itself in vain against the 1 Parachute Division: Heidrich's men stood firm and yielded not a yard. This sequence of disappointing failures caused great consternation among the Allied staffs. For Clark in particular it was especially painful. The new offensive had been launched with a blare of propaganda and a welter of confident prophesy, and Clark's name had been blazoned throughout the world as the man who was directing it. That the troops who had tried and failed were not Americans, but British and Empire troops, over whom he could exercise little influence, made no difference. His was an American Army, and the American Army would be blamed for any failure that occurred. On 22 March, General Juin noted:

The position of the New Zealand Corps in Cassino and its immediate vicinity has not improved since 19 March. The Germans continue to defend the ruins of the town with the same tenacity and lose no opportunity of launching counter-attacks. Each house has to be captured separately, and in this type of fighting, in which the German and Allied positions are interlocked and the New Zealanders can be supported only with difficulty, the Germans, and particularly their paratroops are by no means the least skilful of fighters. The stubborn and, apparently, unexpected opposition is causing consternation in the Allied High Command. General Clark, who called me to his battle headquarters yesterday, 21 March, is most anxious and nervous. His position is no simple one. In this Cassino affair, only British forces have been engaged. Their losses, without being particularly high, have been severe enough. The two attacking divisions (i.e. the N.Z. and Indian) are exhausted and, because from the outset they have been able to show no success, they have lost their *élan*. In these circumstances the question must be asked: Should the battle continue, regardless of casualties suffered, or would it not be wiser to call off the attacks at present in progress? General Clark asked me for my opinion.

I said that to me it seemed inadvisable to commit oneself too deeply to a local operation which had already proved to be costly and which would become more costly every day—and all for the sake of a meagre success. I mentioned again my own ideas regarding large-scale, comprehensive operations as the only manner in which a break-through in depth could be achieved and such formidable obstacles as Cassino overcome by means of an enveloping movement. I felt that in his heart of hearts General Clark agreed entirely with what I had said.

But for him the problem also contains a personal aspect. He is in command of the army conducting these painful operations, and although the troops engaged are British, over whom he exercises no great influence, while doing his utmost to assist them in every way, he himself remains in the eyes of the world as the man who failed to take Cassino. This aspect depresses him greatly. Furthermore, there is also the question of prestige. Such a fuss has been made about the first great bombardment that the enterprise has assumed the character of a new major operation, and he is reluctant to see it end in failure. . . .

I can only hope that the affair will come to a swift and victorious conclusion, for, from the broader aspect, I cannot but ask myself in what sort of condition will the British troops emerge from the battle . . . and I greatly fear that the major spring offensive will find us in somewhat of a dilemma.*

Alexander, however, had no intention of letting things get out of hand to that extent. When Freyberg's last attempt failed, he at once called off the attack on both town and hill.

The Gurkhas, however, were still in the same precarious situation on Height 435, and, surrounded though they were, somehow or other they had to be withdrawn. The Gurhkas themselves supplied the answer. Heavily bandaged and with a prominent display of a Red Cross flag, they made their way in small groups and in broad daylight to Rocca Janula. From there they slipped through the 200-yard gap between the castle and Cassino. The paratroops let them pass unmolested, and the commander magnanimously refrained from prying too closely into the nature and severity of their wounds. Consideration for a gallant enemy could not have done more!

Like the first, the second Cassino battle ended in an undeniable victory for the defence. But it was a victory dearly bought. The German casualties, caused primarily by the attack on 15 March and the continuous and exceptionally heavy artillery fire, had been severe. Precise figures are not available, but XIV Corps' War Diary for 23 March states that the strength of the battalions engaged at Cassino on that day varied from forty to 120 men. The New Zealand Corps, too, had suffered heavily. Basing his figures on a report from General Maitland Wilson, Churchill says its losses amounted to 1,050 New Zealanders, 1,160 Indians and 190 British of the 78 Division—a total of 2,400 men. This was the depressing balance sheet of an enterprise upon which such high hopes had been pinned and which ended in so sorry a failure.

The resistance put up by the German paratroops made a profound impression on the Allies. In his report to the Minister of War, General Marshall says: 'Determined attempts to capture the town failed in the face of the fanatical resistance by crack German units—notably the 1 Parachute Division, which General Alexander termed the best German division on any front' (War Reports). And General Maitland Wilson:

* Jacques Mordal, Cassino.

'The German paratroops, the defenders of Cassino, gave our troops an example of stubborn resistance similar to that which we encountered against the Japanese in the Pacific.'

It was not, however, the paratroops' powers of resistance alone that wrecked Freyberg's plans. The Allies had deliberately refrained from attempting to bring about the fall of the monastery hill by means of an enveloping movement or even to split up the German defence by a feint attack. Instead they again launched a frontal attack on a bastion, which they well knew would be stubbornly defended, convinced that with the use of overwhelming air and artillery power they could simply sweep the defenders out of their path. Clark himself remarks: 'I felt that the New Zealand Corps had failed because it placed too much reliance on the overpowering weight of bombing to reduce the enemy defences. The enemy was too well protected and too determined. Maximum advantage of the powerful aerial and artillery support which was provided could be taken only by speedy, aggressive action by infantry and armour, using the maximum available force. Piece-meal action, committing a company or a battalion at a time, merely invited failure against the German veterans.'*

It is certainly true that the New Zealand Corps indulged in far too much 'penny-packeting'. First the 25th Battalion assaulted Rocca Janula, then the 24th and 26th advanced to the attack, and the Gurkhas were expected to capture the monastery single-handed. It was only when they had to go to ground on Height 435 that it was decided to launch the Essex Regiment and the Rajputana Rifles also against the abbey.

But the cardinal error was undoubtedly the erroneous reliance placed on the effects of the aerial and artillery bombardment. For this error of judgement it would be unfair to blame Freyberg alone. Since El Alamein the artillery and, even more so, the massing of bombers had been regarded by the Anglo-American High Command as the sovereign panacea and the means which hitherto had always carried them to their goal; and it was probably the capture of Pantelleria that had convinced the last waverers of the correctness of this fundamental principle. Fuller, on the other hand, who often passes quite merciless judgement on the conduct of the Mediterranean operations, declares, with regard to Pantelleria: 'But the truth is, now that Allied ammunition production was approaching its peak, tactics were fast retrogressing to battles of attrition, based on weight of metal and high explosives, in contradistinction to battles of movement, based on audacity and imagination. In 1915–17 the saying was: "Artillery conquers, infantry occupies." Now it reads: "Bombing conquers, all else follows up".'†

* *Calculated Risk.*　　　† *The Second World War.*

And now at Cassino for the first time this procedure failed to be of any help. But this is by no means a proof that massed bombing attacks are ineffective. At Cassino a great deal of luck saved the paratroops from complete annihilation, and the men who survived the inferno recovered from the shock with quite remarkable swiftness. In reality, massed air bombardments of this nature usually tore great holes in the German defences, provided always that it did not, as at Cassino, create an insuperable obstacle through which armour could find no way. Of this St Lô affords a classic example.

Regardless of whether these devastating air bombardments catch the enemy in the open or in a built-up area, they always create a furnace, in which even the finest divisions are incinerated. For not only is the individual man subjected to an all but intolerable strain and almost invariably destroyed in the process, but weapons and supplies are also destroyed with equal certainty and completeness. Field-Marshal von Kluge, who succeeded Rommel on the Western Front, in a report submitted to Hitler on 22 July 1944, for example, says: 'The psychological effect of such a mass of bombs coming down with all the power of elemental nature upon the fighting troops, especially the infantry, is a factor which has to be given particularly serious consideration. It is immaterial whether such a bomb-carpet catches good troops or bad, they are more or less annihilated.'*

But in the monastery, on the other hand, not one single weapon was even scratched, thanks to the consideration Eaker showed for it now that he had destroyed it. Had he set his bombers at the abbey and destroyed its defenders instead of using them to block the Via Casilina for Freyberg's armour, the Allies would probably have marched into Rome in April instead of June.

As it was, the deluge of bombs at Cassino had either destroyed or buried practically all the weapons and most of the ammunition of the forward companies. Of the five guns of the only anti-tank unit in the line, all but one had been buried, and the one surviving gun was damaged and rendered immobile. The heavy infantry weapons—machine-guns and mortars—were nearly all buried under mountains of rubble. The only weapons remaining to those who had survived were their small arms, which they had kept clutched to their bodies during the bombardment, and a few light machine-guns. It is astonishing to think that these meagre resources, in the hands of a small band of determined and experienced veterans, sufficed to hold up so magnificent a body of troops as the New Zealand Corps until German reinforcements arrived.

But the assumption that the stubborn defence at Cassino had any effect on the date of the invasion of France is incorrect. Eisenhower had

* Wilmot, *The Struggle for Europe.*

already fixed the 31 May as D Day before the second Cassino battle started, and the prior capture of Rome was not in any way regarded as a *conditio sine qua non*. Desirable though it may have been, Overlord would have gone ahead, regardless of events in Italy. German propaganda, on the other hand, attached great importance to the Cassino battle, attributing to it a significance which gave the German people the impression that the West Wall would be able to withstand the attacks of the Allied armies and air fleets as Cassino had done. But it discreetly omitted to mention that the waves which for months had been beating in vain against Cassino could not be compared with the tornado that was preparing to hit the north-west coast of France. Cassino may have awakened great hopes of success; but St Lô was the turning point on the road to catastrophe.

Chapter 12

The Defenders of Town and Abbey

The successful defence of the town and hill of Cassino is one of the outstanding feats of arms accomplished by German troops in the Second
World War. This impressive victory won by the 1 Parachute Division and
the army units placed under its command evoked the astonished admiration
of the world, and it is all the more impressive in that it occurred in the
fifth year of the war, at a time when the German armies were no longer
striding victoriously forward and no longer enjoyed the advantage of
superior armaments. Cassino was fought against an enemy who had long
since seized the initiative and who possessed an overwhelming superiority
on land, at sea and in the air. The Germans, on the other hand, had been on
the defensive and hard-pressed for a year and more, their divisions had
been bled white and their resources in armaments weakened by aerial
bombardment.

As their fathers had stood up to the fury of Verdun and the battles of the
Somme a quarter of a century before, their sons now stood fast in the face
of the terrifying material onslaught with which the enemy was destined to
destroy them. The paratroops well knew what was at stake. The order that
Cassino was to be held in all circumstances meant a struggle to the death;
but they also knew that very pregnant reasons had been responsible for the
order. Their task was not simply to hold up the enemy for a while, but to
bar the way to Rome. For Rome in the hands of the enemy meant airfields

not far from the German frontiers and more and more bombs on the already hard-pressed homeland.

Kesselring had good reasons, after the first battle of Cassino, for entrusting the defence of this vital key-point to the 1 Parachute Division. Heidrich's Division personified the hard core of the German parachute arm. It was the successor to the 7 Flying Corps Division, the 'womb' of the parachute arm, which had been raised with such great difficulty by General Student. With this division were connected those names which have gone down in the history of war as the first operations ever to be conducted by means of parachute landings—Stavanger and Dombas in Norway, Rotterdam, Dordrecht and Moerdijk in Holland, Eben Emael and the Albert Canal in Belgium, and last but by no means least, Crete.

Yet Crete all but became the graveyard of the German parachute arm. The severe casualties suffered persuaded Hitler that the days of the paratroops were over and that their initial successes had been due solely to the novelty of the arm and the surprise it achieved. Churchill, on the other hand, after the conquest of Crete, ordered the strength of the British paratroops to be raised from 500 to 5,000!

Crete was the first milestone on 7 Flying Corps' unhappy road. From there its regiments and battalions were pitched into Russia, where they were for the most part split up into small units and placed under the command of army divisions. Some went to Leningrad, some to Stalino and Yuhkno, and by the time the exhausted remnants were crouching frozen in the hard winter of 1941/42, most of the veterans of Crete lay buried in the snowy deserts of Russia. It was only the summer of 1942 that the last remnants—scattered elements of the 2 Parachute Regiment, the machine-gun battalion and the anti-tank sections—returned from Russia. Hitler had sacrificed one of the keenest weapons in his armoury to plug up a few holes on the Eastern Front, while the Allies were busily engaged in creating a mighty airborne army. Nor is that the end of the story. While the last of the paratroops were being decimated at Volkhov, Hitler sent the 'Ramcke Brigade' to Africa—without its aircraft, as infantry! And in Africa they remained, lost for ever to the parachute arm.

This senseless waste of an *élite* body of men is a tragic chapter in the history of Hitler, Master of the Art of War.

It was not until the spring of 1942 when, after the fall of Tobruk, it was decided to capture Malta, that the parchute arm was restored to favour in Hitler's eyes. For now he had sudden and urgent need of Student's experts. But the Malta enterprise, like that at Tuapse, where the paratroops were to open up the Caucasian passes from the south, failed to materialize.

Then, in the autumn of 1942, the 7 Flying Corps Division returned to Smolensk. General Heidrich, who had been commanding the 3 Parachute

Regiment, now assumed command of the division under its new title of 1 Parachute Division. But once again many experienced parachutists and other specialists were left buried in the wide plains of Russia, before the Division was withdrawn into tactical reserve and transferred to France. From France it went to Sicily, where it delivered its last attack from the air. From then onwards, the Division had fought like any other infantry division, inadequately provided with motor transport, but comparatively well armed; only in artillery was it really weak.

Now the Division was at Cassino. Behind it lay 220 days of continuous fighting. Only for a short while, after the evacuation of Sicily, had it enjoyed a brief rest in Calabria and Apulia; since Salerno it had been uninterruptedly in the front line, the fierce storm of battle had swept over it, and its ranks had been very greatly depleted. The men had fought till they could fight no more. They were worn out, and most of them were suffering from malaria. Many had had no leave since quitting Russia. Yet their fighting spirit remained unbroken. The superior enemy strength had taken heavy toll of them, but they had proved their ability to stand up to odds, and the success they had achieved bred in them a fine measure of self-confidence. Come what might at Cassino, they'd take good care that the enemy did not get a walk-over.

Though the pages that follow offer the reader an anthology of outstanding deeds that bear witness to the gallantry of the Cassino warriors, they represent only a small selection, taken from a host of individual achievements which, in combination, led to the German victory. War diaries and operational reports have for the most part been destroyed or lost; such as survive are not yet available for scrutiny by German military historians. What follows is based on later accounts by officers and men who were in the Cassino furnace and on the personal recollections of the author. Many deeds have been forgotten, for those who accomplished them live no more. Many a deed and act of sacrifice passed unnoticed, since none was there to bear witness to them.

The first story concerns the fate of No. 7 Company, 3 Parachute Regiment. Only a handful survived the seven-hour preliminary bombardment; most of them had died and been buried beneath the ruins; and those who had survived were at the end of their tether when the barrage at last lifted to engage targets in the rear areas. But when they heard the clatter of on-coming tanks, their fighting spirit burst once more into flame. A fresh hour of trial was at hand, and they were ready to meet it.

Through the slowly clearing smoke and dust Lieutenant Schuster's men suddenly saw the first three Sherman tanks a bare fifty yards away. They were twisting and turning this way and that in an effort to find a way through the mass of craters and rubble. Behind them came infantry, without a care in the world and confident that nothing could harm them in this desolation of ruins. Without bothering about cover, the men clambered over the piles of rubble, and no shot, no burst from the dreaded German machine-gun, Mk. 42, broke the peace. The tank commanders, too, felt quite secure. They lounged unconcernedly out of their turrets, joking with each other over the inter-com. There was not a 'Jerry' to be seen anywhere!

Suddenly the first shots rang out from among the ruins, and the tank commanders ducked hastily back into their tanks. The infantry dived into craters or sought cover behind the armoured vehicles. That was the first blow. The second, aimed at the leading Sherman, followed at once. Lance-Corporal Blum supplied it with a 'Panzerfaust' (the German anti-tank bazooka). The crew leapt out, but were plastered with rifle grenades as they dashed for cover behind the remnants of a wall. The two remaining monsters ground their way laboriously towards Schuster's men. The infantry crept cautiously forward under cover of their armoured escort, throwing hand grenades haphazardly into the ruins around them. But the paratroops were on the alert, and prevented any further advance. The tanks stuck fast in the rubble, until darkness enabled them to get back. The infantry, however, remained where they were. Despite his successful parrying of the first thrust, Schuster's position was highly dangerous. He knew that the enemy had broken into No. 10 Company's position on his right. In the evening he heard that the only assault gun in the sector had been buried beneath the ruins. His means of communication had been destroyed, runners could not get through, and he had lost touch with battalion headquarters. The enemy, he thought, was probably sitting on top of the company, on Rocca Janula. Isolated and cut off, he and his men crouched in the ruins and waited.

The night passed quietly. The Company Commander distributed a little bread and sugar, the only food they had left. But the men were desperately thirsty. For twelve hours they had had nothing to drink, and clinging chalk dust and the heat of battle had parched their throats. In front of them they could hear the murmur of the Rapido, but between them and it were the New Zealanders.

Throughout the next day, the enemy contented himself with pinning the paratroops down with gunfire and grenades, hoping in this way to force them to surrender. Indeed, a tank called on them to do so, but the demand was ignored. While they still had ammunition, Schuster's men had no intention of giving up; there they were, and there they'd stay and fight. Lance-Corporal Kny and Rifleman Boching stalked a Sherman tank and crippled it. This effort put new heart into the men. But by evening both food and ammunition were coming to an end. Schuster had still been unable to establish contact with the Battalion, but in the meanwhile he had confirmed that the enemy had occupied the Rocca Janula. Thirst had now become an intolerable burden. Haggard and exhausted the men crouched in their holes. The Battalion, obviously, had written them off, and no help could be expected from that quarter. Everything looked pretty grim and hopeless.

But there was still just one course open to Schuster—a break-through to his own lines, and he decided to have a shot at it. He divided his forlorn little band into three groups, and at 10 p.m. the groups rose and set out at ten-minute intervals.

Schuster himself with six men started off westwards in the direction of Monte Cairo and, though fired upon from two sides, got through the town without loss. The way before him now rose steeply and, pouring with sweat, their parched throats afire, the paratroops climbed painfully up the barren, shell-pitted slopes. Danger lurked all round them; any and every shadow might be concealing a Tommy. The chances of getting through seemed slender indeed. But the will to do so, to avoid being captured, drove them onwards.

North of Cassino they came across a field telephone post, but the connexions had been cut. A little later they ran into an enemy sentry, but his burst of tommy-gun fire passed harmlessly over their heads. Luck seemed to be with them. But thirst had now become a torture, and in the bare rocks not a drop of water was to be found. When dawn came, Schuster realized that he was still behind the enemy lines and had not got through, as he had hoped. To try and go on in daylight was out of the question. There was nothing for it but to lie up all day and wait for darkness to fall. Very close to them Indian troops were at work, broadening a hill path. In the valley below were row upon row of tents. The enemy, seemingly, was massing an imposing force for the capture of Monte Cassino.

Impatiently the paratroops awaited the blessed cloak of darkness. At last, after hours of dangerous and agonizing waiting, at about ten o'clock the groups set out once again. Stiff and cramped by hours of lying, the men stumbled forward, and almost at once ran into an Indian company moving forward in relief. Like a flash the paratroops disappeared, as though the earth had swallowed them. Then they moved on again. Soon the clink of equipment and the low murmur of voices caught Schuster's ear. They were now obviously very close to the enemy lines. With the utmost caution they crept on. Then suddenly: 'Halt! Who goes there?' 'Captain Brown,' answered Schuster and continued to advance. A shadow detached itself from the darkness of the night, a steel-helmeted figure with a tommy-gun at the ready. Schuster continued calmly towards him. 'I'm

Captain Brown, on special duty,' he said in faultless English. 'I've been ordered to go through and pick up some German prisoners.' 'Sorry,' replied the Tommy, he didn't know anything about that, his suspicions aroused by the sight of the unfamiliar but distinctive paratroop helmet. The officer would have to come along, please, and see the guard commander, he said, and Schuster realized he would have to do something quickly. Pretending to follow the sentry, he whispered urgently to his men: 'Knock him out—quick! But no noise!' And the next instant a sizeable piece of rock hit the sentry on the back of the head. As he fell, however, he pressed the trigger, and a burst of fire caught Schuster in the chest and arm. 'What now?' muttered Sergeant-Major Richter, bending over him. 'Beat it! and get back to the lines,' Schuster managed to say. Richter hesitated. He was loth to leave his officer lying there. Then, with an effort, 'And that's an order,' Schuster added.

And beat it they did, pursued by rifle fire and the chatter of tommy-guns. Summoning their last remnants of strength, they hastened in the direction of the German lines and at about 2.30 a.m. they stumbled into the positions of No. 11 Company, north of Albaneta. At last they had reached safety—and a drink.

The next morning they were taken before General Heidrich, who questioned them closely. This was an exploit after his own heart, the sort of thing he expected of his paratroops. A medal and a bit of leave in the Dolomites was the just reward given to these six survivors of No. 7 Company. But one thought continued to depress them—the uncertainty about the fate of their company commander. Was he still alive? How was he getting on?

By this time Schuster was safely in hospital in Caserta. Here, on the Allied lines of communication he had been quite one of the sights. Neither doctors nor nurses had ever set eyes on so forlorn-looking a warrior. His uniform hung in shreds round him; his hands and face were scratched and torn; from his haggard cheeks sprouted a straggling, incipient beard and from head to foot he was covered in mud and blood—a truly horrible personification of the murderous battle of Cassino. But Schuster was patched up, and medical care and skill saved him from any permanent ill-effects.

While the remnants of No. 7 Company were slipping away through the mountains, determined officers in Cassino below were laboriously creating a fresh defensive position. In this, Rennecke, who was in command, Foltin, the O.C. 2nd Battalion, and Jamrowski were the prime architects.

When last mentioned, Jamrowski was just emerging from the tomb from which he had freed himself. At once he set off towards No. 8 Company observation post on the slopes of Height 193. On the way he ran into some

New Zealanders, but after a brief exchange of shots they retreated, and Jamrowski and his little band went on. Again they encountered an enemy patrol, and again Jamrowski beat it off. At last he approached the post, only to find it surrounded by the enemy. The enemy on the slopes below Rocca Janula were a particular menace to him, and he decided to have a go at them. Throughout the night he kept on attacking and driving off small enemy patrols, and by morning he had the block of houses on the slopes of Height 193 firmly in his hands; and from there he could dominate the whole northern sector of Cassino.

This was important. For now he was on the flank of the New Zealanders pressing forward towards the centre of the town. But to open fire on them presented great difficulties. The New Zealanders were as alert as gun-dogs; at the slightest sign of movement their snipers came into action, and those snipers were devilish good shots, as the paratroops well knew from Cretan days. Whenever the enemy spotted a position, he at once put the artillery or tanks on to it. Jamrowski therefore hardly dared to use his machine-gun at all—it kicked up too much dust, gave the position away and drew immediate fire. But the Germans, too, had their snipers. As their targets they singled out officers, incautious tank commanders and infantry moving under cover of the armoured vehicles, and their fire obviously got on the New Zealanders' nerves.

But Jamrowski was by no means content to sit meekly on the receiving end; he was determined to wage an aggressive form of defence, such as Heidrich had preached in 1940. He therefore decided on the evening of 16 March to attack a New Zealand strongpoint, held by tanks. Under cover of darkness, he hoped, he would stand a good chance of knocking the monsters out. While he was making his plans, he heard a well-known voice—Jansen, the runner whom he had sent out after the first wave of bombers and whom he had given up as dead!

Scarcely had Jansen got clear of the dug-out on the morning of 15th than the second wave came in. He could not get back, so he threw himself down under cover of the nearest bit of wall, which promptly collapsed on top of him, leaving a small crevice through which he was just able to breathe. Otherwise, he was completely penned in, unable to move either hand or foot. For hours he lay there, trying in vain to loosen the grip of even one stone. Then at last, as the dust trickled away, something began to move, and he was able to shift a little. After thirty-three hours of indescribable torment he had freed himself. Bruised, battered and bleeding, he staggered over the rubble. Most men would have made straight for the nearest field-dressing station; but not Jansen. His one thought was to rejoin his hard-pressed comrades. And now—there he was.

The first thing he had to do, Jamrowski told him, was to have a rest and regain his strength. There'd be plenty of time for that later, Jansen retorted; now he wanted to be in on the attack—the Lieutenant hadn't too many men, as it was. After the New Zealanders had been winkled out, then he'd take a nap.

Powers of resistance! This was the spirit displayed by the defenders of Cassino. Their efforts had been all but superhuman. Jamrowski, in a letter to the author, said: 'The night was our friend. By night we were able to move. But there wasn't a hope of any rest. First we had to rebuild and improve our positions, establish communication between the various strongpoints, get the wounded away and bring up ammunition, food and water. When you consider that half the small force was engaged on these fatigues, and the position still had to be held with the other half—for there was always the danger of a sudden attack—and when you think that from the few men left I had to send some on reconnaissance, then you'll realize what these fellows accomplished. . . .'

Their position, a rock cavern, was immediately behind the front line. On 18 March it was the objective of a massed attack. With the aid of flame-throwers the enemy advanced right up to the mouth of the cavern. But the paratroops prevailed in the end, and twenty-one New Zealanders surrendered to them.

From then onwards, Staff-Sergeant Israel, a veteran of Heidrich's old regiment in the days of the Reichswehr, kept watch like a Cerberus on the mouth of the cave. If the enemy attacked again, they would find Israel ready and waiting. And over in the 'Continentale' stood the other 'tiger' of No. 6 Company, Sergeant-Major 'Charlie' Neuhoff. He dominated the centre of the town like a monarch and brushed aside repeated attacks by whole New Zealand battalions. Try as they would, they could not get across to the south side of the Via Casilina.

Above, on the slopes of the monastery hill, the enemy had made no progress either. After their first failure, the Gurkhas had had enough. The staff of the 1st Parachute Battalion and its No. 4 Company under Lieutenant Voight had transformed the monastery into a veritable fortress. Four heavy and two light machine-guns and two medium mortars had been installed amid the ruins; a comprehensive telephone system had been established and a whole army of artillery observing officers had taken up their position in the shell-proof subterranean passages.

When the men of No. 4 Company first occupied the abbey in February, it had presented a shattering spectacle. It was not only the inanimate desolation of the ruined buildings which impressed them, but also the living misery that confronted them—Brother Carlomanno wandering light-headed among the ruins, sheep and donkeys in the Priory courtyard, starving and reduced to skeletons, which had somehow survived since the bombardment with nothing to eat save the shredded fronds of the palm trees. Everywhere as they worked, the men came across the corpses of civilians, often arms and legs were found, sticking out of the ground; and then, when the rains ceased and the March sun shone again, it was quickly followed by the intolerable stench of decaying bodies.

But even worse than that was the smoke screen. From the 20 March Freyberg had enveloped town and abbey from morning till night in an impenetrable smoke screen. So concentrated was the fire of the smoke shells, that the men had to wear their gas-masks to shield their throats. Eating became a difficult and tiresome business, and only at night was there a little respite. But at night they were plagued by another kind of pest. The continuous and heavy artillery fire sent huge clouds of chalk dust high into the air, and when firing ceased, this dust gradually settled, causing violent fits of coughing and in many cases loss of voice. And to put a seal on the general discomfort, the water supply began to give out. The main cistern in the central courtyard was still there, but it had been badly damaged, the water had become polluted and had to be laboriously filtered before it could be drunk.

Considering the vast amount of metal hurled at them—the German gunners estimated that at least 300,000 shells had been fired at the monastery—the losses of the garrison, No. 4 Company, had been negligible—three dead and eleven wounded. But No. 2 Company on Rocca Janula and Height 165 had suffered severely. The company had been hard hit by the bombardment, and the remnants that had survived were annihilated by the infantry. Of the whole company there was but one survivor. Most had been killed, and the remainder had been wounded and taken prisoner.

The great hole torn in the German defences by the attack of the New Zealand 25th Battalion had been partly plugged by the 1st Battalion, 4 Parachute Regiment's attack on 19 March. The salient feature of this hard fight had been the chivalry displayed by both sides. When the German attack on Rocca Janula failed, the British Commander at once agreed to a two-hour truce, and Indians and Germans worked side by side, gathering the dead and tending the wounded. With great difficulty the paratroops carried their wounded up to the abbey, and many died on the way. Of inestimable value were the supplies of blood which the Allies had tried to drop on the Gurkhas, but which had fallen in the German lines. With the primitive means at their disposal the doctors gave blood transfusions and performed many major operations, for Cassino was too far away, stretcher bearers were lacking and it was not possible swiftly to evacuate the severely wounded to the hospitals below.

Exactly the same decency was shown by both sides when the second German attack on 22 March also failed. The garrison of the castle handed over the German wounded, and the British medical officer even gave the Germans four stretchers to help with their evacuation. The Gurkhas gave their opponents—and not only the wounded—cigarettes, chocolate, offered them a swig from their water-bottles and in many other small ways demonstrated the esteem in which they held a worthy foeman. But the moment the truce ended, the fighting continued as bitterly as ever. The next day, however, when the German medical orderlies returned the stretchers they had borrowed, the Gurkhas received them with all the courtesy that is characteristic of their race.

On the same day that the Germans had delivered these abortive attacks on Rocca Janula, a company of the New Zealand 20 Armoured Regiment launched the attack that has already been mentioned against Massa Albaneta, up in the mountains. Towards midday a report had reached the battle headquarters of the 2nd Battalion, 4 Parachute Regiment, of an enemy tank said to be approaching Massa Albaneta. The news was received with astounded incredulity, particularly at regimental head-quarters, where it was regarded as a feeble joke. No one thought it possible for enemy armour to have penetrated into the steep, rugged, mountain country. But Major Grassmehl, who was officiating in command, knowing that all sorts of improbable things occur in war, sent Lieutenant Eckel, commanding the anti-tank company, to investigate.

Accompanied by one of his men and a war correspondent who happened to be there, Eckel set out. Carefully, making use of every scrap of available cover the three men advanced like stalkers towards Albaneta, 300 yards away. From the shelter of a rock they suddenly caught sight of a number of enemy tanks, rattling along a narrow mountain path. Eckel counted seventeen of them, Grants and Commandos—sixteen-tonners, that is, with one 3·7 cm. gun, a machine-gun and an anti-tank machine-gun. It was obvious, too, that they had been specially modified to enable them to operate in mountain country.

There could be no doubt about the object of the enterprise. These tanks were going to make a thrust at the abbey and try and relieve the hard-pressed Gurkhas on Height 435.

By this time, the advanced artillery observation posts had also observed this unusual attack and had telephoned to their batteries, and very quickly the first salvoes were bursting round the tanks. When the smoke cleared, six of the tanks were seen to have been immobilized. The rest were circling round the fortress-like Albaneta, firing wildly in all directions. Eckel and his companions crawled forward. From where they were he could not reach the tanks with his bazooka. They had to get closer. . . .

Calmly Kammermann took aim and pressed the trigger. Misfire! The second round was also a misfire. He now had only one round left; if that failed, then the golden opportunity would be lost. But this time, the shot, well and truly aimed, hit the tank, which burst into flames.

Three of the tanks now turned in the direction of the monastery. On that course, Eckel rightly foresaw, they would be confined to a narrow hill path, the steep sides of which precluded any possibility of deviation. Eckel set off in pursuit. He had no short-range anti-tank weapon, but he hoped he might be able to lob a hand grenade into an open turret. But when his party were close to Albaneta, they found, quite by accident, three T-mines. That was indeed a find, and it did not take Eckel long to make up his mind how to use them. Hastening forward at their best speed on the flank of the tanks, the little party managed to get sufficiently ahead to enable them to plant the mines in the hill path. All unsuspecting the leading tank came on; from their cover all that Eckel and his men could see of it was the antennae of its wireless. Would it . . . or wouldn't it? . . .

Suddenly an ear-splitting explosion rent the air and a black cloud enveloped the tank. Eckel leapt to his feet with a yell of triumph. The trap had closed. The tracks of the leading tank had been blown to pieces, leaving it incapable of movement and blocking the way, for the other two could now neither go forward towards the monastery nor back, since to reverse along the very narrow path was all but impossible.

The other tanks then tried to shift their crippled companion out of the way. The crew of the second tank leapt out, intending to fasten a tow-wire to the 'lame duck'. But they were at once caught in the well-directed fire of the paratroops, who had been watching events from the nearby hill-top. The crew of the crippled tank then went berserk and opened a furious fire in all directions with everything they had. A few faithful mules, grazing peacefully on the fresh spring grass and oblivious of the evil intentions of the men around them, were the first victims.

Eckel wondered how he could put a stop to it. A hand grenade? And indeed, using a rifle grenade as a hand grenade, he succeeded in putting the tank's machine-gun out of action. But its other gun continued to fire furiously. Desperate situations demand drastic action. Eckel now had nothing left with which to continue the fight; but he knew that at battalion headquarters there was a dump of explosives. He dashed off at once, being hit on the way by a shell splinter; but 'his engine was still running', and on he went.

Breathless, he reached his destination, grabbed a few T-mines, some detonators and a length of fuse and ran back to give his booty the *coup de grâce*. With great skill he stalked his way nearer and nearer to the prey. To leap on its back, tear open the turret and drop an already primed mine into the interior was the work of a moment. He leapt off and dived for cover, closely followed by two terror-stricken members of the tank's crew. Then, with a sharp crack the tank burst asunder. The mine had blown it to pieces.

Eckel's exploit was too much for the watching paratroops above. The fever of the chase gripped them and they, too, wanted to be 'in on it'. Two of them, Wielun and Sack, managed to find some T-mines, worth their weight in gold at that moment, and rushed boldly at the other tanks and put two of them out of action exactly as Eckel had done. Hufnagel and Gudd accounted for one more apiece.

Twelve tanks were now out of action, six of them completely destroyed. The remaining five were still firing furiously, mostly at Albaneta, which they obviously took to be either a command post or a well-fortified strong-point. Eckel now turned to the one nearest to him, stalking it like a hunter. The tank's entire attention was concentrated on Albaneta, and his approach was not noticed. He fixed a primed mine behind the turret and leapt for safety. Tank number thirteen had been accounted for.

The fourteenth was blown up in the same way by Eckel and Wielun working together. Panic now gripped the crews of the surviving tanks. Never in their lives had they seen anything like this. The devil himself must have been taking a hand in the game. Turrets were torn open, the crews poured out and sought safety in headlong flight. But they did not get very far. From all sides a murderous fire was opened on them; some fell at once, others tried to put up a fight, but they quickly realized the hopelessness of their position and surrendered.

Better safe than sorry, Eckel thought, and as twilight fell he called up a party from his own company to blow up the abandoned tanks. The tank hunt had lasted a good hour, and it had given the enemy a sharp reminder that to 'muck about' with the 4 Parachute Regiment, 'the tigers of Cassino', was a foolhardy thing to do.

But now, in the main battle, the paratroops no longer stood alone. Behind them, strong artillery forces, intervening with ever increasing effectiveness, had put stiffening into the defence, and the guns from neighbouring sectors were also giving their support.

Though General Heidrich was exercising overall control of the artillery fire plan in person, Colonel Heilmann still had plenty of batteries with which to put in a word or two. Heidrich had established himself at the battle headquarters of the 3 Parachute Regiment and was directing the defence from there. The situation facing him demanded that the operations should be conducted primarily by means of artillery fire. Both he and Heilmann were directing their efforts with the same object in view—to pin down the enemy by gunfire and, if possible, to establish a fire superiority, if only for the time being, over the enemy. This is how Colonel Heilmann saw things:

I well knew that the few men I had in the front line, however gallantly they fought, could not win the battle alone. My best and most trustworthy leaders had already gone forward into Cassino itself. . . . My object, however, was to decide the issue by gunfire, and I thought I saw a chance of doing so. We had, of course, fewer guns than the enemy, and those that we had were somewhat partworn. But war always demands a whole series of improvisations. . . .

I now demanded of the artillery a lavish and unrestricted expenditure of ammunition and even went as far as to harrow them into compassion for the poor infantryman, when I laid down the amount to be expended in accordance with my fire plan for the day. . . . There were grouses, of course. Some batteries did not want to fire by day, because their positions would be given away; ammunition could only be brought up at night, and the waggons frequently got bogged down in the soft ground; according to Army instructions, mine-throwers were to be used only for direct fire, because their ammunition was so expensive, and so on. But from the front I was constantly receiving reports of suspected enemy concentrations, and on those areas I wanted fire to be brought to bear. Accordingly I brushed all these objections aside. I was determined to show my lads at the front that we behind were doing our utmost to support them.

There now began a struggle for fire superiority such as seldom occurred during the war. On the other side, batteries stood wheel to wheel; and their supplies of ammunition seemed to be inexhaustible. The battle for Cassino had now been raging for months, and the enemy artillery fire was daily becoming more accurate. Any movement, any fresh target revealed in our main defensive position drew immediate fire. From early morning till darkness fell, an observer aircraft, 'Iron Gustav', the men called it, cruised unimpeded over our positions. . . .

Yet in this second battle of Cassino we achieved the great feat of gaining, for a while at least, superiority of fire. This is how it was done: With great skill and by using every possible means of communication, the artillery liaison officer with the 3 Parachute Regiment succeeded in co-ordinating the fire of more and more batteries in the sector and even in integrating the artillery of the division next to us. . . . The heavy machine-gun and mine-thrower platoons of the division were brigaded and their fire co-ordinated in a single, homogenous fire plan. The heavy machine-guns made good use of dummy positions—an art, incidentally, that seemed to have been forgotten in this war. The fire plan was gradually broadened to embrace every type of weapon available, and even rifles and rifle-grenades were allotted their specific tasks. . . .

What the German gunners accomplished at Cassino is worthy of a place beside the feats of their comrades in the front line. The artillery positions had for the most part been pin-pointed by the enemy, and as soon as a battery opened fire, the enemy guns were on it in a flash. Whenever 71 Mortar Regiment fired its salvoes, the men hardly had time to take cover before a shower of shells descended upon them. Whole batteries of the New Zealand artillery had been given as a sole task this constant engagement of the mortar batteries. Even so, the stout-hearted gunners of

71 Regiment fired salvo after salvo, and the manner in which they stood up to the enemy counter-battery fire evoked everyone's admiration. Their battery positions were like ploughed fields, and there was not a square yard that had not been ploughed up by a shell.

The defensive victory at Cassino, then, had been won thanks to the co-operation between the army units engaged and the paratroops. But the 1 Parachute Division was one corporate assault entity, as it had been in Crete, when paymasters, clerks and lorry drivers, who had never made a parachute jump in their lives, had slipped into the transport aircraft, in order not to be left out. Now at Cassino, they pressed forward in the same way. 'The great thing about this battle,' says General Heidrich in his last report, 'was the spirit in which it was fought. At the outset soldier's luck had smiled on me, and it was quite by chance that I found myself in the front line when the battle began. But for that I should not have been able to draw the artillery so swiftly into the fight. No one who participated in the battle will ever forget the spirit shown. To this very day, the memory of the manner in which every man hastened forward moves me deeply. Clerks abandoned their desks, drivers vied with each other, even under the heaviest fire, in their efforts to keep the troops supplied with everything they needed. In their care of the wounded the medical personnel displayed the same devotion to duty.'

Equal tribute must be paid to the doctors in the casualty clearing stations and field hospitals, who worked without respite day and night to save those who could be saved. They were the silent heroes of the battle, as were the lorry drivers who night after night groped their way through a corridor of shell-holes into a crater-bespattered Cassino. How often, their tyres slashed by splinters, were they compelled to stop and change a wheel on the open road, or with radiator or engine hit, to wait for a tow! And all this in pitch-black darkness, at a snail's pace and by the flickering light of bursting shells.

But on the very fringe of the battle itself stood the stoutest of all the front troops' friends—the stretcher bearers, the men in charge of the pack animals and the trusty, though often damnably stubborn, mules themselves. To these men fell the most hazardous task of all. While the riflemen in the front line were comparatively safe in their dug-outs, these others had to continue their good work in the open and, as often as not, under fire. From the point on the Via Casilina where they took over from the lorries, the pack-animal personnel night after night carried supplies up the hillsides. Their only way lay through the dreaded 'Dead Man's Gully', which was under constant and concentrated fire, was strewn with the corpses of man and beast and filled with the odours of decay. On every journey through the gully death took its toll. It took two hours to reach Albaneta and an hour and half to get to the monastery, and every second could bring death. The narrow mountain path was littered with boulders, rocks frequently came tumbling down, and disaster lurked round every corner. If the column were caught by enemy fire, the men, of course, took what cover they could, but the animals often broke loose and went hurtling down the precipitous hill-sides; or some animal would be hit, and then the man had to take over its heavy load himself.

In this way, with untold effort and sacrifice, the front line was kept well supplied. Nor were the return journeys any picnic. Once again man and beast had to traverse the fire zone, and this time the personnel had their own wounded to get down into the valley, where ambulances waited to take them along the fire-swept Via Casilina to the field hospitals; and many a wounded man, feeling safe at last in the hands of the medical orderlies, was killed on the way to safety.

To obviate this danger, General Heidrich ordered that the wounded men were to be transported by day, in armoured troop carriers and under the protection of the Red Cross. Even then, there were still casualties, and many a troop carrier was destroyed by enemy fire. The observation officers of the New Zealand artillery were not to blame; but they often unintentionally directed fire on these vehicles because in the smoke and mist they had been unable to see the Red Cross flag.

The pity of it is that after the war slanderous assertions were made—and by no means only by the other side—that 1 Parachute Division had abused the Red Cross and used their armoured vehicles to take ammunition to Monte Cassino. These people refused to believe that supplies could possibly have been carried forward along a Via Casilina under constant fire in any other way. Such slanderers do not deserve the dignity of rebuttal. Suffice it to say that the Germans guilty of them merely fouled their own nests.

The gallant stand made by the 1 Parachute Division was given its due recognition by the other side—and not by the armed forces alone. Responsible journalists made no secret of their admiration for the defenders of Cassino and not infrequently gave expression to it. *The Times* of 19 March says: 'From statements made by prisoners taken during this desperate struggle it is possible to form some picture of life in Cassino today. Men of the 1 Parachute Division are seldom brought in as prisoners; they are that type of soldier who would rather fight and die than surrender, and when by chance one of them is brought in, he will say nothing. . . .'

On 23 March *The Times* correspondent in Italy reported: 'Cassino has been transformed into a heap of rubble. But rubble furnishes ideal fighting material for bold and determined troops; and such are the troops whom the

Germans have sent to Cassino with the specific object of holding the town for as long as possible. . . .

'In the aerial bombardment and the subsequent artillery barrage some of their companies were annihilated and a great mass of material was destroyed. But the men who emerged from the shambles were men possessed of a desperate determination to resist and to hold Cassino for as long as it could be held. They emerged from deep cellars that had with-stood the hail of bombs and shells; some shovelled their way out of the ruins, and even when they were brought to battle, they refused to give in. Such are the men of the 1 Parachute Division, whom our armies met in Sicily, at Ortona and now again at Cassino. Their numbers are growing steadily smaller, and they have paid dearly for their implacable defence of Cassino—and with their fighting qualities, they are all but irreplaceable.'

Straightforward words, unequivocal in their assessment of the morale and fighting efficiency of the German paratroops! A broadcast by Naples radio on 21 March was in a somewhat different tone: 'The German paratrooper today has but one object—to die for Adolf Hitler. He is a fanatic, seldom more than twenty years of age. At Cassino he is sacrificing his life for the Führer and his cause. . . .'

A great number of Allied sources talk about the 'fanatical Nazis', the paratroops so imbued with Hitler's doctrines that they would rather be killed than surrender. Only in this way, they say, can their success at Cassino be explained. But let us get this quite straight. The young men of the 1 Parachute Division, exactly like the young men of all the other German divisions, had spent years going through the school of the Hitler Youth movement. When the 'Third Reich' emerged, they had been anything between eight and fifteen years old; they knew nothing but the lies and phrases drilled into them by a dogmatic and one-sided propaganda; from the time they were little toddlers it had been instilled into them that the national socialist concept was the one and only panacea for all evil. Is it then surprising that they, like all the rest of German youth, should have been filled with faith in Hitler? And in the circumstances, who could blame them? The Allies themselves after the end of the war made their own attitude towards this question perfectly clear when they granted amnesties to the younger generation.

But to assert that the defenders of Cassino, these paratroops 'rotten with Nazi-ism', had performed this unique feat of arms simply and solely because of their ideological outlook, is nothing but twaddle, eye-wash and an excuse with which to cover up a military blunder. It could with equal justice to be asserted that the Allied Commandos owed their impressive feats to their fundamental outlook on life. Would anyone care to attribute the stubborn defence of Bastogne to the fact that the American paratroops must have been particularly fanatical Democrats? The values which gave Heidrich's paratroops the strength and ability to stand up to the onslaughts of the Fifth Army were very different. The secret of their success can be summed up in three qualities—comradeship, *esprit de corps*, efficiency. Those were the foundations upon which the German parachute arm was built; and they are the foundations of every *corps d'élite*.

The word comradeship looms large in the vocabulary of the German parachute arm. Nor does it do so fortuitously. It was inevitably inherent in the character of this corps of specialists, composed, up to 1944, exclusively of volunteers. When paratroops go into action, officer and man sit side by side in the same aircraft, the officer is the first to jump—and lands as often as not in the midst of the enemy. He runs the same risks in jumping and is in the same danger of being shot while coming down as his men; he lands on the same hard ground and is just as likely to suffer broken bones as they are. His haversack contains the same modest rations, his water-bottle is filled with the same thin coffee as theirs.

Paratroops know nothing about lines of communication. From the general to the latest joined recruit, they are all always 'up in the line'. When they come down, the staff officers join in the fight, using the same arms as the men, securing the dropping zone and ensuring that those that follow will be able to unload the containers. Maintenance and supply personnel and specialists all jump and land in the same zone, as do also the medical services, the field dressing stations and the field hospitals. The fact that twenty-three medical officers of the parachute arm were among the casualties in Crete speaks for itself.

This experience of jumping together, this sharing of all the hazards of battle and this knowledge that they are all dependent on each other have forged a particularly close bond between officer and man, a bond similar to that which exists in the submarine service, the Panzer arm and the air arm. The officer is just one of the team, of which every member does his best for the good of his side.

The German parachute arm was imbued with a splendid *esprit de corps*. The knowledge that, once they had done their quota of instructional jumps, they were members of a *corps d'élite* of whom so much was expected as a matter of course, was, of itself, enough to give the men a feeling of pride. They knew that exceptional feats of arms were always expected of them, and they did their utmost to prove worthy of the confidence placed in them. And so it was at Cassino. To the men of the 1 Division to surrender town and hill to the enemy was unthinkable. The high repute of their division was at stake, and to preserve that no sacrifice was too great. They were determined to defend Cassino until they could fight no more.

Fighting spirit alone, however, cannot achieve everything. Behind it there must be sound military knowledge and training. These the 1 Parachute had in good measure. It was not for nothing that Heidrich's reputation as an instructor was known far beyond the confines of his own division and, indeed, of the whole parachute arm. He had but little use for the dull drill on the barrack square. Individual and collective field training, mostly with ball ammunition, was his speciality, his 'home ground' the manœuvre areas of Germany, the forests and plains of Russia, the dunes of the Normandy coast and the mountains of southern France. Here he trained his paratroops with ruthless energy, here he equipped them with every quality they would need in battle. His ultimate object was to turn out each individual as a skilled, self-reliant fighter, and each unit as a fighting entity which functioned with the precision of clockwork. He deliberately trained his men to be individualists, and he wisely encouraged a spirit of self-reliance. To his mind the paratrooper had to be an 'all purposes soldier', an infantryman, a pioneer and an anti-tank expert rolled into one; he had to be familiar with all the infantry arms, light and heavy alike; he had to be able to ride a horse, drive a car and be at home on skis.

In the demands General Heidrich made of his men he was quite ruthless. In training he tolerated no weakness, gave no thought to comfort. Officers and men groaned—and often cursed heartily. Frequently he would roar at them, when his eye detected slackness or inefficiency, and he never tired of telling them that seventy-five per cent of success in battle was achieved on manœuvres. But there was nothing of the slave-driver or the cold, impersonal military pedant about him. He enjoyed the personal devotion of his men to a degree that is rare for so senior a commander. Beneath his rugged, ruthless exterior he had a soft heart for his men and their families, and he spared no pains to do what he could for their material comfort and moral well-being. He was really the father of his men; and the latter loved and respected him as sons will love and respect a good father.

That, then, was the secret, in its final analysis, which accounted for the success at Cassino, the very essence of a body of men who had astonished the world.

Chapter 13

The Third Battle of Cassino

After Freyberg's failure, General Maitland Wilson at once set about preparing for the next round. The comprehensive regrouping of the 15 Army Group did not, it is true, permit of any immediate land operations, but fine weather made it possible for him to throw the full might of his air forces into the battle. Now, however, they were not called upon to deliver any major attacks in the Cassino manner, but were ordered to concentrate on disorganizing the lines of communication of the German armies and to 'strangle' Kesselring's divisions. This was the aim and object of 'Operation Strangle', which began in the third week in March and continued throughout the spring offensive, though with fluctuating fortune, as will be seen.

Day after day, formations of the British I and the U.S. 12 Tactical Air Fleets were sent against central Italy where, in close formation, they attacked the railway system south of the line Pisa–Florence–Rimini. More heavily than ever before they struck at the important junctions, Pisa, Florence and Arezzo, Terni, Perugia and Viterbo, and at the same time extended their attacks to include bridges, exposed sections of the line, repair shops and locomotive sheds. Fighters and fighter-bombers hunted supply trains both on the move and in sidings; their most eagerly sought prey were the locomotives, which were so hard to replace. Strategic bombers attacked the Alpine passes, notably the Brenner, and the more important junctions in northern Italy.

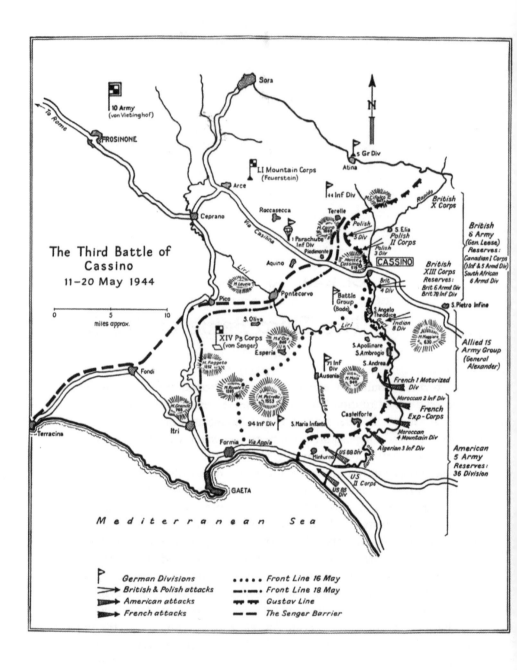

The Third Battle of Cassino
11–20 May 1944

0   5   10
miles approx.

Mediterranean Sea

German Divisions
British & Polish attacks
American attacks
French attacks

Front Line 16 May
Front Line 18 May
Gustav Line
The Senger Barrier

Eaker by no means confined his efforts, however, to the disruption of the Italian railway system. He paid equal attention to the roads in the vicinity of the front, in the rear areas and up as far as Florence, along which German supply columns moved. His aircraft smashed bridges and blocked defiles, and rendered impassable a large number of towns through which the roads passed. The fighters swept along the roads in central and southern Italy and ruthlessly shot up every German vehicle they saw. Very soon movement by day on both roads and railways became absolutely impossible. Only when the weather was bad did train or lorry dare to move in daylight. The ports on the Tyrrhenian Sea and the Adriatic also became the targets of the Allied airmen, for part of the supplies for Tenth Army and Fourteenth Army were still being sent by sea to Genoa, La Spezia and Leghorn, to Venice and Ancona.

The Allied High Command expected great things from Operation Strangle. Even though it might not cause complete or even widespread dislocation, they were confident that it would have a decisively throttling effect on the southern front. This optimism is reflected in Fuller's statement: 'This fiasco [the bombing of Cassino, March 15th] was followed by a period of true strategic bombing. . . . There can be no doubt that these uninterrupted attacks against the enemy's supply system, which not only interfered with his traffic, but forced him to restrict movement to the night, did more damage than had ever been done by one of the "colossal cracks".'* Fuller estimates the number of daily interruptions at twenty-five, a figure which rose by the middle of May to seventy-five.

Operation Strangle did not produce the results expected of it. Eaker certainly succeeded in disrupting very severely the supply lines of Kesselring's Army Group, but he failed entirely to disorganize them. Months before, when the Allied air attacks on the German lines of communication had started to become more marked, those responsible for supplying the armies had set up a subsidiary system, which now became of great value.

As early as December 1943 Army Group had extended its supply and administrative area, which had originally been confined to northern Italy, southwards as far as the area Arezzo–Lake Trasimeme. A comprehensive network of installations—workshops, supply dumps, hospitals and the like—and a great quantity of stores had been shifted to the south, and these new supply dumps were now well stocked. This meant that the armies could be kept more or less well supplied until such time as any damage to road or rail could be repaired. During the winter months any lengthy dislocation of the railway system had not been possible; but the situation would change now that spring, good flying weather and longer hours of daylight were at hand.

* *The Second World War.*

The heavy raids during the week before the Anzio landing had very seriously interfered with the supply of the German armies. Even at that time, it had proved impossible to meet the daily requirement of 3,500 tons by means of lorry transport and by sea. When Army Group C urged the O.K.W. to postpone the attack against the beach-head, the argument used was: On account of the difficult railway situation, we doubt whether the requisite volume of ammunition for the Fourteenth Army can be guaranteed, particularly as Tenth Army is demanding a very considerable allotment for Cassino.

In Italy, as in all theatres of war, the railways were the vital arteries of the fighting fronts. But how was railway traffic to be maintained in the face of this constant tearing up of the lines? In addition to repairing the damage as quickly as possible, a system of transfer was introduced in good time. If the line had been badly damaged ahead of an important supply train and repairs would entail a very considerable delay, the train's load would be transferred to lorries and taken to an empty train, waiting on the other side of the break, provided there was an uninterrupted stretch of at least forty miles ahead of the empty train. This complicated procedure naturally took time, required a considerable number of men to operate it and was generally practicable only at night.

The methodical manner in which the Allies delivered their air attacks made the task of repairing the damage done very much easier. Generally speaking, the Allied air forces repeatedly cut the lines in the same places, with the result that, at least as far as the main lines were concerned, maintenance detachments stationed permanently in the vicinity of known danger spots were able to complete repairs relatively much more quickly than would normally have been the case. It was, however, very difficult, and in some cases impossible, to repair damage to those stretches of line which contained any considerable amount of structural work such as bridges. The moment a bridge had been laboriously repaired, it would promptly be attacked again—and the Italian railway system contained a plethora of bridges! And it was against such vulnerable targets as these that General Eaker increasingly concentrated his attacks during the spring of 1944.

Despite Allied superiority at sea and in the air, a very considerable proportion of supplies for the southern front continued to go by sea. During the period 1 January–1 April 1944, 4,000–6,000 tons of supplies per month for Tenth Army and 8,000–12,000 tons for Fourteenth Army were delivered by sea. This represents some twelve to eighteen per cent of the total supplies delivered.

From the base ports already mentioned cargoes were carried to Civitavecchia and Ancona, where they were transferred to barges and other small craft for onward transit to Gaeta and Anzio, San Benedetto and Pescara. But the farther north the front advanced, the more difficult it became to maintain the flow between the transfer ports and the ultimate ports of destination. On 30 January, for example, the very valuable port of Civitavecchia had to be abandoned, the port installations were blown up and San Stefano had to be used instead. At the same time, thanks to the sharp watch kept on it by enemy surface patrols, Pescara, too, had to be abandoned.

As a rule, the barges and small craft moved only by night, hiding up in coastal waters by day. Arrival at destination was always at night, and cargoes were unloaded at once, to enable the craft to be clear of the harbour by daylight. This, of course, was not always possible, particularly when major operations demanding an increase of supplies were in progress.

The Anzio landing had confronted the German supply services with a new situation. They were now called upon to supply two fighting fronts, demands from both of which increased rapidly after the landing had taken place and the Cassino battles had begun. Very considerable dislocation became inevitable, but the supply and ordnance services of the Army Group were not unduly embarrassed. They concentrated on speeding up repair to railway lines by massing more construction units in the danger areas, on protecting particularly vulnerable stores by concentrating strong protective anti-aircraft forces, and on making the maximum use of the railways by accelerating the processes of loading and unloading.

To minimize losses in those areas where lorry transport was used, Army Group directed that on roads south of a line Piombino–Ancona all lorries would travel by night and without lights. While these measures undoubtedly went a long way towards making good loss of tonnage, they inevitably led to an irrational use of the transport facilities available. Throughout the day columns remained stationary, and the time required for any return journey was greatly increased. The journey Florence–Perugia–Florence, for example, took four nights, while that from Arezzo to Orte and back required six nights. Army Group hoped further to reduce the loss of lorry-tonnage by decreasing the volume of traffic along the main thoroughfares and making more use of subsidiary roads. But the Allied airmen very quickly got on to these new channels and blocked them —at least for day traffic.

The throttling of supply by rail could be counter-balanced only by an increase in lorry transportation; and after the Anzio landing, one of the most urgent of Army Group C's tasks had been the elimination of the supply bottle-neck, and this had been accomplished by commandeering Italian civilian transport. By this means the military supply tonnage of Army Group C rose from 4,500 tons in December to 12,000 tons in April.

The accumulations which had resulted from these precautionary measures proved to be a great asset, once Operation Strangle had started. For whereas before, nine supply trains daily had successfully been run in the Orte–Arezzo and Orte–Foligno areas, now more and more trains dropped out, despite feverish efforts to keep the lines open. Losses in lorries increased to some six per cent of the total number in operation.

But despite the ruthless grip of the Mediterranean Allied Air Force, despite the carpet-bombing of railways, bridges and roads, the stalking of locomotives, lorries and coastal craft, the German supply system remained intact up to and right through the Allied spring offensive. That the May offensive did not end in catastrophe for the German Army is due in no small measure to the organizational ability of the supply and administrative staffs and the spirited willingness shown by supply personnel and railway pioneers. Where, despite all their efforts, the troops in the front line suffered any shortage of supplies, it was due primarily to the critical situation of the German armament and equipment industry as a whole, and only in a lesser degree to the effects of Operation Strangle.

The German supply organization in Italy deserves all the more praise when it is remembered that the army, on orders from Field-Marshal Kesselring, was further burdened with the task of helping to feed Rome. With the general dislocation of railway traffic, the Italian authorities found themselves unable to solve the problem of feeding the civilian population of the capital. The Vatican State and the great industrial concerns came to their aid with contributions of transport. But when it was found that, despite this help, the food stocks in Rome were diminishing rapidly, Kesselring ordered bread and flour to be transported to the city by Army Group lorries. This demanded the transportation of an additional 800–1,000 tons per day, approximately one-tenth of the whole transport tonnage at the disposal of the Commander-in-Chief, South-West, which had to be found at the expense of the fighting forces.

Operation Strangle was a clear indication of Allied intentions. It was correctly interpreted by the German High Command as the prelude to an attempt to decide the issue by means of a general offensive. But when and where Alexander would strike remained a puzzle. Would the Allies try to lever out the whole of the southern front by means of a fresh landing, perhaps at Civitavecchia or even farther north at Leghorn? Or would General Alexander support his offensive by means of large-scale airborne landings in the Liri valley? 'By imagining himself in the enemy's shoes, Kesselring came to the conclusion that the almost complete absence of German naval forces and the weakness of the *Luftwaffe* would enable a major landing to be made in the La Spezia–Leghorn area without significant hindrance before or during disembarkation. The Allies would then be able not only to set foot on land, but also to block the passes of the Apennines before the German divisions, the majority of whom had to travel on foot, would be able to traverse the 350 kilometres separating them from the landing area. Such an operation would have brought about the collapse of the front in Middle Italy and delivered a fatal blow to the Army Group.'*

Despite the paucity of aerial reconnaissance, Field-Marshal Kesselring was fairly accurately informed as regards the overall picture of the activities of the Allied armies. He thought it improbable that any attack from the Anzio beach-head would start before the Cassino offensive had been launched, and he felt that an attack on a broad front by Fifth and Eighth Armies against the centre and right wing of Tenth Army was a more likely opening.

Neither the offensive preparations on the Garigliano nor the signs indicative of an imminent thrust in the Cassino area and to the north of the town had escaped the notice of the German High Command. But the question still remained: Where would Alexander deliver his main blow? Kesselring expected that the main offensive would take the form of an advance through the Auruncian Mountains to the Cassino massif, to be followed by a wheeling movement into the Liri valley; a direct thrust at the Liri valley, as the main operation, he regarded as improbable.

But the ultimate answer to this question would be revealed only when the offensive started. A significant pointer would have been the whereabouts of the French Corps. It had long since left the area north of Cassino, but where it had gone was not known. But wherever Juin popped up, there, for sure, Alexander was planning something special; and no one knew that better than Kesselring himself. 'The whereabouts of the French Corps was a constant source of great anxiety to me. Tenth Army and its subordinate commanders were directed to regard as a matter of urgent importance any information on the subject and to report it forthwith to Army Group, whose ultimate decisions might well depend upon it' (extract from a report by Field-Marshal Kesselring).

His fears proved to have been well founded, for it was Juin who shattered the right wing of Tenth Army and showed the Allies the way to Rome. It was his Corps which ultimately burst open the gates to the Eternal City which the Allies had been battering for so many months.

Another factor which caused Kesselring some anxiety was the possibility of airborne landings. The possibility that Alexander would drop paratroops in the Liri valley, perhaps at Frosinone, could not be lightly dismissed, particularly as such an operation could be made to coincide, both as regards time and place, with a breakout from the beach-head.

As regards the attack from the Anzio beach-head, the Field-Marshal

* Westphal, *The German Army in the West.*

was inclined to believe that the U.S. VI Corps would by-pass Velletri and thrust at Valmontone. Such a move would lend effective support to the offensive of the Fifth and Eighth Armies, with which it would join hands on the Via Casilina, with the object of surrounding the Tenth Army and achieving a 'Little Stalingrad', or at least of driving the German main forces into the mountains away from their lines of retreat and there destroying them at will. For an eccentric attack on Rome itself Kesselring thought that U.S. VI Corps was too weak.

The broad outlines of Army Group C's task were clear. It had to defend the area south of Rome. How long it could do so would depend on the course of the battle or on whether the enemy made a large-scale landing in its rear. First and foremost, however, it had to stand and fight where it was, and this meant that the defensive positions would have to be strengthened by every possible means—more and stronger installations and stock-piling of ammunition on the one hand, and a strengthening of the front between the Tyrrhenian Sea and Cassino on the other, and the formation of a mobile reserve of four divisions in the hands of Army Group.

To withdraw further troops into reserve from an already over-stretched front presented a difficult problem. Since the Anzio landing, the German troops had been all too thin on the ground. The relief of the 15 Panzer Grenadier Division on the Rapido by the Bode Battle Group—composed mostly of units of 44 Infantry Division—had been a stop-gap expedient, as had also been the reinforcement of 71 Division by elements of the Hoch und Deutschland Division. Yet the ultimate use to which the 15 Division was put was unprofitable. At the instigation, apparently, of O.K.W. and during the absence of the divisional commander, it was split up and its battalions were put far forward in the second line, behind the right wing of XIV Panzer Corps. In General von Senger's view, it would have been better to have concentrated the division under its own commander in the Fondi–Pico area as a mobile reserve, with the ability to operate on the 'Senger Barrier',* to cover the retirement of 71 Division and the 94 Infantry Division, should they be defeated, and thus ensure the orderly occupation of the Senger Barrier position.

After the transfer of LXXVI Panzer Corps to the Anzio front, the 'Hauck Corps Group'—305 and 324 Infantry and 114 Rifle Divisions— took over the Adriatic coastal sector. The LI Mountain Corps was put in

---

* The 'Senger Barrier', originally named the 'Adolf Hitler Line', was organized in depth as a barrier to the Liri valley and the Auruncian Mountains. It ran from Terracina on the coast via Fondi to Pico, and from there via Pontecorvo–Aquino– Piedmonte to Monte Cairo. With the help of Slovak and Russian labour battalions it had been built up by the Todt Organization into a system of permanent fortifications. The southern sector, however, had been only partly completed.

between Alfadena and Liri, and the XIV Corps sector was confined to the Auruncian Mountains and the Tyrrhenian coast.* This reorganization was undertaken deliberately by Tenth Army on the strength of its experience in the first battle of Cassino†, in order to enable XIV Corps to exercise more influence on the conduct of the battle on the Army's right wing.

The key position of the Cassino front—the town and hill and the Monte Cairo massif—remained, as before, in the hands of 1 Parachute Division. But the sectors within the Division itself had been altered. Now the 4 Parachute Regiment, with the 1st Machine-gun Parachute Battalion under command, was responsible for the defence of the town and the *Monte*; to its north-west was the 3 Parachute Regiment, with its 1st Battalion on the Calvary Mount (the key to the monastery) and its 2nd Battalion north-west of Colle Santo Angelo, where it joined hands with the von Ruffin Battle Group (4th Mountain Battalion and 2nd Battalion, 100 Mountain Regiment), which was also under command of 1 Parachute Division; and beyond this was the 44 Infantry Division. In reserve in rear was the 1 Parachute Regiment, reinforced by 2nd Battalion, 721 Grenadier Regiment, and 2nd Battalion, 741 Grenadier Regiment.

Apart from the heavy casualties it had suffered, Heidrich's Division had been further greatly weakened by numerous transfers. After the March battle, it had had to transfer one-third of its strength to France to form the nucleus of new units being raised there; its regiments now consisted of only two weak battalions with an average strength of 200 to 300 men. But it was strong in anti-tank weapons and artillery.‡

While coming events on the Cassino front could be awaited with a measure of calm and confidence, the situation at the Anzio beach-head was

---

* Order of Battle of the German forces on the Cassino front on 11.5.44 from north to south:

LI MOUNTAIN CORPS	General Feuerstein
5 Mountain Division	Lieutenant-General Schrank
44 Infantry Division (Hoch und Deutschmeister)	Lieutenant-General Franek
1 Parachute Division	Lieutenant-General Heidrich
Bode Battle Group	
XIV PANZER CORPS	General von Senger-Etterlin.
71 Infantry Division	Lieutenant-General Raapke
94 Infantry Division	Lieutenant-General Steinmetz
15 Panzer Grenadier Division (Corps Reserve)	Lieutenant-General Rodt

† Tenth Army expected a repetition of the British X Corps' attack of 17 January on the Garigliano.

‡ On 11.5.44 the following anti-tank and artillery units were under command:
242 Section Assault Artillery
525 Anti-Tank Section ('Hornets'—8·8 cm. self-propelled guns)
Army Artillery Sections 53, 450, 602, 992
4th Battalion, 190 Artillery Regiment
One heavy anti-aircraft section with 8·8 A.A. guns

less clear. In contrast to Army Group, the Fourteenth Army did not anticipate a direct attack on Valmontone and did not therefore act on Kesselring's advice that the Cisterna arc should be reinforced. The southern front of the beach-head was weakly held, since any attack there was regarded as unlikely, and the heavily decimated 715 Infantry Division was considered strong enough for the purpose. The situation of 362 Division was very different. It was in the Cisterna arc, in the sector, that is, in which the main attack was expected. So far the division had fought with somewhat varying degrees of success. Kesselring would therefore have preferred to see a more reliable division in this vital sector and had, indeed, thought of putting in the 4 Parachute Division. But eventually he decided against any change, since he himself had gradually come to the conclusion that 362 Division, in its strongly constructed, first-class defensive position, well organized in depth, had fully regained its self-confidence and determination; in addition to that, the sector also contained the Lehr Infantry Regiment, fully recovered from its first unhappy experience, the 1027 and 1028 Panzer Grenadier Regiments and strong tank, artillery and anti-aircraft forces.

The general reserve was in the hands of Army Group, and Kesselring had decided that it would be held back until the offensive had been launched, the situation had become clearer and the danger of its being used either at the wrong place or the wrong time had been minimized. As far as the front-line divisions were concerned, this meant that they would have to withstand the first onslaught themselves, without, in the initial phases, being able to count on the intervention of Army Group reserve.

If Alexander combined his offensive with a large-scale landing on the Tyrrhenian coast, his troops would come up against the newly arrived 92 Infantry Division at Civitavecchia or the Hermann Göring Panzer Division at Leghorn. The 26 and 29 Panzer Divisions were in the vicinity of the beach-head, ready to intervene either against a fresh landing or against an attack launched from the beach-head itself. The task allotted to the 90 Panzer Grenadier Division was to defeat the anticipated airborne attack on Frosinone. If this failed to materialize, the divisions would be available either for the Cassino front or the beach-head operations, as might be required.

In central and northern Italy was the von Zanger Army Group, with two main tasks: to hold and improve the coastal fronts and to strengthen the fortifications of the Alpine position, the 'Green Line', or, as the Allies called it, the 'Gothic Line', which ran from Viareggio to Pesaro on the Adriatic coast. From this Army Group a further five divisions, if required, could be sent as a second wave to the southern front.

On 10 May the German regrouping was nearing completion, and two or three more nights were required to carry out the final moves on the Cassino front, when, on the night of 11/12 May, the great Allied offensive was launched.

General Alexander had been preparing for a long time for the blow which would give him possession of Rome and bring about the destruction of Kesselring's Army Group. As early as 5 March, before the second Cassino battle, he had issued his preliminary orders for the regrouping of the Allied armies, and a month later he had allotted their tasks to the Commanders-in-Chief of the Fifth and Eighth Armies. On 1 May, at a conference at his headquarters in Caserta, the operations of the two armies had been co-ordinated, and on 5 May 'Operation No. 1 Allied Armies in Italy' laid down that the intention was 'to destroy the right wing of the German Tenth Army and to drive the remnants of the Tenth and Four-teenth Armies into the area north of Rome; to pursue the enemy to the line Pisa–Rimini, at the same time inflicting upon him the maximum possible losses'.

The tasks allotted to the individual armies were:

(*a*) EIGHTH ARMY

(1) To break through the enemy positions in the Liri valley in the general direction of Highway No. 6 and reach the area east of Rome.

(2) To pursue the enemy in the general direction Terni–Perugia.

(3) Thence to advance on Ancona and Florence.

(*b*) FIFTH ARMY

(1) To take the Ausonia defile and then advance on an axis parallel to that of the Eighth Army, but south of the rivers Liri and Sacco.

(2) To launch an attack from the Anzio beach-head via Cori on Valmontone with the object of cutting Highway No. 6 in the vicinity of Valmontone and thus preventing the reinforcement and retirement of those German forces which were opposing the Eighth Army.

(3) To pursue the enemy north of Rome and capture the Viterbo airfields and the port of Civitavecchia.

(4) To advance on Leghorn. . . .*

In order to ensure that the Gustav Line would be breached and that these far distant objectives could be attained, General Alexander had transferred the mass of the Eighth Army to the Cassino area and had con-centrated a mighty force between the Abruzzi Mountains and the mouth of the Garigliano.

Juin's Corps had been moved far to the south, to the upper reaches of the Garigliano, between Liri and Castelforte. Its place in the mountains

* Extracted from 'Operation Order No. 1 Headquarters, Allied Armies in Italy', dated 5 May 1944.

north of Cassino had been taken by the Polish II Corps, while the U.S. II stood ready on the west bank of the Garigliano. The British X Corps, placed under the direct command of Army Group, was on the Sangro. It was not itself to launch any attack, but was simply to follow up the anticipated German withdrawals.

The superiority of the Allies in both numbers and materiel was now more impressive than ever. Major formations had arrived from the Near East, the United States and Canada. Twenty-one Allied divisions and eleven independent brigades in, or in the immediate vicinity of, the front faced fourteen German divisions and three brigades. When the difference in the strength of the German and Allied divisions is taken into consideration, the superiority of the Allies becomes even more marked. Whereas the German divisions had six infantry battalions (Panzer divisions only four), nearly all the Allied divisions were organized on a nine-battalion basis. Alexander's divisions had been rested and reinvigorated, and most of them were up to full strength; the German divisions on the other hand had been bled white, were battle-weary and under strength. As a net result, the Allied divisions were three to four times as strong in infantry and certainly ten times as strong in weapons and fire power as the Germans. When to all this is added absolute command of the air and inexhaustible supplies of ammunition, the severity of the battle confronting Kesselring's troops can well be imagined.

The evening of 11 May passed very quietly. The Allied artillery fired intermittently, and the German batteries remained all but silent, in order not to draw fire; for up in the mountains, on this night, too, reliefs were still in progress. Suddenly, along the whole Cassino front, the Allied artillery fire stopped—a most unusual occurrence.

Then, at 11 p.m., with equal suddenness the whole front burst into a furious roar. From Aquafondata to the Tyrrhenian Sea a fiery snake writhed across the landscape—the bursting shells from 2,000 guns. The mighty spectacle of flickering fireworks stretched as far as the eye could see, and the angry thunder of the guns reverberated from the mountains all round. The whole artillery of the Fifth and Eight Armies had opened fire with mathematical precision on a time signal sent out by the B.B.C. in London. Once more thousands of shells ploughed up the German positions, and once again the German artillery—and this time the infantry positions as well—became the targets of the Allied heavy guns. At 11.45 p.m. the British on the Rapido, at 1 a.m. the Poles north-west of Cassino, the French in the Auruncian Mountains and the Americans in the coastal sector, all advanced to the attack.

As soon as daylight broke, swarms of fighter-bombers dived down on their targets or cruised endlessly over the positions of the German

artillery. Tenth Army Headquarters in Avezzano and the battle headquarters of XIV Corps were buried under a carpet of bombs and put out
of action. Generals von Vietinghoff and von Senger were on leave in
Germany, and Tenth Army entered the third battle of Cassino without
its commanders. They were, of course, recalled forthwith, but by the time
they had gathered the reins in their hands, the battle had already been
decided.

The decision was swiftly achieved by the French Corps.* Juin's Corps
had been ordered to open the Ausente valley, capture Monte Maio, break
into the Liri valley from the south and take Pico. With all the fury they
could command, Juin's troops hurled themselves at the 71 Infantry
Division on the upper Garigliano. The effect of the preliminary bombardment had been so devastating, that forty-five minutes passed before the
Moroccan 2 Infantry Division, delivering the main attack, came under
fire from the German artillery. Raape's Grenadiers defended desperately
against the superior numbers of these mountain-warfare experts. But by
3 a.m. Monte Faito was already in the hands of the Moroccan 4 Mountain
Division, and the way to Monte Maio was open. But before that, Monte
Girofano had to be captured, in order to cover the left flank of the French
1 Motorized Division. Here, however, surprise did not achieve success.
Throughout the 12 May the fight raged to and fro, before the Moroccans
at last captured the mountain on the morning of 13 May. By midday the
8 Rifle Regiment had taken Monte Feuci, and shortly afterwards, at 4 p.m.
and in the face of feeble German resistance, it captured Monte Maio.
Forty hours after the start of the offensive the southern pillar of the Cassino
gateway had been burst asunder. But on the northern side, the Poles were
laying down their lives in vain.

After the fall of Monte Girofano the French 1 Division pressed on northwards and captured Sant' Andrea on the evening of 13 May. In quick
succession Sant' Ambrogio and Sant' Appolinari fell, and the French had
reached the Liri valley. The northern wing of the 71 Division had been
breached, and the position further south became untenable. Here, too,
Juin's troops had gained ground. Both the Moroccan 4 Mountain and the
Algerian 3 Infantry Divisions had broken into the Gustav Line, and Castelforte and Damiano were in French hands. The door into the Ausente
valley had been pushed open, and Juin did not hesitate for an instant. His

---

* French Expeditionary Corps Order of Battle, third battle of Cassino:

Corps Commander	General Juin
French 1 Infantry Division (motorized)	General Brosset
Moroccan 2 Infantry Division	General Dody
Algerian 3 Infantry Division	General de Monsabert
Moroccan 4 Mountain Division	General Sevez
Three Tabors, Goumiers	
One armoured brigade	

finest hour had come! From the south he immediately thrust at the flank of the 71 Division, and on 13 May Moroccans and Algerians together captured Monte Ceschito. The French 1 Division was tearing hotfoot for San Giorgio, the Algerians were aiming at Ausonia and the Moroccan 4 Mountain Division was girding itself for its surprise thrust deep into the Gustav Line, through the mountains and on to the Petrella massif. The decisive breach had been made. The fate of Monte Cassino had been decided on the Garigliano.

The U.S. II Corps in the coastal sector had not stormed forward with the same speed as the French. Keyes's troops, who had only recently arrived from the United States, did not possess the battle experience of Juin's veterans and in mountain country found themselves confronted with a formidable task. Keyes had been ordered, with strong support from the artillery and the guns of the fleet, to break through astride the Via Appia, break the Senger Barrier and join forces with the Anzio Corps. His objectives were the Brachhi Mountains, Santa Maria Infante and Colle San Martino, after which he was to take Castelonorato and Spigno, in order to open the way for the Moroccans to the Petrella massif.

The preliminary bombardment did not have much effect on the 94 Division, and when the Americans advanced, they found Steinmetz's division ready for them. There ensued a furious fight for Santa Maria Infante and Sollaciano, where the American attacks were repulsed by the 1st Battalion, 267 Grenadier Regiment, and the 94th Fusilier Battalion. Neither the U.S. 351 Regiment here, nor the 85 Division, attacking in the immediate coastal strip, could make any headway at all.

It was only on the afternoon of 13 May that the 88 Division resumed its offensive. Taking advantage of the deep penetration achieved into 71 Division's position, the Americans captured Santa Maria Infante, but were thrown out again by the 94th Fusiliers on the 14th. Although the Fusiliers took prisoner a complete American battalion, they were unable to maintain their position, and the place was finally lost to the enemy on the evening of the same day.

But now the 94 Infantry Division was forced to evacuate its well-fortified positions as a result of French pressure. During the night of 14/15 May the Division was withdrawn to a position on either side of Castelonorato, and twelve hours later the Moroccans attacked Monte Civita from the rear and dislodged its garrison. And now, too, the 94 Division paid dearly for having concentrated its reserves in the coastal area instead of on the Petrella massif, as Kesselring had advised.

XIV Panzer Corps, still under its officiating commander, had allowed control of the operations to slip from its grasp. Its own weak reserves did not suffice to plug the holes torn by the French Corps, and its front became more and more extended; for the British XIII Corps was making relatively slow progress in the Liri valley, and the Poles were still not yet masters of Monte Cassino.

The plan of attack of the British XIII Corps* was as follows: The Corps was to cross the Rapido with two divisions. The 4 Infantry Division, reinforced by 1 Guards and 26 Armoured Brigades, was given the task of forming a bridge-head between Cassino railway station and Santo Angelo. Similarly the Indian 8 Division, in co-operation with the Canadian 1 Armoured Brigade, was to establish another bridge-head between Santo Angelo and Liri. The whole Corps was then to continue the attack and reach the Via Casilina in the vicinity of Piedimonte, where it would link up with the Poles advancing down from the mountains.

After a barrage put down by twenty-one artillery regiments, Kirkman's divisions advanced to the assault. Though the German artillery had suffered considerably, the infantry seem to have got off lightly. Along the whole front the attackers came up against extensive minefields, wire and strongly held German positions. When dawn came, the 10 and 28 Brigades of the 4 Division were holding only a narrow strip of the river bank, but had failed to bridge it. The 28 Brigade was caught by a counter-attack and flung back across the river.

The Indian 8 Division's start had been more auspicious. Its two leading brigades, the 17 and 19, were firmly established across the river. Behind them the engineers had put two thirty-ton bridges in position, and by 8 a.m. a Canadian armoured regiment was on its way across.

On 13 May General Ward launched a fresh attack south of Cassino. This time the attack succeeded in extending 10 Brigade's bridge-head to within a mile of a point north-west of Santo Angelo. During the night of 13/14 May the engineers threw another bridge across the river in 4 Division's sector, and a little later the British took Santo Angelo, which the U.S. 36 Division had tried so hard to capture as long ago as the January before.

General Kirkman felt that the scene was now set for the launching of his main attack, designed to surround and cut off the town and monastery; he accordingly ordered his reserves to cross the river. (Among them was the British 78 Division, which knew all about the Cassino battlefield from its experiences in the March fighting.)

* Order of Battle, British XIII Corps, third Cassino battle:

Corps Commander	General Kirkman
British 4 Infantry Division	General Ward
British 78 Infantry Division	General Keightley
Indian 8 Infantry Division	General Russell
British 6 Armoured Division	General Evelegh
British 1 Guards Brigade	
Canadian 1 Armoured Brigade	

The German Tenth Army now threw all its available reserves into the battle. Part of 90 Panzer Grenadier Division had already been sent into the Liri valley, where the anticipated airborne attack had failed to materialize. The 305 Infantry Division was brought across from the Adriatic to bolster the crumbling Bode Battle Group. The 1 Parachute Regiment was already in action south of Cassino, guarding the heavily menaced flank of Heidrich's Division. Two battalions of the 114 Rifle Division and anti-tank units, pioneers and grenadiers from a variety of divisions now began to pour into the battle area. Holes were being plugged everywhere, but the damage could not be repaired.

The German artillery continued to concentrate its fire on the bridges over the Rapido. But they were hard put to it. From Trocchio the Allied air liaison officers were directing the operations of their 'killer' formations. As soon as any battery opened fire, it was at once overwhelmed by a swarm of fighter-bombers. Although the Allies ruled the sky, German aircraft in formations of about twenty repeatedly tried, with great spirit but with little success, to press through and bomb the river bridges. Then XIII Corps advanced once more, to the attack.

The 78 Division, leap-frogging the 4 Division, reached the Pignataro–Cassino road on 15 May. At the same time the Indians advanced and after a short fight captured Pignataro during the night, and the French Corps pushed forward into San Giorgio. While the Indian 8 Division gained ground comparatively quickly, the British 4 Division on the right wing could only make slow and difficult progress against a stubborn defence. But in Cassino the British made no progress at all. Although the 1st Parachute Machine-gun Battalion had been all but completely annihilated, the right wing of Heidrich's Division held. There the imperturbable Lieutenant Schimpke with No. 1 Anti-Tank Company not only repulsed every infantry attack made against the southern entrance into Cassino, but by 17 May had also destroyed twenty heavy tanks.

Further to the west, too, the British could at first make but little headway towards the Via Casilina. The road to Cassino was still open, and the monastery hill was still in German hands. But by this time its effectiveness had been greatly curtailed; since the beginning of the battle, an impenetrable sea of smoke had enveloped both the Rapido and the Liri valleys and the monastery itself.

As a result of the swift advance of the French Corps, the right wing of LI Mountain Corps had now started to crumble. General Alexander was quick to seize the chance offered to him and at once threw the Canadian I Corps (General Burns) into the battle on Kirkman's left flank. The Canadians' objective was Pontecorvo. They did not wait for the Poles to capture Monte Cassino, but advanced at once on 16 May, and by 18th they had reached the Senger Barrier.

The Poles had been very unlucky. In spite of their massed attacks, they had not succeeded in taking the monastery hill and linking up with XIII Corps on the Via Casilina. The misfortune which had dogged their footsteps since 1939 seemed to be still with them at Cassino. Behind them the men of the Polish II Corps had a truly tragic history. General Anders, their commanding officer, had fought against the Germans on the Vistula and in Warsaw and had been taken prisoner by the Russians at Lemberg on 30 September. The Russians at first put him in the Lemberg prison and then transferred him to the notorious Lubianka prison in Moscow. There, for more than twenty months, he was treated like a criminal and was at last released on 4 August 1941, six weeks after the start of the German invasion of Russia. The Treaty of London, signed on 30 July 1941, which restored relations between Poland and Russia to normal, had also brought freedom to Anders.

A decree issued by the President of the Soviet Union on 12 August 1941 promised 'an amnesty to all Polish nationals at present in the Soviet Union who, either as prisoners-of-war or for other reasons, had been deprived of their liberty'. In the Russo-Polish Military Agreement signed in Moscow on 14 August 1941, it was expressly stated that 'a Polish army will be raised in the territories of the Soviet Union in the shortest possible time . . . this army will form part of the armed forces of the independent republic of Poland . . . which, in conjunction with the armed forces of the U.S.S.R. and the other Allied powers, will participate in the common struggle against Germany. . . .'

It was further stated in the agreement that arms, equipment, rations, etc., for the Polish Army would be supplied by the Government of the U.S.S.R. from its own stocks and issued on a lend-lease basis by the Polish Government.

Conservative estimates put the number of Poles forcibly removed to the Soviet Union between 1939 and 1941 at one and a half million men, women and children. The *Red Star*, official journal of the Red Army, stated that on 17 September 1940 the number of Polish prisoners-of-war in Soviet hands amounted to 181,000 men. Precise and authoritative figures, however, are not available.

General Anders, a personal friend of the Polish Prime Minister, General Sikorski, accepted the difficult task of raising and training this army in Soviet territory. Stalin, however, took his time over releasing the Polish P.O.W.s. The Polish Government made repeated representations, but even in October 1941 great numbers of Poles were still vegitating in camps in the Arctic regions of Russia. Such prisoners as were released had to fend entirely for themselves. The Russians had no intention whatever of fulfilling their treaty obligation to provide transport and take them to the agreed assembly areas. Barefooted, in rags and starving, the Poles trudged wearily to the training camps in Tetskoye and Tatishchevo.

When Anders had safely gathered together some 46,000 men, it was found that the percentage of officers among them was unusually small. Gradually the fact emerged that between 9,000 and 10,000 officers, definitely known to have been in Russian captivity, had not been accounted for. Representations on the subject elicited the laconic reply, dated 14 November 1941: 'All Polish officers in Soviet territory have been released.' The Polish Government, of course, did not let the matter rest there. When the Polish Prime Minister visited Moscow in December a sharp controversy arose between him and Stalin on the subject of the vanished officers. Stalin twisted and turned and resorted to the most improbable evasions. He presumed, he said, that these officers must have fled to Manchuria! But all the time he well knew that they had been brutally put to death a year before at Katyn.

There was yet another problem awaiting solution. So far, the Russian authorities had not lifted a finger to assist in the raising of the Polish Army. They had even sequestrated deliveries which had arrived from the United States, clearly marked: 'For the Polish Army.' But the Poles remained as before—barefooted, in rags and starving. Stalin had no intention of creating on Russian territory a Polish army which might later impede the gangster projects he had in view. He sought to justify his neglect of the Poles on the grounds of the great difficulty the Russians were experiencing in maintaining the fight against the Germans. The Russians themselves, he declared, were very short of war material and in the current critical situation—the Germans were knocking at the gates of Moscow—the Soviet Union could do nothing to help the Poles.

Sikorski then proposed that, in view of Russian 'difficulties', the Polish Army should be transferred to the Near East, where it would be closer to sources of help from the Western allies. Only with great reluctance did Stalin agree, eventually consenting to the transfer of two or three divisions.

But it was March 1942 before the Poles were at last able to leave Russia, accompanied by a great number of women and children, whom the Russians regarded as 'useless mouths'. Russian ships carried these unfortunate wretches to Pahlevi in north Iran, where they came under the care of the British Ninth Army, commanded at the time by General Sir Henry Maitland Wilson. Those fit for training were sent to the training camp at Khanikin; the unfit, the women and children were housed in a camp near Teheran. Iran now became the assembly area for more Polish formations. The Poles who had left France before the capitulation and had fought at Narvik, the Carpathian Brigade, which, under General Kopanski, had distinguished itself at Tobruk, were now all sent to Iran. In this way, the Polish II Corps, consisting of 3 Carpathian, 5 Kresova Divisions and 2 Armoured Brigade, came into being.

And now it was on service in Italy. General Anders had arrived in Naples on 6 February 1944 to confer with the Commander-in-Chief, Eighth Army, under whose command the Poles had been placed. By that time the Carpathian Division was already fighting on the Sangro, and the Kresova was disembarking at Tarento.

The Poles were eager to get into action, and on 16 February General Leese told Anders that if Freyberg's second attack failed, 'it would be up to the Poles to take the place'. In this way, Anders's Corps was given the task of cracking the hard nut on which Americans, Britons, Frenchmen, Indians and New Zealanders had broken their teeth in vain. The Poles, too, shared the same fate. It was only after the paratroops had evacuated the monastery on direct orders from Kesselring that Anders's men were able to set foot in the ruins of the abbey.

To return, however, to the battle, with the Poles still at the foot of Monte Cassino. Anders and his men found themselves confronted with a difficult task, and they had no idea that the allies with whom they were to strive, shoulder to shoulder, to capture this grim bastion had, many months before at the Teheran conference, made Stalin a present of large portions of their homeland—that the Western powers, with Great Britain in the van, had thrown eastern Poland into the jaws of the Russian bear in order to appease the Red colossus. And certainly no Polish soldier, girding himself for the attack on Cassino, ever dreamt that the day would come when the Western powers themselves, albeit unintentionally, would bar the way for them to return to their own homes. For this, in blunt terms, was the frightful result of the recognition of the Lublin 'Government' by Britain and the United States. The Western powers' policy of appeasement knew no bounds, to the tragic misfortune of Poland and the Baltic States and, indeed, of the whole free world.

How fortunate it was that the Polish soldiers knew nothing of all these evil matters! If they had, they would certainly have advanced with much less enthusiasm to the attack on Cassino. Linklater says that the Polish commanders almost came to blows over who was to have the honour of spear-pointing the attack. One drew attention to the manner in which he and his men had distinguished themselves at Tobruk, another pointed out that he was the senior. . . . Battalion competed with battalion for the chance to win the great victory; yet all this ardour was to sink, overwhelmed in a sea of blood.

The Poles' chances of success were certainly better than those of their unfortunate predecessors. In the Liri valley below, the British attack had drawn off strong German forces, and the planned feint attack by British X Corps on Atina promised to tie down the German reserves. This time, too, there was to be no immediate, frontal attack on the monastery itself, for Eighth Army had been ordered to isolate Monte Cassino and push down to the Via Casilina via the high ground north-west of the monastery. Only when this had been done was Anders to launch his attack. In the second phase of the battle, once the monastery was in Polish hands, the Poles, according to plan, were to attack the northern sector of the Senger Barrier.

The keypoint of the Monte Cassino massif, as will be remembered from the first Cassino battle, was the hotly contested Height 593, the Calvary Mount. Here Anders put in the 3 Carpathian Division on a very narrow front, convinced that with such overwhelming force he would swiftly overcome the defenders of both mount and Albaneta. Further north, he proposed sending forward the 5 Division with Colle Santo Angelo as its objective. The path leading up from Cairo, along which the New Zealand tanks had advanced to their destruction on 19 March, had in the meantime been considerably widened by Polish engineers and was now passable for heavy armour. The Polish 2 Armoured Brigade was ordered to use this path and support the attack on the Calvary Mount and Albaneta. After the Carpathian Division had taken Height 593 and the 5 Division had advanced as far as the Via Casilina, the former was to assault the monastery from the north-west.

The Polish attack was planned to the last detail. Vast dumps of ammunition were established well forward. The Poles, of course, had their own supply columns, but in addition and prior to the attack, five companies of Cypriot porters stocked dumps in the mountains with everything that the assaulting troops could require. In the vicinity of Venafro alone no less than 15,000 tons of stores had been accumulated, and arrangements had been made to blanket the entire upper Rapido in smoke, in order to blind the German artillery observation officers who were still occupying Monte Cifalco and had a good view of the area over which the Poles were to attack. According to Linklater, 18,000 smoke canisters were used in the upper Rapido valley between 11 and 24 May, and these were supplemented by a great number of smoke-shells fired by the artillery.

Anders, then, was well justified in awaiting the 11 May with confidence. Punctually at 11 p.m., on a B.B.C. time signal, the Polish artillery opened fire. The bombardment continued for two hours, and then the Poles advanced to the attack. The 6 Lemberg Brigade launched a subsidiary attack on Passo Corno, but encountered stiff opposition from the von Ruffin Battle Group. To the south of Monte Castillone the 5 Vilna Brigade advanced against Colle Santo Angelo. Two of its companies pressed forward as far as Height 517, the 'false crest', only to be caught by the fire of the 2nd Battalion, 3 Parachute Regiment, and driven back with heavy loss. The German artillery fire hit the closely packed masses attacking Colle Santo Angelo with devastating effect and tore great holes in their ranks. The Polish artillery, on the other hand, was groping in the dark; by dawn nearly all its observation officers had been either killed or wounded. Colonel Heilmann, whose battle headquarters had been plastered by fighter-bombers shortly after daybreak, once again showed proof of his mastery of the art of fire direction and control. As in Cassino town two months previously, it was now the artillery under his direction which brought decisive relief to the defence. The Polish losses before Colle Santo Angelo were frightful, and as early as the evening of 12 May Anders was compelled to withdraw the 5 Division back to its assembly area.

The Carpathian troops were equally exhausted. The attack on Albaneta and Height 593 had collapsed and brought grievous casualties. The 2nd Battalion of the 15 Carpathian Rifle Brigade had, admittedly, stormed and captured the Calvary Mount and established itself on the northern slopes of Height 569; and that had been a most auspicious beginning. In the defence of the Calvary Mount, No. 1 Company of the 3 Parachute Regiment had lost more than half its complement; at once the 2nd Battalion sprang to its aid and sent its No. 7 Company to join in the attempt to recapture the position. The attempt failed, and its leader was killed. Four times the reserves of the 1st and 2nd Battalions stormed the lost position, and four times the Poles repulsed them. The Carpathian riflemen put up a magnificent defence, but paid a heavy price. By midday the Poles holding the mount had been reduced to one officer and seven men, but a reinforcement from the reserve company of the battalion restored the balance.

In the evening the paratroops launched their fifth and final assault. This time they were successful, and the blood-drenched crest was once more in German hands and remained so until the paratroops later evacuated it of their own accord.

As darkness closed over the battlefield, General Anders also withdrew the Carpathian riflemen. Despite superior numbers, the support of heavy artillery fire and the protection afforded by a constant smoke screen, the Poles, at the end of a fierce day, had gained no ground at all. They had fought gallantly, but the paratroops had thwarted all their efforts. With a bare 700 men the latter had withstood the onslaughts of two full-strength divisions and survived one of the most dramatic and bloodiest actions of the whole Cassino campaign.

Major Veth, commanding the 2nd Battalion, 3 Parachute Regiment, noted in his war diary; 'A Polish regiment is attacking Height 593 and has taken No. 1 Company by surprise. Four counter-attacks failed. The fifth succeeded. 130 enemy dead counted. Battalion battle headquarters filled with wounded.'

On 13 and 14 May the Poles delivered four more vain and costly attacks on the Calvary Mount. By this time the defenders were in dire straits. Major Veth noted: 'Impossible to get wounded away . . . enveloped in a smoke screen. Great number of dead on the slopes—stench—no water—no sleep for three nights—amputations being carried out at battle headquarters. . . .' Once again smoke compelled the paratroops to wear their gas-masks, and in the hot May sun the stench from corpses was intolerable.

'But the German paratroops had every right to feel pleased with themselves. Monte Cassino remained unconquerable, and they have withstood the onslaughts of two divisions of an army which consisted solely of veteran and proven fighters.'* Nevertheless, the paratroops gazed anxiously at the Liri valley below, and what they saw boded nothing but evil. An unbroken stream of Allied tanks and vehicles was flowing westwards. Battery followed battery in endless array. It was a superb spectacle of material power, and for the first time the German private soldier caught a comprehensive glimpse of the immense material wealth of the Allies. How, they wondered, could anyone stand up to such odds? Very soon the British would close the gates in their rear, and here on the Cassino front Heidrich's Division was sitting in the trap.

The danger threatening the 1 Parachute Division grew hourly. On 17 May the 78 Division captured Piumarola, and to its north the 4 Division reached the Via Casilina. After months of bitter fighting the vital artery of the Cassino front had been severed. The ring was beginning to close. But the Germans had at least been able to occupy in good time the Senger positions in LI Mountain Corps' sector. At Pontecorvo the 361 Panzer Grenadier and the 376 Grenadier Regiments were firmly established. But Aquino and Piedimonte were only weakly held.

In the Auruncian Mountains, in XIV Panzer Corps' sector, however, the situation was even worse than in the Liri valley. When General Senger arrived back from leave on 17 May, all he found was one vast shambles. His Corps had been decisively defeated, the 71 Division had been practically destroyed, the 94 all but annihilated and the 15 Panzer Grenadier Division very hard hit. And the Fifth Army was on the threshold of the Senger Barrier. What had happened since 14 May on XIV Corps front baffles description.

After the deep penetration into 71 Division's position on 14 May,

* Jacques Mordal, *Cassino.*

General Juin had at once realized what an opportunity had been presented to him up in the mountains. His eye was fixed on the 5,000-foot Monte Petrella massif, deep in the German defensive system, and he decided to push his Moroccan mountain-warfare experts through the Auruncian Mountains to the Itri–Pico road, twelve miles behind the Gustav Line. On 13 May he had assembled a force drawn from the 4 Moroccan Division and the Goumiers of 12,000 men with 4,000 pack animals and placed it under the command of General Guillaume. On 14 May, after capturing Monte Ceschito, Guillaume had advanced in the direction of Petrella. By the night of 14/15 May the Goumiers had been clambering up Monte Fammera, north of Spigno, and on 16th Guillaume had captured Monte Petrella (4,700-foot) and Monte Rivole (4,200 foot). Supplies had then been dropped for them by thirty-six Baltimore bombers, and on the 17th the advance had continued. By the evening Serra del Lago, Monte Faggeto and Monte Calvo had all passed into the Moroccans' hands, and the Itri–Pico road, XIV Corps' vital diagonal line of communication, lay at the feet of the French colonial troops.

The right wing of the French Corps had also made rapid progress. After the fall of Monte Maio and Vallemaio, Dody's Division had captured Castelnuovo after a stiff fight, and Moroccans and Algerians together took Ausonia. The next objective had been Esperia; but east of the town the Algerians had been somewhat held up by the counter-attack of the 200 Panzer Grenadier Regiment. The Grenadiers, however, had been too weak to bring the advance to a standstill, and on 17 May the Algerians had taken Esperia and the French 1 Division had captured the commanding height of Monte d'Oro. The next day San Olivia had fallen, and on 19 May the French had reached the southern outskirts of Pico, and Guillaume's Moroccans took Campodimale on the Itri–Pico road.

XIV Corps threw in its last weak reserves in an attempt to prevent any further advance by the French Corps. The German formations were inextricably intermingled, battalions and remnants from various divisions fighting side by side in a confused mass. On 18 May Headquarters 44 Infantry Division had assumed command of one sector, and on 20th the 26 Panzer Division took over the sector previously held by 71 Division. But by the time General von Lüttwitz assumed command in the new sector, his battle headquarters were already under fire from French heavy machine-guns and mortars.

As a result of this surprise success of the French Corps, 94 Infantry Division's position on the coast had become untenable, and the U.S. II Corps had thus been presented with a relatively easy victory. Throughout the 16 and 17 May Steinmetz's Division had fought desperately against the 85 Division to hold Formia, but on the evening of the 17th the town had been lost. Meanwhile the U.S. 88 Division had been pressing swiftly forward through the mountains towards Itri. The remnants of the 267 Grenadier Regiment put up a hard fight, but Itri and the Gaeta peninsula both fell, and on 19 May the Americans were in occupation of Monte Grande to the west of the Itri–Pico road.

The first—and most difficult—stage of the road to Anzio had been overcome, and in less than a week Clark was able to announce that the beachhead and the southern front had been fused together.

Meanwhile, the northern wing of the front had also been on the move. Since 10.20 a.m. on 18 May the Polish flag had been flying over the ruins of the monastery. The German paratroops had vacated the abbey on the previous night.

Before this, however, the Poles had had to endure another hard blow from the men of Heidrich's Division. When they again advanced to the assault on 17 May the paratroops gave them as hot a reception as they had done on 12 May. Once more the Colle Santo Angelo and the Calvary Mount had been the focal points of the attack. Here and there the Kresova Division managed to penetrate into the positions on Colle Santo Angelo and the false crest, only to be thrown back by counter-attacks. For ten hours the fighting had continued, and the Poles had again suffered heavily. General Anders had become desperate; his reserves had been exhausted, and he was still as far as ever from his objective. He threw in the last thing he had —a weak battalion made up of drivers, mechanics and clerical personnel; but that, too, failed to turn the scales.

The Carpathian Division's objective had once again been the Massa Albaneta and Calvary Mount, and once again there occurred a bloody fight for Height 593. Losses on both sides had been severe. But victory had been denied to the Poles, despite effective support from the 2 Armoured Brigade. The latter had succeeded in destroying most of No. 3 Company of the 3 Parachute Regiment, but had failed to isolate the Calvary Mount as completely as the infantry had failed to capture it. Despite Allied assertions to the contrary, neither Colle Santo Angelo, the false crest, nor the Calvary Mount were captured in battle. It was only after the general situation on the Tenth Army front had necessitated the withdrawal of the paratroops that Anders's men set foot on the heights.

The German dispatch rider, who on the evening of 17 May brought up the order to evacuate, found only sorry remnants of their companies. The German casualties, and particularly those of the 1st Battalion, 3 Parachute Regiment, had been severe in the extreme. Of No. 1 Company, which for six days had been in the forefront of the fight for the Calvary Mount, only one officer, one non-commissioned officer and one man remained.

So, on the night of 17/18 May the paratroops with heavy hearts evacuated their Cassino positions, in which they had suffered so severely, but had also fought so impressively. Against odds, for three months they had repulsed all attacks and had drawn the attention of the whole world to this field of battle; and now they had to slip away, silently and by night. That was a bitter blow, for defeated they had not been. The British had already reached the Via Casilina, and the only way of escape lay through the mountains. The 2nd Battalion, 4 Parachute Regiment, which had defended the town, had to retire up and over the slopes of Monte Cassino itself. 'Dead Man's Gully' claimed its last victims, and through intermittent artillery fire the paratroops hastened over the rugged mountain slopes north of the Via Casilina in the direction of Piedimonte.

When the 12 Podolski Regiment launched its assault on the morning of 18 May and stormed its way into the ruins, not a shot was fired. All that the Poles found were a few German wounded, whom it had been impossible to move and who remained there in the care of medical orderlies. After four months of the most bitter and costly fighting, the Allied flag flew over the Mount of St Benedict. But—at what cost!

The U.S. Fifth Army alone, between the 15 January, when the battle for Monte Cassino started, and the 4 June, when the Allies marched into Rome, lost 107,144 men. To those must be added the casualties suffered at Cassino in the spring offensive (those of the British XIII Corps amounted to 4,056 and the Polish II Corps lost 3,779)—a grand total of 118,979 dead, wounded and missing.

To Washington and London these figures, the bill for the Quebec 'lawyers agreement', were horrifying. Had more attention been paid to Churchill, then perhaps the Balkan States would not now be groaning under the knout of the Communist tyrants.

The fall of Monte Cassino, a bastion regarded as impregnable, was an event of the very highest importance. Like the fall of Rome, it occurred at a very opportune moment, shortly before Eisenhower launched the cross-Channel enterprise. Alexander announced the capture of town and hill in a special communiqué: 'Cassino and the monastery have been conquered. The last attack against the town was delivered by British troops, while the Poles took the abbey. . . . After the unique feat of the Fifth Army in penetrating the Gustav Line on 14 May, and thanks to the swift advance of French and American troops into the mountains, the enemy has been completely out-manœuvred by the Allied armies in Italy. . . . The I Parachute Division, the best fighting unit in the German Army, is estimated to have lost half its strength.'

To Churchill Alexander telegraphed: '. . . Capture of Cassino means a great deal to me and both my armies. Apart from its Foreign Office value, it seems to me to have great propaganda possibilities.'*

The Poles were immensely proud of being hailed as the conquerors of Monte Cassino, and the Polish Government in exile struck a special medal with the inscription 'Monte Cassino'.

* Churchill, *The Second World War*, Vol. V.

Chapter 14

Rome at Last!

The pattern that had emerged from the opening days of the spring general offensive had made it clear that there was now very little likelihood of any sea or airborne landing. The hazards involved in the moving and commitment of reserves had therefore been greatly minimized, and the German High Command was now able to devote the whole of its attention to the land battle in progress. This fact had already led, on 13 May, to the release of the 90 Panzer Grenadier Division which, although it had delivered no counter-attack in divisional strength in the Liri valley, had nevertheless made a vital contribution to the stabilization of LI Mountain Corps' front.

Had he received earlier information regarding the strength and direction of the French thrust, Kesselring would perhaps have sent Baade's Division to reinforce Tenth Army's left wing, rather than into the Liri valley. But in spite of his strict orders that any information regarding Juin's movements was to be reported forthwith to Army Group, he heard nothing of the disaster that had befallen XIV Corps until the third or fourth day of the battle. Even so, the situation was by no means irreparable, and the fact that the Petrella massif had been lost did not mean that Tenth Army's right wing would have to be withdrawn, but it did cause Kesselring to intervene personally in the conduct of operations. His first act was to give orders for the evacuation of Monte Cassino, and his second was to release

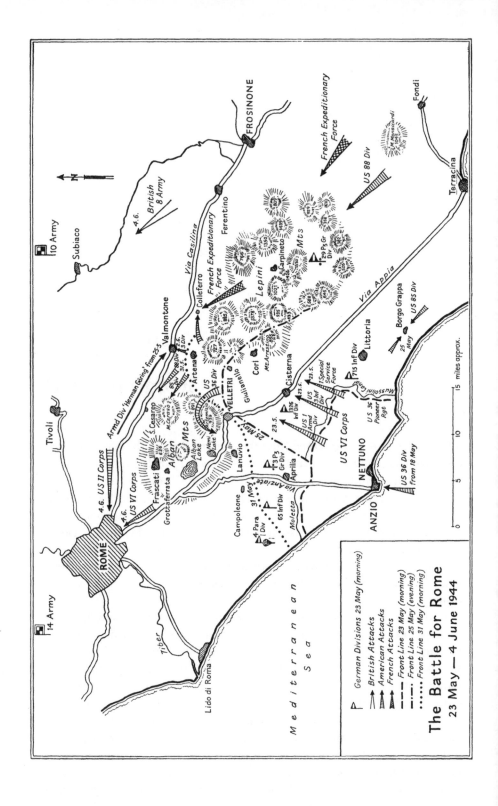

The Battle for Rome
23 May — 4 June 1944

Legend:

- △ German Divisions 23 May (morning)
- British Attacks
- American Attacks
- French Attacks
- ——— Front Line 23 May (morning)
- ——— Front Line 25 May (evening)
- ········· Front Line 31 May (morning)

Map labels:

14 Army
10 Army
Subiaco
British 8 Army
FROSINONE
French Expeditionary Force
M. Monacundi
Fondi
Terracina
US 88 Div
29 Pz Gr Div
Lepini Mts
Carpineto
US 85 Div
Borgo Grappa
Via Appia
Littoria
715 Inf Div
Colleferro
Ferentino
Via Casilina
Tivoli
Valmontone
US II Corps
US VI Corps
Armd Div 'Herman Göring' from 25.5.
Artena
3 Div
36 Div
US
VELLETRI
Cori
M. Artemisio
Cisterna
1 Special Service Force
US 36 Pioneer Rgt
US VI Corps
25 May
ROME
Tiber
Frascati
Grottaferrata
Alban Mts
Alban Lake
Lanuvio
Campoleone
4 Para Div
65 Inf Div
Moletta
Via Anziate
3 Pz Gr Div
Aprilia
Mussolini Canal
US 1 Armd Div
3 Inf Div
1 Armd Div
36 Inf Div
US VI Corps
NETTUNO
US 36 Div from 18 May
ANZIO
Lido di Roma
Mediterranean Sea

0 5 10 15 miles approx.

the 26 Panzer Division from the general reserve and send it into action in the Pico area.

By 18 May the front from Monte Cairo to Pico was firmly stabilized, and in this sector the Senger Barrier was occupied from end to end, fully and with no gaps. But the situation between Pico and Terracina was causing some anxiety. The sector was weakly held by the remnants of the 94 Infantry Division and some individual battalions of 15 Panzer Grenadier Division. There was, however, still a chance that Fifth Army's thrust might be stopped and the threatened break-through to the beach-head prevented. In the beach-head itself all was quiet, the Tenth Army's left wing had not been attacked, and it was quite safe to withdraw troops from that area, as the transfer of 305 Infantry Division to the Liri valley had proved. But even if an offensive were to be launched from the beach-head, the 29 Panzer Grenadier, the 92 Infantry and the Hermann Göring Panzer Division would still be available. But Tenth Army's whole anxiety was focused on Pico. It was here that von Vietinghoff feared a deadly stab in the back of the Senger Barrier, and in his mind's eye he already saw the French advancing on Ceprano and Frosinone. If that happened, the Senger Barrier would have to be abandoned forthwith.

Kesselring held a different view. 'Regardless of whether we fight on the Senger Barrier or have to withdraw, help for the right wing must be the primary consideration' (extract from a memorandum by the Field-Marshal).

But in either case, further operations would not be possible unless more troops became available. The 334 Infantry Division and the rear elements of the 305 Division were on their way from the Adriatic, but on its left wing the Tenth Army remained markedly static. Was Tenth Army counting on the release of troops from Army Group reserve? Did they not realize the danger that would threaten their flank if Fifth Army succeeded in linking up with the beach-head?

Be that as it may, on 19 May Kesselring himself intervened and ordered the 29 Panzer Grenadier Division to move into the Fondi area. The Division was ready to move and could have been in position in its new area during the course of 20 May. But once more the Field-Marshal had the same experience as he had had the previous October over Termoli. When he returned to his battle headquarters on the evening of 29 May, he was told that Fourteenth Army had protested against the removal of the 29 Division and that the Division had therefore not yet started to move southwards. This was too much of a good thing! And Fourteenth Army was not even being attacked! Kesselring insisted that his orders be forthwith obeyed, for he knew that any delay in the timely arrival of 29 Division would not only have the gravest consequences for Tenth Army, but might well also lead to the crumbling of Fourteenth Army's right wing.

The rapid advance made by U.S. II Corps had no place in Alexander's original concept. The Commander-in-Chief, 15 Army Group, had other plans. Just as Fifth Army was poised to launch its blow, Clark heard that it was Alexander's intention that an attack should be delivered on 21 May from the beach-head via Cori in the general direction of Valmontone. At the same time, he wished the U.S. II and the French Corps to attack northwards via Ceprano, in order to take in rear the German forces opposing the advance of the Eighth Army. General Leese with the latter, however, was to mark time until the attacks on Valmontone and Ceprano had borne fruit.

Clark was somewhat taken aback by this new plan, which was so completely contrary to his own intentions. Less than thirty miles lay between Fifth Army and the beach-head. Why should he be asked to play a supporting role to the Eighth Army, when the great prize was beckoning to him from the coast? Why give precedence to the attack on Valmontone, when the linking-up of Fifth Army and VI Corps in the beach-head presented an excellent chance of taking Rome by direct assault? For Rome was the great prize that Clark's Army was after, and all other operations, as far as the Americans were concerned, were of minor importance. Clark frankly admits: 'We not only wanted the honour of capturing Rome, but we felt that we more than deserved it; that it would to a certain extent make up for the buffeting and the frustration we had undergone in keeping up the winter pressure against the Germans. My own feeling was that nothing was going to stop us on our push towards the Italian capital. Not only did we intend to become the first army in fifteen centuries to seize Rome from the south, but we intended to see that the people back home knew that it was the Fifth Army that did the job and knew the price that had been paid for it.'*

It was with some reluctance that Alexander gave Clark a free hand. It was not easy for him to refuse any American request. The Americans in Italy had to be kept happy, for very soon their help was going to be urgently needed when, after the fall of the Italian capital, the great question arose: landing in southern France, or advance into the Balkans? Clark did not hesitate for a moment, but forthwith set II Corps in motion. On the afternoon of 20 May the U.S. 88 Division captured Fondi at the first attempt and pushed on at once into the mountains. There then followed a typical example of the uninhibited zeal and zest with which the Americans go

---

* *Calculated Risk.* General Clark's historical reference is to Belisar, who, having captured Naples in A.D. 536, marched through the Liri valley and occupied Rome without a fight.

about a task of this nature. They were not content with having taken Fondi or even with having occupied the dominating Monte Monsicardi beyond it; they rushed impetuously forward through the mountains, regardless of the situation on their flanks, and by 23 May they had reached Roccasecca dei Volsci, fifteen miles north-west of Fondi.

The U.S. 85 Division, too, had been fighting with penetrative effect. One battalion, which landed from the sea at Sperlonga, met with as little opposition as did the regiments attacking to the south of the Via Appia. In rapid succession the heights dominating Terracina, Monte San Stefano and Monte Leano, fell, and on 23 May, attacking from the north, the Americans threw the battalion of the 15 Panzer Grenadier Regiment and the 103 Reconnaissance Section out of Terracina and occupied the town.

The Germans had thus lost an area of high ground which had been regarded as impregnable. The 29 Panzer Division had done its best, but had been unable to prevent it. Clark, on the other hand, exploited his success at once and to the full. He sent the 85 Division forward through the Pontine marshes, and from the beach-head a combat group of the U.S. 36 Engineer Regiment, reinforced by the reconnaissance section of the British 1 Division, set off in a south-easterly direction and joined hands with the 85 Division at Borgo Grappa on 25 May.

A tenuous contact with the beach-head had thus been established, but it was wide enough to allow reinforcements to be sent to VI Corps by the land route. But the French Corps, which would have enabled Clark to widen the passage and strike swiftly at the left flank of Fourteenth Army, was not available to him, since it was already in action at Pico.

In spite of its initial difficulties, the 26 Panzer Division had established itself firmly in the Senger Barrier on each side of Pico. The importance of the sector and the threat to LI Mountain Corps' rear that had resulted from the French thrust were sufficient reason for the employment here of a *corps d'élite*; and once again von Lüttwitz's seasoned division did all that the High Command expected of it. The French made no progress.

The French 1 Division's first attempt to capture Monte Leucio to the east of Pico failed. The next day, 20 May, Juin put in the 3 Algerian Division, which captured the mountain after a hard fight. Brosset's Division at once set off in pursuit and pushed forward as far as San Giovanni in the Liri valley. Its success, however, was short-lived. On 21 May General von Lüttwitz hit back in strength. His armoured reserves fell upon the French and drove them back to Monte Leucio. The Algerians, who in the meanwhile had fought their way into Pico, were also thrown back. But Juin was not to be denied. On 22 May he delivered a concentric attack on Pico, with the Algerians thrusting from the east and the Moroccan 4 Mountain Division from the south, and by midday the town was in

French hands. The next day the French maintained their pressure northwards, but were not able to get beyond Pico. Meanwhile, on the German side, the 334 Division, which had been brought over from the Adriatic, had joined in the battle, and Juin's prospects of capturing Ceprano swiftly were very considerably diminished. On 23 May, just at the right moment, the Canadian attack on Pontecorvo, where General Burns broke through the Senger Barrier, relieved the pressure on the French, and on 25 May the Algerians captured San Giovanni without much trouble. The next day Vallecorsa on the French left fell to the Moroccan Division.

The French attack on Pico had very materially held up the operations of Fifth Army. Between the two Corps was a gap of no less than twenty-five miles. While Keyes was joining hands with Truscott at Borgo Grappa, Juin was still only six miles north of Fondi, and only then was the way to the beach-head open to the French General. The objective given to him was Colleferro, five miles east of Valmontone, where he was to cut the Via Casilina and bar the way to any German withdrawal.

Alexander, however, relegated the French Corps to the subsidiary roads, in order to leave Eighth Army a clear passage along the Via Casilina. Clark would have preferred to see the French on the main road, and he therefore urged Alexander not to refuse sanction for a French attack on Ferentino. To this Alexander gave the somewhat oracular reply that Juin could certainly attack Ferentino, that he himself would, indeed, welcome such an operation as being of great assistance to the Eighth Army, but that the Via Casilina would, of course, have to be kept free for the British forces, in order to ensure their timely intervention in the battle for Rome.

The French thus had perforce to make their way laboriously through the Lepini Mountains, with the River Sacco as the dividing line between them and the Eighth Army. Immediately south of the river the Moroccan 2 Infantry Division led the way through the mountains via Carpentino, with Sevez's 4 Mountain Division following behind it. The French had played the principal role in the battle for the Gustav Line, but now they had to be content to play second fiddle. To Juin this was a bitter disappointment. It had been his Corps that had burst open the gates through which the Allied armies were now streaming towards the great prize of Rome, which, he felt, should really have gone to the French.

Meanwhile the Eighth Army had also been on the move. On 20 May by a *coup de main* the Carpathian Division had captured Piedimonte, a strongly fortified and important keypoint in the Senger Barrier. But a counter-attack by the 1st Battalion, 4 Parachute Regiment, threw the Poles out again; and the Kresova Division had been attacking Monte Cairo without success.

A glance at the front line held by the Tenth Army on 24 May, the day on which Terracina fell and the Canadians started to break through the

Senger Barrier, will show more clearly than ever how great the success of the U.S. Fifth Army had been. When the 85 Division troops hoisted the Stars and Stripes in Terracina twenty-five miles behind the Gustav Line, the British Eighth Army had gained a mere four and a half miles at Cassino itself and at Pontecorvo had penetrated the German defences to a depth of only eight miles. The British attributed their slow advance firstly to the stiff opposition which they encountered and secondly to an alleged dearth of roads and the immense mass of some 20,000 vehicles which blocked the Liri valley. The impression given, however, is that the Eighth Army had been deliberately held back in order to allow Fifth Army's success south of the Liri valley to come to full fruition, and that it did not intend to set about the task of breaking through the Senger Barrier until after the French had taken Pico.

On 18 May Monte Cassino had fallen and the Canadians were close to Pontecorvo. But General Leese took his time. It was not until 23 May that he advanced against the Senger Barrier, and then not with the concentrated force of the whole Eighth Army, but simply with a single division of the Canadian Corps. At 6 a.m. on 23 May the Canadian 1 Infantry Division advanced on a 2,000-yard front between Pontecorvo and Aquino. It was only with difficulty that the Canadians made any progress against Baade's Division; but by midday they had reached the Pontecorvo–Aquino road, and by the evening Pontecorvo was in their hands.

Now the Canadian 5 Armoured Division took over the lead and by 24 May had reached the River Melfa, south-west of Roccasecca railway station. The Senger Barrier had been broken, and the way to Ceprano was free. But 1 Parachute Division was still in position between Aquino and Monte Cairo. Major Schram swung part of his artillery in position on the Cairo massif through an angle of 180 degrees and brought fire to bear from the rear on the Canadians, who were then striving to cross the Melfa. But Schram, of course, could not maintain fire in two directions for very long. The Poles were thrusting with all their might against the northern flank of the Senger Barrier. On 25 May the Kresova Division took Monte Cairo, and on the same day the 3 Division took Piedimonte at the fourth attempt.

It was now high time for Heidrich to move into position in the Melfa sector if he wished to avoid being surrounded from the south and north. The Indian 8 and British 78 Divisions followed closely on the heels of the withdrawing paratroops and in rapid succession occupied Aquino, Castrocielo and Roccasecca as soon as they were evacuated. On 25 May the Canadian 5 Armoured Division entered Ceprano, and on 28 May the British 6 Armoured Division, in action for the first time since the start of the spring offensive, captured Monte Grande, south of Arce, which had been tenaciously defended by 1 Parachute Regiment.

The holding of Arce had been of paramount importance, since it was vital to keep open the road to Avezzano, LI Mountain Corps' only line of retreat. The 1 Parachute Regiment accomplished the task, holding on grimly till the evening of 29 May, when they abandoned the town to the advancing Indians.

The main objective of the Eighth Army, however, was still Frosinone. The Canadian 5 Armoured Division was still leading the attack. After mopping-up the Ceprano area, the Canadians took Pofi on 29 May, and two days later General Burns reported that he had captured Frosinone, that important keypoint, which had been on Clark's programme since December.

During the next two days General Leese swung the mass of the Eighth Army round to the north, for in the meanwhile the operations in the beach-head area had proved decisive. Clark's divisions were hastening towards the capital, and there was no need for Leese to hurry to the assistance of Fifth Army, as Alexander would have liked to see him do.

Despite the narrowness of the Anzio beach-head, U.S. VI Corps had gradually been built up to Army strength. At the front, the U.S. 36 Engineer Regiment was on the right, the U.S. 34 and 45 Divisions in the centre and the British 1 and 5 Divisions on the left. Behind them, organized in depth and ready to move, stood the U.S. 1 Armoured and 3 Infantry Divisions and the 1 Special Service Force. The task allotted to these proven formations was to break through to Valmontone. Since the 18 May the U.S. 36 Division had been disembarking, and it had been Clark's intention to send the 85 Division also by sea to Anzio. But the plan had been overtaken by events. Four days nevertheless elapsed, before the one Allied division with its great concourse of vehicles had been disembarked in the small ports of Anzio and Nettuno. The capture of Terracina, however, meant that the 85 Division would now presumably be able to reach the beach-head as quickly by the land route as by sea.

The German Fourteenth Army, too, was now well prepared for the decisive battle—at least as far as its right wing and centre were concerned. At Cisterna and on the outskirts of the Pontine marshes, however, the situation gave rise to not a little anxiety. The formations under the command of 1 Parachute Corps—the 4 Parachute, the 65 Infantry and the 3 Panzer Grenadier Divisions—were all seasoned veterans. Pfeiffer's Division (65th) and Graeser's Division (3 Panzer Grenadier) had recovered with astonishing speed from their reverses on the Sangro and in the Reinhard Line respectively and were regarded as thoroughly reliable, hard-fighting troops. The 4 Parachute Division, which in reality had only been raised in the beach-head area, had also done well; the efficiency and morale of the older paratroops in it had endowed the Division with the traditional spirit of the Parachute arm.

The left sector in the beach-head area was under command of LXXVI Panzer Corps, the weaknesses of whose formations was known. The 362 Infantry Division had been comparatively recently raised—in November 1943—and it had not recovered from the mauling and severe losses it had incurred in its counter-attacks in the February operations. The same applied to the 715 Division, which had also suffered heavily in February and was also rather weak in other respects.*

Field-Marshal Kesselring did all he could to stiffen the backbone of Fourteenth Army. After the departure to the southern front of the 29 Panzer Grenadier Division, he transferred the 334 Infantry Division to the beach-head and took steps to ensure that the Hermann Göring Panzer Division would be available to Fourteenth Army, if required.

As before, the Commander-in-Chief, South-West, was still expecting VI Corps to attack Valmontone. This coincided in all respects with the tactical conception of his opposite number, General Alexander, who fully appreciated the opportunities for an encircling movement which possession of Valmontone would offer. His object was not confined solely to blocking the Via Casilina and driving the Tenth Army away from Rome; he had more far-reaching plans. The exceptionally favourable positions of the beach-head was nothing less than an invitation to make a thrust into the deep flanks of the Tenth Army, and such an operation would inevitably lead to the encirclement and destruction of strong German forces. Valmontone was the starting line, the keypoint for the implementation of that 'little Stalingrad' of which Churchill had spoken at Teheran; and Rome, on the periphery of the battle, would automatically fall into Allied hands.

As will be seen, it was the Americans who completely upset Alexander's plans. Their one and only objective was Rome. They were not in the least

* Order of Battle, German Fourteenth Army, Anzio–Nettuno, mid-May 1944:

Commander-in-Chief, Fourteenth Army	General von Mackensen
I PARACHUTE CORPS	General Schlemm
4 Parachute Division	Colonel Trettner
65 Infantry Division	Lieutenant-General Pfeiffer
3 Panzer Grenadier Division	Lieutenant-General Graeser
LXXVI PANZER CORPS	General Herr
362 Infantry Division	Lieutenant-General Greiner
715 Infantry Division (partly motorized)	Lieutenant-General Hildebrant
ARMY RESERVE	Lieutenant-General Goeritz

The following formations joined Fourteenth Army during the course of the battle and were placed under its command:

29 Panzer Grenadier Division	Lieutenant-General Fries
334 Infantry Division	Lieutenant-General Böhlke
Hermann Göring Panzer Division	Major-General Schmalt

interested in any battle of encirclement. Once they'd captured Rome, they'd soon deal with the Germans!

By 23 May the scene was set. At 6.30 a.m. Truscott struck on both sides of Cisterna. After a forty-five-minute artillery barrage, 700 bombers and fighters attacked targets in 362 Infantry Division's sector, and at the same time the assaulting troops emerged from their positions and advanced to the attack. Under cover of a thick smoke-screen, the Americans moved forward with great determination and flung the German regiments out of their positions. By evening the 1 Special Service Force was on the farther side of the Via Appia, the U.S. 3 Division in the southern outskirts of Cisterna, and the 1 Armoured Division had captured the railway station west of the town. The 24 May brought Truscott further successes. Cisterna was surrounded, and the 1 Armoured Division sent one detachment forward towards Cori and a second to Velletri to broaden the extent of the penetration. On the evening of the next day, the 3 Division took Cisterna. The 955 Grenadier Regiment had stubbornly defended the town for forty-eight hours, until lack of ammunition put an end to further resistance.

The 362 Division had been severely mauled. Its 954 and 956 Regiments had been decimated, and the 955 Regiment completely annihilated. After that, it was easy for the Americans to gain ground swiftly. By the evening of 25 May the 1 Special Service Force was in possession of Monte Arrestino, and the 1 Armoured Division had taken Cori and Guilianello and at its most northernly point the thrust had penetrated more than ten miles.

On the left flank, however, the attack had been less successful. Here Truscott had put in the 34 Division on 25 May, but its attack had come to a standstill south of Velletri. There the Americans had come up against a new opponent—the 12 Parachute Regiment, the 'assault regiment', whose commander, Major Timm, gave nothing away. But Truscott had to capture Velletri and Monte Artemesio, if he were to continue his attack on Valmontone without exposing his left flank to the danger of unpleasant surprises.

Fourteenth Army reacted 'in the grand manner' to the Cisterno penetration. It closed up its left flank at once and withdrew 715 Division into the Lepini Mountains, but failed to synchronize these measures with the movements of 29 Panzer Grenadier Division. And now Clark had a secure land-bridge to VI Corps.

The remnants of 362 Division climbed up to 'C Position' in the Alban Hills north of Velletri.* Its losses had been very severe. Up to 25 May the U.S. VI Corps had taken 2,450 prisoners, most of them men of Greiner's Division.

---

* The 'C Position', the last line south of Rome, ran from the Alban Hills diagonally across the peninsula to Pescara on the Adriatic coast.

The struggle for Valmotone could now be continued only if further troops became available. The inexperienced 92 Infantry Division, until now in army reserve, tried desperately but in vain to plug the yawning gap between the Lepini Mountains and the Alban Hills. The Division was, in any case, too weak to stand any chance of succeeding; but apart from that, it was not put in as a corporate entity, but was committed to battle in driblets, as its elements reached the battle area.

Then at last, on 25 May, the reconnaissance section, the advanced guard of the Hermann Göring Panzer Division, reached Valmontone. When the 29 Panzer Grenadier Division had been committed to battle at Fondi on 21 May, Kesselring had released the Hermann Göring Division and placed it under Fourteenth Army's command. Truscott had then not yet launched his attack, and it was anticipated that the Division would reach Valmontone by 24 May at the latest. But unforeseen delays had occurred. While on the march the Division had been repeatedly attacked from the air, and the speed of its progress had been greatly diminished. But at last, on 27 and 28 May, the main body arrived and joined in the battle. But valuable time had been irretrievably lost. Kesselring had done everything possible to ensure the success of this pre-eminently well-armed division. Together with the divisional commander he had sent his principal staff officer, Colonel Beelitz, to Headquarters, Fourteenth Army, to discuss in detail the manner in which the Division was to be used. He himself hoped to see it go into action forward of Artina, in conjunction with the remnants of the 362 and 715 Infantry Divisions.

The Allied air forces had, of course, put an almost complete stop to all traffic by day on the roads leading south. On 25 May alone they had destroyed 655 vehicles in the Fourteenth Army's sector, and in the beach-head battle the U.S. 12 Tactical Air Fleet had scored its biggest success to date. Its efforts had very considerably accelerated the fall of the Italian capital.

The delay in the arrival of the Hermann Göring Division could have had more serious repercussions if it was not for the fact that Clark had changed the priority of his objectives. On 25 May he gave Truscott orders to advance forthwith through the Alban Hills on Rome. The British Eighth Army was advancing along the Via Casilina, and although it was still a long way to the south, Clark had a sneaking feeling that the British were determined to march into Rome with the Americans. To continue to force the pace against Valmontone as he had been doing would be of assistance primarily to the Eighth Army, and Clark was in no hurry to reach the Via Casilina. That, he felt, could wait until after the Alban Hills had been captured. Then it would be the Americans, and not the British who would rush forward from Valmontone into Rome.

Alexander got wind of Clark's intentions on 26 May, when he was talk-ing to the latter's Chief of Staff, Gruenther, at Fifth Army Battle Head-quarters. He agreed to the proposed attack on the Alban Hills, but, return-ing to the subject a few minutes later, he remarked: 'I'm sure that the Army Commander will maintain his pressure on Valmontone. Will he do that?' But Fifth Army's dispositions already showed quite clearly that Clark had relegated the Valmontone attack, at least for the time being, to the status of a purely subsidiary operation.

The main attack was delivered against the Alban Hills by Truscott on 26 May. His 34 Division attacked Velletri and Lanuvio, and the 45 Division was directed against Campoleone, but gained very little ground from the divisions of the I Parachute Corps. This caused Truscott to put in the 1 Armoured Division the next day, but it, too, failed to give any additional impetus to the attack. A further attempt by the 1 Division on 28 May ended with the putting out of action of thirty-seven tanks.

The 28 May had brought impressive success to the German defence. But—'It is a great pity that the admirable efforts of the troops on the right wing [4 Parachute, 65 Infantry and 3 Panzer Grenadier Divisions] were not emulated by the formations on the left' (Kesselring). In fact catastrophe on the left flank lay only a few days ahead. There the U.S. 3 Division had driven its spearhead still farther to the north and had taken Artena on 26 May. But the attempt to reach the Via Casilina had failed, for three days the Americans were held up before Valmontone, and the door of the trap which Alexander had set for the Tenth Army was left open.

Churchill at once intervened. On 28 May he telegraphed to Alexander: '. . . At this distance it seems much more important to cut their line of retreat than anything else. I am sure you have considered moving more armour by the Appian Way up to the northernmost spearhead directed against the Valmontone–Frosinone road. A cop is much more important than Rome, which would anyhow come as its consequence. The cop is the the one thing that matters.'* The thought of Valmontone was robbing the British Prime Minister of his peace of mind. It was here that he saw the great chance for which he had been waiting so long. The Russians were contriving one battle of encirclement after another, and it was only the Western allies who, except for Tunis, had so far failed to achieve a 'Stalin-grad'; and the greater the number of German divisions destroyed south of Rome, the greater would be the chance of a swift move into the Balkans.

Scarcely had Churchill sent off his first telegram than he followed it with another: '. . . but I should feel myself wanting in comradeship if I did not let you know that the glory of this battle, already great, will be measured, not by the capture of Rome or the juncture with the beach-head, but by

* *The Second World War*, Vol. V.

the number of German divisions cut off. I am sure you will have revolved all this in your mind, and perhaps you have already acted in this way. Nevertheless I do feel I ought to tell you that it is the cop that counts.'*
But Clark had already moved his pieces on the board in a way which precluded any possibility of a 'cop' such as Churchill desired. As early as 27 May he had put in the 36 Division north of Velletri, and in the meanwhile the British division on the left flank had also joined in the attack. Clark's compass bearing was set directly at Rome.

It was the U.S. 36 Division that was destined to strike the decisive blow. On 30 May one of its very numerous reconnaissance groups found a gap in the German line near Monte Artemisio and immediately pushed through it. During the night of 30/31 May the 142 Regiment climbed the steep slopes of the mountain; behind it came the whole of the rest of the division, and the next morning Walker's troops reached the Velletri-Nemi road in rear of the defence and on the flank of the I Parachute Corps.

At once Clark gave the signal for the general attack, Truscott concentrated his whole force on the assault of the Alban Hills, and Rome prepared to receive its new occupiers.

The blunder at Artemisio could very easily have been avoided. The existence of this gap on the Artemesio spur between 362 Division and the Hermann Göring Division was known to Fourteenth Army Command. Kesselring himself had intervened to ensure that no unpleasant surprises occurred in this important sector. He himself has the following to say on the matter:

I was well informed regarding developments at the point of penetration, as I personally visited the various command posts nearly every day. On one of these visits I noticed the gap between the 362 and the Hermann Göring Divisions and drew Fourteenth Army's attention to it on 29 May. The next day, when I found that not only had the gap been not closed, but that nothing at all had been done to cover it, I personally telephoned to the Commander-in-Chief, Fourteenth Army, and spoke sharply about this unpardonable omission, stressing that what could easily be accomplished today by a single battalion might well prove impossible to do with a whole division tomorrow.

On 31 May, when I received a report direct from an artillery command post on the reverse slopes of the Artemisio spur—once again before any report from Fourteenth Army—that infantry was advancing against the command post, the tactical and strategical consequences were at once obvious to me. The fact that Fourteenth Army was then able to make available two or three battalions only proves that it could easily have done so earlier. A complete restoration of the situation was impossible. Once again Fourteenth Army had to pay dearly for its blind confidence. At this advanced stage, after four years of war, no one has the

* The Second World War, Vol. V.

right to rely on the strict, one hundred per cent obedience of orders; in cases such as this, the responsible commander should either go in person or send an officer to see that his orders have been properly carried out. To have done so in this instance would not only have been possible, but was an absolute duty! This was the last straw which decided me to recommend to Hitler a change in the command of Fourteenth Army or Army Group C.*

The 36 Division had made a typical American 'raid'. With the same light-hearted insouciance with which they had advanced to Persano in the Salerno battle they now sped on winged feet into the German positions north and west of Velletri. But this time they scored a resounding success and brought about the collapse of the whole German front from the Alban Hills to the coast; for on 1 June they made a determined thrust into the flank of 1 Parachute Corps, and Lanuvio and Campoleone could be held no longer. This meant—for the Germans a general retreat, and for the Americans a pursuit to Rome.

On 2 June the U.S. 1 Armoured Division started up its engines to lead Fifth Army into the Eternal City. On the same day the 88 Division was in San Cesareo on the Via Casilina, ready to set out on the march to Rome. At Valmontone, too, the German front had collapsed, and there was now nothing between the Americans and the goal they had so eagerly sought.

The attack against the Lepini Mountains and the Alban Hills had been carried out by U.S. II Corps. Clark had summoned it and the 85 and 88 Divisions from the Pontine marshes, and Keyes had arrived on 31 May. On 2 June the 3 Division had taken Valmontone, the 1 Special Service Force had established contact with the French Corps and the 85 and 88 Divisions, attacking northwards, had captured Monte Ceraso and Cesareo.

In the Allied camp it was widely assumed that Clark would march into Rome with colours flying and bands playing; and it seemed only right and proper that representatives of the other contingents fighting in Italy should be there to receive their share of the cheers of the Roman populace. The Polish Government in exile demanded that a Polish contingent should participate in the march, and from Jugoslavia Tito sent a deputation of officers in good time to be present at the victory celebrations in the capital of his arch-enemy. Thoroughly exasperated by all this nonsense, Clark sent for his Chief of Staff. 'As politely as you can, please tell everybody, including the Swedes, if need be,' he said angrily, 'that I will not frame the tactical occupation of Rome.' And he added: 'God and the Boche dictate these measures.'

In this way, the march into Rome on 4 June became an exclusively American affair, with the new 88 Division leading the way. At 7.15 p.m.

* Extract from a memorandum by Field-Marshal Kesselring.

its advanced guard reached the Piazza Venezia in the centre of Rome.

The Fourteenth Army had withdrawn swiftly behind the Tiber and the Amine sector, with 4 Parachute Division as rear-guard and the last German troops to march through Rome. When the Americans entered the city, they were astonished to find that not one of the numerous bridges over the Tiber had been demolished. Kesselring, as was disclosed only after the war had ended, had given strict orders on the subject and had once again given free rein to his consideration for Italian works of art, deliberately accepting military disadvantages, simply to preserve the Eternal City from damage. His consideration was poorly rewarded, and the Venice verdict is no credit to British justice.

The conquest of Rome was, of course, an event of world-wide significance. At last the bells could peal again! Many and bitter had been the disappointments which the Allies had suffered since Salerno. First they had expected to be in Rome by October, then it was Christmas or January at the latest; and in the end it had occurred in the following June. Nine long months had passed since the Allied armies first set foot on Italian soil. With horror they looked back on the severe winter, on such places as Monte Camino, Ortona, the Garigliano, Anzio and, above all, Monte Cassino.

Two days before the launching of the great invasion of Normandy the Americans hoisted their flag over Rome. But they and their allies had paid dearly for the privilege. Since the 11 May, the start of the offensive, the Fifth Army had suffered 18,000 casualties, the Eighth Army 14,000 and Juin 10,000. Forty-two thousand men—a grim tribute to the determination with which the German forces had defended themselves against great odds!

The German casualties, too, had naturally been very heavy. Although Alexander had not succeeded in trapping and destroying any major formations, the 20,000 German prisoners alone represented a loss of two whole divisions, and to this must be added at least half as many dead and wounded. German material losses, particularly in motor vehicles, had also been severe. For days on end the Subiaco Pass, through which the main body of the Tenth Army had had to squeeze its way, resembled a huge snake of burning vehicles, and all the other roads along which the German forces retreated were strewn with wrecked tanks, lorries and cars.

Field-Marshal Kesselring comments on the Allied offensive:

The battles during this period were of exceptional severity. That the troops, with few exceptions (which unfortunately proved disastrous as regards the ultimate outcome), stood up to the test is a tribute to their good quality. In general, the same can be said of the leadership. Many errors and failures could perhaps, have been avoided; but we are still too close to events to be able to pass a completely objective verdict.*

Here is an Allied view:

The Allied armies were opposed by generals and soldiers of supreme ability ... and though the cause for which they fought was abominable ... a German army in the field was a formidable and brilliant instrument. ... In the proper emotions of war it was difficult to recognize in the German infantry who held the bitter heights of Cassino and fought so desperately in the channelled chaos of the ruins below, a courage equal to the valour of the soldiers whose death and heroism filled our hearts; and so long as German tactics were a villainous obstacle that had to be overwhelmed or circumvented, it was not easy to appreciate, and impossible to admire, them . . .; and nowhere did the Germans more convincingly show their profound and finished aptitude for war ... and their remarkable faculty for reshaping from broken battalions and the rabble of defeat a rear-guard of unimpaired morale.†

From the German side, tribute must be paid to the Allied troops. They fought gallantly, even though they had an easier task than the Germans, who were almost invariably on the receiving end. It is easier to fight well when advancing than when marching along the road to defeat. If, from the host of Allied troops, from an army composed of Americans, Britons, French, Indians, New Zealanders and Poles, Canadians, South Africans and Italians, some formations merit special mention, then the laurels must go to the French Expeditionary Corps, the U.S. 3, 36, and 88 Divisions and the troops of General Anders.

With the capture of Rome the first chapter of the Italian campaign came to an end. There now followed a series of rear-guard actions in central Italy, which continued until the Green Line was reached in the late summer. But while the Allied armies were storming northwards, a fresh tug-of-war 'at the highest level' began. Again it was Churchill who urged that the Italian campaign should be crowned with an advance into the Balkans; and again it was the Americans who thwarted him. Once more Overlord and its satellite, 'Anvil', ruined the Mediterranean campaign, and once more it was Stalin who had the last laugh and who was to derive untold advantage from the divergencies of opinion in the camp of the Western allies.

* *Soldat bis zum letzten Tag.*   † Linklater, *The Campaign in Italy.*

Chapter 15

A Lost Victory

After the fall of Rome, the German armies found themselves in an extremely critical situation. Fourteenth Army was in particularly dire peril, and at first it did not seem as though it would be possible to halt the hotly pursuing Americans west of the Tiber. Tenth Army's situation was a little better; but its divisions had been withdrawn so far from Rome and the Tiber that a concentration of any considerable strength west of the Tiber was impossible.

But by the time it reached Lake Bolsena, the Fourteenth Army had begun to regain its cohesion, and by the middle of June Kesselring had established a solid defensive front on either side of Lake Trasimene. Here it was not until the end of the month that the Allies were able to make any progress. On 16 July the British captured Arezzo, the next day the Poles were in Ancona and on the 19th the Americans took Leghorn. Meanwhile, the French had marched into Siena.

The 15 Army Group continued to maintain its pressure. The Americans occupied the whole of the lower reaches of the Arno, and on 12 August the New Zealanders entered Florence.

Alexander's forces were now only a few miles south of the Green Line; but he lacked the numbers which would have enabled him to attack the position at once. A great deal of regrouping was necessary before any further offensive could be launched.

In two months, the Allies had advanced nearly 250 miles in spite of the severity with which their wings had been clipped. At the beginning of July Alexander had received orders to make available forces for Operation 'Anvil'—the landing in the South of France. The final strength of which he was deprived grew, eventually to seven divisions. Particularly hard hit was the Fifth Army, whose strength was reduced from 250,000 to 153,000 men.

With a complete disregard for the great opportunities of the hour, the Combined Chiefs of Staff crippled Alexander's victorious progress and hamstrung the victory of Cassino and the capture of Rome. From the Fifth Army they took away its best divisions and made no adequate replacements. From the United States came one solitary division, the U.S. 92 (coloured) Division, and it was later followed by the Brazilian Corps. That, of course, did not begin to compensate for the loss of the French Expeditionary Corps and the U.S. VI Corps, which had formed the nucleus of the Fifth Army.

Despite these hard blows, which hit him just when he was winning all along the line, the Allied Commander-in-Chief followed closely on the heels of the retreating Germans and adhered firmly to his own and Churchill's plans. In the same way as Overlord had been an inexorable drag-weight on the Italian campaign from its very start, now Anvil was to frustrate completely all British plans for the further prosecution of the war in the Mediterranean theatre.

It will be remembered that the decision to mount Anvil (later renamed 'Dragoon') had been taken at the Teheran conference. At Stalin's suggestion and with his concurrence, the cross-Channel invasion, the capture of Rome, the occupation of Italy up to the line Pisa–Florence–Rimini and Operation Anvil, the landing in southern France, had been accepted as the main operations to be conducted by the Western allies in 1944. Anvil was to be launched before, or at the latest at the same time as, the cross-Channel invasion, in order to draw off as strong German forces as possible from northern France to the south. Since it was considered that any smaller force would be unable to achieve the desired object, it was agreed that ten divisions should be earmarked for Anvil. These divisions, it was further agreed, would have to be drawn from the forces already in the Mediterranean theatre, and only the question of when they would have to be made available was left open. The final answer, obviously, depended upon the progress of the Italian campaign. At the time of the Teheran conference the Allies, certainly, had counted on capturing Rome in the near future and hoped, or at least thought it possible that, once Rome had fallen, Kesselring would withdraw without further ado direct to the Alpine positions.

Were these expectations fulfilled, then the withdrawal from Italy of the forces required for Anvil would present no problem (remembering that at

Teheran the line Pisa–Rimini had been accepted as the final objective). The situation, however, had not developed in the least as anticipated. Instead of February, it had been June before the Allies entered Rome, and there seemed to be no sign that Kesselring intended to surrender central Italy without a fight. Churchill glumly telegraphed to Harry Hopkins: 'The decision to land at Anzio and the delays at Cassino have forced us to postpone Anvil again and again.' The question now arose whether it was worth while mounting Anvil at all. Eisenhower had crossed the Channel two days after the capture of Rome, and there was therefore no prospect of being able to give him immediate support of the type originally envisaged, and if the landing on the French Riviera were not to take place for several weeks, it seemed doubtful whether by that time it would serve any useful purpose at all.

When General Marshall arrived in London on 7 June for consultations with the British Chiefs of Staff, the question of Anvil was on the agenda. But discussion on the subject was now not confined to drawing off German troops from Normandy, for in the meanwhile another, and perhaps more important, problem had arisen. In the United States the vast mass of troops awaiting transportation to Europe was growing steadily greater. Forty to fifty divisions were already standing-by, but before they could cross the Atlantic, the Allies had to have possession of adequate and efficient European ports at which to land them. It was, admittedly, anticipated that Cherbourg would fall in the near future, and Eisenhower's plans included the capture of the Breton ports of Brest, Lorient and St Nazaire; but it was by no means certain when these ports would fall or how long it would be before their dismantled docks were once more in working order. And in Marshall's view it was of paramount importance to the success of Overlord that the maximum possible strength should be concentrated in the minimum possible time.

He therefore put before his British colleagues the proposal that completely new bases should be captured on the western and southern coasts of France. He was thinking primarily, he said, of Bordeaux and Marseilles, through which the awaiting U.S. divisions could stream into the European mainland and flood across the whole of France. The proposal met with the immediate approval of Churchill and his Chiefs of Staff. But the British were unwilling to embark on any enterprise which might jeopardize Alexander's victory in Italy; they were determined resolutely to oppose any weakening of their forces there and were prepared to agree only to a solution which would not in any way interfere with the full exploitation of their victories in the Italian theatre.

On 14 June the Combined Chiefs of Staff finally agreed that preparations for a new landing should be taken in hand, and General Maitland Wilson was directed to work out plans for amphibious landings on the west coast of France, on the Côte d'Azur and at the head of the Adriatic. The final choice between them would depend upon developments in the strategic situation as a whole.

When Marshall met Maitland Wilson in Italy on 17 June, the Commander-in-Chief, Mediterranean, while fully appreciating the necessity for an increase in American bases in France, made no secret of his aversion to Operation Anvil and expressed a strong preference for Alexander's plan to maintain close and intense pressure on the Germans and break through into the Po valley. Maitland Wilson went even further. He suggested that after the break into the Po valley the proper course would be a landing across the Adriatic in Istria and thence a thrust through the Laibach depression into the plains of Hungary and the Danubian basin. Marshall was not a little shocked by the suggestion and told Maitland Wilson that 'it was not the policy of the Combined Chiefs of Staff to use U.S. troops for a campaign in south-east Europe, but to use them exclusively in France, and that such U.S. troops as were sent to the Mediterranean would be sent there solely for the purpose of launching an attack against the south coast of France'. To this, Maitland Wilson, strongly supported by Alexander, Eaker and John Cunningham, retorted that an extension of the Italian campaign into Hungary offered the best chance of defeating the enemy decisively in 1944 instead of in the first half of 1945.

When Maitland Wilson incorporated his ideas in a memorandum addressed to the Combined Chiefs of Staff and the British Chiefs supported his proposals, the Americans were taken so completely aback that they sharply demanded the immediate mounting of Anvil in accordance with the decisions reached at Teheran.

Eisenhower, understandably, took the same line. On 23 July he suggested to the Combined Chiefs of Staff that all forces becoming available in the Mediterranean should be used in direct support of the coming decisive battle in Normandy. An advance into the Laibach depression, he agreed, might well tie down German forces, but would not be able to draw off one single division from France. With equal emphasis Eisenhower expressed his aversion to an attack on Bordeaux. While admitting that this port was nearer to the States than Marseilles, he felt that Marseilles would not only be easier to capture, but would also open a direct route for operations against the Ruhr.

In the event, it was Operation Anvil that completely wrecked the operations against the Ruhr. After the break out of the Normandy beach-head, Montgomery, it will be remembered, argued with all the emphasis he could command that a concentrated thrust through northern France and Belgium should be directed against the Ruhr and that the position in central and southern France should be allowed to remain static. But it was the troops advancing up the Rhone valley who contributed more than a little to the great hold-up that occurred on the frontiers of Germany. Eisenhower's armies extended their flank further and further southwards in order to join up with the Anvil forces as quickly as possible. The Allied front became wider and wider, and Montgomery's thrust, which had started so auspiciously, became weaker and weaker.

To the Americans this broadening of the Allied front was more than welcome. The possibility of out-manœuvring the Germans by a series of bold and skilful operations played no part in their strategic thinking. What they wished to do was to crush and destroy the enemy by means of a frontal assault delivered along the whole line by 'the giant military steam-roller manufactured in the training camps and factories of the U.S.A.' And it was to this end that Eisenhower deployed the whole of his forces from the Swiss frontier to the North Sea.

Roosevelt, too, was inclined to take the same view. In Teheran he had told his son: 'Of one thing our Chiefs of Staff are convinced: the best way to kill the maximum number of Germans with the minimum loss of American soldiers is to concentrate on one vast and furious offensive and smash them with everything we've got. And to me that makes sense.' Churchill and his advisers had never regarded such a course with favour. It is therefore not surprising that when the question: Bay of Biscay, Côte d'Azur or Vienna arose, the British and American Chiefs of Staff could not agree. And here the decisive and, as later transpired, fatal last word rested with one man—Roosevelt.

In the meantime fresh impetus was given to Churchill's opposition to Anvil by a telegram he received from General Smuts, who was in Italy, visiting the South African Division. In it Smuts hit the nail squarely on the head:

... As regards plans for Alexander's advance, he and Wilson agreed that there will be no difficulty in his break-through to the Po and thereafter swinging east towards Istria, Liubliana and so on to Austria. Alexander favours an advance both by land and sea, while Wilson favours the latter and thinks three seaborne divisions with one or two airborne divisions would suffice and make possible the capture of Trieste by the beginning of September. Thereafter the advance will reopen eastwards, gathering large partisan support and perhaps forcing the enemy out of the Balkans. The co-operation between our and the Russian advance towards Austria and Germany would constitute as serious a threat to the enemy as Eisenhower's advance from the west, and the three combined are most likely to produce early enemy collapse.*

These and other views of a similar nature Churchill incorporated in a

* Churchill, *The Second World War*, Vol. VI.

memorandum which he sent to the President on 28 June. Roosevelt's reply was as prompt as it was adverse. He made it quite clear that he was determined to adhere to the 'grand strategy' enunciated at Teheran, in accordance with which all available forces were to be concentrated for Overlord. Stalin, he said, had been emphatically in favour of Anvil and had brushed aside as purely subsidiary any other operations in the Mediterranean theatre. Reading between the lines, it was obvious that Roosevelt did not feel he could agree to any alteration in Mediterranean strategy without Stalin's prior concurrence:

... I agree that the political considerations you mention are important factors, but military operations based thereon must be definitely secondary to the primary operations of striking at the heart of Germany.... My interest and hopes centre on defeating the Germans in front of Eisenhower and driving on into Germany, rather than on limiting this action for the purpose of staging a full major effort in Italy.... I cannot agree to the employment of United States troops against Istria *and into the Balkans*, nor can I see the French agreeing to such use of French troops.... Finally for purely political considerations over here, I should never survive even a slight setback in Overlord, *if it were known that fairly large forces had been diverted to the Balkans.**

So that was it! In November the United States would go to the presidential polls, and Roosevelt's chances of re-election would probably be gravely jeopardized if, in addition to those engaged in France and Italy, he committed further American troops to battle in south-east Europe. That Roosevelt was building up strong American forces in France was acceptable even to those—and there were more than a few of them—who thought that the war against Japan should be given priority over the struggle for Europe. The American people as a whole felt that there was a close bond between the United States and France, and Americans were unanimous in their desire to liberate the French people, who had so materially helped the British colonies to gain their freedom in 1776. If, in liberating France, they were at the same time treading the path that would lead to the swift collapse of Germany, then even the Republicans could not withhold their support.

To the employment of U.S. troops in south-east Europe the American people would react very differently. This, they would feel, would be an unwarranted interference in internal European affairs; but more important than that would be the suspicion that they were creating a British sphere of influence in the Balkans—with the help of American troops. But, to have made the American people realize—even before the elections and even if recognition of the desirability of so doing had existed—that it was not the

* Churchill, *The Second World War*, Vol. VI. The italics are Sir Winston's.

British but the Communists who were striving to ensure political primacy for themselves in the Balkans—that was something that was beyond the bounds of possibility.

It was, of course, Roosevelt himself who did everything he could to avoid giving offence to Stalin—to whom, since Teheran, he always referred affectionately as 'Uncle Joe'—by intervening militarily in the Balkans. And his reason for this was twofold. Firstly, because at Teheran Stalin had promised that on the conclusion of hostilities in Europe he would take part in the war against Japan; and secondly, because Roosevelt was naïve enough to believe that he would be able usefully to incorporate the Soviet Union as a valuable pillar of the future and, as it turned out, very fragile edifice of peace which he had in view. Furthermore, the President feared that if the Western allies gave any visible signs of mistrust towards the U.S.S.R., the latter would dissociate itself from his plans for the betterment of the world and entrench itself behind a *cordon sanitaire*.

That Churchill took a much more realistic view was of no avail. The Russians had for a long time been intriguing busily in both Italy and the Balkans, so much so that on 4 May 1944 Churchill asked his Foreign Minister to draw up a memorandum setting forth 'the brute issues between us and the Soviet Government which are developing in Italy, in Rumania, in Bulgaria, in Yugoslavia and above all in Greece. . . . Are we going to acquiesce in the Communization of the Balkans and perhaps of Italy? . . . I am of the opinion . . . that we ought to come to a definite opinion on it, and if our conclusion is that we resist the Communist infusion and invasion, we should put it to them pretty plainly at the best moment that military events permit.'*

The capture of Rome presented him with just such a moment. The time for action had come. But Roosevelt and his Chiefs of Staff cast aside Alexander's victory—irresponsibly and at the very moment when deadly blows were raining down on Hitler from all sides. In the east the Russians were pouring into Poland, in the west a mighty flood was about to burst its bonds and rush from the coasts of Normandy to Paris, and in the south Alexander was advancing to the valley of the Po. It looked as though Hitler was bound to be knocked out, but at the last moment he was saved by the gong. It was not his own armies, however, but Roosevelt and his generals who gave the signal for the end of the round; and in the interval Hitler recovered in an astonishing manner.

At the end of June Churchill for the first time had admitted that the game was lost. But his name would not have been Churchill if he had tamely accepted defeat, and it was not long before he was once again in action. Maitland Wilson's preparations for the invasion of southern France were

* *The Second World War*, Vol. VI.

in full swing when General Bradley suddenly burst with irresistible fury out of the Normandy beach-head and Patton strode with seven-league boots to the Seine and into Brittany. Thus in a flash the whole situation changed drastically, and it was obvious that a landing on the Riviera would now be too late to be of the slightest assistance to the Normandy advance. The British Chiefs of Staff therefore suggested that the forces concentrating for Anvil should be transferred to Brittany. On 7 August, to discuss the situation and to try to gain Eisenhower's support for his Adriatic plans, Churchill went to Supreme Command Headquarters in Portsmouth.

He argued that, in view of the favourable developments in northern France, occupation of Marseilles had now become unnecessary, and he made the further point that, since the divisions in readiness in the United States would shortly be able to proceed direct to the Breton ports, there was now no need for fresh bases in the Bay of Biscay. Therefore, instead of sending Wilson's forces to western or southern France, it would be far better, he suggested, to use them in Italy and, later, for a thrust into the Danubian basin.

To this Eisenhower replied that the comprehensive demolitions in the Breton ports made it unlikely that American troops would be able to make swift use of them; that Marseilles was very much closer to Metz than was Brest, and that a thrust up the Rhone valley offered a unique opportunity of surrounding and destroying the German forces in south-western France.

Churchill prophesied that the divisions advancing from Marseilles would have 'a bloody fight on their hands', and expressed the fear that it might be three months before they reached Lyons and that Marseilles might well become a second Anzio. Although Churchill brought all his scintillating and persuasive powers of oratory to bear and despite the support he received from Eisenhower's Chief of Staff, Bedell-Smith, and the First Sea Lord, Sir Andrew Cunningham, the Supreme Commander remained adamant. 'Ike' felt 'that the Prime Minister's real concern was possibly of a political rather than a military nature. . . . I well understood that strategy can be affected by political considerations, and if the President and the Prime Minister should decide that it was worth while to prolong the war, thereby increasing its cost in men and money, in order to secure the political objectives they deemed necessary, then I would instantly and loyally adjust my plans accordingly.'*

There was nothing more to be said. Eisenhower refused to change his mind and 'said "no" and went on saying "no" all the afternoon in every way known to the English language'.

On 8 August Roosevelt put a final end the two months' controversy and cabled to Churchill: 'I have consulted by telegraph with my Chiefs of

* Eisenhower, *Crusade in Europe*.

Staff, and am unable to agree that the resources allocated to "Dragoon" should be considered available for a move into France via ports on the coast of Brittany. On the contrary, it is my considered opinion that "Dragoon" should be launched as planned at the earliest possible date, and I have full confidence that it will be successful and of great assistance to Eisenhower in driving the Huns from France.'*

The invasion of the Côte d'Azur was duly launched on 15 August. It accomplished exactly nothing. The moment the U.S. Seventh Army under General Patch landed east of Toulon, Hitler at once withdrew all German forces from south and south-western France; and most of the ports in western France were already in Allied hands before the Franco-American forces advancing up the Rhone valley had reached Lyons. The German First and Ninth Armies extracted themselves so skilfully that General Patch had little prospect either of surrounding any major formations or of exercising any influence at all on the operations in northern France and Belgium.

The reverse side of the medal was even less alluring. In Italy, Field-Marshal Alexander† was being ridden on a tight rein. As a result of the removal of the French Expeditionary Corps and the U.S. VI Corps—seven first-class divisions in all—the battles for the Apennines dragged on until the winter. Alexander now had no chance of being able to advance to the Italo–Yugoslav frontier before the spring, and long before that Eisenhower would certainly be in Germany—and the Russians in Austria. The fruits of the Rome victory had been irretrievably cast aside, greatly to the advantage of Stalin.

Churchill was not alone in foreseeing what was to come. On 30 August Smuts wrote to him: '. . . From now on it would be wise to keep a very close eye on all matters bearing on the future settlement of Europe. This is the crucial issue on which the future of the world for generations will depend. In its solution your vision, experience, and great influence may prove a main factor.'‡

Today, the full extent of the tragedy that subsequently befell Europe is plain for all to see. Unimpeded, the Red Army was able to sweep over the whole of south-eastern Europe, and the freedom of the Balkan peoples was drowned in a sea of blood and tears. Nor it is difficult to imagine what a great service would have been rendered to the free world had the Western allies advanced straightway into the Balkans after the fall of Rome, instead of dissipating their forces in an enterprise which brought them more harm than good.

---

* Churchill, *The Second World War*, Vol. VI.
† After the fall of Rome, General Alexander was promoted to Field-Marshal.
‡ Churchill, *The Second World War*, Vol. VI.

As regards the damage done, the one man best qualified to assess it, the Commander-in-Chief of the U.S. Fifth Army and later Military Governor of Austria, General Mark Clark, is uncompromisingly emphatic. He writes:

A campaign that might have changed the whole history of relations between the Western world and Soviet Russia was permitted to fade away, not into nothing, but into much less than it could have been. . . . Not alone in my opinion, but in the opinion of a number of experts who were close to the problem, the weakening of the campaign in Italy in order to invade southern France instead of pushing on into the Balkans was one of the outstanding political mistakes of the war. . . . Our government had committed itself to an attack, decided upon a year earlier at Teheran, without re-evaluating the strategic situation in the light of new Allied successes in France and Italy. Stalin, it was evident, throughout the Big Three meeting and negotiations at Teheran was one of the strongest boosters of the invasion of southern France. He knew exactly what he wanted in a political way as well as a military way; and the thing that he wanted most was to keep us out of the Balkans, which he had staked out for the Red Army. If we switched our strength from Italy to France, it was obvious to Stalin, or anyone else, that we would be turning away from central Europe. From France the only way we could get into the Balkans was through Switzerland. . . In other words, Anvil led into a dead-end street. It is easy to see, therefore, why Stalin favoured Anvil at Teheran and why he kept right on pushing for it; but I never could understand why, as conditions changed and the war situation changed, the United States and Britain failed to sit down and take another look at the overall picture. . . . It was generally understood that President Roosevelt toyed with the idea for a while, but was not encouraged by Harry Hopkins. . . . I later came to understand, in Austria, the tremendous advantage we had lost by our failure to press on into the Balkans. . . . Had we been there before the Red Army, not only would the collapse of Germany have come sooner, but the influence of Soviet Russia would have been drastically reduced.*

To Hitler, of course, the emasculation of the Fifth Army and the failure of the Allies to push on into the Balkans were of inestimable value. He was naturally well aware of the strategic importance of northern Italy, and he fully realized that possession of the Po valley opened up a whole series of new possibilities for the prosecution of the strategic bombing of the war industries that had been transferred to east Germany. Nor was he ignorant of the dangers that would have threatened had the Allies advanced into the Balkans. Not only would there have been a threat of a stab in the back of the Eastern Front, but also the probability that Germany would be deprived of those sources of raw materials, in which south-eastern Europe was so rich and which were vital to the German war effort. Hitler knew, therefore, that he could not afford to expose these territories to the possibility of an Allied surprise attack.

Calculated Risk.

As regards southern France, the situation was very different. The destruction of the railway system had in any case made it impossible for Germany to import wolfram from Spain and bauxite from Portugal, and air bases in southern France were of very minor importance to the Allies, in comparison with those in northern Italy. It was, then, an area that Hitler could afford to evacuate without undue loss from either the military or the economic point of view—particularly as the submarine bases on the Bay of Biscay were no longer of any significance. On balance, therefore, he was far readier to strengthen the front in Italy than to put up a fight for the possession of Provence and south-western France.

Furthermore, Anvil was an unmistakable indication of Allied intentions. Hitler knew that he need not worry any more about Italy and the Balkans. Accordingly, he promptly withdrew the Hermann Göring Panzer Division from the Italian front and transferred it to Poland, where the whole central sector of the Eastern Front was aflame; and he sent the 3 and 15 Panzer Grenadier Divisions to France to oppose Patton's onslaught against the upper Moselle.

Anvil not only made a nonsense of the whole Italian campaign, but also threw the whole Allied strategy in western Europe out of gear; and both these repercussions were to have tragic consequences for Europe. They presented Hitler with a chance to stabilize the Western Front and to sacrifice his last strategic reserves in his ill-fated Ardennes offensive—those reserves which, a little later, would have been able to hold up the Red flood from the east. And in that case, it would have been Eisenhower and not Zhukov who marched into Berlin. Then again, had not Anvil snatched the spear from Alexander's hand, it would most probably have been the Union Jack and the Stars and Stripes that would have flown victoriously over the Ballhausplatz in Vienna.

The stubborn opposition of the German forces in Italy at Cassino had decisively delayed the mounting of Anvil and by so doing had given the Allies a unique, but also a last, chance of putting their strategic helm about and setting course for the Balkans. The victories at Cassino and Anzio had paved the way for the frustrating of Stalin's plans and the transfer of Alexander's armies to the areas where the freedom of the peoples of south-eastern Europe was at stake. But for Roosevelt's veto, Alexander's victory and Kesselring's defeat would in reality have been a genuine victory for the whole of Europe, and, in the ultimate analysis, the German and Allied soldiers who died at Cassino would at least have given their lives in a worthy cause—the freedom of Europe.

As it is, Monte Cassino remains for the free world a tragedy of world-wide historical significance.

Epilogue

The Resurrection of Monte Cassino

In the meanwhile, nearly twenty years have gone by, years of hard work for the inhabitants of the land of St Benedict. The scars of war have healed, the destroyed villages have risen afresh and the traffic flows smoothly along the asphalt roads at the foot of Monte Cassino. The Liri valley has blossomed once again into all its erstwhile fertility, oxen patiently plough the heavy, clay soil, and Cassino itself resounds with the cries of bargaining peasants, buying and selling in the market-place.

But it is a completely new Cassino. The old town still lies in ruins, beneath which lie the men of the 1 Parachute Division and many a young yeoman from far distant New Zealand. The town which died on 15 March 1944 has never been rebuilt. The new town has moved farther into the plain. It is very modern, and with its huge office buildings, its shops, banks and hotels it is almost typically American in its style. It is a busy and industrious town, and with justifiable pride the Italians say: 'Cassino is the symbol of the regeneration of our country.'

With equal zest the Italians have obliterated all traces of war for miles around. Many of the villages have changed their sites; some, which, before they were destroyed, were perched high up in the mountains, have moved down into the valley, nearer to the springs and the roads.

And in the valley, too, the soldiers of Germany and the allied nations lie peacefully, side by side, at rest in the earth which they had died to hold or to capture, their graves piously tended by friend and foe alike; for human hatreds perish, but Christian charity is immortal. For the fifth time the House of St Benedict has risen from the dead and a new sprig has burgeoned from the evergreen trunk that is the eternal symbol of Monte Cassino.

But when war had passed on its way, the monastery had presented a most pitiable spectacle, and it seemed as though many decades would be required to restore it to its pristine glory.

One of the first to return to the monastery hill had been Don Ildefonso Rea, the Abbot of Cava and now the Bishop and Abbot of Monte Cassino and the 298th successor to St Benedict. Very shortly afterwards the monks returned from Rome, with the fragile and ancient Don Gregorio Diamare at their head. But before the monks returned and while the ruins remained unguarded, 'the human hyenas had fallen upon it, ransacking the ruins and pillaging everything they could lay their hands on' (Leccisotti). Souvenir hunters, too, were rampant, and in this way such remnants as had been spared by bomb and shell were lost for ever.

The monks at first installed themselves in the cellars, and their efforts to breathe new life into their abbey were splendidly supported by the British. Italian officials, Italian and Polish soldiers also came to their aid. The first and most urgent task was to clear and repair the Via Serpentina and restore communication with the valley below. As soon as the road was usable, the work of clearing the monastery itself began. This was indeed a formidable and arduous task, and half a million cubic yards of rubble had to be cleared before a start could be made with the rebuilding of the abbey on its original site. The greatest possible care was taken to examine the débris and to search for any remnants of the great number of works of art which had not previously been removed because it had not been possible to move them. With loving toil many sculptures, mosaics and reliefs were rescued, repaired, restored and incorporated in the new building. Every stone, every fragment of wood was scrutinized before it was carried away. Careful search, too, was made for the graves of German soldiers; and when these were located in the Priory courtyard, their wooden crosses all bore the date of 15 February 1944.

The whole mountain was now pulsating with new life. In the ruins Italian soldiers and workmen laboured side by side with German prisoners-of-war who had volunteered their services in the good cause; and soon it was the turn of an army of builders, carpenters and stone masons to set to work, as their ancestors in bygone centuries had done, restoring the monastery to its pristine glory.

The Italians are master-builders and craftsmen, as they proved once more in this rebuilding of Monte Cassino. In no time a small chapel was built over the graves of St Benedict and St Scholastica, and the monks were able once more to celebrate divine service. The official laying of the foundation stone took place on 15 March 1945, the anniversary of the destruction of Cassino town, in the presence of a distinguished gathering of statesmen, diplomats and dignitaries of the Church. The first section to be rebuilt was the Torretta, which had been only partially destroyed; then, in succession, followed the Basilica, the south-eastern wing and, finally, the north-west trancept. The new building adheres closely to the original plan, which had been rescued by German soldiers and taken to safety in Rome.

It will be a long time, however, before the decorations are completed. To reconstruct the walls and roofs was a comparatively simple matter; but to embellish the rooms with frescoes, mosaics and reliefs and to restore the Basilica and the Sacristy to even a vestige of their former glory will be the work of a lifetime or even of generations.

The new monastery cost many thousands of millions of lire. By far the greater portion of the huge sum required was provided by the Italian Government, which, notwithstanding the heavy damage that Italy suffered during the war, was anxious to do all in its power to recreate this national memorial as quickly as possible. Generous contributions flowed in, too, from Europe and from countries farther afield, and the Order of St Benedict dedicated much of its wealth to the swift restoration of its founder's monastery.

Sir Winston Churchill, in the dedication of his history of the Second World War, has written the words:

IN PEACE—GOOD WILL

Monte Cassino is pre-eminently suited to become a symbol of good will. Not in vain should the word 'PAX', which in huge letters embellishes the portals of the monastery, be allowed to call upon mankind to honour peace, good will and mutual forgiveness.

One last word. St Benedict's Hill is the ideal place for the holding of reunions by the enemies of yesterday. It is above all the fighting men who, nearly two decades ago, fought and bled for their country, who are called upon to build new bridges between their peoples. As the old soldiers of the First War reunite and foregather in France and in Belgium, so the warriors of all nations who fought at Cassino should foregather there and help to bring the world at last to that state of grace, towards which the monks of Cassino have for centuries dedicated all their efforts:

PEACE AMONG MEN

Bibliography and Sources

I would like to express my thanks to the authors, publishers and proprietors of those of the books and publications listed below from which I have very kindly been allowed to reproduce some short extracts.

Alexander, Viscount: *The Alexander Memoirs*. Cassell 1962.
Badoglio, Pietro: *Italy and the Second World War*. Oxford U.P. 1948.
Bradley, Omar N.: *A Soldier's Story*. Eyre and Spottiswoode. 1952.
Butcher, Harry S.: *My Three Years with Eisenhower*. New York 1946.
Churchill, Sir Winston: *The Second World War*. Cassell 1950–4.
Ciechanowski, Jan: *Vergeblicher Sieg*. Zürich 1948.
Clark, Mark: *Calculated Risk*. Harrap 1951.
Cunningham, Viscount: *A Sailor's Odyssey*. Hutchinson 1951.
Distruzione di Montecassino, la; Documenti e Testimonianze. Monte-cassino 1950.
Der Deutsche Fallschirmjaeger, Nos. 2, 5 and 9. 1953.
Deutsche Allgemeine Zeitung. February–March 1944.
Eisenhower, Dwight D.: *Crusade in Europe*. Heinemann 1949.
Fuller, J. F.: *The Second World War*. Eyre and Spottiswoode 1954.
Kesselring, Alnert: *Soldat bis zum letzten Tag*. Bonn 1953.
Leccisotti, Tommaso: *Montecassino*. Basle 1949.
Linklater, Eric: *The Campaign in Italy*. H.M.S.O. 1951.
Macmillan, Norman: *The Royal Air Force in the World War*, vol. 3. Harrap 1949.

Montgomery, Viscount: *El Alamein to the River Sangro*. Hutchinson 1948.
                    From Normandy to the Baltic. Hutchinson 1947.
Mordal, Jacques: *Cassino*. Paris 1952.
Munding, P. Emmanuel: *Der Untergang von Montecassino*. Beuron 1954.
Neue Zürcher Zeitung. February–March 1944.
Die Oesterreichische Furche, Nos. 45–50. 1951.
Reports—Kesselring.
Reports on the defensive operations of the Tenth Army in Italy.
von Rintelen, Enno: *Mussolini als Bundesgenosse*. Tübingen/Stuttgart 1951.
Rommel, Erwin: *Krieg ohne Hass*. Heidenheim/Br. 1950.
Sherwood, Robert E.: *The White House Papers of Harry Hopkins*. Eyre and
    Spottiswoode 1950.
War Reports, The—of General Marshal, General Arnold, Admiral King.
    Philadelphia/New York 1947.
Westphal, Siegfried: *Heer in Fesseln*. Bonn 1952.
                  The German Army in the West. Cassell 1951.
Wilmot, Chester: *The Struggle for Europe*. Collins 1952.
Wilson, Lord: *Eight Years Overseas 1939–47*. Hutchinson 1948.

Index